MATHEMATICS OF

INVESTMENT
and
CREDIT

Second Edition

Samuel A. Broverman, ASA, Ph.D.
University of Toronto

ACTEX Publications, Inc.
Winsted, Connecticut

Requests for permission should be addressed to
  ACTEX Publications
  P.O. Box 974
  Winsted, CT 06098

Manufactured in the United States of America

10 9 8 7 6 5 4 3 2

Cover design by MUF

Library of Congress Cataloging-in-Publication Data

Broverman, Samuel A., 1951-
    Mathematics of investment and credit / Samuel A. Broverman.
        p. cm.
    Includes bibliographical references and index.
    ISBN 1-56698-218-9 :
    1. Interest--Mathematical models. 2. Interest--Problems,
 exercises, etc. I. Title
HG4515.3.B76   1991
332.8'2--dc20   91-20310
                                                                  CIP

ISBN: 1-56698-218-9

CONTENTS

CHAPTER 5   251
THE INTEREST RATE AS A RANDOM VARIABLE

CHAPTER 6   293
TOPICS IN FINANCE AND INVESTMENT

PREFACE

In teaching an intermediate level university course in mathematics of finance over a number of years, I found an increasing need for a textbook that provided a thorough and modern treatment of the subject, while incorporating theory and applications. This book is an attempt to satisfy that need. It is based, to a large extent, on notes that I developed while teaching and using a number of textbooks for the course.

As in many areas of mathematics, the subject of mathematics of investment has aspects that do not become outdated over time, but rather become the foundation upon which new developments are based. The traditional topics of compound interest and cashflow valuation, and their applications, are developed in the first few chapters of the book. In addition, a number of modern topics are included. There is a chapter devoted to interest rates as random variables, and a final chapter covering a number of topics that have traditionally been regarded as belonging to the field of finance, such as derivative investments and bond duration and immunization of investment portfolios.

The numerical calculations required in the practical application of this subject have led, in the past, to a number of awkward computational techniques based on compound interest tables. With the increased availablity of rapid and efficient computational capabilities, this text emphasizes a more direct calculation approach.

The mathematical background required for the book is a course in calculus at the Freshman level. Chapter 5 on stochastic interest rates also requires a background in probability and statistics. The topics in the book are arranged in an order that is similar to traditional approaches to the subject, with Chapter 1 introducing interest rates, Chapter 2 developing methods for valuing annuities, Chapter 3 considering amortization of loans, and Chapter 4 concerning bond valuation. Chapter 5 on stochastic interest rates and Chapter 6 on finance-related topics are areas where this text goes beyond the traditional approach to the subject.

The second edition has been expanded to include discussion and examples of investment derivatives, a rapidly developing aspect of financial markets.

I would like to acknowledge the support of the Actuarial Education and Research Foundation, which provided support for the early stages of development of the book.

I would like to thank John Mereu, Michael Gabon, and Professors Steve Linney, Walter Lowrie, David Promislow, Srinivasa Ramanujam, and Peter Ryall who reviewed a first draft of the book. Their insightful comments and suggestions were most helpful in the book's development. I am also grateful to Robert Marcus of Altamira Investments, with whom I had several conversations regarding practical aspects of the bond market.

My appreciation is also expressed to the people at ACTEX Publications who saw the project through from manuscript to textbook. Specifically, Marilyn J. Baleshiski, format and layout editor, Sandi Lynn Fratini, style editor, Dick London, FSA, mathematics editor, and Marlene Lundbeck, graphic arts.

Finally, I have had the continuous support of my wife, Sue Foster. I thank her for her patience and the inspiration she has provided.

March 1996   Samuel A. Broverman

To Sue, Alison, Amelia, and Andrea

MATHEMATICS OF

INVESTMENT
and
CREDIT

Second Edition

Neither a borrower nor a lender be . . .

W. Shakespeare

*The Tragedy of Hamlet,
Prince of Denmark, act i, scene iii*

INTRODUCTION TO INTEREST RATES

1.1   INTRODUCTION

Almost everyone, from time to time, will be a saver, borrower, or investor, and will have access to insurance, pension plans, or other financial benefits. There is a wide variety of financial transactions in which individuals, corporations, or governments can become involved. The range of available investments has broadened over time, accompanied by an increase in the complexity of many of these investments.

Financial transactions invariably involve numerical calculations, and, depending on their complexity, may require detailed mathematical formulations. It is therefore important to establish fundamental principles upon which these numerical calculations and mathematical formulations are based. The objective of this book is to systematically develop insights and mathematical techniques which lead to these fundamental principles upon which financial transactions can be modeled and analyzed.

An initial step in the analysis of a financial transaction is to translate a verbal description of the transaction into a mathematical model. Unfortunately, in practice a transaction may be described in language which is somewhat vague and which may result in disagreements as to its interpretation. The need for precision in the mathematical model of a financial transaction requires that there be a correspondingly precise and unambiguous understanding of the verbal description before the translation to the model is made. To this end, terminology and notation, much of which is in standard use in financial and actuarial practice, will be introduced.

A component that is common to virtually all financial transactions is *interest*, the "time value of money." Most people are aware that interest rates play a central role in their own personal financial situations as well as in the economy as a whole. Many governments and private enterprises employ economists and analysts who make forecasts regarding the level of interest rates. It is not unusual to see immediate and significant effects on the various financial markets, particularly stock and bond markets, when new forecasts of interest rate levels are released by prominent economists.

To analyze financial transactions, a clear understanding of the concept of interest is needed. Interest can be defined in a variety of contexts, and most people have at least a vague notion of what it is. In the most common context, interest refers to the consideration or rent paid by a borrower of money to a lender for the use of the money over a period of time. Other definitions may be found in dictionaries and legal statutes, and, in essence, they agree with this definition.

This chapter provides a detailed development of the mechanics of interest rates: how they are measured and applied to amounts of principal over time to calculate amounts of interest. In the next section of the chapter a standard measure of interest rates is defined and two common growth patterns for investments, simple and compound interest, are discussed. Later in the chapter various alternative standard measures of interest, such as nominal rate of interest, rate of discount, and force of interest, are discussed. Also developed in this chapter is the general way in which a financial transaction is modeled in mathematical form, using the notions of present value and equation of value.

1.2   INTEREST ACCUMULATION AND EFFECTIVE RATES OF INTEREST

An interest rate is most typically quoted as an annual percentage. If interest is credited or charged annually, the quoted annual rate, in decimal fraction form, is multiplied by the amount invested or loaned to calculate the *amount of interest* that accrues over a one-year period. It is generally understood that as interest is credited or paid, it is reinvested. This reinvesting of interest leads to the process of *compounding interest*. The following example illustrates this process.

EXAMPLE 1.1

The current rate of interest quoted by a bank on its savings account is 9% per annum, with interest credited annually. Smith opens an account with a deposit of 1000. Assuming that there are no transactions on the account other than the annual crediting of interest, find the account balance just after interest is credited at the end of 5 years.

SOLUTION

After one year the interest credited will be 1000(.09), resulting in a balance (with interest) of $1000 + 1000(.09) = 1000(1.09) = 1090$. This balance then earns interest in the second year, producing a balance of $1090 + 1090(.09) = (1090)(1.09) = 1188.10$ at the end of the second year. The balance at the end of the third year will be $1188.10 + 1188.10(.09) = 1188.10(1.09) = 1295.03$. It will be $1295.03 + 1295.03(.09) = 1295.03(1.09) = 1411.58$ after four years, and $1411.58 + 1411.58(.09) = 1411.58(1.09) = 1538.62$ at the end of the fifth year. □

It is clear from Example 1.1 that with an interest rate of i per annum and interest credited annually, an initial deposit of X will earn interest of $X \cdot i$ for the following year. The accumulated value at the end of the year will be $X + X \cdot i = X(1 + i)$. If this amount is left on deposit for another year, the interest earned in the second year will be $X(1 + i) \cdot i$, so that the accumulated balance is $X(1+i) + X(1+i) \cdot i = X(1+i)^2$ at the end of the second year. The account will continue to grow by a factor of $1 + i$ per year, resulting in a balance of $X(1 + i)^n$ at the end of n years. This is the pattern of accumulation that results from compounding, or reinvesting, the interest as it is credited. (Note that $X(1 + i)^n$ might produce a different result than $X(1 + i)(1 + i)(1 + i) \cdots$, if each multiplication in the latter approach is rounded - see Exercise 1.2.8.)

In Example 1.1, if Smith were to observe the accumulating balance in the account by looking at regular bank statements, he would see only one entry of interest credited each year. It would be generally understood, however, that interest is accruing on the account throughout the year, so that if Smith were to close the account between interest credit dates, a fraction of that year's interest would be paid. It is useful to regard the underlying accumulation of interest as a continuous process for which the annual (or quarterly or monthly) crediting of interest reflects the practical aspect of administering the accumulation. This is discussed more fully in the text following Example 1.2.

It is possible that the rate of interest will change from one year to the next. If the interest rate is i_1 in the first year, i_2 in the second year, and so on, then after n years an initial amount X will accumulate to $X(1 + i_1)(1 + i_2) \cdots (1 + i_n)$, where the growth factor for year t is $1 + i_t$ and the interest rate is i_t.

In practice interest may be credited more frequently than once per year. For example many bank accounts pay interest monthly and credit cards generally charge interest monthly on previous outstanding balances. If an initial deposit is allowed to accumulate in an account over time, the algebraic form of the accumulation will be similar to the one given above for annual interest. At interest rate j per compounding period, an initial deposit of amount X will accumulate to $X(1 + j)^n$ after n compounding periods. At an interest rate of $\frac{3}{4}\%$ per month, with interest credited monthly, an initial deposit of X would accumulate to $X(1.0075)^n$ at the end of n months. The growth factor for a one-year period at this rate would be $(1.0075)^{12} = 1.0938$. The account earns 9.38% over the year. This interest rate of 9.38% is called the ***effective annual rate of interest*** earned on the account. In general, the effective annual rate of interest earned by an investment during a one-year period is the percentage change in the value of the investment from the beginning to the end of the year without regard to the investment behavior at intermediate points in the year. Comparisons of investment performance are often done by comparing the respective effective annual interest rates earned by the investments over a particular year.

If the monthly compounding at .75% described above were to continue for another year, the accumulated value after two years would be $X(1.0075)^{24} = X(1.0938)^2$. We see that over an integral number of years a month-by-month accumulation at a monthly rate of .75% is *equivalent* to annual compounding at an annual rate of 9.38% in the sense that they result in the same accumulated value. Two rates of interest are said to be ***equivalent*** if they result in the same pattern of growth over the same time period. For some transactions, a standard way of comparing interest rates is to find and compare their equivalent effective annual rates. It is a common practice to have rates quoted on an annual basis, with compounding taking place more frequently than once per year. Thus the monthly rate of .75% would be quoted as 9% *per year compounded monthly*. This leads to the notion of *nominal* annual rates of interest, which are considered in detail in Section 1.4.

When compound interest is in effect and transactions, either deposits or withdrawals, are occurring in an account, the resulting balance at some future point in time can be found by accumulating all transactions to that time. The next example illustrates this.

| EXAMPLE 1.2 |

Smith deposits 1000 into an account on January 1, 1990. The account credits interest, at effective annual rate 5%, every December 31. Smith withdraws 200 on January 1, 1992, deposits 100 on January 1, 1993, and withdraws 250 on January 1, 1995. What is the balance in the account just after interest is credited on December 31, 1996?

| SOLUTION |

One approach is to recalculate the balance after every transaction. On December 31, 1991 the balance is $1000(1.05)^2 = 1102.50$; on January 1, 1992 the balance is $1102.50 - 200 = 902.50$; on December 31, 1992 the balance is $902.50(1.05) = 947.63$; on January 1, 1993 the balance is $947.63 + 100 = 1047.63$; on December 31, 1994 the balance is $1047.63(1.05)^2 = 1155.01$; on January 1, 1995 the balance is $1155.01 - 250 = 905.01$; and on December 31, 1996 the balance is $905.01(1.05)^2 = 997.77$. An alternative approach is to accumulate each transaction to the December 31, 1996 date of valuation and combine all accumulated values, adding deposits and subtracting withdrawals. Then we have $1000(1.05)^7 - 200(1.05)^5 + 100(1.05)^4 - 250(1.05)^2 = 997.77$ for our balance on December 31, 1996. Exercise 1.2.21 shows that the two approaches in this solution are equivalent for any sequence of deposits and withdrawals, as long as compound interest is in effect. □

The pattern for compound interest at rate i per period described above results in an accumulation factor of $(1 + i)^n$ over n periods. Examples 1.1 and 1.2 have interest credited every year, and the implication from those examples is that n must be a positive integer corresponding to a completed number of years or interest credit periods. Let $S(t)$ represent the accumulation, or growth factor from time 0 to time t. Then a more general definition of compound interest accumulation at rate i per period is

$$S(t) = (1 + i)^t \tag{1.1}$$

over t interest periods, where t is any positive real number. If, in Example 1.1, Smith closed his account in the middle of the fourth year, the accumulated value at time $t = 3\frac{1}{2}$ would be $1000(1.09)^{3.5} = 1000(1.09)^3(1.09)^{1/2} = 1352.05$, which is the balance at the end of the third year accumulated to the middle of the fourth year. If the interest compounding period is one year, a fraction of a year is generally described as either an integral number of months, for example m months, or an exact number of days, for example d days. In the first case t is formulated as

$t = \frac{m}{12}$, although not all months are exactly $\frac{1}{12}$ of a year, and in the second case t is formulated as $t = \frac{d}{365}$.

In practice, when calculating accumulation over a fraction of an interest period, a variation on compound interest is often used. This variation is commonly known as *simple interest*. At a rate of i per year, an amount of 1 invested at the start of the year grows to $1 + i$ at the end of the year. If t represents a fraction of a year, then under simple interest the accumulated value at time t of the initial amount of 1 is

$$S(t) \;=\; 1 + i \cdot t. \tag{1.2}$$

As in the case of compound interest, for a fraction of a year t is either $\frac{m}{12}$ or $\frac{d}{365}$ (or $\frac{d}{360}$ in some special cases), depending on whether time is described in months or days. Short term transactions for periods of less than one year are often formulated on the basis of simple interest at a quoted annual rate. The following example refers to a *promissory note*, which is a short-term (generally less than one year) contract requiring the issuer of the note (the borrower) to pay the holder of the note (the lender) a principal amount plus interest on that principal at a specified annual interest rate for a specified length of time, at the end of which the payment is due. It is understood that promissory note interest is calculated on the basis of simple interest.

EXAMPLE 1.3

On January 31 Smith borrows 5000 from Brown and gives Brown a *promissory note*. The note states that the loan will be repaid on April 30 of the same year, with interest at 12% per annum. On March 1 Brown sells the promissory note to Jones, who pays Brown a sum of money in return for the right to collect the payment from Smith on April 30. Jones pays Brown an amount such that Jones' yield (interest rate earned) from March 1 to the maturity date can be stated as an annual rate of interest of 15%. Find the amount that Jones paid to Brown and the yield rate Brown earned quoted on an annual basis.

SOLUTION

We first find the payment required on the maturity date. This is $5000[1 + i \cdot t]$, where $i = .12$ and $t = \frac{89}{365}$, since there are 89 days from January 31 to April 30 in a non-leap year. The payment required on April 30 is 5146.30. Let X denote the amount Jones pays Brown on March 1.

Denote by j_1 the annual yield rate earned by Brown based on simple interest for the period of t_1 years from January 31 to March 1, and denote by j_2 the annual yield rate earned by Jones for the period of t_2 years from March 1 to April 30. Let Z denote the maturity amount paid by Smith on April 30. Then $X = 5000(1 + t_1 \cdot j_1)$ and $X(1 + t_2 \cdot j_2) = Z = 5146.31$. The following time-line diagram indicates the sequence of events.

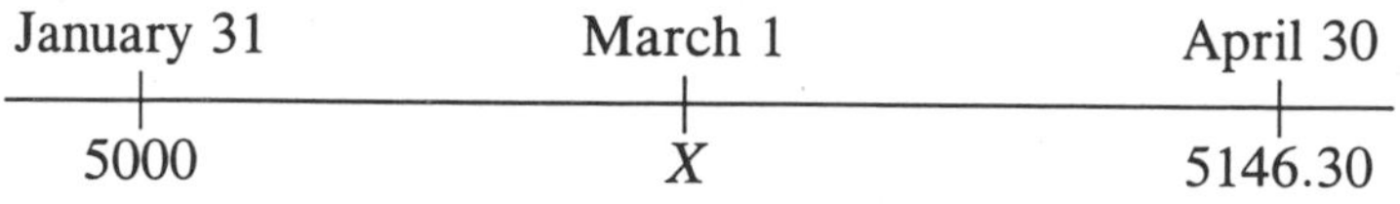

January 31	March 1	April 30
5000	X	5146.30

FIGURE 1.1

We are given $j_2 = .15$, and must solve for $X = \dfrac{Z}{1 + (.15)t_2}$. We have $Z = 5146.30$ and $t_2 = \dfrac{60}{365}$, so $X = \dfrac{5146.30}{1 + (.15)(\frac{60}{365})} = 5022.46$. Now with X known, $j_1 = \left[\dfrac{X}{5000} - 1 \right] \cdot \dfrac{1}{t_1}$, where $t_1 = \dfrac{29}{365}$, so that $j_1 = .0565$. □

Notice that in Example 1.3, if Jones had paid Brown a price which yielded Jones an annual return of 12%, that price would be 5046.75, which would yield Brown 11.77% on an annual basis. The price to yield Jones 15% is 5022.46. This inverse relationship between yield and price (the increased yield of 15% to Jones corresponds to a smaller investment on Jones' part) is typical of "*fixed-income*" investments. A fixed-income investment is one for which the future payments are predetermined (unlike an investment in, say, stocks which involves some risk, and for which the return cannot be predetermined). As interest rates increase, the price that an investor (Jones) will pay for an investment with fixed future payments decreases. An alternative way of describing this is to say that the holder of a fixed income investment (Brown) will see the market value of the investment decrease as the yield rate to maturity demanded by a buyer increases. This can be explained by noting that a higher yield rate requires a smaller investment amount to achieve the same dollar level of interest payments. This will be seen again when the notion of *present value* is discussed later in this chapter.

It is clear that accumulation under simple interest forms a linear function whereas compound interest accumulation forms an exponential function. This is illustrated in the following figure showing the accumulation of an initial investment of 1 at an interest rate of $i = .30$.

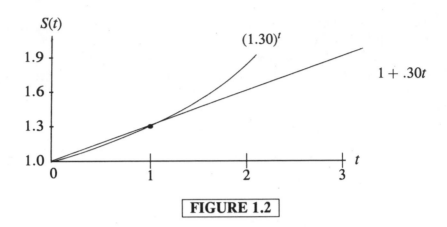

FIGURE 1.2

From Figure 1.2 it appears that simple interest accumulation is larger than compound interest accumulation, at the same interest rate, for values of t between 0 and 1, but compound interest accumulation is greater than simple interest accumulation for values of t greater than 1. In practice the use of simple interest is generally restricted to periods of less than a year ($t < 1$). At $t = \frac{1}{4}$, for example, $1 + (.30)(\frac{1}{4}) = 1.075 > 1.0678 = (1.30)^{1/4}$, but at $t = 3$ we find $1 + (.30)(3) = 1.9 < 2.197 = (1.30)^3$. This relationship between simple and compound interest is verified algebraically in the following example.

EXAMPLE 1.4

Suppose that $i > 0$. Show that (i) if $0 < t < 1$ then $(1 + i)^t < 1 + i \cdot t$, and (ii) if $t > 1$ then $(1 + i)^t > 1 + i \cdot t$.

SOLUTION

We use the following result from calculus: if f and g are differentiable functions such that $f(a) = g(a)$ and $f'(x) < g'(x)$ for $a < x < b$, then $f(b) < g(b)$.

(i) Suppose $0 < t < 1$. Let $f(i) = (1 + i)^t$ and $g(i) = 1 + i \cdot t$. Then $f(0) = g(0) = 1$. If we can show that $f'(i) < g'(i)$ for any $i > 0$, then we can use the calculus result above to conclude that $f(i) < g(i)$ for any $i > 0$. First note that $f'(i) = t \cdot (1 + i)^{t-1}$ and $g'(i) = t$. Since $i > 0$, it follows that $1 + i > 1$, and since $t < 1$, it follows that $t - 1 < 0$. Then $(1 + i)^{t-1} < 1$, so $f'(i) < g'(i)$. This completes the proof of part (i).

(ii) Suppose that $t > 1$. Let $f(i) = 1 + i \cdot t$ and $g(i) = (1 + i)^t$. Again $f(0) = g(0)$. If we can show that $f'(i) < g'(i)$ for any $i > 0$, then we can use the calculus result above to conclude that $f(i) < g(i)$ for any $i > 0$. Since $t > 1$ and $i > 0$ it follows that $t - 1 > 0$ and $1 + i > 1$. Thus $(1 + i)^{t-1} > 1$, and it follows that $f'(i) = t < t \cdot (1 + i)^{t-1} = g'(i)$. This completes the proof of part (ii). $\square$

In practice interest accumulation is often based on a combination of simple and compound interest. Compound interest would be applied over the completed (integer) number of interest compounding periods, and simple interest would be applied from then to the fractional point in the current interest period. Under this approach, at annual rate 9%, over a period of length 4 years and 5 months an investment would grow by a factor of $(1.09)^4[1 + \frac{5}{12}(.09)]$.

When analyzing the accumulation of a single invested amount, the value of the investment is generally regarded as a function of time. For example, $S(t)$ is the value of the investment at time t, with t usually measured in years. Time $t = 0$ usually, although not necessarily, corresponds to the time at which the original investment was made. The amount of interest earned from time t_1 to time t_2 can therefore be written as $S(t_2) - S(t_1)$. Also, with this notation, the effective annual interest rate for the one-year period from time u to time $u + 1$ would be i_{u+1}, where $S(u + 1) = S(u) \cdot (1 + i_{u+1})$, or, equivalently,

$$i_{u+1} = \frac{S(u+1) - S(u)}{S(u)}. \tag{1.3}$$

This relationship for i_{u+1} shows that the effective annual rate of interest for a particular one-year period is the amount of interest (or growth) for the year as a proportion of the value of the investment (or amount invested) at the start of the year. In other words,

effective annual rate of interest for a specified one-year period

$$= \frac{\text{amount of interest for the one-year period}}{\text{value (or amount invested) at the start of the period}}.$$

The accumulated amount function can be used to find an effective interest rate for any time interval. For example, the three-month effective interest rate for the three months from time $3\frac{1}{4}$ to time $3\frac{1}{2}$ would be $\frac{S(3\frac{1}{2}) - S(3\frac{1}{4})}{S(3\frac{1}{4})}$.

From a practical point of view, the accumulated amount function $S(t)$ would be a step function, changing by discrete increments, since interest is credited at discrete points of time, such as every year or month. For more theoretical analysis of investment behavior, it may be useful to assume that $S(t)$ is a continuous, or differentiable, function, such as in the case of compound interest growth on an initial investment of amount 1 at time $t = 1$, where $S(t) = (1 + i)^t$ for any non-negative real number t.

As defined above, the accumulated amount function $S(t)$ refers to the value at time t of a specific investment. A more general representation of accumulation from time t_1 to time t_2 can be made by using a function of the form $s(t_1, t_2)$, which represents the accumulated value at time t_2 of an amount of 1 invested at time t_1. With this notation the accumulated value at time t of an investment of 1 at time 0 is $s(0, t)$.

1.3 PRESENT VALUE AND EQUATIONS OF VALUE

If we let X be the amount that must be invested at the start of a year to accumulate to 1 at the end of the year at effective annual interest rate i, then $X(1 + i) = 1$, or, equivalently, $X = \frac{1}{1 + i}$. Thus $\frac{1}{1 + i}$ is the *present value of an amount of* 1 *due in one year*. The factor $\frac{1}{1 + i}$ is usually denoted by v and is called a *present value factor* or *discount factor*. When a situation involves more than one interest rate, the symbol v_i may be used to identify the interest rate on which the present value factor is based.

The present value factor v is particularly important in the context of compound interest. Accumulation under compound interest has the form $S(t) = S(0) \cdot (1 + i)^t$. This expression can be rewritten as $S(0) = \frac{S(t)}{(1 + i)^t} = S(t) \cdot v^t$. Thus $K \cdot v^t$ is the present value at time 0 of an amount K due at time t under compound interest growth (*i.e.*, $K \cdot v^t$ is the amount that must be invested at time 0 to grow to K at time t under compound interest growth), and the present value factor v acts as a "compound present value" factor in determining the present value. Accumulation and present value are inverse processes.

EXAMPLE 1.5

Ted wants to invest a sufficient amount in a fund in order that the accumulated value will be one million dollars on his retirement date in 25 years. Ted considers two options. He can invest in Equity Mutual Fund, which invests in the stock market. E.M. Fund has *averaged* an annual compound growth rate of 19.5% since its inception 30 years ago, although its annual growth has been as low as 2% and as high as 38%. The E.M. Fund provides no guarantees as to its future performance. Ted's other option is to invest in a zero-coupon bond or "stripped bond" (*i.e.*, a bond with no coupons, only a payment on the maturity date; see Chapter 6), with a guaranteed effective annual rate of interest of 11.5% until its maturity date in 25 years.

(a) What amount must Ted invest if he chooses E.M. Fund and assumes that the average annual growth rate will continue for another 25 years?

(b) What amount must he invest if he opts for the stripped bond investment?

SOLUTION

(a) If Ted invests X at $t = 0$, then $X(1.195)^{25} = 1,000,000$, so that the present value of 1,000,000 due in 25 years at effective annual rate .195 is $1,000,000 \cdot v^{25} = \dfrac{1,000,000}{(1.195)^{25}} = 11,635.96$.

(b) The present value of 1,000,000 due in 25 years at $i = .115$ is $1,000,000 \cdot v^{25} = \dfrac{1,000,000}{(1.115)^{25}} = 65,785.22$. Note that no subscript was used on v in part (a) or (b) since it was clear from the context as to the interest rate being used. □

If simple interest is in effect, then $S(t) = S(1) \cdot [1 + i \cdot t]$ and therefore $S(0) = \dfrac{S(t)}{1 + i \cdot t}$. It is important to note that implicit in this expression is the fact that simple interest accrual begins at the time specified as $t = 0$. The present value based on simple interest accumulation *assumes* that interest begins accruing at the time the present value is being found. There is no standard symbol representing present value under simple interest that corresponds to v^t under compound interest. An important difference between the operation of present value under compound interest and under simple interest is illustrated in the following example.

EXAMPLE 1.6

(a) An amount of 1000 is due on December 31, with accumulation based on compound interest at annual rate $i = .10$. Let P_0 be the present value on January 1 ($t = 0$) and let P_1 be the present value on July 1 ($t = .5$) of the 1000 due on December 31 ($t = 1$). Show that the present value at $t = 0$ of P_1 due at $t = .5$ is equal to P_0.

(b) Suppose the accumulation uses simple interest at $i = .10$. Show that the result in part (a) does not hold in this case.

SOLUTION

(a) We have $P_1 = 1000 \cdot v^{.5} = 953.46$, and $P_0 = 1000 \cdot v = 909.09$. The present value at $t = 0$ of $P_1 = 953.46$ due at $t = .5$ is $953.46 \cdot v^{.5} = 909.09 = P_0$. This must be the case since $P_1 = 1000 \cdot v^{.5}$ implies that $P_1 \cdot v^{.5} = 1000 \cdot v = P_0$.

(b) $P_1 = \dfrac{1000}{1 + (.10)(.5)} = 952.38$, and $P_0 = \dfrac{1000}{1 + (.10)(1)} = 909.09$. But based on simple interest at $i = .10$, the present value at $t = 0$ of $P_1 = 952.38$ due at $t = .5$ is $\dfrac{952.38}{1 + (.10)(.5)} = 907.03$, which is not equal to $P_0 = 909.09$. This is because with simple interest from time $t = 0$, there is no reinvestment at time $t = .5$. (Exercise 1.3.1 generalizes this example.) $\qquad\square$

Given an accumulated amount function $S(t)$, the investment growth from time t_1 to time $t_2 > t_1$ is from $S(t_1)$ to $S(t_2)$. Thus an amount of $\dfrac{S(t_1)}{S(t_2)}$ invested at time t_1 will grow to 1 at time t_2. In other words, $\dfrac{S(t_1)}{S(t_2)}$ is a generalized present value factor from time t_2 back to time t_1.

From a general point of view, when a financial transaction is represented algebraically it is usually formulated by means of one or more equations that represent the values of the various components of the transaction and their interrelationships. Along with the interest rate in effect, the components of the transaction are amounts already disbursed or yet to be disbursed and amounts already received or yet to be received. These amounts are called *dated cash flows*. A mathematical representation of the transaction will be an equation that balances the dated cash outflows and inflows, according to the particulars of the transaction. A transaction will usually consist of a series of one or more payments disbursed in combination with a series of one or more payments received, all at various points in time. The equation balancing these payments must take into account the "time values" of these payments, the accumulated and present values of the payments made at the various time points. Such a balancing equation is called an *equation of value* for the transaction, and its formulation is a central element in the process of analyzing a financial transaction.

In order to formulate an equation of value for a transaction, it is first necessary to choose a reference time point or focal date. At the reference time point the equation of value balances, or equates, the following two factors:

(1) the accumulated value of all payments already disbursed plus the present value of all payments yet to be disbursed, and
(2) the accumulated value of all payments already received plus the present value of all payments yet to be received.

EXAMPLE 1.7

Every Friday in February (the 7th, 14th, 21st, and 28th) Walt places a 1000 bet, on credit, with his bookie, who charges an effective weekly interest rate of 8% on all credit extended. Unfortunately for Walt, he loses each bet and agrees to repay his debt to the bookie in four installments, to be made on March 7, 14, 21, and 28. Walt pays 1100 on each of March 7, 14, and 21. How much must Walt pay on March 28 to completely repay his debt?

Received				Paid			
1000	1000	1000	1000	1100	1100	1100	X
2/7	2/14	2/21	2/28	3/7	3/14	3/21	3/28
0	1	2	3	4	5	6	7

FIGURE 1.3

SOLUTION

The payments in the transaction are represented in Figure 1.3. We must choose a reference time point at which to formulate the equation of value. If we choose February 7 ($t = 0$) as the reference point, the value then of what Walt has already received and is yet to receive (on credit) is $1000(1 + v + v^2 + v^3)$, representing the four weekly credit amounts received in February, where v is the present value factor $\frac{1}{1.08}$ and t is measured in weeks. The value at $t = 0$ of what Walt must pay is $1100(v^4 + v^5 + v^6) + X \cdot v^7$, representing the three payments of 1100 and the fourth payment of X. The equation of value is then

$$1000(1 + v + v^2 + v^3) = 1100(v^4 + v^5 + v^6) + X \cdot v^7. \qquad (A)$$

Solving for X results in

$$X = \frac{1000(1 + v + v^2 + v^3) - 1100(v^4 + v^5 + v^6)}{v^7} = 2273.79. \text{ (B)}$$

If we choose March 28 $(t = 7)$ as the reference time point, then $1000[(1+j)^7 + (1+j)^6 + (1+j)^5 + (1+j)^4]$ is the value of what Walt has received, and the value of what he has repaid is given by $1100[(1+j)^3 + (1+j)^2 + (1+j)] + X$, where $j = .08$. The equation of value is then

$$1000[(1+j)^7 + (1+j)^6 + (1+j)^5 + (1+j)^4]$$
$$= 1100[(1+j)^3 + (1+j)^2 + (1+j)] + X. \text{ (C)}$$

Solving for X results in

$$X = 1000[(1+j)^7 + (1+j)^6 + (1+j)^5 + (1+j)^4]$$
$$- 1100[(1+j)^3 + (1+j)^2 + (1+j)] = 2273.79. \text{ (D)}$$
$$\square$$

We see from Example 1.7 that an equation of value for a transaction involving compound interest may be formulated at more than one reference time point with the same ultimate solution. Notice that Equation C can be obtained from Equation A by multiplying Equation A by $(1+j)^7$. This corresponds to a change in the reference point upon which the equations are based, Equation A being based on $t = 0$ and Equation C being based on $t = 7$. In general, when a transaction involves only compound interest, an equation of value formulated at time t_1 can be translated into an equation of value formulated at time t_2 simply by multiplying the first equation by $(1 + i)^{t_2 - t_1}$. In Example 1.7, when $t = 7$ was chosen as the reference point, the solution was simpler than that required for the equation of value at $t = 0$, in that no division was necessary. For most transactions there will often be one reference time point that allows a more efficient solution of the equation of value than any other reference time point.

When considering transactions that involve simple interest accumulations, more care must be taken in choosing a reference time point for the equation of value as compared with transactions involving compound interest. This is a consequence of the property of present value illustrated in Example 1.6. Under compound interest, any equation of value at time t_1 can be transformed into an equivalent equation of value at time $t_2 > t_1$ simply by multiplying the first equation by $(1+i)^{t_2-t_1}$, since, under compound interest, interest is assumed to be reinvested and the accumulation factor for the period from t_1 to t_2 is $(1+i)^{t_2-t_1}$. Under the operation of simple interest, it is *not* true that the equation of value at time t_2 can be obtained by multiplying the equation of value at time t_1 by $1+i\cdot(t_2-t_1)$ (this being the simple interest accumulation factor for the period from t_1 to t_2 for interest accrual beginning at t_1). This is so because under simple interest the values of the various components can not be regarded as being reinvested at time t_1. Thus in setting up an equation of value when simple interest is in operation, the reference time point that usually is chosen is the time at which the transaction terminates. This is considered in the following example.

EXAMPLE 1.8

Don owns shares in a public company and will receive a dividend payment on the 15th of every March, June, September, and December of this year. On each dividend date he wishes to deposit a level amount X into a bank account earning interest at annual rate $i = .12$, so that the account has an accumulated value of 1000 after interest is credited on December 31 this year. Find X if the account earns simple interest from the date of deposit to the interest credit date of December 31.

SOLUTION

With December 31 as the reference point, the equation of value is

$$X\left[1+(.12)\left(\tfrac{291}{365}\right)\right] + X\left[1+(.12)\left(\tfrac{199}{365}\right)\right]$$
$$+ X\left[1+(.12)\left(\tfrac{107}{365}\right)\right] + X\left[1+(.12)\left(\tfrac{16}{365}\right)\right] = 1000,$$

which produces $X = 238.01$. (If we choose March 15 as the reference time point, a difficulty arises. The equation of value is *not*

$$X+ \frac{X}{1+(.12)(\tfrac{92}{365})} + \frac{X}{1+(.12)(\tfrac{184}{365})} + \frac{X}{1+(.12)(\tfrac{275}{365})} = \frac{1000}{1+(.12)(\tfrac{291}{365})},$$

which leads to $X = 238.26$, which, if deposited on the specified dates, would grow to 1001.06 on December 31.)   ☐

Note that in Example 1.8, with December 31 taken as the reference point for the transaction, the interest earned may be described and calculated as *interest on the average balance outstanding* (or *average balance invested*) throughout the interest period. The average balance is $B = \dfrac{291X + 199X + 107X + 16X}{365}$, and X is found from the relation $4X + .12B = 1000$, leading to $X = 238.01$, as before. Exercise 1.3.2 shows that the use of an average balance is valid whenever the transaction termination date is used as the point of reference in a simple interest transaction.

1.4 NOMINAL RATES OF INTEREST

Quoted annual rates of interest frequently do not refer to the effective annual rate. Consider the following example.

EXAMPLE 1.9

Sam has just received a credit card with a credit limit of 1000. The card issuer quotes an annual charge on unpaid balanced of 24%, payable monthly. Sam immediately uses his card to its limit. The first statement Sam receives indicates that his balance is 1000 but no interest has yet been charged. Each subsequent statement includes interest on the unpaid part of his previous month's statement. He ignores the statements for a year, and makes no payments toward the balance owed. What amount does Sam owe according to his thirteenth statement?

SOLUTION

Sam's first statement will have a balance of 1000 owing, with no interest charge. Subsequent monthly statements will apply a monthly interest charge of $\left(\frac{1}{12}\right)(24\%) = 2\%$ on the unpaid balance from the previous month. Thus Sam's unpaid balance is compounding at an effective one-month rate of 2%. The balance on statement 13 (12 months after statement 1) will have compounded for 12 months to $1000(1.02)^{12} = 1268.23$, with rounding to the nearest penny each month. (The exact value is 1268.24.) The effective annual interest rate charged on the account in the 12 months following the first month is 26.82% and not the quoted 24%, because the quoted rate is a *nominal annual rate*, not an effective annual rate. This example shows that a nominal annual interest rate of 24% compounded monthly is equivalent to an effective annual rate of 26.82%. □

Nominal rates of interest occur frequently in practice. They correspond to situations in which interest is credited or compounded more often than once per year. Example 1.9 illustrates a case in which the quoted nominal annual rate must be transformed into an effective one-month rate. A nominal annual rate can be associated with any interest compounding period, such as six months, one month, or one week. In order to apply a quoted nominal annual rate it is necessary to know the associated interest compounding period, or, equivalently, the number of interest conversion periods in a year. In Example 1.9 the associated interest compounding period is indicated by the phrase "payable monthly," so the effective interest period is one month. This could also be stated in any of the following ways: (i) annual interest rate of 24%, compounded monthly, (ii) annual interest rate of 24%, convertible monthly, or (iii) annual interest rate of 24%, convertible 12 times per year. All of these phrases mean that the 24% quoted annual rate is to be transformed to an effective one-month rate of one-twelfth of the quoted annual rate, $(\frac{1}{12})(.24) = .02$. The compound rate is a fraction of the quoted annual rate corresponding to the fraction of a year represented by the interest compounding period.

In Example 1.9 the quoted nominal annual rate of 24% compounded monthly is equivalent to an effective annual rate of 26.82%. The notion of equivalence of two rates was introduced in Section 1.2, where it was stated that rates are equivalent if they result in the same compound accumulation over any equal periods of time. This can be seen in the case of the nominal annual 24% compounded monthly and effective annual 26.82%. The nominal annual 24% refers to a compound monthly rate of 2%. Then in t years ($12t$ months) the growth of an initial investment of amount 1 will be $(1.02)^{12t} = [(1.02)^{12}]^t = (1.2682)^t$. But $(1.2682)^t$ is the growth in t years at effective annual rate 26.82%, which verifies the equivalence of the two rates. The typical way to verify equivalence is to convert one rate to the compounding period of the other rate, using compound interest. In the case just considered, the compound monthly rate of 2% can be converted to an equivalent effective annual growth factor of $(1.02)^{12} = 1.2682$. Alternatively, an effective annual rate of 26.82% can be converted to a compound monthly growth factor of $(1.2682)^{1/12} = 1.02$.

Once the nominal annual interest rate and compounding interest period are known, the corresponding compound interest rate for the interest conversion period can be found. Then the accumulation function follows a compound interest pattern, with time usually measured in units of effective interest conversion periods. When comparing nominal annual interest rates with differing interest conversion periods, it is necessary to convert the rates to equivalent rates with a common effective interest period. The following example illustrates this.

EXAMPLE 1.10

Tom is trying to decide between two banks in which to open an account. Bank A offers an annual rate of 15.25% with interest credited semiannually, and Bank B offers an annual rate of 15% with interest credited monthly. Which bank will give Tom a higher effective annual growth?

SOLUTION

Bank A pays effective 6-month interest of $\frac{1}{2}(15.25\%) = 7.625\%$. In one year (two effective interest periods) a deposit of amount 1 will grow to $(1.07625)^2 = 1.158314$ in Bank A. Bank B pays an effective monthly interest rate of $\frac{1}{12}(15\%) = 1.25\%$. In one year (12 effective interest periods) a deposit of amount 1 in Bank B will grow to $(1.0125)^{12} = 1.160755$. Bank B has an equivalent effective annual rate that is almost $\frac{1}{4}\%$ higher than that of Bank A.   □

In order to compare quoted nominal annual rates with differing interest conversion periods equitably, it is necessary to transform them to some common time basis, such as an effective annual period as in Example 1.10.

There is standard notation for denoting nominal annual rates of interest. Whereas the symbol i is generally reserved for denoting an effective annual rate, the symbol $i^{(m)}$ is reserved for denoting a nominal annual rate with interest credited (or compounded, or convertible) m times per year. Thus $i^{(m)}$ refers to an interest compounding period of $\frac{1}{m}$ years and compound rate per period of $\frac{1}{m} \cdot i^{(m)} = \frac{i^{(m)}}{m}$. In Example 1.9, $m = 12$, so the nominal annual rate is denoted by $i^{(12)} = .24$. Similarly, in Example 1.10 the nominal annual rates would be $i^{(2)} = .1525$ and $i^{(12)} = .15$ for Banks A and B, respectively.

The nominal annual rate $i^{(m)}$ implies a $\frac{1}{m}$-year compound rate $j = \frac{i^{(m)}}{m}$. Then after t interest conversion periods of length $\frac{1}{m}$ years each (*i.e.*, after $\frac{t}{m}$ years), an initial investment of 1 would accumulate to $(1+j)^t = \left[1 + \frac{i^{(m)}}{m}\right]^t$. The accumulated value after one year (m interest compounding periods) would be $\left[1 + \frac{i^{(m)}}{m}\right]^m$. If we let i denote the effective annual rate equivalent to $i^{(m)}$, then in one year 1 grows to $1 + i$, and this leads to the basic equation linking a nominal annual rate to its corresponding equivalent effective annual rate,

$$1 + i = \left[1 + \frac{i^{(m)}}{m}\right]^m. \tag{1.4}$$

If we are given numerical values for $i^{(m)}$ and m, the equivalent effective annual rate i can be found from

$$i = \left[1 + \frac{i^{(m)}}{m}\right]^m - 1. \tag{1.5}$$

If we are given i and m, then the equivalent $i^{(m)}$ can be found from

$$i^{(m)} = m\left[(1+i)^{1/m} - 1\right]. \tag{1.6}$$

Then $(1 + i)^{1/m}$ is the $\frac{1}{m}$-year growth factor and $(1 + i)^{1/m} - 1 = \frac{i^{(m)}}{m}$ is the equivalent $\frac{1}{m}$-year compound interest rate.

EXAMPLE 1.11

On December 31 Smith deposits 1000 in an account paying interest quarterly. On December 31 of the following year, just after interest is credited, he has a balance of 1114.62. What is the quoted nominal annual rate of interest on his account?

SOLUTION

The effective annual rate is 11.462%, or $i = .11462$. With $m = 4$, the equivalent nominal annual interest rate, convertible quarterly, is

$$i^{(4)} = 4\left[(1+i)^{1/4} - 1\right] = 4\left[(1.11462)^{1/4} - 1\right] = 4[1.0275 - 1] = .1100,$$

or 11%. Then $(1 + i)^{1/4} = (1.11462)^{1/4} = 1.02750$ is the 3-month growth factor, and the 3-month compound interest rate is 2.75%. Alternatively, the 3-month compound interest rate is j, where $(1 + j)^4 = 1.11462$, so that $1 + j = 1.0275$. □

It should be emphasized that $i^{(m)}$ is a notational convenience for describing nominal annual rates. Once the compounding period and rate are known, accumulation follows the pattern of compound interest.

It should be intuitively clear that with a given nominal annual rate of interest, the more often compounding takes place during the year, the larger the year-end accumulated value will be, so the larger the equivalent effective annual rate will be as well. This is verified algebraically in Exercise 1.4.2. It is interesting to observe the relationship between equivalent i and $i^{(m)}$ as m changes.

EXAMPLE 1.12

Suppose the nominal annual rate is 12%. Find the equivalent effective annual rates for $m = 1, 2, 3, 4, 6, 8, 12, 52, 365, \infty$.

SOLUTION

$m = 1$ implies interest convertible annually ($m = 1$ time per year), which implies the effective annual interest rate $i^{(1)} = i = .12$. We use Equation (1.5) to solve for i for the other values of m. The results are given in Table 1.1.   □

The limit in the final line of Table 1.1 is a consequence of l'Hospital's Rule; see Exercise 1.4.2. Note that if $m > 1$, then $.12 = i^{(m)} < i$. Because of compounding, the nominal annual 12% results in effective annual growth of more than 12%. It can also be seen from Table 1.1 that the more frequently compounding takes place (*i.e.*, as m increases), the larger is the equivalent effective annual rate. As compounding goes from annual ($m = 1$) to semiannual ($m = 2$) to monthly ($m = 12$), there are significant increases in the equivalent effective annual rate. The increases are less significant, however, in going from monthly to weekly or even daily compounding, so we see that there is a limit to the benefit of compounding. With a nominal annual rate of 12%, the maximum equivalent effective annual rate that can be attained is 12.75%. No matter how often compounding takes place, the effective annual rate will not exceed 12.75%. The limiting case ($m \to \infty$) in Example 1.12 is called continuous compounding and is related to the notions of *force of interest* and instantaneous growth rate of an investment. This is discussed in Section 1.6.

TABLE 1.1

m (effective period)	$\frac{1}{m}$-year effective interest rate $\frac{i^{(m)}}{m}$	$i = \left[1 + \frac{i^{(m)}}{m}\right]^m - 1$
1 (1 year)	$\frac{i^{(1)}}{1} = \frac{.12}{1} = .12$	$(1.12)^1 - 1 = .12$
2 (6 months)	$\frac{i^{(2)}}{2} = \frac{.12}{2} = .06$	$(1.06)^2 - 1 = .1236$
3 (4 months)	$\frac{i^{(3)}}{3} = \frac{.12}{3} = .04$	$(1.04)^3 - 1 = .124864$
4 (3 months)	$\frac{i^{(4)}}{4} = \frac{.12}{4} = .03$	$(1.03)^4 - 1 = .125509$
6 (2 months)	$\frac{i^{(6)}}{6} = \frac{.12}{6} = .02$	$(1.02)^6 - 1 = .126162$
8 (1.5 months)	$\frac{i^{(8)}}{8} = \frac{.12}{8} = .015$	$(1.015)^8 - 1 = .126593$
12 (1 month)	$\frac{i^{(12)}}{12} = \frac{.12}{12} = .01$	$(1.01)^{12} - 1 = .126825$
52 (1 week)	$\frac{i^{(52)}}{52} = \frac{.12}{52} = .0023$	$\left(1+\frac{.12}{52}\right)^{52} - 1 = .127341$
365 (1 day)	$\frac{i^{(365)}}{365} = \frac{.12}{365} = .00033$	$\left(1+\frac{.12}{365}\right)^{365} - 1 = .127475$
∞	$\lim_{y \to \infty}\left(1+\frac{.12}{y}\right)^y - 1 = e^{.12} - 1 = .127497$	

Example 1.12 illustrated the behavior of the equivalent effective annual interest rate i as the frequency of compounding increases, based on the fixed nominal annual rate $i^{(m)} = .12$. The following example illustrates the behavior of the equivalent $i^{(m)}$ as m increases while the effective annual rate i is held fixed.

EXAMPLE 1.13
Suppose that $i = .12$. Find the equivalent nominal rates $i^{(m)}$ for $m = 1, 2, 3, 4, 6, 8, 12, 52, 365, \infty$.
SOLUTION
We use Equation (1.6) to solve for $i^{(m)}$. The results are shown in Table 1.2. □

In Table 1.2 the second column shows the equivalent compound rate for the corresponding compound interest period. For example, for $m = 2$, .0583 is the half-year, or 6-month compound rate equivalent to an effective annual rate of 12%. Example 1.13 shows that as compounding takes place more frequently, a *lower* nominal annual rate is required in order to be equivalent to the fixed effective annual rate of 12%. This is verified algebraically in Exercise 1.4.2, where it is shown that for a fixed value of i, $i^{(m)}$ is a decreasing function of m. In other words, for $m > n > 1$, nominal rates equivalent to i satisfy the relationship $i^{(\infty)} < i^{(m)} < i^{(n)} < i$.

A nominal rate, although quoted on an annual basis, may refer to only the immediately following fraction of a year. For instance, in Example 1.10 Bank B's quoted nominal annual rate of 15% with interest credited monthly might apply only to the coming month, after which the quoted rate (still credited monthly) might change to 13.5%. Thus when interest is quoted on a nominal annual basis, the actual rate may change during the course of the year, from one interest period to the next.

In the past few sections of this chapter we have characterized investment growth by means of interest accumulating into the future based on amounts invested at the present time. It is sometimes convenient to measure investment growth in terms of present or "discounted" values of specified amounts due at specified points in the future, and we have already seen this to a certain extent in the discussion of present value in the previous section.

TABLE 1.2

m	$(1 + i)^{1/m} - 1$	$i^{(m)} = m[(1 + i)^{1/m} - 1]$
1	.12	.12
2	.0583	.1166
3	.0385	.1155
4	.0287	.1149
6	.0191	.1144
8	.0143	.1141
12	.0095	.1139
52	.00218	.1135
365	.000311	.113346
∞	$\lim_{m \to \infty} m[(1 + i)^{1/m} - 1] = ln(1 + i) = .113329$	

1.5 EFFECTIVE AND NOMINAL RATES OF DISCOUNT, AND INTEREST-IN-ADVANCE

To this point interest amounts have been regarded as paid or charged at the end of an interest compounding period, and the corresponding interest rate is the ratio of the amount of interest paid at the end of the period to the amount of principal invested or loaned at the start of the period. Interest rates and amounts viewed in this way are sometimes referred to as *interest payable in arrears* (*i.e.*, payable at the end of an interest period). This is the standard way in which interest rates, effective and nominal, are quoted and amounts are calculated, and in many situations it is the method required by law.

Occasionally a transaction calls for *interest payable in advance*. In this case the quoted interest rate is applied to obtain an amount of interest which is payable at the *start* of the interest period. For example, if Smith borrows 1000 for one year at a quoted rate of 10% with interest payable in advance, the 10% is applied to the loan amount of 1000, resulting in an amount of interest of 100 for the year. However, the interest is payable in advance, at the time the loan is made. Thus Smith receives the loan amount of 1000 and must immediately pay the lender 100, the amount of interest on the loan. One year later he must repay the loan amount of 1000. The net effect is that Smith receives 900 and repays 1000 one year later. Regarding the loan amount of 1000 as the principal in this transaction, Smith receives an amount (900) that is *discounted* (by 10%) from the principal (1000), and must repay the principal one year later. This rate of 10% payable in advance is called the *rate of discount* for the transaction. It is also possible to regard the discounted amount received by the borrower at the time of the loan as the principal (900 in this case). One should be clear as to which amount is considered to be the principal.

From the lender's point of view, a loan with principal amount 1000 has just been made, 100 is paid now and 1000 is to be paid one year from now. If we assume that the 100 received now can be loaned out in a similar manner at the same rate, the lender will now receive 10 (as interest-in-advance) on the 100 and will receive 100 (as well as the original 1000) one year from now. This can be done again, with the lender making a loan of 10 repayable one year from now with interest-in-advance of 1 due now. Continuing this indefinitely, we see that the lender can arrange the loan so that the total repaid one year from now is $1000 + 100 + 10 + 1 + .1 + .01 + \cdots = 1111.11$, so the lender receives an equivalent effective annual return of 11.11% on the original loan of 1000. This is the concept of *interest-in-advance*. The 10% rate of interest-in-advance is equivalent to an effective interest rate (in arrears) of 11.11%. The concepts of interest-in-advance and discount are very similar, and mathematical calculations involving them are identical.

Smith's transaction has an effective annual interest rate of $\frac{100}{900} = .1111$, or 11.11%. Measured as an *effective annual interest rate* (interest in arrears), the loan rate is 11.11% (100 is 11.11% of 900), but measured as an *effective annual discount rate*, the rate is 10% (100 is 10% of 1000). Both descriptions, arrears and advance, refer to the same transaction. They are different but equivalent ways of measuring interest on a transaction. Thus we see that an effective annual interest rate of 11.11% is equivalent to an effective annual discount rate of 10%.

In terms of an accumulated amount function, the general definition of the effective annual rate of discount from time $t = 0$ to time $t = 1$ is

$$d = \frac{S(1) - S(0)}{S(1)}. \tag{1.7}$$

This definition is in contrast with that for the effective annual rate of interest, given earlier in this chapter, which has the same numerator but has a denominator of $S(0)$. Effective annual interest measures growth on the basis of the initially invested amount, whereas effective annual discount measures growth on the basis of the year-end accumulated amount. Both measures can be used in the analysis of a financial transaction.

Equation (1.7) can be rewritten as $S(0) = S(1) \cdot (1 - d)$, so $1 - d$ acts as a present value factor. The value at the start of the year is the principal of $S(1)$ minus $d \cdot S(1)$, the interest payable in advance. On the other hand, on the basis of effective annual interest we have $S(0) = S(1) \cdot v$. Then for d and i to be equivalent rates, we must have $\frac{1}{1+i} = v = 1 - d$, or, equivalently, $i = \frac{d}{1-d}$ or $d = \frac{i}{1+i}$. With $d = .10$ in the situation outlined above, we have $i = \frac{d}{1-d} = \frac{.1}{1-.1} = .1111$, or 11.11%. The relationships between equivalent interest and discount rates for periods of other than a year are similar, for example $d_j = \frac{j}{1+j}$.

From a practical point of view, $S(0)$ in Equation (1.7) will not be less than 0. Then assuming $S(1) > S(0)$, an effective rate of discount can be no larger than 1. (Note that effective discount of 100% implies a present value factor of $1 - 1 = 0$ at the start of the period.) In the equivalence between i and d we see that $\lim_{i\to\infty} d = 1$, so that very large effective interest rates correspond to equivalent effective discount rates near 100%. The following example further outlines the relationship between equivalent interest and discount rates.

EXAMPLE 1.14

Among the various securities issued by governments are *treasury bills* (or *T-bills*). A T-bill issued at time 0 with duration t and face amount F is an obligation to pay the T-bill holder an amount F at time t. Suppose Smith buys a 91-day T-bill with face amount 1,000,000 for a purchase price of 979,640. Find the effective 91-day interest and discount rates and verify their equivalence.

SOLUTION

The amount of interest earned by Smith over the 91-day period is $1,000,000 - 979,640 = 20,360$. Then $d_j = \dfrac{20,360}{1,000,000} = .02036$ is the 91-day discount rate, and $j = \dfrac{20,360}{979,640} = .02078$ is the 91-day interest rate. Then

$$d_j = .02036 = \frac{.02078}{1 + .02078} = \frac{j}{1+j}. \qquad \square$$

T-bills are often sold with durations of 91 days (13 weeks) or 182 days (26 weeks), and are issued every Thursday with maturities 13 or 26 weeks later so that the issue and maturity days of the week coincide. There is an active secondary market in T-bills and they are a popular short-term and low risk investment vehicle. When T-bill sales are reported in the financial press, they are described in terms of a nominal annual interest rate and also by a purchase price per 100 of face amount. For the T-bill in Example 1.14, the quoted price would be 97.964 and the interest rate would be quoted as a nominal annual rate convertible every 91 days, $i^{\left(\frac{365}{91}\right)}$ (see Exercise 1.4.4). The rate $i^{\left(\frac{365}{91}\right)}$ must satisfy $\dfrac{91}{365} \cdot i^{\left(\frac{365}{91}\right)} = .02078$, the 91-day interest rate, so the quoted rate would be $\left(\dfrac{365}{91}\right)(.02078) = .0834$, or 8.34%. In the United States the yield may also be quoted on a nominal annual discount basis using a 360-day year, so the quoted annual yield as a discount rate would be $\left(\dfrac{360}{91}\right)(.02036) = .0805$.

Prices are quoted to the nearest one-tenth of a cent per 100 of face amount, and nominal annual interest rates are quoted to the nearest .01%. (See Exercise 1.5.2 which considers the potential for roundoff error in the quoted rate and price.) The U.S. government's Truth in Lending legislation requires that financial institutions making loans based on discount rates make clear to borrowers the equivalent interest rate being charged. Thus a discount rate of 8% cannot be presented as a loan rate of 8%, but must rather be presented as the equivalent interest rate, $i = \dfrac{d}{1-d} = 8.7\%$.

Corresponding to an effective annual discount rate d is the present value factor $1 - d = v$. The present value of 1 due in n years can then be represented in the form $v^n = (1-d)^n$, so that present values can be represented in the form of *compound discount*. This underlines the fact that the notions of discount rate and compound discount form an alternative to the notions of interest rate and compound interest in characterizing the behavior of an investment. (See Exercise 1.5.5.)

The calculation of present value over durations of less than one year is sometimes based on *simple discount*. At a quoted annual simple discount rate of d, the present value of 1 due in t years is given by $1 - d \cdot t$, where $0 < t < 1$. Note that there is an inherent restriction on t, in that it only makes sense for the present value, $1 - d \cdot t$, to be greater than 0. Therefore, $t < \dfrac{1}{d}$. The considerations regarding the measurement of t (day count, etc.) are the same as those for simple interest.

Promissory notes are occasionally sold based on simple discount from the maturity value, as illustrated in the following example.

EXAMPLE 1.15

On June 18 Jones borrows 5000 from Smith and gives Smith a promissory note at annual interest rate 8% with a maturity date of April 18 in the following year. Brown buys the note from Smith on August 3, based on simple discount at annual rate 9%. Determine Brown's purchase price and the equivalent effective annual interest rates earned by each of Brown and Smith on the transaction.

SOLUTION

The note's maturity value is $5000\left[1 + \left(\dfrac{304}{365}\right)(.08)\right] = 5333.15$, so Brown pays

$5333.15\left[1 - \left(\dfrac{258}{365}\right)(.09)\right] = 4993.87$. He earns a 258-day interest rate of

$\dfrac{5333.15 - 4993.87}{4993.87} = .067939$, for an equivalent effective annual rate of

$(1.067939)^{365/258} - 1 = .097452$, or 9.75%. Smith's 46-day rate is

$\dfrac{-6.13}{5000} = -.001226$, since Smith lost money on the transaction. His equivalent effective annual rate is given by $(1-.001226)^{365/46} - 1 = -.009687$, or about -1%. $\qquad\qquad\qquad\qquad\qquad\qquad\qquad\qquad\qquad\qquad\qquad\qquad\qquad$ $\square$

Discount rates may be quoted on a nominal annual basis in the same way as interest rates. The relationship between equivalent nominal and effective annual discount rates parallels in a reverse way the relationship between nominal and effective annual interest rates. The symbol $d^{(m)}$ implies a $\frac{1}{m}$-year compound discount rate of $\frac{d^{(m)}}{m}$. The $\frac{1}{m}$-year present value factor is then $1 - \frac{d^{(m)}}{m}$. This would compound m times in a year, resulting in an annual present value factor of $\left(1 - \frac{d^{(m)}}{m}\right)^{m}$. If d is the equivalent effective annual discount rate, then

$$1 - d = \left(1 - \frac{d^{(m)}}{m}\right)^{m}. \qquad\qquad (1.8)$$

This outlines the relationship between equivalent nominal and effective annual discount rates. The following example illustrates the relationship numerically.

EXAMPLE 1.16

Suppose that $d = .107143$. Find the equivalent nominal annual discount rates $d^{(m)}$ for $m = 1, 2, 3, 4, 6, 8, 12, 52, 365, \infty$.

SOLUTION

Using Equation (1.8) we solve for $d^{(m)} = m[1 - (1-d)^{1/m}]$. The numerical results are tabulated below in Table 1.3. $\qquad\qquad\qquad\qquad\qquad\qquad$ $\square$

TABLE 1.3

m	$1 - (1-d)^{1/m}$	$d^{(m)} = m[1 - (1-d)^{1/m}]$
1	.107143	.107143
2	.0551	.1102
3	.0371	.1112
4	.0279	.1117
6	.0187	.1123
8	.0141	.1125
12	.0094	.1128
52	.0022	.1132
365	.0003	.11331
∞		.11333

Note that as m increases, $d^{(m)}$ increases with upper limit $d^{(\infty)}$; thus if $m > n$, then $d^{(m)} > d^{(n)}$ for equivalent rates. This is the opposite of what happens for equivalent nominal interest rates (see Example 1.13). This can be explained by noting that interest compounds on amounts increasing in size whereas discount compounds on amounts decreasing in size (see Exercise 1.5.4).

The effective annual discount rate used in Example 1.16 is $d = .107143$, which is equivalent to an effective interest rate of $i = .12$. It was chosen to facilitate comparison with Table 1.2 in Example 1.13. Exercise 1.5.5 examines in more detail the numerical relationship between equivalent nominal annual interest and discount rates, and refers to the equivalent rates in the tables from Examples 1.13 and 1.16. Note that the nominal annual interest rate convertible continuously from Example 1.13 is $i^{(\infty)} = .1133$, which is equal to $d^{(\infty)}$ in Example 1.16. In general, for equivalent rates i and d it is always the case that $d^{(\infty)} = i^{(\infty)}$, referred to earlier as the *force of interest* (see Exercise 1.5.4).

It is not practical to have interest compounding continuously in the sense of actually updating accumulated values every few minutes or hours. The continuous function $(1 + i)^t$ would be approximated by a step function, where interest is credited at certain points of time, such as daily, monthly, or semiannually. Nevertheless, the notion of force of interest is useful and important in the creation of mathematical models of financial transactions and for other theoretical purposes. The next section is concerned with the force of interest.

1.6   FORCE OF INTEREST

In the discussion of nominal rates of interest (Section 1.4) it was pointed out that a quoted nominal annual rate may refer only to a fraction of a year. For example, if a bank credits interest at a 3-month compound rate of 2% for the three-month period of January - February - March, the nominal annual rate convertible quarterly quoted by the bank would be found from the relationship $\frac{i^{(4)}}{4} = .02$, so that $i^{(4)} = .08$ for those three months. It is possible that for April - May - June the 3-month compound interest rate credited by the bank (and therefore the quoted nominal rate) may be adjusted, so that although quoted on an annual basis, a specified nominal annual interest rate might only be valid for a particular fraction of a year.

In general, with accumulated amount function $S(t)$, the accumulation from time t to time $t + \frac{1}{m}$ is from amount $S(t)$ to amount $S\left(t + \frac{1}{m}\right)$, and the $\frac{1}{m}$-year compound rate for that period is $\frac{S(t + \frac{1}{m}) - S(t)}{S(t)}$. If $i^{(m)}$ is the corresponding nominal annual rate convertible m times per year, then we have $\frac{i^{(m)}}{m} = \frac{S(t + \frac{1}{m}) - S(t)}{S(t)}$, or, equivalently,

$$i^{(m)} = \frac{S(t + \frac{1}{m}) - S(t)}{\frac{1}{m} \cdot S(t)}. \tag{1.9}$$

In this context $i^{(m)}$ is the quoted nominal annual rate of interest based on the investment performance from time t to time $t + \frac{1}{m}$.

If m is increased, the time interval $\left[t, t + \frac{1}{m}\right]$ decreases, and we are focusing more and more closely on the investment performance immediately following time t. Taking the limit as $m \to \infty$ in Equation (1.9) results in

$$i^{(\infty)} = \lim_{m \to \infty} \frac{S(t + \frac{1}{m}) - S(t)}{\frac{1}{m} \cdot S(t)}. \tag{1.10a}$$

Replacing $\frac{1}{m}$ with h on the right hand side, and noting that $h \to 0$ as $m \to \infty$, we see that Equation (1.10a) becomes

$$i^{(\infty)} = \frac{1}{S(t)} \cdot \lim_{h \to 0} \frac{S(t + h) - S(t)}{h} = \frac{1}{S(t)} \cdot \frac{d}{dt} S(t) = \frac{S'(t)}{S(t)}. \tag{1.10b}$$

The symbol $i^{(\infty)}$ can be regarded as a nominal annual rate of interest *compounded infinitely often* or *compounded continuously*. $i^{(\infty)}$ is a measure of the *instantaneous* rate of growth of the investment at time point t. The instantaneous rate of growth at time t is also called the *force of interest at time t*. Note that $S'(t)$ represents the absolute instantaneous rate of growth of the investment at time t (just as $S(t+1) - S(t)$ is the absolute *amount* of growth from t to $t + 1$), whereas $\frac{S'(t)}{S(t)}$ is the relative instantaneous rate of growth per unit amount invested (just as

$\frac{S(t+1) - S(t)}{S(t)}$ is the relative amount of growth from t to $t+1$ per unit invested at time t).

The force of interest may change as t changes, and the notation δ_t is used in place of $i^{(\infty)}$ to denote the force of interest at time t. It is clear that in order for the force of interest to be defined, the accumulated amount function must be differentiable and thus continuous. (A common situation is that $S(t)$ is continuous and differentiable except for finitely many points of discontinuity.)   In the following example the force of interest corresponding to each of simple and compound interest accumulation is derived.

| **EXAMPLE 1.17** |

Derive an expression for δ_t if accumulation is based on (a) simple interest, and (b) compound interest at annual rate i.

| **SOLUTION** |

(a) $S(t) = S(0) \cdot [1+i \cdot t]$, so $S'(t) = S(0) \cdot i$. Then $\delta_t = \frac{S'(t)}{S(t)} = \frac{i}{1+i \cdot t}$.

(b) $S(t) = S(0) \cdot (1+i)^t$, so that $S'(t) = S(0) \cdot (1+i)^t \cdot ln(1+i)$ which shows that $\delta_t = ln(1+i)$. In the case of compound interest growth, the force of interest is constant as long as the effective annual rate is constant. In the case of simple interest, δ_t decreases as t increases.   □

The force of interest is another measure that can be used to characterize investment growth.   Using Equation (1.10b) we have $\delta_t = \frac{1}{S(t)} \cdot \frac{d}{dt} S(t) = \frac{d}{dt} ln[S(t)]$. Integrating from $t = 1$ to $t = n$ results in $\int_0^n \delta_t \, dt = \int_0^n \frac{d}{dt} ln[S(t)] \, dt = ln[S(n)] - ln[S(0)] = ln\left[\frac{S(n)}{S(0)}\right]$. This can be rewritten in the form

$$S(n) = S(0) \cdot exp\left[\int_0^n \delta_t \, dt\right] \qquad (1.11a)$$

or

$$S(0) = S(n) \cdot exp\left[-\int_0^n \delta_t \, dt\right]. \qquad (1.11b)$$

Thus the n-year accumulation factor based on force of interest δ_t is $exp\left[\int_0^n \delta_t\, dt\right]$ and the n-year present value factor is $exp\left[-\int_0^n \delta_t\, dt\right]$. The general accumulation factor from time t_1 to time t_2 would be $exp\left[\int_{t_1}^{t_2} \delta_t\, dt\right]$. In the special case where δ_t is constant with value δ from t_1 to t_2, the accumulation factor simplifies to $e^{(t_2-t_1)\cdot\delta}$.

Another identity involving the force of interest is based on the relationship $\frac{d}{dt} S(t) = S(t) \cdot \delta_t$, so that integrating both sides from time 0 to time n results in

$$\int_0^n S(t) \cdot \delta_t\, dt = \int_0^n \frac{d}{dt} S(t)\, dt = S(n) - S(0), \qquad (1.12)$$

the amount of interest earned from time 0 to time n. In the integral, $S(t) \cdot \delta_t\, dt$ is the amount of interest earned at instant t.

EXAMPLE 1.18

Given $\delta_t = .08 + .005t$, find the accumulated value over five years of an investment of 1000 made at (a) time 0, and (b) time 2.

SOLUTION

(a) In this case, $S(0) = 1000$ and $S(5) = S(0) \cdot exp\left[\int_0^5 \delta_t\, dt\right]$, so that the accumulated value is

$$1000 \cdot exp\left[\int_0^5 (.08 + .005t)\, dt\right]$$

giving

$$1000 \cdot exp[(.08)(5) + (.0025)(25)] = 1000 \cdot e^{.4625} = 1588.04.$$

(b) This time we have $S(2) = 1000$ and $S(7) = S(2) \cdot exp\left[\int_2^7 \delta_t\, dt\right]$, so that the accumulated value over 5 years is

$$1000 \cdot exp\left[\int_2^7 (.08 + .005t)\, dt\right],$$

leading to

$$1000 \cdot exp[(.08)(7-2) + (.0025)(49-4)] = 1669.46. \qquad \square$$

It was shown in Example 1.17 that if the effective annual interest rate i is constant then $\delta_t = ln(1 + i)$. Now suppose the force of interest δ_t is constant with value δ from time $t = 1$ to time $t = n$. Then

$$S(n) = S(0) \cdot exp\left[\int_0^n \delta_t \, dt\right] = S(0) \cdot e^{n\delta} = S(0) \cdot (e^{\delta})^n. \quad (1.13)$$

This accumulation is similar to compound interest accumulation which is of the form $S(n) = S(0) \cdot (1 + i)^n$. In fact if $e^{\delta} = 1 + i$ then the two growth patterns are identical. In other words, a constant force of interest δ is equivalent to a constant effective annual interest rate i if they satisfy the relationship $e^{\delta} = 1 + i$, or, equivalently, $\delta = ln(1 + i)$. Example 1.17 illustrates the relationship that δ and i must satisfy in order to be equivalent rates. This relationship was already seen in Example 1.13, where an effective annual rate of $i = .12$ was used to find equivalent nominal annual rates $i^{(m)}$ for various values of m. For $m = \infty$ in that example, the rate $i^{(\infty)}$ was found to be $i^{(\infty)} = ln(1 + i) = .1133$, the force of interest equivalent to $i = .12$.

In Example 1.16 the nominal annual discount rates equivalent to $d = .107143$ (which is equivalent to $i = .12$) were found for various values of m. In particular it was seen that $d^{(\infty)} = .1133$ is the same as the $i^{(\infty)}$ equivalent to $i = .12$. Exercise 1.5.4(f) investigates why $i^{(\infty)}$ and $d^{(\infty)}$ are always equal for equivalent i and d. $d^{(\infty)}$ can be regarded as a *force of discount* similar in nature to the force of interest. This is examined in more detail in Exercise 1.6.1 where it is shown that $d^{(\infty)}$ can also be represented as $\dfrac{S'(t)}{S(t)}$.

| EXAMPLE 1.19 |

Find the accumulated value after 5 years of an initial investment of 10,000 if (a) $i = .12$, (b) $i^{(12)} = .12$, (c) $\delta = .12$, (d) $d^{(12)} = .12$, and (e) $d = .12$.

| SOLUTION |
(a) $10,000(1.12)^5 = 17,623.42$
(b) $10,000(1.01)^{60} = 18,166.97$
(c) $10,000(e^{.12})^5 = 18,221.19$
(d) $10,000(.99)^{-60} = 18,276.30$
(e) $10,000(.88)^{-5} = 18,949.01$ □

The explicit use of the force of interest does not often arise in a practical setting. However, for transactions of very short duration (a few days or only one day), a nominal annual interest rate convertible daily, $i^{(365)}$, might be used. This rate is approximately equal to an equivalent force of interest of $i^{(\infty)} = \delta$.

| EXAMPLE 1.20 |

Smith requires a one-day loan of 100,000 and is quoted a nominal rate of interest convertible daily of 12%. Find the amount of interest Smith must pay for the one-day loan. Suppose the loan was quoted at an annual force of interest of 12%. Find the interest Smith must pay in this case.

| SOLUTION |

With $i^{(365)} = .12$, the one-day effective rate of interest is $\frac{.12}{365}$, so that interest on 100,000 for one day will be 32.88 (to the nearest cent). If $\delta = .12$, then one day accumulation is from 100,000 to $100,000 \cdot e^{(1/365)(.12)} = 100,032.88$, so the interest for one day is again 32.88. (If calculations were taken to the nearest one-tenth of a cent, the amounts of interest would differ; see Exercise 1.6.2.) □

Using the more general accumulation function $s(t_1,t_2)$ described in Section 1.2, the more general force of interest function

$$\delta(t_1,t_2) = \frac{\frac{\partial}{\partial t_2} s(t_1,t_2)}{s(t_1,t_2)} \qquad (1.14)$$

can be defined.

Measuring investment growth by the force of interest is important in developing models of financial transactions. This is due to the continuous-differential nature of many theoretical financial models and the relative ease with which exponential factors can be combined algebraically. Examples of this will be seen in the consideration of stochastic (uncertain) rates of return in Chapter 5 and in the subject of cash flow matching in Chapter 6.

1.7 INFLATION AND THE "REAL" RATE OF INTEREST

Along with the level of interest rates, one of the most closely watched indicators of a country's economic performance and health is the rate of inflation. A widely used measure of inflation is the change in the *Consumer Price Index* (CPI), generally quoted on an annual basis. The change in the CPI measures the annual (effective) rate of change in the cost of a specified "basket" of consumer items. Alternative measures of inflation might be based on more specialized sectors in the economy.

Inflation rates vary from country to country. They may be extremely high in some economies and almost insignificant in others. It is sometimes the case that an economy experiences deflation for a period of time (negative inflation), characterized by a decreasing CPI. Politicians and economists have been involved in numerous debates on the causes and effects of inflation, its relationship to the country's economic health, and how best to reduce or prevent inflation.

Investors are also concerned with the level of inflation. It is clear that a high rate of inflation has the effect of rapidly reducing the value (purchasing power) of currency as time goes on. It is not surprising then that periods of high inflation are usually accompanied by high interest rates, since the rate of interest must be high enough to provide a "real" return on investment. The study of the cause and effect relationship between interest and inflation is the concern of economists. We are concerned here with analyzing the relationship between interest and inflation in terms of the measurement of return on investments.

We have used the phrase *real return* a few times already without being very specific as to its meaning. The real rate of interest refers to the *inflation-adjusted* return on an investment. The simple and commonly used measure of the real rate of interest is $i - r$, where i is the annual rate of interest and r is the annual rate of inflation. This measure is often seen in financial newspapers or journals. As a precise measure of the real growth on an investment, or real growth in purchasing power, $i - r$ is not quite correct. This is made clear in the following example.

EXAMPLE 1.21

Smith invests 1000 for one year at effective annual rate 15.5%. At the time Smith makes the investment, the cost of a certain consumer item is 1. One year later, when interest is paid and principal returned to Smith, the cost of the item has become 1.10. The price of the item has experienced annual inflation of 10%. What is the annual growth rate in Smith's purchasing power with respect to the consumer item?

SOLUTION

At the start of the year, Smith can buy 1000 items. At year end he receives $1000(1.155) = 1155$, and is able to buy $\frac{1155}{1.10} = 1050$ items. Thus Smith's purchasing power has grown by 5% (*i.e.*, $\frac{50}{1000}$). Regarding the 10% increase in the cost of the item as a measure of inflation, we have $i - r = .155 - .10 = .055$, so, in this case, $i - r$ is not a correct representation of the "real" return earned by Smith.   □

In Example 1.21 Smith would have to receive 1100 at the end of the year just to stay even with the 10% inflation rate. He actually receives interest plus principal for a total of 1155. Thus Smith receives $1000(1+i) - 1000(1+r) = 1000(i - r) = 55$ more than necessary to stay even with inflation, and this 55 is his "real" return on his investment. To measure this as a percentage, it seems natural to divide by 1000, the amount Smith initially invested. This results in a rate of $\frac{55}{1000} = .055 = i - r$, the simple measure of real growth mentioned before Example 1.21. A closer look, however, shows that the 55 in real return earned by Smith is paid in year-end dollars, whereas the 1000 was invested in year-beginning dollars. The dollar value at year end is not the same as that at year beginning, so that to regard the 55 as a percentage of the amount invested, we must measure the real return of 55 and the amount invested in equivalent dollars (dollars of equal value). The 1000 invested at year beginning is equal in purchasing value to 1100 at year end. Thus, based on year-end dollar value, Smith's real return of 55 should be measured as a percentage of 1100, the inflation-adjusted equivalent of the 1000 invested at the start of the year. On this basis the real rate earned by Smith is $\frac{55}{1100} = .05$, the actual growth in purchasing power.

In general, with annual interest rate i and annual inflation rate r, an investment of 1 at the start of a year will grow to $1 + i$ at year end. Of this $1 + i$, an amount of $1 + r$ is needed to maintain dollar value against inflation, *i.e.*, to maintain purchasing power of the original investment of 1. The remainder of $(1+i) - (1+r) = i - r$ is the "real" amount of growth in the investment, and this real return is paid at year end. The investment of 1 at the start of the year has an inflation-adjusted value of $1 + r$ at year end in year-end dollars. Thus the percentage growth in the investment, based in terms of year-end dollars, is

$$i_{real} = \frac{value\ of\ amount\ of\ real\ return\ (yr\text{-}end\ dollars)}{value\ of\ invested\ amount\ (yr\text{-}end\ dollars)} = \frac{i - r}{1 + r}, \quad (1.15)$$

which is a more accurate measure of the real rate of interest. Then the real growth factor is given by $1 + i_{real} = 1 + \frac{i-r}{1+r} = \frac{1+i}{1+r}$, so that $(1 + i_{real})(1 + r) = 1 + i$.

Notice that the lower the inflation rate r, the closer $1 + r$ is to 1, and so the closer $i - r$ is to $\frac{i-r}{1+r}$. On the other hand, if inflation is high, and it has been known to reach levels of a few hundred percent in some countries, then the denominator $1 + r$ becomes an important factor in

$\frac{i - r}{1 + r}$. For instance, if inflation is at a rate of 100% ($r = 1$) and interest is at a rate of 120% ($i = 1.2$), it usually being the case that interest is greater than inflation (see Exercise 1.7.1), then $i - r = .21$ but $\frac{i - r}{1 + r} = .10$.

One more point to note when considering the combination of interest and inflation to determine a real rate of interest is that inflation rates are generally quoted as the rate that has been experienced in the year just completed, whereas interest rates are usually quoted as those to be earned in the coming year. In order to make a meaningful comparison of interest and inflation, both rates should refer to the same one-year period. Thus a projected rate of inflation for the coming year should be used in conjunction with the interest rate for the coming year.

1.8   NOTES AND REFERENCES

Standard International Actuarial Notation was first adopted in 1898 at the 2nd International Actuarial Congress, and has been updated periodically since then. The current version of the notation is found in the article "International Actuarial Notation," on pages 166-176 of Volume 48 (1947) of the Transactions of the Actuarial Society of America. Although some texts in mathematics of finance use "*A*" for the accumulation function, it is more consistent with Standard International Actuarial Notation to use "*S* " or "*s* " for accumulation, and to use "*A*" or "*a*" for present value.

The representation of an accumulated amount function as a function of two variables in the form $S(s,t)$ is considered in detail in the papers "Accumulation Functions," published by the Society of Actuaries in the 1985.1 issue of ARCH, and "Actuarial Equivalence," in the 1988.2 issue of ARCH.

Governments at all levels (federal, state, provincial, and even municipal) have statutes regulating interest rates. These include usury laws limiting the level of interest rates and statutes specifying interest rate disclosure and interest calculation. For example, the Canadian Criminal Code contains a law limiting interest to an effective annual rate of 60%, and the U.S. Government's Truth in Lending legislation of 1968 requires nominal interest disclosure for most consumer borrowing.

Vaguely worded statutes regulating interest rates can result in legal disputes as to their interpretation. Section 4 of Canada's century-old *Interest Act* states that "Except as to mortgages on real estate, whenever interest is ... made payable at a rate or percentage per day, week, month, or ... for any period less than a year, no interest exceeding ... five per cent per annum shall be chargeable ... unless the contract contains an express statement of the yearly rate or percentage to which such other rate ... is equivalent." This legislation has resulted in numerous civil suits over which of nominal and effective annual rates are to be interpreted as satisfying the requirement of being equivalent to an interest rate quoted per week or month. The Canadian courts have mostly ruled that either nominal or effective annual rates satisfy the requirements of Section 4.

The book *Standard Securities Calculation Methods* published by the Securities Industry Association in 1973 was written as a reference for "the entire fixed-income investment community" to provide a "readily available source of the formulas, standards and procedures for performing calculations." Included in that book are detailed descriptions of the various methods applied in practice in finding t for simple interest calculations.

1.9 EXERCISES

Exercises 1.2

1.2.1 Smith needs to borrow 5000 for one year. He is offered the loan at an annual rate of 5%. He is also offered a loan of 10,000 at a lower rate of interest. If he borrows the 10,000, he can invest the excess 5000 for one year at 3%. How low must be the rate on the 10,000 loan in order for Smith to prefer it to the 5000 loan?

1.2.2 Smith has 1000 with which she wishes to purchase units in a mutual fund. The investment dealer takes a 9% "front-end load" from the gross payment. The remainder (910 in this case) is used to purchase units in the fund, which are valued at 4.00 per unit at the time of purchase. Six months later the units have a value of 5.00 and the fund managers claim that "the fund's unit value has experienced 25% growth in the past 6 months." When units of the fund are sold, there is a redemption fee of 1.5% of the value of the units redeemed. If Smith sells after 6 months, what is her 6-month return for the period? Suppose instead of having grown to 5.00 after 6 months, the unit values had dropped to 3.50. What is Smith's 6-month return in this case?

1.2.3   (a) Jones invests 100,000 in a 180-day short term guaranteed investment certificate at a bank, based on simple interest at annual rate 7.5%. After 120 days, interest rates have risen to 9% and Jones would like to redeem the certificate early and reinvest in a 60-day certificate at the higher rate. In order for there to be no advantage in redeeming early and reinvesting at the higher rate, what early redemption penalty (from the accumulated value of the investment certificate to that point) should the bank charge at the time of early redemption?

   (b) Jones wishes to invest funds for a one-year period. Jones can invest in a one-year guaranteed investment certificate at a rate of 8%. Jones can also invest in a 6-month GIC at annual rate 7.5%, and then reinvest the proceeds at the end of 6 months for another 6-month period. Find the minimum annual rate needed for a 6-month deposit at the end of the first 6-month period so that Jones accumulates at least the same amount with two successive 6-month deposits is she would with the one-year deposit.

1.2.4   At time 0, Al borrows 1 from Bob and issues Bob a promissory note for the loan, with payment due at time $t < 1$ (years) at interest rate i per annum. At time $t_1 < t$, Bob sells the promissory note to Carl. Carl pays Bob an amount X so that Bob's yield during the time he held the promissory note (from time 0 to time t_1) can be quoted as j_1 per annum and Carl's yield can be quoted as j_2 per annum.

   (a) Derive an expression for X in terms of j_1.
   (b) Derive an expression for X in terms of j_2 and i.
   (c) Show that if $j_1 = j_2$ then they are less than i.
   (d) Show that if j_2 increases then j_1 decreases, so that as prevailing interest rates rise and Carl's yield increases, the value of Bob's promissory note decreases.
   (e) Suppose that time 0 is March 15, time t is November 30, and time t_1 is June 12. Suppose also that $i = .13$. Find X and j_2 for each of the following values of j_1: .03, .08, .13, .18, .23. Note the pattern in the behavior of j_2 as it relates to j_1.

1.2.5   Smith deposits 1000 in Bank A on January 1. Bank A credits interest at annual rate $i = .15$. If Smith closes his account, he receives simple interest up to the time of withdrawal. Smith visits Bank B across the street and is told that he can open an account anytime that year and receive simple interest at annual rate $i = .145$, paid from the date of deposit to December 31. Smith consults his math of finance text and realizes that if he chooses the right day to close his account at Bank A and immediately redeposit the proceeds in a new account in Bank B he will maximize the return on his 1000 over that year. What is that day?

1.2.6   Smith has just filed his income tax return and is expecting to receive, in 60 days, a refund cheque of 1000. The tax service that helped Smith fill out his return offers to buy Smith's refund cheque from him. Their policy is to pay 85% of the face value of the cheque. What annual simple interest rate is implied? Smith negotiates with the tax service and sells his refund cheque for 900. To what annual simple interest rate does this correspond? Smith decides to deposit the 900 in an account which earns simple interest at annual rate 9%. What is the accumulated value of the account on the day he would have received his tax refund cheque? How many days would it take from the time of his initial deposit of 900 for the account to reach 1000?

1.2.7   (a) Smith's business receives an invoice from a supplier for 1000 with payment due within 30 days. The terms of payment allow for a discount of 2.5% if the bill is paid within 7 days. Smith does not have the cash on hand 7 days later, but decides to borrow the 975 to take advantage of the discount. What is the largest simple interest rate, as an annual rate, that Smith would be willing to pay on the loan?
        (b) Repeat part (a) with 30 replaced by n, .025 replaced by j, and 7 replaced by m ($< n$).

1.2.8   (a) With interest at six-month compound rate .0325, calculate the accumulated value after one year of an initial deposit of 1 if (i) the accumulation is calculated exactly, with fractions of a cent (to several decimal places) retained after the first interest payment, (ii) rounding to the nearest cent is done after interest is credited, and (iii) rounding to the nearest 1.

(b) Calculate compound interest accumulations each year for 20 years based on an effective annual interest rate of 10% by each of the two methods in part (a), based on initial invested amounts of 10, 1000, and 1,000,000.

1.2.9   Suppose that $i > 0$. Prove each of the following inequalities.
(a) $(1+i) + (1+i)^3 > 2(1+i)^2$
(b) $(1+i)^{10} + (1+i)^{30} > 2(1+i)^{20}$
(c) $(1+i)^n + (1+i)^m > 2(1+i)^{\frac{n+m}{2}}$, if $m > n \geq 0$

1.2.10 At an effective annual compound interest rate of $i > 0$, it is found that an investment doubles in a years, triples in b years, and 1 grows to 5 in c years.
(a) Is c greater than, equal to, or less than $\frac{3a+b}{2}$?
(b) To what amount does 10 grow in $3a + 2b$ years?
(c) In how many periods will 1000 grow to 1200?

1.2.11 2500 is invested. Find the accumulated value of the investment 10 years after it is made for each of the following rates.
(a) 4% annual simple interest
(b) 4% effective annual compound interest
(c) 6-month interest rate of 2%
(d) 3-month interest rate of 1%

1.2.12 For each of the following pairs of rates, determine which one results in more rapid investment growth.
(a) 17-day rate of $\frac{3}{4}$% or 67-day rate of 3%
(b) 17-day rate of $\frac{3}{2}$% or 67-day rate of 6%

1.2.13 If 1 is invested at periodic interest rate j, show that the amount of interest earned in the second period exceeds the amount of interest earned in the first period by j^2. Give a verbal explanation for this.

1.2.14 (a) For an investment whose accumulation is based on simple interest, show that doubling the interest rate has the same effect on the accumulated amount as doubling the time for accumulation.

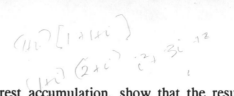

(b) For compound interest accumulation, show that the result in part (a) does not hold, and determine which has a greater effect on the accumulated amount.

1.2.15 (a) Show that at an effective annual compound interest rate of i, the amount of interest earned in successive years on an investment of 1 grows by a factor of $1 + i$ and these amounts are i, $(1 + i) \cdot i$, $(1 + i)^2 \cdot i$, $\ldots$, $(1 + i)^{n-1} \cdot i$ for the first, second, third, $\ldots$, n^{th} year, respectively.

(b) Using the fact that the amount of interest earned from time 0 to time n is $(1 + i)^n - 1$, derive a formula for the sum $1 + (1 + i) + (1 + i)^2 + \cdots + (1 + i)^{n-1}$.

1.2.16 If the 3-month compound interest rate is -3%, what is the accumulated value after 1 year of an initial investment of 1?

1.2.17 (a) Unit values in a mutual fund have experienced annual growth rates of 10%, 16%, -7%, 4%, and 32% in the past five years. The fund manager suggests the fund can advertise an average annual growth of 11% over the past five years. What is the actual average annual compound growth rate over the past five years?

(b) A mutual fund advertises that average annual compound rate of returns for various periods ending Dec. 31, 1995 are as follows:
10 years - 13%; 5 years - 17%; 2 years - 15%; 1 year - 22%.
Find the 5 year average annual compound rate of return for the period January 1, 1986 to December 31, 1990, and find the annual rate of return for calendar year 1994.

(c) Using the fact that the geometric mean of a collection of positive numbers is less than or equal to the arithmetic mean, show that if annual compound interest rates over an n-year period are i_1 in the first year, i_2 in the second year, $\ldots$, i_n in the nth year, then the average annual compound rate of interest for the n-year period is less than or equal to $\frac{1}{n} \cdot \sum_{k=1}^{n} i_k$.

1.2.18 AAA Mutual Fund started up on January 1, 1994 with a unit value of 10.00. The fund has issued quarterly dividends of 3% every March 31, June 30, September 30 and December 31 in 1994 and 1995. Some past unit values are: January 31, 1994 - 10.50, January 31, 1995 - 10.30, July 31, 1995 - 11.80, October 31, 1995 - 12.90, December 31, 1995 - 12.80, January 31, 1996 - 13.20.
As of Jan. 31, 1996 determine the return for the past 1-month, 3-months, 6-months, 1 year and average compound 2-year return (assume reinvestment of dividends whenever they are paid).

1.2.19 Investment growth is sometimes plotted over time with the vertical axis transformed to an exponential scale, so that the numerical value of y is replaced by e^y or 10^y at the same position on the vertical axis. Show that the graph of compound interest growth over time with the vertical axis transformed in this way is linear.

1.2.20 (a) Smith is quoted an annual interest rate of i. He opens a special account which allows him to pick any point in the coming year as a reinvestment date, to which he will be paid simple interest from the start of the year and from which simple interest will be paid to the end of the year. Show that the reinvestment date that maximizes Smith's year-end accumulated value is the midpoint of the year.

(b) Let the situation be similar to that in part (a), but with Smith allowed to pick two reinvestment dates. Show that the dates which maximize Smith's year-end accumulated value are the equally-spaced dates $t = \frac{1}{3}$ and $t = \frac{2}{3}$.

(The results of parts (a) and (b) can be generalized, using mathematical induction, to n dates, showing that with $n - 1$ allowable reinvestment dates, the maximum year-end accumulated value occurs when the dates are equally spaced at $t = \frac{1}{n}, \frac{2}{n}, \ldots, \frac{n-1}{n}$.)

1.2.21 Suppose compound interest is in effect on an account at effective annual rate i. The account is opened at time 0 with deposit X_0, and a series of transactions (deposits or withdrawals) takes place in the account. The transactions are $X_1, X_2, \ldots, X_n$ (positive for deposit and negative for withdrawal), taking place at times $0 < t_1 < t_2 < \cdots < t_n$. Use mathematical induction to show that the two approaches in the solution of Example 1.2 result in the same balance in the account at time t_n, immediately after the transaction at that time. (Hint: Assume that the two methods give the same balance after the transaction at time t_k and show it then follows that the two methods give the same balance at time t_{k+1}.)

1.2.22 Suppose that the effective annual rate of interest is 12% from time $t = 0$ to time $t = 4$, and it is 10% from time $t = 4$ to time $t = 8$. Show that the appropriate two-variable representation for the accumulated value at time t, of an investment of 1 made at time s, is

$$s(t_1, t_2) = \begin{cases} (1.12)^{t-s} & \text{for } 0 \leq s \leq t \leq 4 \\ (1.12)^{4-s} \cdot (1.10)^{t-4} & \text{for } 0 \leq s \leq 4 \leq t \leq 8 \\ (1.10)^{t-s} & \text{for } 4 \leq s \leq t \leq 8 \end{cases}$$

1.2.23 Show that if $t_1 < t_2 < t_3$, then for compound interest $s(t_1, t_2) \cdot s(t_2, t_3) = s(t_1, t_3)$, but for simple interest the equality does not hold.

Exercises 1.3

1.3.1 A payment of amount K is due at time $t > 0$. Let P_0 be the present value of K at time 0, and for $0 < s < t$, let P_s be the present value of K at time s.

(a) If interest is calculated at rate i on a compound basis, show that P_0 is the present value at time 0 of amount P_s due at time s. Show that if u is any point in time then $P_0(1 + i)^u = P_s(1 + i)^{u-s} = K(1 + i)^{u-t}$, so that under compound interest, if payments are equivalent based on one focal date (in the sense that one is the present or accumulated value of another at some specified rate of interest), they are equivalent based on any focal date.

(b) If interest is calculated on a simple interest basis, with time t as the focal date, express the relationships between P_0 and P_s, between P_0 and K, and between P_s and K. Repeat this using time 0 as the focal date. This shows that under simple interest, equivalent payments based on one focal date may not be equivalent using another focal date.

(c) Suppose that $K = 1000$, $i = .10$, $s = \frac{1}{2}$, and $t = 1$. Find P_0 and P_s in each of parts (a) and (b) above.

1.3.2   At time 0 a balance of amount B_0 is in an account earning simple interest at rate i per period. Various deposits and withdrawals are made during the period, with a transaction of amount a_k made at time t_k for $k = 1, 2, \ldots, n$, where $0 < t_k < 1$. ($a_k > 1$ indicates a deposit to the account, and $a_k < 1$ indicates a withdrawal.) Assume that $t = 1$ is the reference point (focal date) for the account and interest on deposits and withdrawals begins accruing at the time of the deposit or withdrawal.

(a) Find an expression for B_1, the account balance at $t = 1$.

(b) Find an expression for $\overline{B}$, the average balance in the account during the period from time 0 to time 1.

(c) Show that $B_1 \ = \ B_0 + \sum_{k=1}^{n} a_k + \overline{B} \cdot i.$

1.3.3   Smith borrows 1200 at annual rate 6%. He makes a payment of 500 one year later ($t = 1$). One year after that ($t = 2$) Smith borrows an additional 600, still at the 6% rate. Assuming simple interest, what amount would be required to completely repay the loan at time $t = 3$?

1.3.4   Fisheries officials are stocking a barren lake with pike, whose number will increase annually at the rate of 40%. The plan is to prohibit fishing for two years on the lake, and then allow the removal of 5000 pike in each of the third and fourth years, so that the number remaining after the fourth year is the same as the original number stocked in the lake. Find the original number, assuming that stocking takes place at the start of the year and removal takes place at midyear.

1.3.5 A person has debts of 200 due July 1, 1989 and 300 due July 1, 1991. A payment of 100 was made on July 1, 1986 to reduce those debts. What additional amount payable on July 1, 1990 would cancel the remaining debts, assuming effective annual interest at rate 4%?

1.3.6 Starting in 1989, Smith receives a dividend cheque on the 15th of each January, April, July, and October. He immediately deposits it into an account earning a monthly interest rate of .75%, crediting interest on the last day of each calendar month, and paying simple interest for amounts on deposit for less than a month. The dividend cheques are 100 each in 1989, and increase to 105 each in 1990. What is the account balance just after interest is credited on December 31, 1990?

1.3.7 Ed buys a TV from Al for 480 by paying 50 in cash, 100 every three months for one year (four payments of 100), and a final payment in 15 months (three months after the final quarterly payment). Find the amount of the final payment if Al earns a 3-month compound interest rate of 3%. What is the final payment if Al earns a one-month rate of 1%?

1.3.8 Smith lends Jones 1000 on January 1, 1987 on the condition that Jones repay 100 on January 1, 1988, 100 on January 1, 1989, and 1000 on January 1, 1990. On July 1, 1988, Smith sells to Brown the rights to the remaining payments for 1000, so Jones makes all future payments to Brown. Let j be the 6-month rate earned on Smith's net transaction, and let k be the 6-month rate earned on Brown's net transaction. Are j and k equal? If not, which is larger?

1.3.9 A magazine offers a one-year subscription at a cost of 15 with renewal the following year at 16.50. Also offered is a two-year subscription at a cost of 28. What is the effective annual interest rate that makes the two-year subscription equivalent to two successive one-year subscriptions?

1.3.10 What is the present value of 1000 due in 10 years if the effective annual interest rate is 6% for each of the first 3 years, 7% for the next 4 years, and 9% for the final 3 years?

1.3.11 A manufacturer can automate a certain process by replacing 20 employees with a machine. The employees each earn 24,000 per year, payable on the last day of each month, with no salary increases scheduled for the next 4 years. If the machine has a lifetime of 4 years and interest is at a monthly rate of .75%, what is the most the manufacturer would pay for the machine (on the first day of a month) in each of the following cases?

(a) The machine has no scrap value at the end of 4 years.

(b) The machine has scrap value of 200,000 after 4 years.

(c) The machine has scrap value of 15% of its purchase price at the end of 4 years.

1.3.12 A contract calls for payments of 750 every 4 months for several years. Each payment is to be replaced by two payments of 367.85 each, one to be made 2 months before, and one to be made at the time of, the original payment. Find the 2-month rate of interest implied by this proposal if the new payment scheme is financially equivalent to the old one.

1.3.13 Smith wishes to buy a T.V. set and is offered a time payment plan whereby he makes 24 monthly payments of 30 each starting now. Smith wants the payments to start in 2 months rather than now. If interest is at a one-month interest rate of 1%, what is the present value now of the saving to Smith if the seller agrees to Smith's terms?

1.3.14 Calculate each of the following derivatives.

(a) $\frac{d}{di}(1+i)^n$ (b) $\frac{d}{di}v^n$ (c) $\frac{d}{dn}(1+i)^n$ (d) $\frac{d}{dn}v^n$

1.3.15 Smith receives a paycheck of 3500 on the last day of each month, and immediately deposits all but 1000 of it in a bank account. The first deposit is on December 31, 1989. Smith deposits an additional 1000 on the 15th of every month. The account pays an annual interest rate of 10%. Find the balance in the account on March 31, 1990, after the deposit is made and interest is credited, in each of the following cases.

(a) Simple interest based on minimum monthly balance and credited on the last day of March (no interest in Jan. , Feb.).

(b) Simple interest based on minimum daily balance and credited on the last day of March (no interest in Jan. , Feb.).

(c) Same as (a) but with interest credited on the last day of every month.

(d) Same as (b) but with interest credited on the last day of every month.

It follows from Exercise 1.3.2 that use of minimum daily balances for simple interest calculations is equivalent to using average balances. That is, minimum daily balances with interest credited at the end of each quarter is equivalent to basing interest for the quarter on the average balance, and minimum daily balances with interest credited at the end of each month is equivalent to basing interest for the month on the average balance for the month.

1.3.16 Let $0 < t < 1$. Find the present value at time t of an amount 1 due at time 1, under each of the following methods.

(a) Present value at simple interest from time t to time 1.

(b) Present value at compound interest.

(c) Present value to time 0 then accumulation to time t at simple interest. Show that the relative size of the results is (a) < (b) < (c).

1.3.17 On February 5 Vera makes a deposit to a bank account with a quoted annual interest rate of 12%. The account balance grows to 1000 on December 31 of the same year.

(a) Suppose that interest is credited quarterly, on the last day of each March, June, September, and December, and simple interest is credited for amounts on deposit less than a full quarter. What is the amount of Vera's deposit?

(b) What is the amount of the deposit if interest is credited only every December 31 on the basis of simple interest for periods of less than a year?

(c) Repeat part (b) with the interest basis being compound interest for periods of less than a year.

(d) Find the present value on December 31 of 1000 due on the following December 31, and then accumulate this with simple interest to February 5.

1.3.18 A loan of 1000 is made at the start of a year ($t = 0$). It is repaid by 3 equal payments of 350 each, made every 4 months (*i.e.*, at $t = \frac{1}{3}, \frac{2}{3}$, and 1).
  (a) If calculation is on the basis of simple interest with $t = 1$ as the focal date, what is the annual interest rate i?
  (b) How would (a) be solved if the focal date were $t = 0$? How would the rate compare to the one found in part (a)?
  (c) If calculation is on the basis of compound interest, how would the rate compare with those in parts (a) and (b)?

1.3.19 The parents of three children aged 1, 3, and 6 wish to set up a trust fund that will pay 25,000 to each child upon attainment of age 18, and 100,000 to each child upon attainment of age 21. If the trust fund will earn interest at 10%, what amount must the parents now invest in the trust fund?

1.3.20 Smith has debts of 1000 due now and 1092 due two years from now. He proposes to repay them with a single payment of 2000 one year from now. What is the implied effective annual interest rate if the replacement payment is accepted as equivalent to the original debts?

Exercises 1.4

1.4.1 Bank A has an effective annual rate of 18%. Bank B has a nominal annual rate of 17%. What is the smallest whole number of times per year that Bank B must compound its interest in order that the rate at Bank B be at least as attractive as that at Bank A on an effective annual basis? Repeat the exercise with a nominal rate of 16% at Bank B.

1.4.2 (a) Show that if $j > 0$ then the function $f(m) = \left(1 + \frac{j}{m}\right)^m$ is an increasing function of m.
  (b) Show that if $j > 0$ then $g(m) = m[(1+j)^{1/m} - 1]$ is a decreasing function of m.
  (c) Use l'Hospital's Rule to show that $\lim_{m\to\infty} f(m) = e^j$ for the function $f(m)$ defined in part (a).
  (d) Show that $\lim_{m\to\infty} g(m) = \ln(1+j)$ for the function $g(m)$ defined in part (b).

1.4.3 (a) Smith buys a one-year *guaranteed investment certificate* with principal of X. (A GIC has an interest rate guaranteed for the term of the certificate, a significant penalty for redemption prior to the specified maturity date, and principal and interest usually secured by a government deposit insurance program.) The annual interest rate quoted on the certificate is 9%, with interest payable monthly, on the monthly anniversary date of the certificate. Immediately upon receiving an interest payment Smith reinvests it in an account earning a nominal annual rate of 9% convertible monthly, with interest compounded from the first deposit date. Show that after one year Smith has the same total that she would have had if she had deposited the full X in the account and left it on deposit for the year.

    (b) Smith is considering two one-year guaranteed investment certificates. The first pays 9.75% on the maturity date and the second has an annual rate of 9.5% with interest paid semiannually. Suppose in the case of the second GIC Smith is able to reinvest the first interest payment for the rest of the year. What equivalent effective annual rate does Smith require for the reinvested interest payment in order that the two GIC's be equivalent?

1.4.4 Nominal interest can be defined even if m is not an integer. The algebraic definition is still valid. Suppose a bank advertises an annual rate of 10% on short-term deposits. An investor chooses a term of 45 days with interest calculated on the basis of simple interest. This nominal rate of 10% can be expressed as $i^{(m)}$ for an appropriate m. Find m and the equivalent effective annual rate of interest.

1.4.5 The nominal interest rate $i^{(m)}$ can be defined for values of $m < 1$. Algebraically the definition follows the relationship in Equation (1.4).

    (a) If $i = .10$, find the equivalent $i^{(.5)}$, $i^{(.25)}$, $i^{(.1)}$, and $i^{(.01)}$. Rank the values in increasing size, and compare with the relationship $i^{(m)} < i$ for $m > 1$.

    (b) Find the equivalent effective annual i if (i) $i^{(.5)} = .11$, (ii) $i^{(.25)} = .10$, (iii) $i^{(.1)} = .10$, and (iv) $i^{(.01)} = .10$.

    (c) For the functions $f(m)$ and $g(m)$ defined in Exercise 1.4.2, find the limits as m approaches 0.

1.4.6   Find the present value of 1000 due at the end of 10 years if
        (a) $i^{(2)} = .09$,   (b) $i^{(6)} = .09$,   and   (c) $i^{(12)} = .09$.

1.4.7   Mountain Bank pays interest at rate $i^{(2)} = .15$.   River Bank pays
        interest compounded daily.   What minimum nominal annual rate
        must River Bank pay in order to be as attractive as Mountain Bank?

1.4.8   Smith receives income from his investments in Japanese currency
        (yen).   Smith does not convert the yen to dollars, but invests the
        yen in a term deposit that pays interest in yen.   He finds a bank that
        will issue such a term deposit, but it charges a 1% commission on
        each placement and on each rollover.   The current interest rate on
        the yen deposits is a nominal annual rate of 3.25% for a 3-month
        deposit.   To keep his yen available, Smith decides to roll over the
        deposit every 3 months.   What is the effective annual after-
        commission rate that Smith earns?

1.4.9   Express i in terms of a series expansion in $i^{(m)}$.

1.4.10 Smith buys a 1000 Canada savings bond, with an issue date of
        November 1, paying interest at 11.25% per year.   The bond can be
        cashed in anytime after January 1 of the following year, and it will
        pay simple interest during the first year of $\frac{1}{12}$ of the annual interest
        for every completed month since November 1.   The government
        allows purchasers to pay for their bonds as late as November 9,
        with full interest still paid for November.   Smith pays 1000 on
        November 9 and cashes in the bond on the following January 1.
        What is his equivalent effective annual rate of interest for his
        transaction?

Exercises 1.5

1.5.1   Let j be the compound interest rate for the T-year period from r to
        $r + T$, and let d_j be the corresponding rate of discount.   Show that

        (a) $d_j = \dfrac{j}{1 + j}$ and   (b) $j = \dfrac{d_j}{1 - d_j}$.

1.5.2   A 182-day T-bill for 100 has a quoted price of 94.771 and a quoted yield rate of 11.07%. Show that any price from 94.767 to 94.771 inclusive has a corresponding yield rate of 11.07%. This shows that the yield rate quote to .01% is not as accurate a measure for the T-bill as is the price to 10^{ths} of a cent.

1.5.3   Given an effective annual discount rate of d, show that, with compounding, the accumulated value after n years of an initial investment of amount 1 is $(1 - d)^{-n}$. In other words, if an amount X due in n years has present value 1, then $X = (1 - d)^{-n}$.

1.5.4   (a) Suppose the nominal rate of discount compounded semi-annually is 100%, so that the 6-month discount rate is 50%. What is the present value at time 0 of an amount of 1 due in 1 year? What is the amount of discount from time $t = 1$ back to time $t = \frac{1}{2}$? What is the amount of discount from time $t = \frac{1}{2}$ back to time $t = 0$?   Note that the further back in time discounting is applied, the smaller the actual amount of discount for the corresponding period, so that although the 6-month effective discount rate is 50% for both halves of the year, the amount of discount in the second half is .50 but the amount in the first half is only .25, for a total of .75 (and an equivalent effective annual discount rate of .75). This is the opposite of what occurs when compounding interest forward, and it accounts for the fact that an equivalent effective rate of discount is smaller than the corresponding nominal rate of discount.

   (b) What is the largest that $d^{(m)}$ could be?

   (c) Show that the function $f(m) = \left(1 - \frac{d}{m}\right)^m$ is increasing (i.e., $f'(m) > 0$).

   (d) Show that $g(m) = m\left[1 - (1 - d)^{1/m}\right]$ is increasing.

   (e) Show that $\lim_{m \to \infty} f(m) = e^{-d}$.

   (f) Show that $\lim_{m \to \infty} g(m) = d^{(\infty)} = -\ln(1 - d)$.   Suppose d and i are equivalent discount and interest rates. Recall from part (d) of Exercise 1.4.2 that $i^{(\infty)} = \ln(1 + i)$. Show that $d^{(\infty)} = i^{(\infty)}$.

1.5.5   Show that equivalent nominal interest and discount rates $i^{(m)}$ and $d^{(m)}$
satisfy the relationships (a) $d^{(m)} = \dfrac{i^{(m)}}{1 + \dfrac{i^{(m)}}{m}}$ and (b) $i^{(m)} = \dfrac{d^{(m)}}{1 - \dfrac{d^{(m)}}{m}}$,
and show that these relationships are consistent with the results of
Exercise 1.5.1.

1.5.6   A store has a normal markup of 30% on the purchase price of
goods bought at wholesale. During a promotion the markup is only
15%. What percent reduction in the retail price will result?

1.5.7   (a) Show that for equivalent i and d, $i = d + d^2 + d^3 + \cdots$. This
generalizes the comment on page 23 that a rate of interest-in-
advance of 10% is equivalent to an interest rate of
$.1 + .01 + .001 + \cdots = .1111\ldots$.
(b) If i and d are equivalent, express d as a series in i.

1.5.8   For each of the following expressions for equivalent rates i and d,
either show that the expression is valid or find a numerical example
that contradicts the expression. (Assume i and d are equivalent
rates.)

(a) $id = i - d$

(b) $v = 1 - d$

(c) $\dfrac{1}{d} - \dfrac{1}{i} = 1$ if $i \neq 0$

(d) $\dfrac{i+d}{2} < \sqrt{id}$ if $i > 1$

(e) $d\left(1 + \dfrac{i}{2}\right) = i\left(1 - \dfrac{d}{2}\right)$

(f) $d\sqrt{1+i} = i\sqrt{1-d}$

(g) $\left(1 + \dfrac{i}{2}\right)^n < \left(1 - \dfrac{d}{2}\right)^{-n}$ if $i > 1$

1.5.9   Show that $\dfrac{\left(1 + \dfrac{i^{(3)}}{3}\right)\left(1 + \dfrac{i^{(2)}}{2}\right)\left(1 - \dfrac{d^{(6)}}{6}\right)}{\left(1 - \dfrac{d^{(3)}}{3}\right)\left(1 - \dfrac{d^{(2)}}{2}\right)\left(1 + \dfrac{i^{(6)}}{6}\right)} = \left(1 + \dfrac{i^{(12)}}{12}\right)^{16}$,
assuming that all rates in the expression are equivalent.

1.5.10 Repeat Exercise 1.4.5 for nominal discount rates, replacing i by d.

1.5.11 If the 3-month compound interest rate is 3%, find the equivalent 1-
month, 2-month, 3-month, 4-month, 6-month, and 1-year compound interest and discount rates.

1.5.12 If $0 < k < 1$ and $n > 0$, rank the following quantities in order of increasing size: $(1 - k)^{-n}$, $(1 + k)^n$, $\left(1 - \frac{k}{2}\right)^{-2n}$, $\left(1 + \frac{k}{2}\right)^{2n}$.

1.5.13 For the identity $i - d = id$, what is the analogy for nominal rates (*i.e.*, what is $i^{(m)} - d^{(m)}$)?

1.5.14 (a) Smith has a promissory note due in n days. A bank will buy the note from Smith using a simple discount rate d. What is the equivalent simple interest rate i earned by the bank over the period? What happens to i as n increases?
  (b) A lender wishes to earn interest at an annual simple rate of 11%. What annual simple discount rate should be charged on a loan for 1 year? for 6 months? for 1 month?

1.5.15 A 1000 182-day Treasury bill has sold for 941.42. Find the exact equivalent effective annual interest rate to the nearest .001%, assuming a 365-day year.

1.5.16 Bob borrows 1000 from Ed at effective annual interest rate i, agreeing to repay in full at the end of one year. When the year is up, Bob has no money, but they agree that he can repay one year later in such a way that the effective annual discount rate d in the second year is *numerically equal* to the interest rate i in the first year. At the end of the second year Bob pays 1200. What is i in the first year?

1.5.17 Given any set of equivalent positive rates $d^{(6)}$, $d^{(12)}$, $i^{(6)}$, and $i^{(12)}$, show that $\dfrac{d^{(12)}}{d^{(6)}} > \dfrac{i^{(12)}}{i^{(6)}}$.

1.5.18 Smith buys a 182-day T-bill at a price which corresponds to a quoted annual yield rate for 182-day T-bills of 10%. 91 days later Smith sells the T-bill, at which time the prevailing quoted annual yield rate for 91-day T-bills is also 10%. Find the actual nominal annual yield (convertible every 91 days) that Smith earned for the 91 days he held the T-bill. To what quoted annual rate would 91-day T-bills have to move in order that he receive a nominal yield of 10% when he sells the T-bill?

1.5.19 Suppose $i^{(m)} < 0$.   Show that the equivalent effective annual
interest rate i is numerically equal to the negative of d, where d is
the effective annual discount rate equivalent to a nominal discount
rate $d^{(m)}$ that is numerically equal to the negative of $i^{(m)}$. Show that
this implies that for negative interest rates, equivalent nominal and
effective annual interest rates also satisfy the inequality $i^{(m)} < i$.

1.5.20 A loan of 1800 is to be repaid by a single payment of 2420.80 two
years after the loan is made.   The interest rate is quoted as
"nominal annual interest of 15%."   Find   (a) the frequency of
compounding, and (b) the equivalent effective annual discount rate.

1.5.21 Smith has 960 to invest on January 1. He has the following two
investment options.
(a) He can buy a 6-month 1000 T-bill for a purchase price of 960,
and reinvest the proceeds on July 1 at a 6-month interest rate j.
(b) He can buy a one-year 1000 T-bill for a purchase price of 920
and invest the remaining 40 in an account earning interest at
the same 6-month interest rate j as in option (a).
If options (a) and (b) result in the same accumulated amount on
December 31, including interest and T-bill maturity, find the value
of j (assuming $j < 1\%$).

1.5.22 A non-interest-bearing note of amount X, due in one-half year, is
valued today at 4992. Find X under each of the following interest
calculation methods.
(a) Compound interest at effective annual rate 8%.
(b) Simple interest at annual rate 8%.
(c) Compound discount at effective annual rate 8%.
(d) Simple discount at annual rate 8%.

1.5.23 Smith just bought a 100,000 182-day T-bill at a quoted nominal
annual rate of 10%.
(a) Find the price, P, that Smith paid for the T-bill.
(b) What is the volatility of the bill's value with respect to the
nominal annual yield rate (*i.e.*, what is $\frac{dP}{di}$)?   Use the
differential to approximate the change in the price of the T-bill
if the yield rate changes to 10.1% immediately after Smith
purchases it.

(c) Suppose the T-bill had a 91-day duration instead of a 182-day duration. Find the price and volatility with respect to the yield rate at a quoted nominal yield of 10%. What happens to the volatility with respect to the yield rate as a T-bill approaches its due date?

1.5.24 In Example 1.15 suppose Brown buys the note from Smith for 5100. Determine the equivalent annual simple and effective annual interest rates earned by Brown and Smith.

1.5.25 For $d < 1$, derive a result describing the relative sizes of $1 - dt$ and $(1 - d)^t$ similar to the result of Example 1.4.

1.5.26 (a) Let the annual discount rate in year 1 be $d_1 = .10$ and in year 2 be $d_2 = .20$. Find a level effective annual d that is equivalent to d_1 and d_2 over the two-year period.

(b) Show that for $d_1, d_2 \geq 1$, it follows that $d \geq \dfrac{d_1 + d_2}{2}$.

1.5.27 Simplify $\dfrac{1}{d^{(m)}} - \dfrac{1}{i^{(m)}}$.

1.5.28 Assuming equivalent rates, find (a) the derivative of $d^{(m)}$ with respect to $i^{(m)}$, and (b) the derivative of i with respect to d.

Exercises 1.6

1.6.1 (a) Find an expression for the $\frac{1}{m}$-year discount rate from time t to time $t + \frac{1}{m}$ in terms of an accumulated amount function S.

(b) If $d^{(m)}$ is the nominal annual discount rate corresponding to the rate in part (a), find an expression for $d^{(m)}$ in terms of S.

(c) Take the limit as $m \to \infty$ of the expression for $d^{(m)}$ in part (b) to show that $d^{(\infty)} = \dfrac{S'(t)}{S(t)} = \delta_t$.

1.6.2 Suppose that the one-day loan in Example 1.20 was for 1,000,000. Find the interest payable for a one-day loan at annual rate 12% (a) if interest is quoted on a nominal annual basis convertible daily, and (b) if interest is quoted on an annual force of interest basis.

1.6.3   (a) Find the series expansion for $d^{(2)}$ in terms of δ.

(b) Repeat part (a) for $d^{(m)}$, $i^{(m)}$, and $\dfrac{i^{(m)} + d^{(m)}}{2}$.

(c) Find the series expansion for δ in terms of $d^{(2)}$.

1.6.4   Show that $\lim\limits_{i \to 0}$ of both $\dfrac{(\delta - d)}{\delta^2}$ and $\dfrac{(i - \delta)}{\delta^2}$ is .50.

1.6.5   A contract calls for payments of 1000 each on January 1, April 1, July 1, and October 1. The four payments are to be replaced by a single payment. Calculate the single payment if it is made on (a) October 1 using $i^{(2)} = .10$, (b) April 1 using $d^{(4)} = .10$, or (c) July 1 using $\delta = .10$.

1.6.6   An investment of 1000 accumulates to 1360.86 at the end of 5 years. If the force of interest is δ during the first year and 1.5δ in each subsequent year, find the equivalent effective annual interest rate in the second year.

1.6.7   (a) Suppose an accumulated amount function is a polynomial of the form $S(t) = a_0 + a_1 \cdot t + \cdots + a_n \cdot t^n$, where $a_n > 0$ and $n > 0$. Show that $\lim\limits_{t \to \infty} \delta_t = 0$.

(b) Let $\delta_t = \dfrac{k}{\sqrt{t}}$, $k > 0$. Find an expression for the accumulation function $S(t)$, where $S(0) = 1$. Show $\lim\limits_{t \to \infty} \dfrac{S(t)}{1 + it} = \infty$ for any $i > 0$, and $\lim\limits_{t \to \infty} \dfrac{S(t)}{(1 + i)^t} = 0$.

1.6.8   On January 1 Smith deposits 1000 in an account earning $i^{(4)} = .08$ with interest credited on the last day of March, June, September, and December. If Smith closes the account during the year, simple interest is paid on the balance from the most recent interest credit date.

(a) What is Smith's close-out balance on July 19?

(b) Suppose all four quarters in the year are considered equal, and time is measured in years. Derive expressions for Smith's accumulated amount function $S(t)$, the close-out balance at time t. Consider separately the four intervals $0 \le t \le .25$, $.25 \le t \le .50$, $.50 \le t \le .75$ and $.74 \le t \le 1$.

(c) Using part (b), show that if $0 \le t \le .25$, then it follows that
$\delta_t = \delta_{t+.25} = \delta_{t+.50} = \delta_{t+.75}$.

1.6.9   Smith forecasts that interest rates will rise over a 5-year period according to a force of interest function given by $\delta_t = .08 + \frac{.025t}{t+1}$ for $0 \le t \le 5$.
(a) According to this scheme, what is the average annual compound effective rate for the 5-year period?
(b) What are the equivalent effective annual rates for each of years 1, 2, 3, 4, and 5?
(c) What is the present value at $t = 2$ of 1000 due at $t = 4$?

1.6.10 (a) It was shown in Example 1.4 that over t years, $0 < t < 1$, accumulation to time t at simple interest exceeded accumulation at compound interest. Show that for a given rate of interest i, the maximum of $(1+it) - (1+i)^t$ occurs at $t_i = \frac{1}{\delta}[\ln i - \ln \delta]$.
(b) Show that $\lim_{i \to 0} t_i = \frac{1}{2}$ and $\lim_{i \to \infty} t_i = 1$.

1.6.11 Show that $\lim_{i \to \infty} \frac{i}{\delta} = \infty$, $\lim_{i \to \infty} \frac{\delta}{d} = \infty$, and $\lim_{i \to \infty} \frac{i/\delta}{\delta/d} = \infty$.

1.6.12 The present value of K payable after 2 years is 960. If the force of interest is cut in half the present value becomes 1200. What is the present value if the effective annual discount rate is cut in half?

1.6.13 If the force of interest is doubled, are the corresponding equivalent effective annual interest and discount rates more or less than doubled?

1.6.14 Show that if δ is the average annual force of interest earned by a fund from time t_1 to time t_2, and if i is the corresponding average effective annual interest rate over the same period, then $\delta = \ln(1 + i)$.

1.6.15 For the equivalent rates i, $i^{(12)}$, $i^{(2)}$, d, $d^{(12)}$, $d^{(2)}$, and δ, calculate each of the others given (a) $i = .10$, (b) $i^{(12)} = .10$, (c) $i^{(2)} = .10$, (d) $d = .10$, (e) $d^{(12)} = .10$, (f) $d^{(2)} = .10$, and (g) $\delta = .10$. In each case verify the inequality $d < d^{(2)} < d^{(12)} < \delta < i^{(12)} < i^{(2)} < i$.

1.6.16 Express $\frac{d}{dt}\,\delta_t$ in terms of $S(t)$ and its derivatives.

1.6.17 $S_1(t)$ is an accumulation function at force of interest $\delta_t^{(1)}$, and $S_2(t)$ is an accumulation function at force $\delta_t^{(2)}$. Let $S_1(0) = S_2(0) = 1$. What is $S(t)$ for $\delta_t = \delta_t^{(1)} + \delta_t^{(2)}$, in terms of $S_1(t)$ and $S_2(t)$?

1.6.18 Find $S(t)$ if $\delta_t = (1+t)^{-k} \cdot \ln B$.

1.6.19 Find the derivatives with respect to δ of i, d, $i^{(m)}$, and $d^{(m)}$.

Exercises 1.7

1.7.1   (a) Suppose that for the coming year inflation is forecast at an effective annual rate of $r = .15$ and interest is forecast at effective annual rate $i = .10$. What will be the corresponding real, or inflation-adjusted rate of interest for the coming year?

(b) Using the values of r and i in part (a), suppose Smith borrows 100,000 for a year at $i = .10$, and buys 100,000 units of a certain item that has a current cost of 1 per unit. Suppose the price of this item is tied to the rate of inflation ($r = .15$). One year from now Smith sells the items at the inflated price. What is his net gain on this transaction? (This illustrates that during times when inflation rates exceed interest rates, there is great incentive to borrow at the negative real rate of interest. This demand by borrowers is a factor in the inevitable correction that leads to the interest rate becoming larger than the inflation rate.)

1.7.2   A person's savings earn an effective rate of $i = .12$ on which 45% income tax is paid. If the inflation rate is 10% per year, what is the annual after-tax real rate of return?

1.7.3   Smith earned gross income of 40,000 last year. According to the income tax structure, taxes are 25% of the first 20,000 of gross income plus 50% of the excess over 20,000. Thus Smith paid 15,000 in taxes and had after-tax income (ATI) of 25,000. Inflation is forecast at 5% this year, and Smith's gross income will rise by 5% to 42,000. The government is considering a new tax structure of 25% of the first 21,000 plus 50% of the excess over 21,000 (full indexing).

(a) Show that if the government adopts the new tax structure then the real annual rate of growth in both Smith's ATI and in his paid taxes is 0%.

(b) Find the real annual rate of growth in Smith's ATI and his taxes paid if the government continues with the old scheme (no indexing).

1.7.4   If the force of interest for the coming year will be δ and the force of inflation will be δ_r, show that the inflation-adjusted force of interest is $\delta - \delta_r$.

1.7.5   The newly independent nation of Falkvinas has a unit of currency called the Britarg. In the coming year inflation in Falkvinas will be 100%, whereas Canada's inflation rate will be 14%. A Canadian investor can earn interest in Canada on Canadian dollars at an annual rate of 18%. What effective annual rate must an investor earn on Britargs in Falkvinas in order that his real rate of interest match the real rate earned by an investor in Canadian dollars?

1.7.6   Smith will need 1000 U.S. dollars one year from now. He can invest funds in a U.S. dollar account for the next year at 9%. Alternatively Smith can now buy Canadian dollars at the exchange rate of 0.73 U.S. = 1 Cdn., and invest in a Canadian dollar account for the next year at 10%. If both of these alternatives require the same amount of currency today, what is the implied exchange rate between the two currencies one year from now?

1.7.7   Show that the present value of $(1 + r)^n$ due in n years at effective annual rate i is equal to the present value of 1 due in n years at effective annual rate $\frac{i - r}{1 + r}$.

1.7.8   (a) In an attempt to reduce interest rates during times of high
             inflation, a government allows banks to issue "indexed term
             deposits" upon which only the "real" interest earned is taxed.
             If inflation is at rate r, and the bank pays interest at real rate
             i', then on a one-year deposit of initial amount 1 an investor
             receives inflation-adjusted principal of $1 + r$, plus "real
             interest" on the inflation-adjusted principal of $i'(1 + r)$, for a
             total amount paid at year end of $(1 + r)(1 + i')$. The investor
             pays tax only on the real interest paid [*i.e.*, on $i'(1 + r)$]. This
             is compared to the usual term-deposit situation in which
             interest at rate i is paid at the end of the year.   Derive
             expressions in terms of i, i', r and t_x (where $0 < t_x < 1$ is the
             investor's tax rate) for the real after-tax rates of return on the
             inflation-adjusted term deposit and on the standard term
             deposit.
         (b) Suppose $r = 12\%$ and a bank offers inflation-adjusted term
             deposits at a real rate of 2%.   What rate of interest would an
             investor have to earn on a standard term deposit in order to
             have the same after-inflation, after-tax return as on the
             inflation-adjusted term deposit if the investor has a tax rate of
             (i) 0%, (ii) 25%, (iii) 40%, (iv) 60%?

━━━━━━━━━━━━━━━━━━━━━━━━━━━━ **CHAPTER 2**

THE VALUATION OF PERIODIC
PAYMENTS - ANNUITIES

2.1   INTRODUCTION

Many financial transactions involve a series of payments, such as periodic
dividend payments on a holding of common stock, monthly payments on a
loan, or annual interest payments on a savings bond. It is often the case
(as in the loan and bond examples) that the payments are made at regularly
scheduled intervals of time. In the examples in Chapter 1 that dealt with
transactions involving more than one payment, each payment was treated
and valued separately. When a transaction involves a number of payments
made in a systematic way, it is often possible to apply algebraic methods to
simplify the valuation of the series.   In this chapter we will develop
methods for valuing a series of payments.

The key algebraic relationship used in valuing a series of payments is
the familiar geometric series summation formula

$$1 + x + x^2 + \cdots + x^k \;=\; \frac{1 - x^{k+1}}{1 - x} \;=\; \frac{x^{k+1} - 1}{x - 1}. \qquad (2.1)$$

This is illustrated in the following example.

| **EXAMPLE 2.1** |

The federal government sends Smith a family allowance payment of 30
every month for Smith's child.   Smith deposits the payments in a bank
account on the last day of each month. The account earns interest at the
annual rate of 9% compounded monthly and payable on the last day of
each month, on the minimum monthly balance. If the first payment is

deposited on May 31, 1988, what is the account balance, including the payment just made, on December 31, 1999?

SOLUTION

The one-month compound interest rate is $j = .0075$.   The balance in the account on June 30, 1988, including the payment just deposited and the accumulated value of the May 31 deposit is $C_2 = 30(1+j) + 30 = 30[(1+j) + 1]$.   The balance on July 31, 1988 is $C_3 = C_2(1+j) + 30 = 30[(1+j) + 1](1 + j) + 30 = 30[(1+j)^2 + (1+j) + 1]$. Continuing in this way we see that the balance just after the mth deposit is $C_m = 30[(1+j)^{m-1} + \cdots + (1+j)^2 + (1+j) + 1]$, the accumulation of those first m deposits.   The balance on December 31, 1999, just after the 140th payment, is

$$30\left[(1+j)^{139} + (1+j)^{138} + \cdots + (1+j) + 1\right]$$

$$= 30\left[\frac{(1+j)^{140} - 1}{(1+j) - 1}\right] = 30\left[\frac{(1.0075)^{140} - 1}{.0075}\right] = 7385.91.$$

The following line diagram illustrates the accumulation in the account from one deposit to the next.   □

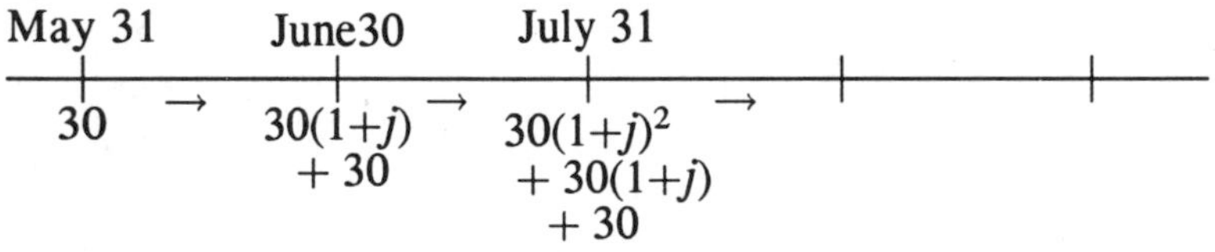

May 31	June30	July 31		
30 →	$30(1+j)$ →	$30(1+j)^2$ →		
	$+ 30$	$+ 30(1+j)$		
		$+ 30$		

FIGURE 2.1

2.2   ACCUMULATED VALUE OF AN ANNUITY

In Example 2.1 the expression for the aggregate accumulated value,

$$30[(1 + j)^{139} + (1 + j)^{138} + \cdots + (1 + j) + 1]$$

$$= 30(1 + j)^{139} + 30(1 + j)^{138} + \cdots + 30(1 + j) + 30,$$

can be interpreted as the sum of the accumulated values of the individual deposits. $30(1+j)^{139}$ is the accumulated value on December 31, 1999 of the deposit made on May 31, 1988, $30(1+j)^{138}$ is the accumulated value on December 31, 1999 of the deposit made on June 30, 1988, and so on. In general, when valuing a series of payments, it is often efficient to consider the corresponding series of values of the individual payments. Let us consider a series of n payments (or deposits) of amount 1 each, made at equally spaced intervals of time, and for which interest is at compound rate i per payment period, with interest credited on payment dates. The accumulated value of the series of payments, valued at the time of (and including) the final payment, can be represented as the sum of the accumulated values of the individual payments, producing

$$(1+i)^{n-1} + (1+i)^{n-2} + \cdots + (1+i) + 1 \; = \; \frac{(1+i)^n - 1}{(1+i) - 1}$$

$$= \; \frac{(1+i)^n - 1}{i}. \qquad (2.2)$$

This is illustrated in the following diagram.

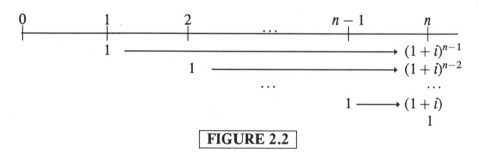

FIGURE 2.2

The generic term used to describe a series of periodic payments is *annuity*. In a life insurance context, an annuity is a "life-contingent" series of payments, which is made contingent on the survival of a specific individual or group of individuals. The more precise term for a series of payments *not* contingent on the occurrence of any specified events is *annuity-certain*. Since this book deals almost entirely with annuities-certain, we shall use the term annuity to refer to an annuity-certain, unless otherwise specified.

The accumulated value of the general annuity considered above has standard notation and terminology associated with it. The symbol $s_{\overline{n}|i}$

denotes the accumulated value, at the time of (and including) the final payment of a series of n payments of 1 each made at equally spaced intervals of time, where the rate of interest per payment period is i. Thus

$$s_{\overline{n}|i} = \sum_{t=0}^{n-1}(1 + i)^t = \frac{(1+i)^n - 1}{i}. \qquad (2.3)$$

If there is no possibility of confusion with other interest rates in a particular situation, the subscript i is dropped and the accumulated value is denoted $s_{\overline{n}|}$. The number of payments in the series is called the *term* of the annuity, and the time between successive payments is called the *payment period*. Note that for any i, $s_{\overline{1}|i} = 1$, but if $i > 0$ and $n > 1$, then $s_{\overline{n}|i} > n$.

The $s_{\overline{n}|}$ notation can be used to express the accumulated value of an annuity provided the following conditions are met.
(1) The payments are of equal amount;
(2) The payments are made at equal intervals of time, with the same frequency as the interest rate is compounded;
(3) The accumulated value is found at the time of and including the final payment.

Equation (2.3) can be rewritten as $i \cdot s_{\overline{n}|} + 1 = (1 + i)^n$. This expression shows that if an amount of 1 is invested at periodic interest rate i, and the interest is reinvested every period for n periods when received, then the accumulation of the reinvested interest, along with the return of the initial amount invested, is equal to the compound accumulation of 1 invested for n periods.

| EXAMPLE 2.2 |

What level amount must be invested on May 1 and November 1 each year from 1988 to 1995, inclusive, to accumulate 7000 on November 1, 1995 if $i^{(2)} = .09$?

| SOLUTION |

If the level amount invested every 6 months is denoted by X, the equation of value on November 1, 1995 is $X \cdot s_{\overline{16}|.045} = 7000$ (2 payments per year for 8 years), where $s_{\overline{16}|.045} = \frac{(1.045)^{16} - 1}{.045}$. Then $X = \frac{7000}{s_{\overline{16}|.045}} = 308.11$.

$\square$

Occasionally after a series of deposits is completed, the accumulated balance continues to accumulate with interest only. The following example illustrates this.

EXAMPLE 2.3

Suppose that in Example 2.1, Smith's child is born in April, 1988 and the first payment is received in May. The payments continue until (and including the month of) the child's 16th birthday. The payments continue until (and including the month of) the child's 16th birthday. The balance in the account then continues to accumulate with interest until the end of the month of the child's 21st birthday. What is the balance in the account at that time?

SOLUTION

At the end of the month of the child's 16th birthday, Smith makes the 192nd deposit (16×12) into the account, with accumulated value $30 \cdot s_{\overline{192}|.0075} = 12{,}792.31$. Five years (60 months) later, at the end of the month of the child's 21st birthday, the account will have grown, with interest only, to $12{,}792.31(1.0075)^{60} = 20{,}028.68$. $\quad\square$

As illustrated in Example 2.3, k payment/interest periods after the final payment is made, the accumulated value of an n-payment annuity can be expressed as $s_{\overline{n}|} \cdot (1+i)^k$, and rewritten as

$$
\begin{aligned}
s_{\overline{n}|}(1+i)^k &= \frac{(1+i)^n - 1}{i}(1+i)^k \\[2mm]
&= \frac{(1+i)^{n+k} - (1+i)^k}{i} \\[2mm]
&= \frac{(1+i)^{n+k} - 1}{i} - \frac{(1+i)^k - 1}{i} \\[2mm]
&= s_{\overline{n+k}|} - s_{\overline{k}|}.
\end{aligned}
\tag{2.4}
$$

An alternative derivation of Equation (2.4) is outlined in Exercise 2.2.1. Using Equation (2.4) the accumulated value of the account on April 30, 2009 (the end of the month of the child's 21st birthday) in Example 2.3 can be written as $30[s_{\overline{252}|} - s_{\overline{60}|}]$.

Figure 2.3 below provides an interpretation for the formulations given in Equation (2.4). If the annuity payments had continued to time $n + k$, the time of valuation, the accumulated value would be $s_{\overline{n+k}|}$. Since there are not actually any payments made for the final k payment periods, $s_{\overline{n+k}|}$ must be reduced by $s_{\overline{k}|}$, which represents the accumulated value of k payments ending at time $n + k$.

Payment Number

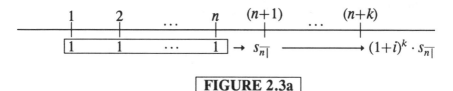

FIGURE 2.3a

Payment Number

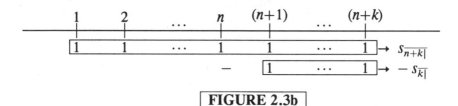

FIGURE 2.3b

Equation (2.4) can be reformulated as

$$s_{\overline{n+k}|} = s_{\overline{n}|}(1+i)^k + s_{\overline{k}|} = s_{\overline{k}|}(1+i)^n + s_{\overline{n}|}. \qquad (2.5)$$

This concept of dividing a series of payments into subgroups and valuing each subgroup separately can be applied to find the accumulated value of an annuity when the periodic interest rate in effect changes during the term of the annuity. This is illustrated in the following modification of Example 2.1.

EXAMPLE 2.4

Suppose that in Example 2.1 the interest rate earned on the account changes to 7.5% (still compounded monthly) as of January 1, 1994. What is the accumulated value of the account on December 31, 1999?

SOLUTION

In a situation in which the interest rate is at one level for a period of time and changes to another level for a subsequent period of time, it is necessary to separate the full term into time intervals over which the interest rate is constant. We first calculate the accumulated value in the account on December 31, 1993, since the interest rate is level at .0075 per month up until this point. This accumulated value is $30 \cdot s_{\overline{68}|.0075} = 2648.50$. From January 1, 1994 onward, the accumulation in the account can be regarded in two separate parts: the accumulation of the 2648.50 that was on balance as of January 1, 1994, and the accumulation of the continuing deposits from January 31, 1994 onward. The 2648.50 accumulates to $2648.50(1.00625)^{72} = 4147.86$ as of December 31, 1999, and the remaining deposits continuing from January 31, 1994 accumulate to $30 \cdot s_{\overline{72}|.00625} = 2717.36$, for a total of 6865.22. Thus the accumulated value on December 31, 1999 can be written as $30\left[s_{\overline{68}|.0075} \cdot (1.00625)^{72} + s_{\overline{72}|.00625}\right].$　　　　□

If we consider an $n + k$-payment annuity with equally spaced payments and with an interest rate of i per payment period up to the time of the nth payment, followed by an effective interest rate of j per payment period from the time of the nth payment onward, the accumulated value of the annuity at the time of the final payment can be found in the following way.

(a) The accumulated value of the first n payments valued at the time of the nth payment is $s_{\overline{n}|i}$.

(b) The accumulated value found in part (a) is accumulated for an additional k periods at compound periodic interest rate j, to a value of $s_{\overline{n}|i}(1+j)^k$ at time $n + k$.

(c) The accumulated value of the final k payments is $s_{\overline{k}|j}$.

(d) The total accumulated value at time $n + k$ is the sum of (b) and (c), and equals $s_{\overline{n}|i}(1+j)^k + s_{\overline{k}|j}$.

Note that if the interest rate is level over the $n + k$ periods, that is if $j = i$, then Equation (2.5) is the same as the expression in (d). This method can be extended to situations in which the interest rate changes more than once during the term of the annuity. (See Exercise 2.2.2.)

The relationship in Equation (2.5) can also be used to find the accumulated value of an annuity for which the payment amount changes during the course of the annuity. The following example illustrates this point.

EXAMPLE 2.5

10 monthly payments of 50 each are followed by 14 monthly payments of 75 each. If interest is at a monthly effective rate of 1%, what is the accumulated value of the series at the time of the final payment?

SOLUTION

Using the same technique as in Example 2.3 for finding the accumulated value of an annuity some time after the final payment, we see that the accumulated value, at the time of the 24th payment, of the first 10 payments is $50 \cdot s_{\overline{10}|.01}(1.01)^{14} = 601.30$. The value of the final 14 payments is $75 \cdot s_{\overline{14}|.01} = 1121.06$, for a total accumulated value of 1722.36. There is an alternative way of approaching this situation. Note in Figure 2.4 below that the original (non-level) sequence of payments can be decomposed into two separate level sequences of payments.

Time	0	1	2	...	10	11	12	...	24
Original series		50	50	...	50	75	75	...	75
New Series 1		50	50	...	50	50	50	...	50
New Series 2						25	25	...	25

FIGURE 2.4

The accumulated value (at time 24) of the alternate form of the series is $50 \cdot s_{\overline{24}|.01} + 25 \cdot s_{\overline{14}|.01} = 1348.67 + 373.69 = 1722.36$. ☐

2.3 PRESENT VALUE OF AN ANNUITY

The discussion in Section 2.2 was concerned with the accumulated value of the payments in an annuity. We now consider the present value of an annuity, which is the value of the payments at the time, or some time before, the payments begin.

Consider again a series of *n* payments of amount 1 each, made at equally spaced intervals for which interest is at effective rate *i* per payment period, with interest credited on payment dates. The present value of the series of payments, valued one period before the first payment, can be represented as the sum of the present values of the individual payments:

$$v + v^2 + \cdots + v^{n-1} + v^n \;=\; v[1 + v + \cdots + v^{n-1}]$$

$$= \; v \cdot \frac{1 - v^n}{1 - v}$$

$$= \; \frac{1}{1 + i} \cdot \frac{1 - v^n}{1 - v}$$

$$= \; \frac{1 - v^n}{i}. \tag{2.6}$$

The symbol $a_{\overline{n}|i}$ is used to denote this present value, so that

$$a_{\overline{n}|i} \;=\; \sum_{t=1}^{n} v^t \;=\; \frac{1 - v^n}{i}. \tag{2.7}$$

As in the case of valuing an accumulated annuity, the $a_{\overline{n}|}$ notation can be used to express the present value of an annuity provided the following conditions are met.
(1) The payments are of equal amount.
(2) The payments are made at equal intervals of time, with the same frequency as the the frequency of interest compounding.
(3) The present value is found one payment period before the first payment is made.

Note that if $i > 0$, then $a_{\overline{n}|i} < n$, but if $i = 0$, then $a_{\overline{n}|i} = n = s_{\overline{n}|i}$.

The present value of an annuity typically arises in the problem of finding the required periodic loan payment, given the loan amount, number of payments, and interest per payment period. This would be solved by setting the loan amount equal to the present value (at the time of the loan) of the loan payments. The following example illustrates this situation.

EXAMPLE 2.6

Brown has bought a new car and requires a loan of 12,000 to pay for it. The car dealer offers Brown two alternatives on the loan:
(a) monthly payments for 3 years, starting one month after purchase, with an interest rate of 12% compounded monthly, or
(b) monthly payments for 4 years, also starting one month after purchase, with an interest rate of 15% compounded monthly.
Find Brown's monthly payment and the total amount paid over the course of the repayment period under each of the two options.

SOLUTION

We denote the monthly payment under option (a) by P_1 and under option (b) by P_2. Since payments begin one month (one payment period) after the loan, the equations of value for the two options are (a) $12{,}000 = P_1 \cdot a_{\overline{36}|.01}$ and (b) $12{,}000 = P_2 \cdot a_{\overline{48}|.0125}$. Then $P_1 = \dfrac{12{,}000}{a_{\overline{36}|.01}} = \dfrac{12{,}000(.01)}{1-(1.01)^{-36}}$

$= \dfrac{12{,}000}{30.107505} = 398.57$, and $P_2 = \dfrac{12{,}000}{a_{\overline{48}|.0125}} = \dfrac{12{,}000}{35.931363} = 333.97$.

The total paid under option (a) would be $36 \cdot P_1 = 14{,}348.52$, and under option (b) it would be $48 \cdot P_2 = 16{,}030.56$. $\qquad\square$

Another context in which the present value of an annuity arises can be considered. Suppose Brown has 12,000 with which he wishes to open an interest earning account and draw monthly income for 3 years. This forms a 3-year annuity payable monthly. Suppose he can deposit (invest) the 12,000 at interest rate $i^{(12)} = .12$, and receive monthly payments for three years (36 payments) starting one month after the deposit. The monthly payment, P, that he receives is found from an equation of value identical to that for P_1 in Example 2.6, an equation that equates the 12,000 deposit with the present value of the payments it generates. Note in this case that after the 36th payment is made, the account becomes exhausted with a balance of zero.

Similar to the case of an accumulated annuity, it may be necessary to find the present value of a series of payments some time before the first payment is made. This is illustrated in the following modification of Example 2.6.

EXAMPLE 2.7

Suppose that in Example 2.6 Brown can repay the loan, still with 36 payments under option (a) or 48 payments under option (b), with the first payment made 9 months after the car is purchased. Assuming interest accrues from the time of the car purchase, find the payments required under options (a) and (b).

SOLUTION

We denote the new payments under options (a) and (b) by P_1' and P_2', respectively. Then the equation of value for option (a) is $12{,}000 = P_1'[v^9 + v^{10} + \cdots + v^{44}] = P_1' \cdot v^8 \cdot a_{\overline{36}|.01}$, which leads to

$$P_1' = \frac{12{,}000}{v^8 \cdot a_{\overline{36}|.01}} = (1.01)^8 \cdot \frac{12{,}000}{a_{\overline{36}|.01}} = (1.01)^8 \cdot P_1 = 431.60. \quad \text{In a simi-}$$

lar manner, $P_2' = (1.0125)^8 \cdot \dfrac{12{,}000}{a_{\overline{48}|.0125}} = (1.0125)^8 \cdot P_2 = 368.86.$

$\square$

Suppose an n-payment annuity of 1 per period is to be valued $k+1$ payment periods before the first payment is made. The present value can be expressed as $v^{k+1} + v^{k+2} + \cdots + v^{k+n}$, which can be reformulated as $v^k[v + v^2 + \cdots v^n] = v^k \cdot a_{\overline{n}|}$. Since $a_{\overline{n}|}$ represents the present value of the annuity one period before the first payment, the value k periods before that (for a total of $k+1$ periods before the first payment) should be $v^k \cdot a_{\overline{n}|}$. With a derivation similar to that for Equation (2.4) (see Exercise 2.3.2) we have

$$v^k \cdot a_{\overline{n}|} = a_{\overline{n+k}|} - a_{\overline{k}|}. \tag{2.8}$$

Such an annuity is called a *deferred annuity*. The annuity considered in Equation (2.8) is an n-payment annuity deferred for k payment periods, usually called a k-period deferred, n-payment annuity of 1 per period. This annuity is denoted by $_k|a_{\overline{n}|}$. Note that for a k-period deferred annuity, the first payment comes $k+1$ periods after the valuation date, not k periods after. Equation (2.8) can be rewritten in the form

$$a_{\overline{n+k}|} = a_{\overline{k}|} + v^k \cdot a_{\overline{n}|} = a_{\overline{n}|} + v^n \cdot a_{\overline{k}|}. \tag{2.9}$$

Just as Equation (2.5) can be used for accumulated annuities, Equation (2.8) can be applied to find the present value of an annuity for which the interest rate changes during the term of the annuity. If we consider an $n + k$-payment annuity with equally spaced payments, with an interest rate of i per payment period up to the time of the nth payment, followed by a rate of j per period from the nth payment onward, the present value of the annuity one period before the first payment can be found in the following manner.

(a) The present value of the first n payments valued one period before the first payment is $a_{\overline{n}|i}$.

(b) The present value of the final k payments valued at time n (*i.e.*, one period before the first of the final k payments) at interest rate j is $a_{\overline{k}|j}$.

(c) The value of (b) valued at time 0 (*i.e.*, one period before the first payment of the entire series) at interest rate i per period over the first n periods is $v_i^n \cdot a_{\overline{k}|j}$.

(d) The total present value at time 0 is the sum of (a) and (c), which is $a_{\overline{n}|i} + v_i^n \cdot a_{\overline{k}|j}$.

This is illustrated in the following line diagram.

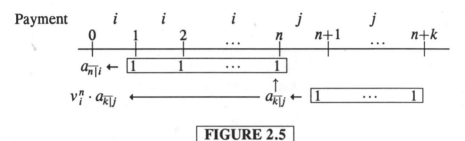

FIGURE 2.5

The valuation point for $s_{\overline{n}|i}$ is the time of the nth payment, and the valuation point for $a_{\overline{n}|i}$ is one period before the first payment, which is n periods earlier. Then it follows that

$$s_{\overline{n}|i} = (1+i)^n \cdot a_{\overline{n}|i} \qquad (2.10)$$

and

$$a_{\overline{n}|i} = v^n \cdot s_{\overline{n}|i}, \qquad (2.11)$$

which can be easily verified algebraically by observing that

$$v^n \cdot s_{\overline{n}|i} = v^n \left[\frac{(1+i)^n - 1}{i} \right] = \frac{1 - v^n}{i} = a_{\overline{n}|i}.$$

For a particular value of i, both $s_{\overline{n}|i}$ and $a_{\overline{n}|i}$ increase as n increases. Furthermore $s_{\overline{n}|i} = 1 + (1+i) + \cdots + (1+i)^{n-1}$ increases as i increases. However, since $v = \frac{1}{1+i}$ decreases as i increases, we can see that $a_{\overline{n}|i} = v + \cdots + v^n$ decreases as i increases. Exercises 2.2.4, 2.2.5, 2.3.5, and 2.3.6 explore the behavior of $s_{\overline{n}|i}$ and $a_{\overline{n}|i}$ as functions of i in greater detail.

It was pointed out in Chapter 1 that if $i > 0$, then v^n decreases as n increases, and, in fact, $v^n \to 0$ as $n \to \infty$. Furthermore it was noted earlier in this section that $a_{\overline{n}|i}$ increases as n increases. As $n \to \infty$ it is easy to see that

$$\lim_{n \to \infty} a_{\overline{n}|i} = \lim_{n \to \infty} \frac{1 - v^n}{i} = \frac{1}{i}.$$

This expression can also be derived by summing the infinite series of present values of payments $v + v^2 + v^3 + \cdots$. The infinite-duration annuity that results as $n \to \infty$ is called a *perpetuity*, and a notation that may be used to represent the present value of this perpetuity is $a_{\overline{\infty}|i} = \frac{1}{i}$. This notion of perpetuity can be considered from another point of view. Suppose that X is the amount that must be invested at interest rate i per period in order to generate a perpetuity of 1 per period (starting one period from now). In order to generate a payment of 1 without taking from the existing principal amount X, the payment of 1 must be generated by interest alone. Therefore $X \cdot i = 1$, or, equivalently, $X = \frac{1}{i}$. It is not possible to formulate the accumulated value of the perpetuity.

2.4 ANNUITY-DUE

The annuity valuations $s_{\overline{n}|i}$ and $a_{\overline{n}|i}$ are called *immediate annuities*; in the singular, one such annuity is called an **annuity-immediate**. The term annuity-immediate refers, in the case of accumulated value, to an annuity valued at the time of the final payment, and in the case of present value it refers to an annuity valued one payment period before the first payment. These are the valuation points for annuities-certain that occur most frequently in practice.

Another standard annuity form is that of the **annuity-due**. This form occurs most frequently in the context of life annuities, but can also be defined in the case of annuities-certain. In the case of present value, an annuity-due refers to the valuation of the annuity at the time of (and including) the first payment. In the case of accumulated value, annuity-due refers to the valuation of the annuity one payment period after the final annuity payment. For n-payment annuities with payments of amount 1 each, the present value is given by

$$\ddot{a}_{\overline{n}|i} = 1 + v + v^2 + \cdots + v^{n-1} = \frac{1 - v^n}{1 - v}$$

$$= \frac{1 - v^n}{d}, \qquad (2.12)$$

and the accumulated value is given by

$$\ddot{s}_{\overline{n}|i} = (1+i) + (1+i)^2 + \cdots + (1+i)^n = (1+i)\left[\frac{(1+i)^n - 1}{i}\right]$$

$$= \frac{(1+i)^n - 1}{d}. \qquad (2.13)$$

Exercise 2.4.1 explores various relationships linking the annuity-immediate and annuity-due forms.

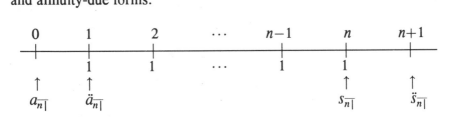

FIGURE 2.6

2.5   PAYMENT PERIOD DIFFERING FROM INTEREST CONVERSION PERIOD

In the annuities considered thus far it has been assumed that the compound interest period is the same as the annuity payment period. In practice it may often be the case that the quoted interest rate has a compounding period which does not coincide with the annuity payment period. For the purpose of a numerical evaluation of the annuity, it is a simple matter to find the interest rate for the annuity payment period that is equivalent to the quoted rate of interest, and assume that interest can be compounded every payment period at that equivalent rate per payment period. The following example illustrates this.

EXAMPLE 2.8

On the last day of every March, June, September, and December, Smith makes a deposit of 1000 into a savings account. The first deposit is March 31, 1985 and the final one is December 31, 2000. Find the balance in Smith's account on January 1, 2001 in each of the following two cases.
(a) $i^{(12)} = .09$, with interest credited on the last day of each month.
(b) $i = .10$, with compound interest credited each December 31.

SOLUTION

Smith makes a total of 64 deposits (4 per year for 16 years). If the 3-month effective rate of interest j were known, then the accumulated value just after the final deposit would be $1000 \cdot s_{\overline{64}|j}$. In case (a), from the quoted nominal annual rate of interest we see that the 1-month effective rate is $\frac{i^{(12)}}{12} = .0075$, so j satisfies the relationship $1+j = (1.0075)^3$, leading to $j = .022669172$. Then $1000 \cdot s_{\overline{64}|j} = 1000 \left[\frac{(1+j)^{64} - 1}{j} \right]$ $= 141,076.09$. In case (b), $1+j = (1+i)^{1/4} = (1.1)^{1/4}$, leading to $j = .02411369$. Then $1000 \cdot s_{\overline{64}|j} = 149,084.32$. $\qquad\square$

There are two types of roundoff error that can occur in calculating the value of an annuity. One is the error that occurs each time interest is credited to an accumulating annuity, since the accumulated value would usually be rounded to the nearest cent. Such an error would not occur in finding the present value of an annuity since the algebraic form for the annuity's present value would be used for calculation purposes. A second type of error will occur if an approximate interest rate is used. Note that in Example 2.8 if we had used approximate values of j rounded to the nearest .01%, for (a) $j \approx .0227$ and for (b) $j \approx .0241$, then the accumulated values would be 141,241.63 in case (a) and 149,005.97 in case (b). Calculators generally have at least 8 digits of accuracy, which is sufficient for all practical purposes. Exercise 2.4.2 considers in more detail the roundoff error in the calculation of annuity values.

There are alternate formulations for the annuity value calculated in Example 2.8 that can reduce the potential for roundoff error. These alternate forms are based on formulations for the annuity value in terms of the quoted rate. In case (a), let $k = \frac{i^{(12)}}{12}$ be the 1-month effective rate of interest. Then $1+j = (1+k)^3$, and the accumulated annuity can be written as

$$1000 \cdot s_{\overline{64}|j} = 1000\left[\frac{(1+j)^{64} - 1}{j}\right] = 1000\left[\frac{(1+k)^{192} - 1}{(1+k)^3 - 1}\right].$$

When the calculations are performed, the denominator is the same as it was in the solution to Example 2.8. In calculating the numerator, however, it is now *not* necessary to first find $j = (1+k)^3 - 1$ and then find $(1+j)^{64}$. We can now find $(1+j)^{64} = (1+k)^{192} = (1.0075)^{192}$ directly, and this avoids the potential error in using a rounded value of j in the calculation of $(1+j)^{64}$. In case (b) of Example 2.8, we have $1+j = (1.1)^{1/4}$, so that the accumulated annuity can be written as

$$1000s_{\overline{64}|j} = 1000\left[\frac{(1+j)^{64} - 1}{j}\right] = 1000\left[\frac{(1.1)^{16} - 1}{(1.1)^{1/4} - 1}\right].$$

The calculation of the denominator is the same as in the solution to case (b) of Example 2.8, but it is no longer necessary to first find j and then use it, or a rounded value of it, to find $(1+j)^{64}$, since we can find $(1.1)^{16}$ directly. Exercises 2.5.1 through 2.5.4 look at the general formulations that can be developed to calculate annuity values when the quoted interest period is not the same as the payment period.

In particular, Exercise 2.5.4 develops the *m-thly payable annuity*, which is illustrated in the following time diagram.

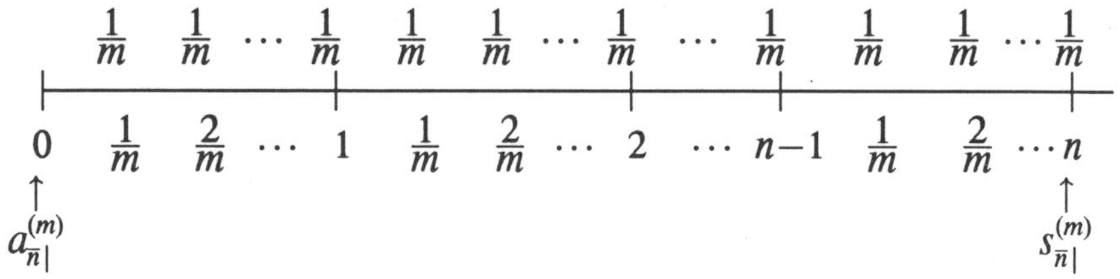

FIGURE 2.7

$a_{\overline{n}|i}^{(m)}$ denotes the present value $\frac{1}{m}^{th}$ of a year before the first payment of a series of payments of $\frac{1}{m}$ each $\frac{1}{m}^{th}$ of a year for n years (total of mn payments) valued at annual effective interest rate i. It is shown that

$a_{\overline{n}|i}^{(m)} = a_{\overline{n}|i} \cdot \frac{i}{i^{(m)}}$, with a similar result for $s_{\overline{n}|i}^{(m)}$. Note that both annuities $a_{\overline{n}|i}^{(m)}$ and $a_{\overline{n}|i}$ involve a total payment of 1 per year $\left(m \text{ payments of } \frac{1}{m} \text{ each} \right.$ in the case of $\left. a_{\overline{n}|i}^{(m)} \right)$, but $a_{\overline{n}|i}^{(m)}$ has fractional payments equally spread throughout the year. These fractional payments will have a larger present value than payments made at the end of the year, so we have $a_{\overline{n}|i}^{(m)} \geq a_{\overline{n}|i}$. This inequality also follows from $a_{\overline{n}|i}^{(m)} = a_{\overline{n}|i} \cdot \frac{i}{i^{(m)}}$, since $i > i^{(m)}$. In case (b) of Example 2.8, the accumulated value can be written in this form as $4000 s_{\overline{16}|.10}^{(4)} = 4000 s_{\overline{16}|.10} \cdot \frac{i}{i^{(4)}}$, where $i = .10$. The total paid per year is 4000, paid in equal quarterly payments of 1000 each.

In its most general form, a series of payments may be made with non-constant payment amounts, times between successive payments not constant, and with varying rates of interest. As pointed out in Section 1.2 of Chapter 1, if $t_1 < t_2$ the symbol $s(t_1, t_2)$ can be used to represent the accumulated value at time t_2 of an amount 1 invested at time t_1. If an annuity consists of n payments of amounts $K_1, K_2, \ldots, K_n$ made at times $t_1 < t_2 < \cdots < t_n$, respectively, then the accumulated value of the series at the time of, and including the final payment is

$$K_1 \cdot s(t_1, t_n) + K_2 \cdot s(t_2, t_n) + \cdots + K_{n-1} \cdot s(t_{n-1}, t_n) + K_n$$

$$= \sum_{r=1}^{n} K_r \cdot s(t_r, t_n), \quad (2.14)$$

and the present value of the series at time $t_0 < t_1$ is

$$\frac{K_1}{s(t_0, t_1)} + \frac{K_2}{s(t_0, t_2)} + \cdots + \frac{K_n}{s(t_0, t_n)} = \sum_{r=1}^{n} \frac{K_r}{s(t_0, t_r)}. \quad (2.15)$$

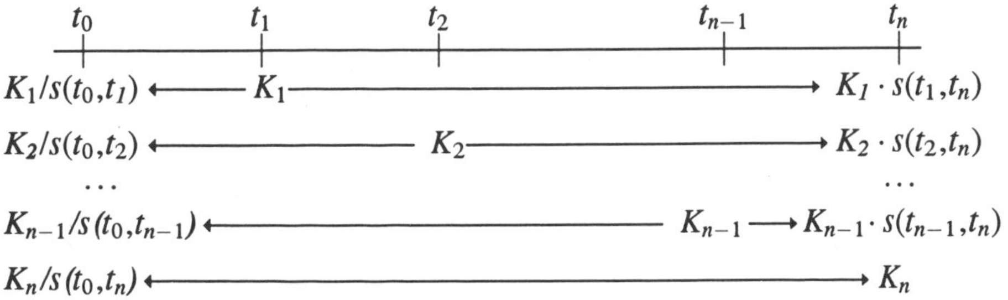

FIGURE 2.8

The annuities considered up to now all have specified individual payments at specified points in time. They are *discrete annuities* and would actually occur in practical situations, such as annuities with annual, monthly, weekly, or even daily payments. For theoretical purposes and for modeling complex situations, it is sometimes useful to consider *continuous annuities*, those which have payments made continuously over a period of time.

2.6   CONTINUOUS ANNUITIES

In part (b) of Example 2.8 a situation is considered in which an annuity has quarterly payments and interest is quoted on an effective annual basis. Exercise 2.5.4 looks at a generalization of this situation in which payments are made every $\frac{1}{m}^{th}$ of a year. As m becomes larger the time between successive payments becomes smaller. Although it would not be physically possible to reach the limit of this payment pattern as $m \rightarrow \infty$, the interpretation of that limit would be an annuity *payable continuously*.

Suppose an annuity has a level rate of continuous payment of 1 per period, and an effective rate of interest of i per period. Then the amount paid during the interval from time t_1 to time t_2 (measured using the period as the unit of time) is equal to $t_2 - t_1$. Suppose the payment continues for n periods, measured from time 0 to time n.   In order to find the accumulated value at time n of the n periods of payment, it is not possible to add up the accumulated values of individual payments as was done for the discrete annuities considered earlier. Because of the continuous nature of the payment, for each time t between 0 and n we can focus on the accumulated value at time n of the infinitesimal amount paid between time t and time $t + dt$. With $t_1 = t$ and $t_2 = t + dt$, the amount paid during the infinitesimal interval from time t_1 to time t_2 is $t_2 - t_1 = dt$.   The accumulated value as of time n of this amount is $(1+i)^{n-t} dt$. These accumulated amounts are "added up" by means of an integral, so that the accumulated value of the continuous annuity, paid at rate 1 per period for n periods,   denoted by $\bar{s}_{\overline{n}|i}$, is given by

$$\int_0^n (1 + i)^{n-t} dt. \qquad (2.16a)$$

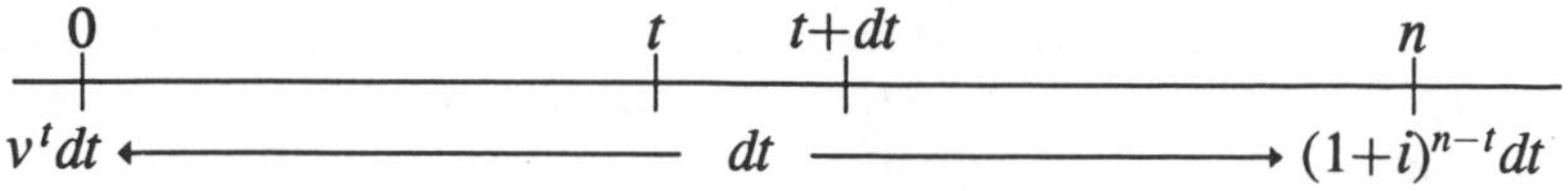

FIGURE 2.9

Integrating the right side of (2.16a) we obtain

$$\bar{s}_{\overline{n}|i} = \left. \frac{-(1+i)^{n-t}}{ln\,(1+i)} \right|_0^n = \frac{(1+i)^n - 1}{\delta}$$

$$= \frac{(1+i)^n - 1}{i} \cdot \frac{i}{\delta} = \frac{i}{\delta} \cdot s_{\overline{n}|i}, \quad (2.16b)$$

where $\delta = ln(1+i)$ is the force of interest equivalent to i.

Continuous annuities are sometimes used to approximate annuities with payments made weekly or daily, as illustrated in the next example.

EXAMPLE 2.9

In 1989 and 1990 Smith deposits 12 every day into an account and in 1991 he deposits 15 every day into the account. The account earns interest quoted as an effective annual rate, with compound interest credited every December 31. The rates are 9% in 1989 and 1990, and 12% in 1991. Find the amount in the account after interest is credited on December 31, 1991 (a) exactly, and (b) using the approximation that deposits are made continuously.

SOLUTION

(a) j_1 and j_2 denote the equivalent daily compound interest rates in 1989 and 1990, and in 1991, respectively. Then it follows that $j_1 = (1.09)^{1/365} - 1 = .000236131$, and $j_2 = (1.12)^{1/365} - 1$. Using the approach illustrated in part (b) of Example 2.8, the accumulated value on December 31, 1991 is

$$12 \cdot s_{\overline{730}|j_1}(1.12) + 15 \cdot s_{\overline{365}|j_2}$$

$$= 12(1.12)\left[\frac{(1.09)^2 - 1}{j_1}\right] + 15\left[\frac{(1.12) - 1}{j_2}\right]$$

$$= 10{,}706.19 + 5{,}796.39 = 16{,}502.58.$$

(b) If deposits are made continuously, then the total paid per year in
    1989-1990 is $12 \times 365 = 4380$, and in 1991 it is $15 \times 365 = 5475$.
    The accumulated value would be

$$4380(1.12) \cdot \bar{s}_{\overline{2}|.09} + 5475 \cdot \bar{s}_{\overline{1}|.12}$$

$$= 4380(1.12)\left[\frac{(1.09)^2 - 1}{\ln(1.09)}\right] + 5475\left[\frac{(1.12) - 1}{\ln(1.12)}\right]$$

$$= 10,707.45 + 5,797.30 = 16,504.75. \qquad \square$$

The present value, at the time payment begins, of a continuous annuity
paying a total of 1 per period at periodic effective interest rate i is

$$\bar{a}_{\overline{n}|i} = \int_0^n v^t \, dt \qquad (2.17a)$$

$$= \frac{1 - v^n}{\ln(1+i)} = \frac{1 - v^n}{\delta}$$

$$= \frac{i}{\delta} \cdot a_{\overline{n}|i}. \qquad (2.17b)$$

Many of the identities valid for discrete annuities also hold for
continuous annuities. The relationships in Equations (2.4), (2.5), (2.6),
(2.8), (2.9), (2.10), and (2.11) are valid if the discrete annuity is replaced
by the corresponding continuous annuity.

Suppose a general accumulation function is in effect, where $s(t_1, t_2)$ is
the accumulated value at time t_2 of an amount 1 invested at time t_1. Then
$\int_{t_0}^{t_e} s(t, t_e) \, dt$ and $\int_{t_0}^{t_e} \frac{1}{s(t_0, t)} \, dt$ represent the accumulated value at time t_e
and the present value at time t_0, respectively, of a continuous annuity of 1
per unit time, payable from time t_0 to time t_e. If accumulation is based on
force of interest δ_r, then

$$s(t_1, t_2) = \exp\left[\int_{t_1}^{t_2} \delta_r \, dr\right], \qquad (2.18)$$

and we have present and accumulated annuity values at time 0 and time n,
respectively, given by

$$\bar{a}_{\overline{n}|\delta_r} = \int_0^n e^{-\int_0^t \delta_r \, dr} \, dt \qquad (2.19a)$$

and

$$\bar{s}_{\overline{n}|\delta_r} = \int_0^n e^{\int_t^n \delta_r \, dr} \, dt, \qquad (2.19b)$$

along with the relationship

$$\bar{s}_{\overline{n}|\delta_r} = \bar{a}_{\overline{n}|\delta_r} \cdot e^{\int_0^n \delta_r \, dr}. \qquad (2.19c)$$

2.7 SOLUTION FOR UNKNOWN TIME OR INTEREST

In this section we consider the following two situations for the basic relationship $L = K \cdot a_{\overline{n}|i}$ (or $M = J \cdot s_{\overline{n}|i}$), or for more complex relationships.

(1) Given L, K (or M, J), and i, find n (an *unknown time problem*).
(2) Given L, K (or M, J), and n, find i (an *unknown interest problem*).

2.7.1 Unknown Time Problem

In its most basic form an unknown time problem has a straight-forward analytic solution. The solution for n in the equation $L = K \cdot a_{\overline{n}|i} = K \cdot \dfrac{1 - v^n}{i}$ is

$$n = \frac{\ln\left[1 - \dfrac{L \cdot i}{K}\right]}{\ln v} = -\frac{1}{\delta} \cdot \ln\left[1 - \frac{L \cdot i}{K}\right], \qquad (2.20a)$$

and for the equation $M = J \cdot s_{\overline{n}|i}$, n is given by

$$n = \frac{\ln\left[\dfrac{M \cdot i}{J} + 1\right]}{\ln(1 + i)} = \frac{1}{\delta} \cdot \ln\left[\frac{M \cdot i}{J} + 1\right]. \qquad (2.20b)$$

In solving for n, the number of payments, both Equations (2.20a) and (2.20b) will usually result in a non-integer value of n. The integer part of n will be the number of full periodic payments required, and there will be an additional fractional part of a payment required to complete the transaction. This additional fractional payment may be paid at the time of the final full periodic payment, or some time (usually one payment period) later.

EXAMPLE 2.10

A loan of 5000 is being repaid by monthly payments of 100 each, starting one month after the loan is made, for as long as necessary plus an additional fractional payment. At interest rate $i^{(12)} = .09$, find the number of full payments required to repay the loan, and the amount of the additional fractional payment required if (a) the additional fractional payment is made at the time of the final regular payment, and (b) the additional fractional payment is made one month after the final regular payment.

SOLUTION

The monthly compound interest rate is $j = \frac{i^{(12)}}{12} = .0075$. We solve the equation $5000 = 100 \cdot a_{\overline{n}|.0075} = 100 \left[\frac{1 - v^n_{.0075}}{.0075} \right]$, so that we find $v^n = 1 - .375 = .625$, or, equivalently, $n = \frac{ln(.625)}{ln(1/1.0075)} = 62.9$.

Thus the repayment will require 62 regular payments of 100 each plus an additional fractional payment. In order to find the amount of the additional fractional payment X, an equation of value must now be set up for each case.

(a) $5000 = 100 \cdot a_{\overline{62}|.0075} + X \cdot v^{62}_{.0075}$, so $X = \dfrac{5000 - 100 \cdot a_{\overline{62}|.0075}}{v^{62}_{.0075}}$,

or $X = 5000(1.0075)^{62} - 100 \cdot s_{\overline{62}|.0075} = 89.55$.

(b) $5000 = 100 \cdot a_{\overline{62}|.0075} + X \cdot v^{63}_{.0075}$, so $X = \dfrac{5000 - 100 \cdot a_{\overline{62}|.0075}}{v^{63}_{.0075}}$.

Note that the value of X in this case is simply 1.0075 times the value of X in case (a), so that $X = 90.22$. It will generally be true that if the additional fractional payment Y is made one payment period after the final full payment, then $Y = X(1+j)$, where X is the additional fractional payment amount if made at the time of the final full payment, and j is the periodic effective interest rate. □

The value for n found from Equation (2.20a) in Example 2.10 was $n = 62.9019$, indicating 62 regular payments of 100 each would be required, plus an additional fractional payment. The amount of the fractional payment will generally be approximately equal to the regular payment multiplied by the fractional part of n. In the case of Example 2.10 this would be $100(.9019) = 90.19$, which is close to the value of X found in both cases, particularly case (b). Exercise 2.7.4 looks at some aspects of this approximate equality.

In the solution for n by Equation (2.20a) it is implicitly assumed that $1 - \frac{L \cdot i}{K} > 0$, since otherwise it would be impossible to find the natural logarithm. Upon closer inspection, if $1 - \frac{L \cdot i}{K} \leq 0$, then $K \leq L \cdot i$, so the loan payment will at most cover the periodic interest due on the loan and will never repay any principal. Therefore the loan will never be repaid and $n = \infty$.

EXAMPLE 2.11

Smith wishes to accumulate 1000 by means of semiannual deposits earning interest at nominal annual rate $i^{(2)} = .08$, with interest credited semiannually. (a) The regular deposits will be 50 each. Find the number of regular deposits required and the additional fractional deposit if the additional fractional deposit is made at the time of the last regular deposit, and if the additional fractional deposit is made six months after the last regular deposit. (b) Repeat the problem with a regular deposit amount of 25.

SOLUTION

(a) Solving the relationship $1000 = 50 \cdot s_{\overline{n}|.04}$ results in a value of $n = \frac{ln(1.8)}{ln(1.04)} = 14.9866$. Thus 14 deposits of the full amount of 50 are required. The accumulated amount on deposit at the time of, and including, the 14th deposit is $50 \cdot s_{\overline{14}|.04} = 914.60$. If the additional fractional deposit is made at the time of the 14th regular deposit, then it must be $1000 - 914.60 = 85.40$, which is actually larger than the regular semiannual deposit. If the account is allowed to accumulate another half-year, then the accumulated amount on deposit six months after the 14th deposit, but *not* including a 15th deposit, is $50 \cdot \ddot{s}_{\overline{14}|.04} = 50(1.04) \cdot s_{\overline{14}|.04} = 951.18$. In this case an additional fractional deposit of amount $1000 - 951.18 = 48.82$ is required to bring the amount on deposit to a total of 1000.

(b) With the problem repeated at a deposit amount of 25, solving $1000 = 25 \cdot s_{\overline{n}|.04}$ results in $n = 24.3624$. The accumulated amount at the time of the 24th deposit is $25 \cdot s_{\overline{24}|.04} = 977.07$, so that the additional fractional deposit required would be 22.93, if it were made at the time of the 24th deposit. The accumulated amount six months after the 24th deposit is $25 \cdot \ddot{s}_{\overline{24}|.04} = 1016.15$. No additional fractional payment would be required since the accumulated value is already 16.15 larger than the target value of 1000.   □

In situations not so elementary as those in Examples 2.10 and 2.11, an unknown time problem may not have an analytic solution for n. In that case some sort of approximation technique must be applied. The following example illustrates this.

EXAMPLE 2.12

Smith makes a gross contribution of 100 per month to a retirement fund earning $i^{(12)} = .09$, with interest credited on the last day of each month. At the time each deposit is made the fund administrators deduct 10 from the deposit for expenses and administration fees. The first deposit is made on the last day of January, 1990. In which month does the accumulated value of the fund become greater than the total gross contribution to that point?

SOLUTION

We wish to solve for the smallest integer n for which the inequality $90 \cdot s_{\overline{n}|.0075} \geq 100n$ is true. The net deposit is 90 and the monthly rate is $\frac{.09}{12} = .0075$. The relationship $90\left[\frac{(1.0075)^n - 1}{.0075}\right] \geq 100n$ is equivalent to $(1.0075)^n \geq 1 + .008333n$, which we cannot solve analytically. An elementary approach to a solution is by "trial-and-error," where we try various values of n until the inequality is satisfied. From an inspection of the inequality, since the exponential factor $(1.0075)^n$ ultimately increases faster than the linear factor $1 + .008333n$, we see that the inequality will eventually be satisfied (*i.e.*, for a large enough n). With the arbitrary choice of $n = 10$, we have $(1.0075)^{10} = 1.077583$ and $1 + .008333(10) = 1.08333$, so the inequality is not satisfied. We try a larger n, say $n = 20$, in which case $(1.0075)^{20} = 1.161184$ and $1 + .008333(20) = 1.1666$, so the inequality is still not satisfied. Continuing in this way we obtain the results shown in Table 2.1.

| | TABLE 2.1 | | |

n	$(1.0075)^n$	$1 + .008333n$	Satisfied
10	1.077583	1.08333	No
20	1.1611843	1.1666	No
30	1.25127	1.2499	Yes
25	1.20539	1.20833	No
28	1.23271	1.23332	No
29	1.24196	1.24166	Yes

Therefore $n = 29$ is the smallest n for which the inequality is satisfied. The 29th deposit occurs at the end of May, 1992. $\qquad\square$

Exercise 2.7.10 looks at other methods of approximation when solving an unknown time problem.

2.7.2 Unknown Interest Rate Problem

We now turn to the situation in which the interest rate is unknown. In most cases it will not be possible to solve for the interest rate analytically from an equation of value, and an approximation method must be used. Usually a method of successive approximation is used in which a sequence of approximations is produced, and the sequence converges to the interest rate being sought. Two frequently used successive approximation methods are the bisection method and the Newton-Raphson method, discussed in detail in Appendix A.

EXAMPLE 2.13

Smith has been buying into a mutual fund by means of annual deposits, and has found that the value of his fund is 91,096.88 just after his 20th deposit. His first 12 deposits were 1000 each and his last 8 deposits have been 1500 each. Find to within .10% the fund's average annual growth rate based on the performance of the deposits using (a) linear interpolation based on rates that are 5% apart, (b) linear interpolation based on rates that are 1% apart, (c) the bisection method, and (d) the Newton-Raphson method.

| SOLUTION |

(a) Linear interpolation requires two interest rates that bracket the true rate. These might be found by trial and error, and we are instructed to use interest rates at intervals of 5%. The accumulated value of Smith's fund as of the 20th deposit can be written as $1000 \cdot s_{\overline{20}|i} + 500 \cdot s_{\overline{8}|i}$ (see Exercise 2.7.24), where i is the interest rate we are trying to find. Setting this equal to 91,096.88, we can write the equation of value as $2 \cdot s_{\overline{20}|i} + s_{\overline{8}|i} = 182.1938$. With an interest rate of 5%, the left hand side is $2 \cdot s_{\overline{20}|.05} + s_{\overline{8}|.05} = 75.68102$, which is too small. We try a larger value of i, say $i = .10$, in which case the left hand side has value 125.9859, which is still too small. With $i = .15$ the left hand side is 218.6140, which is larger than the right hand side. Since $2 \cdot s_{\overline{20}|i} + s_{\overline{8}|i}$ increases as i increases, it is clear that there will be a unique value of i between 10% and 15% which satisfies the equation of value. The interpolation method then sets up the equal ratios $\frac{i - .10}{.15 - .10} = \frac{182.1938 - 125.9859}{218.6140 - 125.9859}$, so that the interpolated value of i is $i \approx .1303$.

(b) With $i = .13$ the left hand side is $174.6509 < 182.1938$, and with $i = .14$ the left hand side is $195.2826 > 182.1938$. We use 13% and 14% to interpolate for i, leading to the equation $\frac{i - .13}{.14 - .13} = \frac{182.1938 - 174.6509}{195.2826 - 174.6509}$, which produces $i \approx .1337$.

(c) In applying the bisection method, we use a starting interval with $a_1 = .10$ and $b_1 = .15$, since, from part (a), we know that $.10 < i < .15$. The absolute error in the nth approximation using the bisection method is no larger than $\frac{b_1 - a_1}{2^n}$. Thus the error bound will definitely be met when $\frac{.15 - .10}{2^n} < .001$ (it may be reached sooner), or, equivalently, when $n = 6$. Successive applications of the bisection method to the function $f(i) = 2s_{\overline{20}|i} + s_{\overline{8}|i} - 182.1938$ result in the sequence of approximations $p_1 = .125$, $p_2 = .1375$, $p_3 = .13125$, $p_4 = .134375$, $p_5 = .1328125$, and $p_6 = .13359375$. (An error of less than .001 is actually reached on the fourth approximation.) If we use $a_1 = .13$ and $b_1 = .14$, then $\frac{.14 - .13}{2^n} < .001$ implies $n = 4$, and $p_1 = .135$, $p_2 = .1325$, $p_3 = .13375$, and $p_4 = .134375$, so the error bound is actually reached on the third approximation.

(d) Newton-Raphson iteration requires a starting value, say i_0, and the successive approximations are then found from $i_{n+1} = i_n - \frac{f(i_n)}{f'(i_n)}$, where $f(i)$ is the function whose zero is being sought. We could use the same $f(i)$ as in part (c), but some simplification occurs if we consider a modified form. Note that $2 \cdot s_{\overline{20}|i} + s_{\overline{8}|i} - 182.1938 = 0$ can be rewritten as $2[(1+i)^{20} - 1] + (1+i)^8 - 1 = 182.1938i$, or, equivalently, as $F(i) = 2(1+i)^{20} + (1+i)^8 - 182.1938i - 3 = 0$. The reason for using this $F(i)$ is that its derivative has a simpler form than that of the equivalent $f(i)$ in part (c). Then

$$i_{n+1} = i_n - \frac{2(1+i_n)^{20} + (1+i_n)^8 - 182.1938i_n - 3}{40(1+i_n)^{19} + 8(1+i_n)^7 - 182.1938}.$$

With a starting value of $i_0 = .10$, the successive approximations are $i_1 = .172032$, $i_2 = .146125$, $i_3 = .135519$, $i_4 = .133839$, $i_5 = .133800$, $i_6 = .133800 = i_7 = \cdots$. The value of i is .134 correct to within .10%. In fact, the exact value of i is .1338. $\qquad\Box$

The smaller the interval of interpolation, the more accurate the approximation found by the method of interpolation will be. With successive approximation any desired level of accuracy can be reached if enough iterations are performed. From a practical point of view, the Newton-Raphson method is the best of the various approximation methods available, due to the relative ease with which it may be applied and its rapid convergence to the root.

Occasionally a situation will allow an algebraic solution for an unknown interest rate. Whether or not such a solution is possible would be determined by analyzing the equation(s) of value associated with the situation. Exercise 2.7.26 is an example of such a situation.

Additional methods of approximation for annuities with level payments are considered in Exercises 2.7.14 through 2.7.16. Note that in both parts (a) and (b) of Example 2.13, the interpolated value of i is smaller than the true value of .1338. There are some general rules that can be formulated regarding the bias of an interpolated interest rate. These are considered in Exercise 2.7.17.

As pointed out in part (d) of Example 2.13 it may be useful to modify the original equation of value when applying the Newton-Raphson method. In Example 2.13 there was a fairly systematic and straightforward solution for the unknown quantity i, and it was clear that there was only one positive interest rate i that satisfied the situation. Many financial transactions will have equations of value that are satisfied by a unique interest rate (see Example 2.18 and Exercises 2.7.21, 2.8.31 and 2.8.32).

Occasionally a complicated situation may arise in which it is not clear whether there is a solution for i, and if so whether it is unique (see Exercise 1.5.21). The considerations of existence and uniqueness of solutions for i in a more general equation of value will be addressed in Chapter 3.

There are a few points to keep in mind when considering a situation involving an unknown rate of interest. Except in unusual circumstances, it can be assumed that interest rates are greater than or equal to -100%, since at a rate of -100% the accumulated value of 1 would be 0 at any future point. One circumstance in which i could be less than -100% would be where an investor has at risk more than the amount invested, such as with "leveraged" investments or when investing on "margin." Another situation would be where the investment consists of a series of varying cashflows both positive and negative (*i.e.*, disbursements and receipts). We will consider the determination of the unknown interest rate, also called the *internal rate of return* in a more general context in Chapter 3.

2.8   ANNUITIES WITH NON-CONSTANT PAYMENTS

We have already considered some situations in which annuity payments were not level over the course of the annuity (see Example 2.5). In order to value the annuity (either present value or accumulated value) if the payment amounts do not follow any uniform pattern, it would probably be necessary to value the payments individually and then add the values of the individual payments. When there is some systematic way in which the payments of an annuity vary, it may be possible to algebraically simplify the present or accumulated value. The simplification will sometimes revolve around the following general procedure. Let X denote the present value at $t = 0$ of a series of payments of amounts K_t at time t for $t = 1, 2, \ldots, n$. In other words, $X = \sum_{t=1}^{n} K_t \cdot v^t$. Then $(1 + i) \cdot X = \sum_{t=1}^{n} K_t \cdot v^{t-1} = \sum_{t=0}^{n-1} K_{t+1} \cdot v^t$, and subtracting the expression for X from the expression for $(1 + i) \cdot X$ gives

$$i \cdot X = K_1 + \sum_{t=1}^{n-1} (K_{t+1} - K_t) \cdot v^t - K_n \cdot v^n.$$

This method is useful in the case where the K_t's are based on a polynomial in t, such as an arithmetic progression, for then $i \cdot X$ involves a series with a polynomial of one less degree than the series of the K_t's.

2.8.1 Annuities Whose Payments Form an Arithmetic Progression

EXAMPLE 2.14

A series of n periodic payments has the tth payment of amount t. Find and simplify the present value one period before the first payment and the accumulated value at the time of the final payment, assuming a periodic interest rate i.

SOLUTION

The present value is $X = v + 2v^2 + 3v^3 + \cdots + (n-1)v^{n-1} + nv^n$. The technique described above produces

$$(1 + i) \cdot X = 1 + 2v + 3v^2 + \cdots + (n-1)v^{n-2} + nv^{n-1},$$

so that after subtraction we have $i \cdot X = 1 + v + v^2 + \cdots + v^{n-1} - nv^n$, which can be simplified to $i \cdot X = \ddot{a}_{\overline{n}|i} - nv^n$, and the present value can be written $X = \dfrac{\ddot{a}_{\overline{n}|i} - nv^n}{i}$. The accumulated value can be similarly found as $\dfrac{\ddot{s}_{\overline{n}|i} - n}{i}$, which is $(1 + i)^n$ times the present value. $\quad\square$

The annuity in Example 2.14 is a special case of an annuity whose payments vary according to an arithmetic progression. In general we consider an n-payment annuity with first payment A and subsequent payments each B larger than the previous one: $A, A + B, A + 2B, A + 3B,$ $\ldots, A + (n-2)B, A + (n-1)B$. The series can be decomposed into two parts, a level series of n payments of amount A each and a series starting at amount B and increasing by amount B each period. The accumulated value of the entire series at the time of the final payment will be equal to the sum of the accumulated values of the series in the decomposition. The accumulated value of the level series is simply $A \cdot s_{\overline{n}|i}$, and following the approach of Example 2.14 we see that the accumulated value of the increasing part of the series is $B\left[\dfrac{\ddot{s}_{\overline{n-1}|i} - (n-1)}{i}\right] = B\left[\dfrac{s_{\overline{n}|i} - n}{i}\right]$.

Note that there are only $n-1$ payments in the series $B, 2B, \ldots, (n-1)B$. Thus the accumulated value of the annuity at the time of the final payment is

$$A \cdot s_{\overline{n}|i} + B\left[\dfrac{s_{\overline{n}|i} - n}{i}\right]. \tag{2.21}$$

The present value of this series one period before the first payment is equal to the accumulated value multiplied by the n-year present value factor v^n, so that the present value one period before the first payment is

$$A \cdot a_{\overline{n}|i} + B\left[\dfrac{a_{\overline{n}|i} - n \cdot v^n}{i}\right]. \tag{2.22}$$

Example 2.14 is a special case of this general relationship in which $A = B = 1$. This special case is denoted in international actuarial notation by $(Ia)_{\overline{n}|i}$ for the present value one period before the first payment of the series $1, 2, \ldots, n$, and $(Is)_{\overline{n}|i}$ for the accumulated value. Thus from Example 2.14 (and Exercise 2.8.1) we have

$$(Is)_{\overline{n}|i} = \dfrac{\ddot{s}_{\overline{n}|i} - n}{i} \tag{2.23a}$$

and

$$(Ia)_{\overline{n}|i} = \dfrac{\ddot{a}_{\overline{n}|i} - nv^n}{i}. \tag{2.23b}$$

The term *increasing annuity* is often used to describe this specific situation for either $(Ia)_{\overline{n}|i}$ or $(Is)_{\overline{n}|i}$, although in this book all references to varying annuities will include a description of the associated payment pattern. Notice that the general form for the annuity whose payments follow an arithmetic progression is given by $A \cdot s_{\overline{n}|i} + B \cdot (Is)_{\overline{n-1}|i}$ for the accumulated value at the time of the final payment, and $A \cdot a_{\overline{n}|i} + B \cdot v \cdot (Ia)_{\overline{n-1}|i}$ for the present value one period before the first payment.

There is a second special case to note, namely an n-payment annuity whose first payment is amount n and whose subsequent payments decrease by 1 each period. This corresponds in the general form to $A = n$ and

$B = -1$.   In this special case the present and accumulated values are denoted $(Da)_{\overline{n}|i}$ one period before the first payment, and $(Ds)_{\overline{n}|i}$ at the time of the final payment, respectively, and could be found and simplified by the method presented at the start of this section.   Alternatively we can apply the general form with $A = n$ and $B = -1$ to obtain

$$(Ds)_{\overline{n}|i} \;=\; n \cdot s_{\overline{n}|i} - (Is)_{\overline{n-1}|i} \;=\; n \left[\frac{(1+i)^n - 1}{i} \right] - \frac{s_{\overline{n}|i} - n}{i}$$

$$=\; \frac{n \cdot (1+i)^n - s_{\overline{n}|i}}{i} \qquad\qquad (2.24a)$$

and

$$(Da)_{\overline{n}|i} \;=\; v^n \cdot (Ds)_{\overline{n}|i}$$

$$=\; \frac{n - a_{\overline{n}|i}}{i}. \qquad\qquad (2.24b)$$

This special case is called the *decreasing annuity*.   The same comments apply here as for the increasing annuity mentioned earlier.

    There are a number of identities involving increasing and decreasing annuities, many of which arise from decomposing the original series of payments illustrated by a time diagram.   Let us consider the present value $(Da)_{\overline{n}|i}$, which represents the value at time 0 of the series shown in Table 2.2.   Below the original decreasing series is shown a decomposition of the series into n separate level annuities, one for each term from length 1 to length n, with present values indicated.

TABLE 2.2

Time	0	1	2	3	$\cdots$	$n-2$	$n-1$	n
Payment	$(Da)_{\overline{n}|}$	n	$n-1$	$n-2$	$\cdots$	3	2	1
	$a_{\overline{n}|}$	1	1	1	$\cdots$	1	1	1
	$a_{\overline{n-1}|}$	1	1	1	$\cdots$	1	1	
	$a_{\overline{n-2}|}$	1	1	1	$\cdots$	1		
	$\vdots$	$\vdots$	$\vdots$	$\vdots$	$\vdots$			
	$a_{\overline{3}|}$	1	1	1				
	$a_{\overline{2}|}$	1	1					
	$a_{\overline{1}|}$	1						

Table 2.2 suggests the identity

$$(Da)_{\overline{n}|i} \;=\; \sum_{k=0}^{n-1} a_{\overline{n-k}|i}. \tag{2.25}$$

Exercise 2.8.4 looks at additional identities involving varying annuities.

2.8.2 Annuities Whose Payments Form a Geometric Progression

Another natural pattern of variation for annuity payments is that of a geometric progression. Such a payment pattern would arise if payments were indexed to a specified rate of inflation.

| EXAMPLE 2.15 |

Smith wishes to purchase a 20-year annuity with annual payments beginning one year from now. The annuity will earn interest at an annual effective rate of 11%. Smith anticipates an annual effective inflation rate over the next 20 years of 4% per year, so he wants to index his annuity at a 4% rate. In other words he would like each payment after the first to be 4% larger than the previous one. If Smith's first payment is to be 26,000, what is the present value of the annuity?

| SOLUTION |

The series of payments is $26{,}000,\ 26{,}000(1.04),\ 26{,}000(1.04)^2, \cdots,$ $26{,}000(1.04)^{19}$, and has present value

$$26{,}000 \cdot v_{.11} + 26{,}000(1.04) \cdot v_{.11}^2 + 26{,}000(1.04)^2 \cdot v_{.11}^3 + \cdots$$
$$+ \,26{,}000(1.04)^{19} \cdot v_{.11}^{20},$$

which can be written $26{,}000 \cdot v \left[1 + 1.04v + (1.04v)^2 + \cdots + (1.04v)^{19}\right]$,

which then simplifies to $26{,}000 \cdot v \left[\dfrac{1 - (1.04v)^{20}}{1 - 1.04v}\right] = 270{,}484.$ □

The important point to note in Example 2.15 is that when payments form a geometric progression, the ratio in the geometric progression combines with the present value factor so that the present value of the annuity reduces to another geometric progression. Another way of viewing an annuity whose payments form a geometric progression is illustrated in the next example.

EXAMPLE 2.16

A series of n periodic payments has first payment of amount 1, and all subsequent payments $(1 + r)$ times the size of the previous payment. At a rate of interest i per payment period, show that the present value of the series at the time of the first payment can be written as $\ddot{a}_{\overline{n}|j}$ for an appropriately defined interest rate j.

SOLUTION

The present value of the series at the time of the first payment is

$$1 + (1+r)v_i + [(1+r)v_i]^2 + \cdots + [(1+r)v_i]^{n-1}$$

$$= \frac{1 - [(1+r)v_i]^n}{1 - (1+r)v_i} = \frac{1 - \left(\frac{1+r}{1+i}\right)^n}{1 - \frac{1+r}{1+i}}$$

We want this to be $\ddot{a}_{\overline{n}|j} = \frac{1 - v_j^n}{1 - v_j}$. If we let $v_j = \frac{1+r}{1+i}$, then the present value will be of the proper form. But if $\frac{1}{1+j} = v_j = \frac{1+r}{1+i}$, then $1+j = \frac{1+i}{1+r}$, so that $j = \frac{i-r}{1+r}$. $\square$

We see from Example 2.16 that the present value of an annuity whose payments form a geometric progression can be formulated as an annuity with level payments valued at a modified rate of interest (an "inflation-adjusted" rate of interest), as described in Section 1.7. In most practical situations i would be larger than r in Example 2.16, so that j would be positive. Algebraically the method of Example 2.16 is valid whenever $i \neq r$. Exercise 2.8.7 considers some variations of the situation given in Example 2.16. In particular, note that for the series of payments in Example 2.16, the present value one period before the first payment can be expressed as $\dfrac{1 - \left(\frac{1+r}{1+i}\right)^n}{i - r}$, and the accumulated value at the time of the final payment can be expressed as $\dfrac{(1 + i)^n - (1 + r)^n}{i - r}$.

It is possible that the geometric increase period and the payment period do not coincide. In such a situation it is usually necessary to modify the payment period to coincide with the geometric increase period; in other words we find an equivalent payment per geometric increase period. We can then apply one of the expressions just given for present and accumulated values. The following example illustrates this.

EXAMPLE 2.17

Smith's child was born January 1, 1981. Smith receives monthly family allowance payments on the last day of each month, beginning January 31, 1981. The payments are increased by 12% each calendar year to meet cost-of-living increases. Monthly payments are constant during each calendar year, being 25 each month in 1981, rising to 28 each month in 1982, 31.36 each month in 1983, and so on. Immediately upon receipt of a payment, Smith deposits it in an account earning $i^{(12)} = .12$ with interest credited on the last day of each month. Find the accumulated amount in the account on the child's 18th birthday.

SOLUTION

The change in payment amount occurs once each year, but the payments are made monthly. The accumulated value on January 1, 1999, the 18th birthday, can be written as the sum of the accumulated values of each of the deposits as

$$25(1.01)^{215} + 25(1.01)^{214} + \cdots + 25(1.01)^{204}$$
$$+ 28(1.01)^{203} + 28(1.01)^{202} + \cdots + 28(1.01)^{192}$$
$$+ 31.36(1.01)^{191} + 31.36(1.01)^{190} + \cdots + 31.36(1.01)^{180}$$
$$+ \cdots + 25(1.12)^{17}(1.01)^{11} + 25(1.12)^{17}(1.01)^{10} + \cdots + 25(1.12)^{17}$$

A way of simplifying this sum is to first group the deposits on an annual basis, and for each year find the accumulated value of that year's deposits at the end of that year, as shown in Table 2.3.

TABLE 2.3

Year	Accumulated Value of Deposits on December 31
1981	$25 \cdot s_{\overline{12}|.01} = X$
1982	$28 \cdot s_{\overline{12}|.01} = 25(1.12) \cdot s_{\overline{12}|.01} = (1.12)X$
1983	$31.36 \cdot s_{\overline{12}|.01} = 25(1.12)^2 \cdot s_{\overline{12}|.01} = (1.12)^2 X$
$\vdots$	$\vdots$
1998	$25(1.12)^{17} \cdot s_{\overline{12}|.01} = (1.12)^{17} X$

The monthly deposits are equivalent to 18 geometrically increasing annual deposits of X, $(1.12)X$, $(1.12)^2X$, ..., $(1.12)^{17}X$. The accumulated value at the time of the final deposit is

$$(1+i)^{17}X + (1+i)^{16}(1.12)X + (1+i)^{15}(1.12)^2X + \cdots + (1+i)^0(1.12)^{17}X, \text{ or}$$

$$(1.12)^{17}X\left[\left(\tfrac{1+i}{1.12}\right)^{17} + \left(\tfrac{1+i}{1.12}\right)^{16} + \left(\tfrac{1+i}{1.12}\right)^{15} + \cdots + 1\right]$$

$$= (1.12)^{17}X\left[\frac{\left(\tfrac{1+i}{1.12}\right)^{18} - 1}{\left(\tfrac{1+i}{1.12}\right) - 1}\right].$$

Since $X = 25 \cdot s_{\overline{12}|.01} = 317.06$ and $i = (1.01)^{12} - 1 = .1268$, the accumulated value is 41,282.55, using values to eight figures. $\square$

The general form of a varying annuity defined at the start of this section had a payment of amount K_t payable at time t. The value of a continuous annuity with varying payments can also be formulated in a general context. In this case the payment pattern is described by a continuous function $h(t)$, which represents the *instantaneous rate* or *density of payment* being made at time t. Then $h(t)\,dt$ would be the instantaneous payment at time t, all of whose present or accumulated values would be "added," in the form of an integral, from time 0 to time n, producing

$$\int_0^n h(t) \cdot v^t\, dt \tag{2.26a}$$

for the present value at time 0, and

$$\int_0^n h(t) \cdot (1+i)^{n-t}\, dt \tag{2.26b}$$

for the accumulated value at time n. Corresponding to the standard increasing annuity ($A = B = 1$) in the discrete case is the continuously increasing annuity, for which $h(t) = t$. The notation used for the present value of this annuity is

$$(\bar{I}\bar{a})_{\overline{n}|i} = \int_0^n t \cdot v^t\, dt, \tag{2.27a}$$

and for the accumulated value is

$$(\bar{I}\bar{s})_{\overline{n}|i} = \int_0^n t \cdot (1+i)^{n-t} \, dt. \tag{2.27b}$$

These can be simplified by applying integration by parts, producing

$$(\bar{I}\bar{a})_{\overline{n}|i} = \frac{\bar{a}_{\overline{n}|} - nv^n}{\delta} \tag{2.28a}$$

and

$$(\bar{I}\bar{s})_{\overline{n}|i} = \frac{\bar{s}_{\overline{n}|} - n}{\delta}, \tag{2.28b}$$

where $\delta = ln(1+i)$. Some other forms of varying continuous annuities are considered in Exercise 2.8.10. If the force of interest is varying as well, say δ_t at time t, then the more general expressions for the present and accumulated values of the annuities at times 0 and n, respectively, are

$$\int_0^n h(t) \cdot e^{-\int_0^t \delta_r \, dr} \, dt \tag{2.29a}$$

and

$$\int_0^n h(t) \cdot e^{\int_t^n \delta_r \, dr} \, dt. \tag{2.29b}$$

In Section 2.7.2 we considered methods of determining the interest rate on an annuity when it is not given. For the cases considered there, and for varying annuities as well, it is generally true that there is a unique solution for i, and it is possible to find i by one of the approximation methods of Section 2.7.2. The following example shows this.

| EXAMPLE 2.18 |

Suppose that an annuity consists of payments $K_1, K_2, \cdots, K_n$ made at times $0 < t_1 < t_2 < \cdots < t_n$, where each $K_r > 0$. Suppose also that $L > 0$. Show that there is a unique $i > -1$ for which L is the present value at time 0 of the given series of payments, where i is the interest rate per time unit measured by t.

| SOLUTION |

With $v = \frac{1}{1+i}$, the present value at time 0 of the series of payments is $f(i) = K_1 \cdot v^{t_1} + K_2 \cdot v^{t_2} + \cdots + K_n \cdot v^{t_n}$. Since the K_r's and t_r's are all > 0, it follows that $f(i)$ is a decreasing function of i, since v^{t_k}

decreases as i increases. But $\lim\limits_{i\to\infty} f(i) = 0$, since each $v^{t_k} \to 0$ as $i \to \infty$, and $\lim\limits_{i\to-1} f(i) = +\infty$, since $v^{t_k} \to +\infty$ as $i \to -1$. Then since $0 < L < +\infty$ and $f(i)$ decreases from $+\infty$ to 0 as i goes from -1 to $+\infty$, it follows that there is a unique $i > -1$ for which $L = f(i)$. Note that $i > 0$ if $L < \sum\limits_{r=1}^{n} K_r$ and $i < 0$ if $L > \sum\limits_{r=1}^{n} K_r$. Exercise 2.8.32 shows that the corresponding result holds for accumulation: given the same assumptions, there is a unique $i > -1$ for which L is the accumulated value of the series at time t_n. $\qquad\square$

In a more general setting a financial transaction may involve a series of disbursements (payments made out) and payments received. Solving for an unknown interest rate, yield rate, or internal rate of return in this general setting is considered in Chapter 3.

2.9 YIELD RATES AND REINVESTMENT RATES

We saw in Section 2.2 that $s_{\overline{n}|i}$ is the accumulated value of a series of n periodic payments of 1 each, invested at periodic rate of interest i, where it is implicitly assumed that interest reinvestment is also at rate i. We saw also that $s_{\overline{n}|i} = (1+i)^n \cdot a_{\overline{n}|i}$ and $a_{\overline{n}|i}$ is the present value of the series one period before the first payment is made. A loan of amount L that is to be repaid with n level payments of amount K each at interest rate i per payment period has equation of value $L = K \cdot a_{\overline{n}|i}$. When a loan transaction is regarded as an investment from the lender's point of view, it appears that to truly earn a (compound) periodic rate of return of i for the n-period term, the lender should have accumulated $L(1+i)^n = K \cdot a_{\overline{n}|i} \cdot (1+i)^n = K \cdot s_{\overline{n}|i}$, with reinvestment of the loan payments as received. Therefore it is implicit in the suggestion that the lender realizes a yield rate of i per period on this investment (loan transaction) that loan payments can be reinvested at rate i.

Consider the case of a 10-year loan of 10,000 at $i = .05$. We look at three ways at which the loan can be repaid.

(1) Ten level annual payments of $\dfrac{10,000}{a_{\overline{10}|.05}} = 1295.05$. If these payments are reinvested at 5% as they are received, the accumulated value at the time of the tenth payment is $1295.05 \, s_{\overline{10}|.05} = 16{,}289$. Since

$10,000(1.05)^{10} = 16,289,$ the lender realizes an annual compound rate of return of 5%.

(2) Ten level annual interest payments of 500, plus a return of the entire 10,000 principal at the end of ten years. If the payments of 500 are reinvested at 5%, the accumulated value after ten years is $500s_{\overline{10}|.05} = 6289.$ Along with the payment of 10,000 at time 10, the accumulated value is again 16,289 (this also follows from the relationship $1 + i \cdot s_{\overline{n}|i} = (1+i)^n$), which indicates an annual compound rate of return of 5%.

(3) A single payment of $10,000(1.05)^{10} = 16,288.95.$ In this case it is clear that the lender receives an annual compound rate of return of 5%.

As long as the reinvestment rate is 5% (or, in general, the interest rate i on the loan), then for any repayment schedule for which the present value of the payments is 10,000 at $i = .05$, the accumulated value of the reinvested payments will be 16,288.95.

Suppose now that the interest rate earned on reinvested payments is 3%. A reinvestment rate is irrelevant in case (3), since no reinvestment takes place. In case (1) the accumulated value of the reinvested payments is $1295.05 \cdot s_{\overline{10}|.03} = 14,846.30.$ In case (2) the accumulated value is $500 \cdot s_{\overline{10}|.03} + 10,000 = 15,731.94.$ In cases (1) and (2) the accumulated value does not give an annual rate of 5% compounded for 10 years on an initial investment of 10,000. The average annual compound rate of interest earned is given by $10,000(1 + i)^{10} = 14,846.30,$ which yields $i = .0403$ in case (1), and is given by $10,000(1 + i)^{10} = 15,731.94,$ or $i = .0464,$ in case (2). The reason the average annual compound interest rate is less than 5% is that the reinvestment rate is less than 5%. Furthermore, the less reinvestment that takes place, the less of a reduction there is below 5%. In other words case (3) has no reinvestment and results in an annual compound rate of 5%, and case (2) has more reinvestment than case (3), but less reinvestment than case (1) which has the lowest average compound return.

We see in the examples above that the yield rate earned on an investment or the *internal rate of* (IRR) *return on a transaction* depends on the point of view from which it is regarded. From the borrower's point of view, case (1) above has a yield rate or IRR of i where $10,000 = 1295.05 \cdot a_{\overline{10}|i}$, so that $i = .05$. From a lender's point of view, taking into account the reinvestment of repayments at 3%, the average annual compound rate of return over the 10 years is i where

$10,000 \cdot (1 + i)^{10} = 14,846.30$, so that $i = .0403$. In general, if the lender is not able to reinvest the repayments at rate i per period, but reinvests them instead at rate j per period, then the accumulated value of the payments at the time of the final payment is $K \cdot s_{\overline{n}|j}$. If $j < i$ then $K \cdot s_{\overline{n}|j} < K \cdot s_{\overline{n}|i}$, and the lender does not realize an average annual compound return of i per period if he initially lends out $K \cdot a_{\overline{n}|i}$. The situation is reversed in the less likely case that $j > i$ (see Exercise 2.9.1).

2.9.1 Book Value and Market Value

An investor considering the purchase of an annuity (or cashflow) at time t_0 will typically calculate the present value of the cashflow at some interest rate, say i_0. This rate would be related to rates in effect for similar investments at the time of valuation. The investor's *yield-to-maturity* on the cashflow is i_0 if the cashflow is held for its entire duration. At any intermediate point during the term of the cashflow, the value of the remainder of the cashflow based on the original rate i_0 is called the *book value* of the cashflow at that time. Such a valuation might be needed for accounting purposes. If the investor decides at time $t_1 > t_0$ to sell the remainder of the cashflow to another investor, an appropriate interest rate called the *market rate*, say i_1, would be used at t_1 for the valuation. The value of the cashflow at t_1 based on the market rate is called the *market value* of the cashflow. These notions of book value and market value arise in the context of loan amortization (Chapter 3) and in the valuation of bonds (Chapter 4).

> **EXAMPLE 2.19**

Smith borrows 10,000 at effective annual interest rate $i_0 = .10$. The loan will be repaid by 10 annual payments of amounts $2000, 1900, 1800, \ldots,$ 1100, with the first payment made one year after the loan. Determine the book value and the market value of the loan payments just after the 5th payment if the market rate of interest then is .12.

> **SOLUTION**

Note that the present value at $t = 0$ of the loan payments at $i_0 = .10$ is $1000 \cdot a_{\overline{10}|.10} + 100 \cdot (Da)_{\overline{10}|.10} = 10,000$. The book value just after the 5th payment is $BV_5 = 1000 \cdot a_{\overline{5}|.10} + 100 \cdot (Da)_{\overline{5}|.10} = 5000$, and the market value is $MV_5 = 1000 \cdot a_{\overline{5}|.12} + 100 \cdot (Da)_{\overline{5}|.12} = 4767.46$. □

2.9.2 The Sinking Fund Method of Valuation

A situation may arise in which a lender is considering the purchase of an annuity (a specified cashflow or series of payments). In previous sections of this chapter we have considered the valuation of the series of payments in the form of the present value of the series at some interest rate i per payment period. However, as noted above, in order to actually realize a return of i per period to the end of the term, we must have a reinvestment rate of i as well. It may be the case that the reinvestment rate j is not equal to i. In practice, the rate i on a loan would tend to be larger than the rate j earned on reinvestment, such as in a deposit account. The *sinking fund method* is a way for an investor to value the annuity or cashflow when $j \neq i$. The sinking fund method of valuing (finding the purchase price for) a level annuity of K per period for n periods allows an investor to receive a periodic return of i per period while recovering his initial investment amount (the principal) in a *sinking fund* (deposit account). The idea is that the investor pays an amount P for the series of payments, and receives a periodic return at rate i on the initial outlay, which would be $P \cdot i$ per period. The actual payment received is K per period, so the amount of the payment in excess of the periodic return is $K - P \cdot i$. This excess is the amount that is deposited into the sinking fund at rate j. At the end of the n-period term, the sinking fund has accumulated to $(K - P \cdot i) \cdot s_{\overline{n}|j}$. This accumulated amount is just enough to repay the investor's initial outlay, allowing him to recover the principal. This scenario is illustrated in Table 2.4.

TABLE 2.4

Time	0	1	2	$\cdots$	n	
Initial outlay	P					
Interest per period		$P \cdot i$	$P \cdot i$	$\cdots$	$P \cdot i$	
Actual payment		K	K	$\cdots$	K	
Sinking fund deposit		$K - P \cdot i$	$K - P \cdot i$	$\cdots$	$K - P \cdot i$	$(K - P \cdot i) \cdot s_{\overline{n}|j} = P$

Then we see that

$$(K - P \cdot i) \cdot s_{\overline{n}|j} = P \tag{2.30a}$$

or, equivalently,

$$P = \frac{K \cdot s_{\overline{n}|j}}{1 + i \cdot s_{\overline{n}|j}}. \qquad (2.30b)$$

This situation is similar to Case (2) on page 95, where the 10,000 loan is repaid by interest alone and the principal is returned at the end of the term. In this case the initial investment of P earns interest of $P \cdot i$ per period, and the principal amount is returned at the end of the term by means of the accumulated sinking fund.

EXAMPLE 2.20

A manufacturer is considering the purchase of some equipment to increase production and generate income of 15,000 per year, payable at the end of the year. The equipment has a lifetime of 8 years and no salvage value. What price should be paid for this equipment in order to realize an annual return of 10% while recovering the principal in a sinking fund earning 7% per annum?

SOLUTION

We can apply Equation (2.30b) with $K = 15,000$, $n = 8$, $i = .10$, and $j = .07$, obtaining $P = \dfrac{15,000 \cdot s_{\overline{8}|.07}}{1 + (.10) \cdot s_{\overline{8}|.07}} = 75,961.77$ as the solution of the equation $(15,000 - .10P) \, s_{\overline{8}|.07} = P$. Note that the income of 15,000 per year can be split into 7596.18 plus 7403.82, and the 8 deposits of 7403.82 accumulate to 75,961.77 at 7%. The present value of the income at $i = .10$ is $15,000 \cdot a_{\overline{8}|.10} = 80,023.89$. $\qquad \square$

Exercises 2.9.2 through 2.9.4 relate to various aspects of the sinking fund approach to valuing a series of payments.

The relationship between the usual present value method (or amortization method) of valuing an annuity and the sinking fund method is considered in the following example.

EXAMPLE 2.21

Let P_1 be the present value of an n-payment level annuity-immediate valued in the usual way at a periodic interest rate of i per period. Let P_2 be the "present" value of the annuity based on the sinking fund method with annual return of $i > 0$ (the same as in the calculation of P_1) to the investor along with recapture of principal in a sinking fund at rate $j > 0$. (The quotation marks around "present" indicate that present value is not being found in the usual sense with a present value factor v at some specified rate of interest.) Derive each of the relationships (a) $i = j \rightarrow P_1 = P_2$, (b) $i > j \rightarrow P_1 > P_2$, and (c) $i < j \rightarrow P_1 < P_2$.

| SOLUTION |

Let the periodic payment be 1. Then $P_1 = a_{\overline{n}|i}$ and $P_2 = \dfrac{s_{\overline{n}|j}}{1 + i \cdot s_{\overline{n}|j}}$. If $i = j$, then $P_2 = \dfrac{s_{\overline{n}|i}}{1 + i \cdot s_{\overline{n}|i}} = \dfrac{s_{\overline{n}|i}}{(1+i)^n} = a_{\overline{n}|i} = P_1$, establishing relationship (a). Note that P_2 can be written (after some simple algebraic manipulation) in the form $P_2 = \frac{1}{i} \cdot \left[1 - \dfrac{1}{1 + i \cdot s_{\overline{n}|j}}\right]$. Then we have the following sequence of implications:

$$i > j \rightarrow s_{\overline{n}|i} > s_{\overline{n}|j} \rightarrow 1 + i \cdot s_{\overline{n}|i} > 1 + i \cdot s_{\overline{n}|j} \rightarrow \dfrac{1}{1 + i \cdot s_{\overline{n}|i}} < \dfrac{1}{1 + i \cdot s_{\overline{n}|j}} \rightarrow$$

$$P_1 = a_{\overline{n}|i} = \frac{1}{i}\left[1 - \dfrac{1}{1 + i \cdot s_{\overline{n}|i}}\right] > \frac{1}{i}\left[1 - \dfrac{1}{1 + i \cdot s_{\overline{n}|j}}\right] = P_2, \text{ which}$$

establishes relationship (b). Relationship (c) is established in the same way as (b), except that all inequalities are reversed. ☐

The sinking fund method of valuation can be applied to a varying series of payments $K_1, K_2, \ldots, K_n$ made at times $1, 2, \ldots, n$. Suppose L is the purchase price of this varying annuity-immediate to provide the purchaser with a return of i per payment period while allowing the recapture of principal in a sinking fund at rate j. Then L must be the accumulated value at time n of the series of sinking fund deposits, where the sinking fund deposit at time t is $K_t - L \cdot i$. Then

$$L = (K_1 - L \cdot i)(1+j)^{n-1} + (K_2 - L \cdot i)(1+j)^{n-2} + \cdots +$$

$$(K_{n-1} - L \cdot i)(1+j)^1 + (K_n - L \cdot i)(1+j)^0$$

$$= \sum_{t=1}^{n} K_t(1+j)^{n-t} - L \cdot i \cdot s_{\overline{n}|j}.$$

Solving for L results in

$$L = \frac{\sum_{t=1}^{n} K_t (1+j)^{n-t}}{1 + i \cdot s_{\overline{n}|j}}. \qquad (2.31)$$

The most general case would also allow for varying rates of return $i_1, i_2, \cdots, i_n$ and sinking fund rates $j_1, j_2, \cdots, j_n$ (see Exercise 2.9.4).

2.9.3 Reinvestment Rates of Interest

When interest compounds at rate i per period it is assumed that as periodic interest is credited it is reinvested at the same rate i. It may be the case, however, that as interest is credited at rate i, it is reinvested at a rate other than i for future compounding. In other words only the initial amount invested earns i per period, and the interest generated by that initial amount is reinvested at rate j.

EXAMPLE 2.22

Smith owns a 10,000 savings bond that pays interest monthly at $i^{(12)} = .06$. Upon receipt of an interest payment, he immediately deposits it into an account earning interest, payable monthly, at a rate of $i^{(12)} = .12$. Find the accumulated value of this account just after the 12th, 24th, and 36th deposit. In each case find Smith's average annual $i^{(12)}$ based on his initial investment of 10,000.

SOLUTION

The savings bond pays interest of 50 per month, so the accumulated values in the account are $50 \cdot s_{\overline{12}|.01} = 634.13$, $50 \cdot s_{\overline{24}|.01} = 1348.67$, and $50 \cdot s_{\overline{36}|.01} = 2153.84$. If j is the average monthly yield rate earned on the initial 10,000 investment, then over 12 months we have $10,000(1+j)^{12} = 10,634.13$, giving $j = .00514$ and $i^{(12)} = 12j = .0616$; over the 24-month period $10,000(1+j)^{24} = 11,348.67$. so that $j = .00529$ and $i^{(12)} = .0634$; over the 36-month period we find $j = .00543$ and $i^{(12)} = .0652$.   □

In general if an amount L is invested and generates interest at rate i per period which is then reinvested at rate j, the accumulated value of the reinvested interest at time n will be $L \cdot i \cdot s_{\overline{n}|j}$, and the total value of the investment will be $L + L \cdot i \cdot s_{\overline{n}|j} = L[1 + i \cdot s_{\overline{n}|j}]$. In Exercise 2.9.10 you are asked to show that the average periodic rate i' earned on the n-period investment lies between i and j.

EXAMPLE 2.23

Suppose that Smith, on a payroll savings plan, buys a bond for 100 at the end of every month, with the bond paying monthly interest at $i^{(12)} = .06$. The interest payments generated are reinvested in an account earning $i^{(12)} = .12$. Find the accumulated value in the deposit account at the end of 12 months, 24 months and 36 months. Find the yield rate in the form $i^{(12)}$ that Smith realizes over each of these time periods on his investment.

SOLUTION

At the end of 12 months Smith will have bought 1200 in bonds. The first 100 bond was bought at the end of the first month, so Smith received interest of 0.50 at the end of the second month, at which time he bought the second 100 bond, bringing his total in bonds to 200. At the end of the third month Smith receives 1.00 (monthly interest on the 200 in bonds), and buys a third 100 bond. At the end of the fourth month he receives 1.50 in interest and buys a fourth 100 bond. Therefore the interest Smith receives from the bonds is $0.50, 1.00, 1.50, 2.00, \ldots, 5.50$ at the ends of months $2, 3, 4, 5, \ldots, 12$. The accumulated value in the deposit account after 12 months is $(.50) \cdot (Is)_{\overline{11}|.01} = 34.13$, after 24 months it is $(.50) \cdot (Is)_{\overline{23}|.01} = 148.67$, and after 36 months the accumulated value is $(.50) \cdot (Is)_{\overline{35}|.01} = 353.84$. Smith's monthly yield j on the 1200 invested over 12 months is the solution of $100 \cdot s_{\overline{12}|j} = 1234.13$, for which the Newton-Raphson method gives a solution of $j = .00508$, or $i^{(12)} = .061$. Over 24 months j is found from $100 \cdot s_{\overline{24}|j} = 2548.67$, which gives $j = .00518$, or $i^{(12)} = .0622$. Over 36 months we have $100 \cdot s_{\overline{36}|j} = 3953.84$, which gives $j = .00529$, or $i^{(12)} = .0634$.

□

As a general approach to the situation in Example 2.23, suppose that a series of n payments of amount 1 each generate interest at rate i per payment period, and that the interest is reinvested as it is received at rate j per period. The first interest payment is i, which comes one period after the first of the original payments. The second interest payment is $2i$ and is paid one period after the second of the original payments. The following table illustrates the original payments and the interest generated by them.

TABLE 2.5										

Time	0	1	2	3	4	$\cdots$	$n-2$	$n-1$	n	
Payment		1	1	1	1	$\cdots$	1	1	1	$\rightarrow$ n
Interest			i	$2i$	$3i$	$\cdots$	$(n-3)i$	$(n-2)i$	$(n-1)i$	$\rightarrow$ $i \cdot (Is)_{\overline{n-1}|j}$

The interest is reinvested at rate j per period, with the payments forming an increasing annuity since interest at rate i is being earned on an increasing principal amount. The total accumulated value of the reinvested interest is $i \cdot (Is)_{\overline{n-1}|j}$, which, along with the original payments, results in a total of $n + i \cdot (Is)_{\overline{n-1}|j}$ at time n.

2.10 NOTES AND REFERENCES

Appendix A presents a review of methods of successive approximation. The book *Numerical Analysis* by Burden and Faires [1] provides a more detailed presentation of numerical methods of solution.

A finite-difference approach to simplifying the present value of a varying annuity is discussed in *The Theory of Interest* by S. Kellison [7]. Chapter 2 of *Compound Interest* by M. Butcher and C. Nesbitt [2] contains an extensive collection of numerical and algebraic problems on annuities.

2.11 EXERCISES

Exercises 2.2

2.2.1 Write the annuity $s_{\overline{n+k}|i}$ in series form (assume n and k are integers). Group separately the accumulated values (as of the time of the final payment) of the first n payments and final k payments. Use this formulation to derive Equation (2.4).

2.2.2 Since June 30, 1986 Smith has been making deposits of 100 each into a bank account on the last day of each month. For all of 1986 and 1987 Smith's account earned nominal interest compounded monthly at an annual rate of 9%. For the first 9 months of 1988 the account earned $i^{(12)} = .105$, and since then the account has been earning $i^{(12)} = .12$. Find the balance in the account on February 1, 1989. Find the amount of interest credited on February 28, 1989.

2.2.3 (a) In a series of 40 payments the first 10 payments are 10 each, the second 10 payments are 20 each, the third ten payments are 30 each, and the final 10 payments are 40 each. The payments are equally spaced and the interest rate is 5% per payment period. Find the accumulated value at the time of the final payment.

   (b) Show that the accumulated value of the series is equal to
$$10\left[s_{\overline{10}|.05} + s_{\overline{20}|.05} + s_{\overline{30}|.05} + s_{\overline{40}|.05}\right].$$

   (c) In a series of $n \cdot m$ payments the first m payments are K each, the second m payments are $2K$ each, and so on, with the final m payments of amount nK each. The payments are equally spaced and interest is at rate i per payment period. Show that the accumulated value of the series at the time of the final payment is $K \cdot \sum_{t=1}^{n} s_{\overline{m \cdot t}|i}$.

2.2.4 (a) Calculate $s_{\overline{10}|i}$ for $i = .01, .011, .012, .013, .014, .015, .02,$ $.03, .04, .05, .10, .15, .20, .25, .50,$ and 1.00. Sketch the graph of $s_{\overline{10}|i}$ as a function of i, based on the calculated values.

(b) Find $\frac{d}{di} s_{\overline{n}|i}$, $\frac{d^2}{di^2} s_{\overline{n}|i}$ and $\frac{d^m}{di^m} s_{\overline{n}|i}$. Relate the first two derivatives to the form of the graph sketched in part (a).

(c) Apply linear interpolation (see Appendix A) to approximate $s_{\overline{10}|}$ at $i = .011$ by (i) using $i = .01$ and $i = .015$, and (ii) using $i = .01$ and $i = .05$. Show that when approximating a value of $s_{\overline{n}|i}$ by linear interpolation, the approximate value is always larger than the true value.

(d) Use the approximation $f(x_0 + h) \approx f(x_0) + h \cdot f'(x_0)$ to find the approximate value of $s_{\overline{10}|i}$ at $i = .011$ based on the true value and derivative at $i = .01$. Repeat this for $i = .101$ based on the true value and derivative at $i = .10$.

2.2.5 Use the values found in part (a) of Exercise 2.2.4 to calculate the values of $\frac{1}{s_{\overline{10}|i}}$ for the various interest rates. Sketch a graph of $\frac{1}{s_{\overline{10}|i}}$ as a function of i.

2.2.6 (a) If $s_{\overline{n}|} = 70$ and $s_{\overline{2n}|} = 210$, find the values of $(1 + i)^n$, i, and $s_{\overline{3n}|}$.

(b) If $s_{\overline{3n}|} = X$ and $s_{\overline{n}|} = Y$, express v^n in terms of X, Y and constants.

(c) If $s_{\overline{n}|} = 48.99$, $s_{\overline{n-2}|} = 36.34$, and $i > 0$, find i.

2.2.7 An $m + n$ year annuity of 1 per year has $i = 7\%$ during the first m years and has $i = 11\%$ during the remaining n years. If $s_{\overline{m}|.07} = 34$ and $s_{\overline{n}|.11} = 128$, what is the accumulated value of the annuity just after the final payment?

2.2.8   Smith opens a bank account, paying interest at rate i, with a
        deposit of R. The bank credits interest annually, but will pay
        simple interest up to the day the account is closed if this occurs
        less than a year after it is opened. Smith gets a bright idea and
        decides that if he closes the account after 6 months and
        immediately opens a new account for six months, his annual return
        will be based on $i^{(2)}$ numerically equal to i. Later Smith realizes
        that if he closes his account and immediately reopens a new
        account n times per year, his annual return will be $i^{(n)}$ numerically
        equal to i. The bank, anticipating such behavior, has in place a
        mechanism that discourages closing and immediately reopening
        accounts. The bank has a service charge of k at the time an
        account is closed if this occurs within one year of the date it was
        opened.
        (a) If Smith's initial deposit is R and he closes and reopens his
            account n times per year, derive an expression in terms of R,
            n, k, and i for the effective annual rate of return that Smith
            realizes on his account.
        (b) If $i = .12$ and $k = 1$ find the value of n that optimizes his
            effective annual return if R is (i) 10,000, (ii) 1000 and (iii)
            100.

2.2.9   Given $s_{\overline{10}|.10} = S$, find the value of $\sum_{t=1}^{10} s_{\overline{t}|.10}$ in terms of S.

2.2.10 A deposit of 1 is made at each of times $t = 1, 2, \dots, n$ to an
        account earning interest at rate i per payment period. Let I_t denote
        the interest payable at time t. Find an expression for I_t, and show
        that $\sum_{t=1}^{n} I_t = s_{\overline{n}|i} - n$. What is the interpretation of this relationship?

2.2.11 In each of the following cases, explain the relationship in terms of
        the amounts deposited, interest, and interest on interest:
        (a) $s_{\overline{3}|i} = 3 + 3i + i^2$,   (b) $s_{\overline{4}|i} = 4 + 6i + 4i^2 + i^3$,
        (c) $s_{\overline{n}|i} = \sum_{k=1}^{n} \binom{n}{k} \cdot i^{k-1}$.

2.2.12 Smith buys 100 shares of stock ABC at the same time Brown buys 100 shares of stock XYZ. Both stocks are bought for 10 per share. Smith receives a dividend of .80 per share, payable at the end of each year, for 10 years, at which time (just after receiving the 10th dividend) he sells his stock for 2 per share. Smith invests his dividends at annual rate 6%, and invests the proceeds of the sale of his stock at the same rate. Brown receives no dividends for the first 10 years, but starts receiving annual dividends of .40 per share at the end of 11 years. Brown also invests his dividends in an account earning 6%. If Brown sells his shares n years after purchase, what should be the sale price per share in order that his accumulated investment matches that of Smith, for each of $n = 15$, 20 and 25 ?

Exercises 2.3

2.3.1 Show that Equation (2.7) can be written as $1 = v^n + i \cdot a_{\overline{n}|i}$, and give an interpretation of this relationship.

2.3.2 Derive Equation (2.8) (a) by means of a line diagram similar to the derivation of Equation (2.4), (b) by considering the series forms of the annuities in Equation (2.8), and

(c) show that $v^m + v^{m+1} + \cdots + v^n = \dfrac{v^{m-1} - v^n}{i}$.

2.3.3 (a) For the situation described in Exercise 2.2.2, find the present value of the series on June 1, 1986.

(b) For the series of part (a) of Exercise 2.2.3, find the present value one payment period before the first payment. Show that this present value can be written as

$10\left[4 \cdot a_{\overline{40}|.05} - a_{\overline{10}|.05} - a_{\overline{20}|.05} - a_{\overline{30}|.05}\right].$

2.3.4 Suppose an annuity of $n + k$ equally-spaced payments (where n and k are integers) of amount 1 each is subject to interest at rate i per payment period until the nth payment, and at rate j per payment period starting just after the nth payment. If Y is the accumulated value of the series at the time of the final payment and X is the present value of the series one period before the first payment, show that $Y = (1+i)^n(1+j)^k \cdot X$.

2.3.5   Repeat parts (a), (c), and (d) of Exercise 2.2.4 for $a_{\overline{10}|i}$, and repeat part (b) for $a_{\overline{n}|i}$.

2.3.6   Use the values found in part (a) of Exercise 2.3.5 to calculate the values of $\dfrac{1}{a_{\overline{10}|i}}$ for the various interest rates. Sketch a graph of $\dfrac{1}{a_{\overline{10}|i}}$ as a function of i.

2.3.7   A loan of 1000 is to be repaid by n equally-spaced payments of amount P_n. If $i = .05$ find the level payment for each of $n = 1$, 2, 3, 4, 5, 10, 15, 20, 25, 50, 100, 200, 500, 1000. Sketch a graph of P_n versus n.

2.3.8   Find expressions for $\dfrac{d}{dn}\, s_{\overline{n}|i}$ and $\dfrac{d}{dn}\, a_{\overline{n}|i}$.

2.3.9   Derive the relationship $\dfrac{1}{a_{\overline{n}|i}} \;=\; \dfrac{1}{s_{\overline{n}|i}} + i$.

2.3.10 Give algebraic proofs for each of the following relationships.

(a) $s_{\overline{90}|} \;=\; s_{\overline{30}|}\left(1 + (1+i)^{30} + (1+i)^{60}\right)$

(b) $a_{\overline{2n}|} \;=\; a_{\overline{n}|}\left(1 + v^n\right)$

(c) $s_{\overline{n}|} + s_{\overline{2n}|} \;<\; s_{\overline{3n}|}$ if both n and i are > 0.

(d) $a_{\overline{n}|} + a_{\overline{2n}|} \;>\; a_{\overline{3n}|}$ if both n and i are > 0.

(e) If $0 = t_0 \le t_1 \le t_2 \le \cdots \le t_{k-1} \le t_k = n$, then

(i) $s_{\overline{n}|} \;=\; \displaystyle\sum_{j=1}^{k}(1+i)^{n-t_j}\cdot s_{\overline{t_j-t_{j-1}}|}$, and

(ii) $a_{\overline{n}|} \;=\; \displaystyle\sum_{j=1}^{k} v^{t_{j-1}}\cdot a_{\overline{t_j-t_{j-1}}|} \;=\; \sum_{j=1}^{k} t_{j-1}|\, a_{\overline{t_j-t_{j-1}}|}$.

2.3.11 (a) A loan of 10,000 is being repaid by 10 semiannual payments, with the first payment made one-half year after the loan. The first 5 payments are K each, and the final 5 are $K + 200$ each. What is K if $i^{(2)} = .06$.

(b) Three schemes are considered for the repayment of a loan of amount L which is to be repaid with 10 annual payments. Scheme (i) has 5 payments of X each followed by 5 payments of $2X$ each, scheme (ii) has 10 payments of Y each, and scheme (iii) has 5 payments of $2Z$ each followed by 5 payments of Z each. For each scheme the first payment is made one year after the loan. Assuming that $i > 0$, show that $X > \frac{2Y}{3} > Z$.

(c) A loan of amount L is to be repaid by $n > 1$ equal annual payments, starting one year after the loan. If interest is at annual effective rate i the annual payment is P_1, and if interest is at annual effective rate $2i$ the annual payment is P_2. Show that $P_2 < 2P_1$.

2.3.12 For each of the factors $\dfrac{s_{\overline{n}|i}}{s_{\overline{m}|i}}$ and $\dfrac{a_{\overline{n}|i}}{a_{\overline{m}|i}}$ find the limits as $i \to 0$ and as $i \to \infty$.

2.3.13 Smith borrows 5000 on January 1, 1990. She repays the loan with 20 annual payments starting January 1, 1991. The payments in even-numbered years are X each and the payments in odd-numbered years are Y each. If $i = .08$ and the total of all 20 loan payments is 10,233, find X and Y.

2.3.14 An accumulated amount function is defined as $S(t) = (1.12)^{\sqrt{t}}$ for $t \geq 0$. Find $s_{\overline{10}|}$ and $a_{\overline{10}|}$, the values at times 10 and 0, respectively, of a series of 10 payments of 1 starting at time 1, and calculate $\dfrac{s_{\overline{10}|}}{a_{\overline{10}|}}$ (strictly speaking the notations $s_{\overline{10}|}$ and $a_{\overline{10}|}$ should not be used since they apply to a situation in which the interest rate is constant in successive periods).

2.3.15 The force of interest has the form $\delta_t = \dfrac{.10}{\sqrt{1 + .10t}}$. An annuity has payments of amount 1 each at times 3 through 7 inclusive. Find the accumulated value of the annuity at time 10.

2.3.16 A loan of 11,000 is made with interest at a nominal annual rate of 12% compounded monthly. The loan is to be repaid by 36 monthly payments of 367.21 over 37 months, starting one month after the loan is made, there being a payment at the end of every month but one. At the end of which month is the missing payment?

2.3.17 Smith makes deposits of 1000 on the last day of each month in an account earning interest at rate $i^{(12)} = .12$. The first deposit is January 31, 1975 and the final deposit is December 31, 1999. The accumulated account is used to make monthly payments of Y each starting January 31, 2000 with the final one on December 31, 2024. Find Y.

2.3.18 A scholarship fund is started on January 1, 1990 with an initial deposit of 100,000 in an account earning $i^{(2)} = .08$, with interest credited every June 30 and December 31. Every January 1 from 1991 on, the fund will receive a deposit of 5000. The scholarship fund makes payments to recipients totaling 12,000 every July 1. What amount is in the scholarship account just after the 5000 deposit is made on January 1, 2000?

2.3.19 For an annuity of $3n$ payments of equal amount at periodic interest rate i, it is found that one period before the first payment the present value of the first n payments is equal to the present value of the final $2n$ payments. What is the value of v^n?

2.3.20 If i is the annual effective interest rate equivalent to force of interest δ, and i' is the annual effective rate equivalent to force of interest $k\delta$, where $k > 0$, show that $a_{\overline{n}|i'} = \dfrac{a_{\overline{kn}|i}}{s_{\overline{k}|i}}$.

2.3.21 Suppose that the effective interest rates in successive periods are i_1, $i_2, i_3, \ldots$.

(a) For an n-payment annuity-immediate of 1 per period starting at the end of the first period, show that

$$s_{\overline{n}|} = 1 + (1+i_n) + (1+i_n)(1+i_{n-1})$$
$$+ \cdots + (1+i_n)(1+i_{n-1})\cdots(1+i_2).$$

(b) For an *n*-payment annuity-due of 1 per period starting at the beginning of the first period, show that

$$\ddot{s}_{\overline{n}|} = (1+i_n) + (1+i_n)(1+i_{n-1}) + \cdots + (1+i_n)(1+i_{n-1}) \cdots$$
$$(1+i_2) + (1+i_n)(1+i_{n-1}) \cdots (1+i_2)(1+i_1).$$

Exercises 2.4

2.4.1 Derive the following identities.

(a) $\ddot{a}_{\overline{n}|i} = (1+i) a_{\overline{n}|i} = a_{\overline{n}|i} + 1 - v^n = 1 + a_{\overline{n-1}|i}$

(b) $\ddot{s}_{\overline{n}|i} = (1+i) s_{\overline{n}|i} = s_{\overline{n}|i} - 1 + (1+i)^n = s_{\overline{n+1}|i} - 1$

(c) $\dfrac{1}{\ddot{a}_{\overline{n}|i}} = \dfrac{1}{\ddot{s}_{\overline{n}|i}} + d$

2.4.2 For each of parts (i) and (ii) of Example 2.8, find the accumulated value of the annuity by rounding the accumulated value to the nearest cent at each interest credit date.

2.4.3 The situation in Example 2.2 is modified so that payments begin on November 1, 1987 and end May 1, 1995, but the accumulated value is still 7000 on November 1, 1995. What is the payment amount in this case? What is the ratio of this payment to the payment found in Example 2.2?

2.4.4 Derive the following identities assuming $t < n$.

(a) $v^t \cdot s_{\overline{n}|} = a_{\overline{t}|} + s_{\overline{n-t}|} = \ddot{a}_{\overline{t+1}|} + \ddot{s}_{\overline{n-t-1}|}$

(b) $(1+i)^t \cdot a_{\overline{n}|} = s_{\overline{t}|} + a_{\overline{n-t}|} = \ddot{s}_{\overline{t-1}|} + \ddot{a}_{\overline{n-t+1}|}$

(c) $v^t \cdot \ddot{s}_{\overline{n}|} = \ddot{a}_{\overline{t}|} + \ddot{s}_{\overline{n-t}|} = a_{\overline{t-1}|} + s_{\overline{n-t+1}|}$

(d) $(1+i)^t \cdot \ddot{a}_{\overline{n}|} = \ddot{s}_{\overline{t}|} + \ddot{a}_{\overline{n-t}|} = s_{\overline{t+1}|} + a_{\overline{n-t-1}|}$

Formulate corresponding expressions for the case $t > n$.

2.4.5 A loan of 5000 can be repaid by payments of 117.38 at the end of each month for *n* years (12*n* payments), starting one month after the loan is made. At the same rate of interest, 12*n* monthly payments of 113.40 each accumulate to 10,000 one month after the final payment. Find the equivalent annual effective rate of interest.

2.4.6 (a) Calculate the values of $s_{\overline{30}|}$ at $i = -.04762$ and $\ddot{a}_{\overline{30}|}$ at $d = .04762$. State and prove algebraically a general principle connecting the two quantities. Do the same for $a_{\overline{n}|}$ at a negative rate of interest and $\ddot{s}_{\overline{n}|}$.

(b) If $n > 0$ use the formulations in Equations (2.3) and (2.7) to describe $s_{\overline{-n}|i}$, $a_{\overline{-n}|i}$, $\ddot{s}_{\overline{-n}|i}$, and $\ddot{a}_{\overline{-n}|i}$.

2.4.7 (a) A perpetuity pays 1 every January 1 starting in 1994. The annual effective rate of interest will be i in odd-numbered years and j in even-numbered years. Find an expression for the present value of the perpetuity on January 1, 1993.

(b) A perpetuity starting January 1, 1994 pays 1 every January 1 in even years and 2 every January 1 in odd years. Find an expression for the present value at rate i per year of the perpetuity on (i) January 1, 1993, and (ii) January 1, 1994.

2.4.8 Verify the identities

$$s_{\overline{n+1}|} \cdot a_{\overline{n}|} = s_{\overline{n}|} \cdot \ddot{a}_{\overline{n+1}|} = \frac{s_{\overline{n+1}|} - \ddot{a}_{\overline{n+1}|}}{i} = \frac{\ddot{s}_{\overline{n}|} - a_{\overline{n}|}}{i}.$$

Exercises 2.5

2.5.1 An annuity has n annual payments of amount 1 each. Interest is quoted at a nominal annual rate of $i^{(m)}$.

(a) Let $j = \frac{i^{(m)}}{m}$. Express the equivalent annual effective rate of interest i in terms of j.

(b) Show that (i) $s_{\overline{n}|i} = \frac{(1+j)^{m \cdot n} - 1}{(1+j)^m - 1}$, (ii) $a_{\overline{n}|i} = \frac{1 - v_j^{m \cdot n}}{(1+j)^m - 1}$,

(iii) $\ddot{s}_{\overline{n}|i} = \frac{(1+j)^{m \cdot n} - 1}{1 - v_j^m}$, and (iv) $\ddot{a}_{\overline{n}|i} = \frac{1 - v_j^{m \cdot n}}{1 - v_j^m}$.

(c) Let $P = \frac{1}{s_{\overline{m}|j}}$ be the payment required every $\frac{1}{m}^{th}$ of a year for one year to accumulate to 1 at the end of the year (*i.e.*, at the time of the mth payment of P) at interest rate j per $\frac{1}{m}^{th}$ of a year. Show that $s_{\overline{n}|i}$ from part (b) is equal to $P \cdot s_{\overline{m \cdot n}|j} = s_{\overline{m \cdot n}|j} s_{\overline{m}|j}$.

(d) Find appropriate m^{thly} replacement payments for the other three annuities in part (b) and verify the following relationships:

(i) $a_{\overline{n}|i} = \dfrac{a_{\overline{m \cdot n}|j}}{s_{\overline{m}|j}}$, (ii) $\ddot{s}_{\overline{n}|i} = \dfrac{s_{\overline{m \cdot n}|j}}{a_{\overline{m}|j}}$, (iii) $\ddot{a}_{\overline{n}|i} = \dfrac{a_{\overline{m \cdot n}|j}}{a_{\overline{m}|j}}$.

(Note that $\ddot{s}_{\overline{n}|i} \neq \dfrac{\ddot{s}_{\overline{m \cdot n}|j}}{s_{\overline{m}|j}}$, but $\ddot{s}_{\overline{n}|i} = (1+j)^m \cdot s_{\overline{n}|i}$ and $\ddot{a}_{\overline{n}|i} \neq \dfrac{\ddot{a}_{\overline{m \cdot n}|j}}{s_{\overline{m}|j}}$, but $\ddot{a}_{\overline{n}|i} = (1+j)^m \cdot a_{\overline{n}|i}$.) Note that these formulations apply whenever the payment period is an integral multiple of the interest period. They are *algebraically* valid even if m is not an integer, in which case a meaning must be assigned to $s_{\overline{m}|j}$ for nonintegral m. This is discussed in Exercise 2.5.3.

(e) If the quoted rate is $i^{(\infty)} = \delta$, the annual force of interest, show that $s_{\overline{n}|i} = \dfrac{e^{n\delta} - 1}{e^{\delta} - 1}$.

(f) Repeat parts (b) and (d) for the present value of perpetuities, both immediate and due.

2.5.2   12 payments of 2000 each are made at 2-year intervals. Find the value of the series (a) 2 years before the first payment at annual effective interest rate $i = .08$, (b) 8 years before the first payment at nominal annual interest rate $i^{(2)} = .08$, (c) at the time of the final payment at nominal annual discount rate $d^{(4)} = .08$, (d) 18 months after the final payment at nominal annual interest rate $i^{(8)} = .08$, and (e) at the time of the first payment at nominal annual interest rate $i^{(4/3)} = .08$.

2.5.3   (a) For any positive real number m, define the function $s_{\overline{m}|j} = \dfrac{(1+j)^m - 1}{j}$. If m is not an integer, then it can be written as $m = m_0 + t$, where m_0 is the greatest integer less than or equal to m, denoted $m_0 = [m]$, and $0 < t < 1$. Show that $s_{\overline{m}|j}$ can be written in the form $s_{\overline{m}|j} = s_{\overline{m_0 + t}|j} = s_{\overline{m_0}|j} \cdot (1+j)^t + s_{\overline{t}|j}$. This suggests that for non-integral m, $s_{\overline{m}|j}$ can be regarded as the accumulated value of the m_0 full payments of amount 1 each (valued at time t measured from the final payment) plus the fractional payment $s_{\overline{t}|j}$ made at time $m_0 + t$.

(b) Using the same approach as in part (a), show that
$$a_{\overline{m}|j} = a_{\overline{m_0+t}|j} = a_{\overline{m_0}|j} \cdot v_j^t + a_{\overline{t}|j} = a_{\overline{m_0}|j} + v^m \cdot s_{\overline{t}|j}$$
$$= v^m \cdot s_{\overline{m}|j}.$$

(c) An annuity consists of 10 annual payments of 100 each, followed by a payment of 50 to be made 6 months after the 10th payment of 100. At an annual effective interest rate of $i = .075$, what is the difference between the accumulated value of the actual series at the time of the payment of 50 and the quantity $100 \cdot s_{\overline{10.5}|.075}$?

(d) Repeat part (c) for $0 < t < 1$, with 50 replaced by $100t$, 6 months replaced by t years, and 10.5 replaced by $10 + t$.

(e) Repeat parts (a) and (b) for the corresponding annuity-due forms.

2.5.4 An annuity has level payments of $\frac{1}{m}$ every $\frac{1}{m}^{th}$ of a year for n years (a total of $n \cdot m$ payments). Interest is at effective annual rate i. Let j denote the interest rate for $\frac{1}{m}^{th}$ of a year that is equivalent to i.

(a) Show that the accumulated value of the annuity at the time of the final payment is
$$\frac{1}{m} \cdot s_{\overline{n \cdot m}|j} = \frac{1}{m} \cdot \frac{(1+i)^n - 1}{(1+i)^{1/m} - 1}.$$

(b) If the series is valued one payment period (*i.e.*, $\frac{1}{m}^{th}$ of a year) before the first payment, show that this present value is
$$\frac{1}{m} \cdot a_{\overline{n \cdot m}|j} = \frac{1}{m} \cdot \frac{1 - v_i^n}{(1+i)^{1/m} - 1}.$$

(c) Show that the accumulated value one payment period after the final payment is
$$\frac{1}{m} \cdot \ddot{s}_{\overline{n \cdot m}|j} = \frac{1}{m} \cdot \frac{(1+i)^n - 1}{1 - v_i^{1/m}},$$

and the present value at the time of the first payment is
$$\frac{1}{m} \cdot \ddot{a}_{\overline{n \cdot m}|j} = \frac{1}{m} \cdot \frac{1 - v_i^n}{1 - v_i^{1/m}}.$$

(d) Show each of the following:

(i) $\frac{1}{m} \cdot s_{\overline{n \cdot m} | j} = \frac{(1+i)^n - 1}{i^{(m)}} = s_{\overline{n}|i} \cdot \frac{i}{i^{(m)}}$

(ii) $\frac{1}{m} \cdot a_{\overline{n \cdot m} | j} = \frac{1 - v_i^n}{i^{(m)}} = a_{\overline{n}|i} \cdot \frac{i}{i^{(m)}}$

(iii) $\frac{1}{m} \cdot \ddot{s}_{\overline{n \cdot m} | j} = \frac{(1+i)^n - 1}{d^{(m)}} = s_{\overline{n}|i} \cdot \frac{i}{d^{(m)}}$

(iv) $\frac{1}{m} \cdot \ddot{a}_{\overline{n \cdot m} | j} = \frac{1 - v_i^n}{d^{(m)}} = a_{\overline{n}|i} \cdot \frac{i}{d^{(m)}}$

(e) The standard actuarial notation used for the annuity forms in (a) through (d) is

$$\frac{1}{m} \cdot s_{\overline{n \cdot m}|j} = \frac{(1+i)^n - 1}{i^{(m)}} = s_{\overline{n}|i} \cdot \frac{i}{i^{(m)}} = s_{\overline{n}|i}^{(m)},$$

$$\frac{1}{m} \cdot a_{\overline{n \cdot m}|j} = \frac{1 - v_i^n}{i^{(m)}} = a_{\overline{n}|i} \cdot \frac{i}{i^{(m)}} = a_{\overline{n}|i}^{(m)},$$

$$\frac{1}{m} \cdot \ddot{s}_{\overline{n \cdot m}|j} = \frac{(1+i)^n - 1}{d^{(m)}} = s_{\overline{n}|i} \cdot \frac{i}{d^{(m)}} = \ddot{s}_{\overline{n}|i}^{(m)}, \text{ and}$$

$$\frac{1}{m} \cdot \ddot{a}_{\overline{n \cdot m}|j} = \frac{1 - v_i^n}{d^{(m)}} = a_{\overline{n}|i} \cdot \frac{i}{d^{(m)}} = \ddot{a}_{\overline{n}|i}^{(m)}.$$

Derive the following identities:

(i) $\ddot{s}_{\overline{n}|i}^{(m)} = \left(1 + \frac{i^{(m)}}{m}\right) \cdot s_{\overline{n}|i}^{(m)} = s_{\overline{n}|i} \cdot \left(\frac{i}{i^{(m)}} + \frac{i}{m}\right)$

$$= s_{\overline{n}|i}^{(m)} + \frac{(1+i)^n - 1}{m}$$

(ii) $\ddot{a}_{\overline{n}|i}^{(m)} = \left(1 + \frac{i^{(m)}}{m}\right) \cdot a_{\overline{n}|i}^{(m)} = a_{\overline{n}|i} \cdot \left(\frac{i}{i^{(m)}} + \frac{i}{m}\right)$

$$= a_{\overline{n}|i}^{(m)} + \frac{1}{m}(1 - v_i^n).$$

(f) Show $\ddot{s}_{\overline{n}|i}^{(m)} = s_{\overline{n+1/m}|i}^{(m)} - \frac{1}{m}$ and $\ddot{a}_{\overline{n}|i}^{(m)} = a_{\overline{n-1/m}|i}^{(m)} + \frac{1}{m}$. It

is possible to use the "upper m" notation to represent $s_{\overline{k/m}|i}^{(m)}$.

Show that this is equal to $\frac{1}{m} \cdot s_{\overline{k}|j}$.

(g) Prove the identities $\frac{1}{a_{\overline{n}|i}^{(m)}} = \frac{1}{s_{\overline{n}|i}^{(m)}} + i^{(m)}$ and $\frac{1}{\ddot{a}_{\overline{n}|i}^{(m)}} = \frac{1}{\ddot{s}_{\overline{n}|i}^{(m)}} + d^{(m)}$.

(h) Use the binomial expansion for $(1+i)^{1/m}$ to show that $a_{\overline{n}|i}^{(m)}$ is

approximately equal to

$$a_{\overline{n}|i} + \frac{m-1}{2m}(1-v^n) = \frac{1}{2m}[(m+1)a_{\overline{n}|i} + (m-1)\ddot{a}_{\overline{n}|i}].$$

Calculate the exact values and the approximate values for
$i = 0, .01, .025, .05, .10, .20,$ and $.50$.

2.5.5 Payments of 25 each are made every 2 months from June 1, 1988
to April 1, 1994, inclusive. Find the value of the series (a) 2
months before the first payment at annual effective interest rate
$i = .06$, (b) 10 months before the first payment at nominal annual
rate $i^{(3)} = .06$, (c) 8 months before the first payment at nominal
annual rate $i^{(4)} = .06$, (d) 2 months after the final payment at
nominal annual rate $d^{(2)} = .06$, and (e) 1 year after the final
payment at annual force of interest $\delta = .06$. Express the values in
terms of the notation defined in Exercise 2.5.4 wherever possible.

2.5.6 A perpetuity paying 25 every 3 months has the same present value
as a perpetuity paying Y every month, with each perpetuity valued
at the time of the first payment. Find Y in terms of appropriate
nominal annual rates of discount.

2.5.7 A perpetuity consists of monthly payments. The payment pattern
follows a repeating 12-month cycle of eleven payments of 1 each
followed by a payment of 2. The monthly effective interest rate is
j. Show that the present value of the perpetuity valued one month

before the first payment is $\frac{1}{j}\left[1 + \frac{1}{s_{\overline{12}|j}}\right]$.

2.5.8 (a) Show that $a_{\overline{n}|}$ can be written as the difference between a perpetuity-immediate and an *n*-year deferred perpetuity-immediate.

   (b) Show that payments of 1 each made at times $n, 2n, 3n, \ldots$ (in perpetuity) have a present value at time 0 of

$$\frac{1}{i \cdot s_{\overline{n}|i}} = \frac{1}{n} \cdot a_{\infty|i}^{(1/n)}.$$

2.5.9 Prove the following identities :

   (a) $a_{\overline{n}|}^{(m)} = \frac{1}{m} \cdot \sum_{t=1}^{m} {}_{t/m}|\ddot{a}_{\overline{n}|}$

   (b) $a_{\overline{n}|}^{(2m)} = \frac{1}{2}\left[a_{\overline{n}|}^{(m)} + {}_{1/2m}|\ddot{a}_{\overline{n}|}^{(m)}\right]$

2.5.10 (a) Find $s_{\overline{1}|}^{(m)}$ assuming simple interest at annual rate i.

   (b) Find $a_{\overline{1}|}^{(m)}$ assuming simple discount at annual rate d.

2.5.11 (a) Show that $\lim_{m\to\infty} s_{\overline{n}|i}^{(m)} = \lim_{m\to\infty} \ddot{s}_{\overline{n}|i}^{(m)} = \ddot{s}_{\overline{n}|i}^{(\infty)} = s_{\overline{n}|i}^{(\infty)} = \overline{s}_{\overline{n}|i}.$

   (b) Show that $\lim_{m\to\infty} a_{\overline{n}|i}^{(m)} = \lim_{m\to\infty} \ddot{a}_{\overline{n}|i}^{(m)} = \ddot{a}_{\overline{n}|i}^{(\infty)} = a_{\overline{n}|i}^{(\infty)} = \overline{a}_{\overline{n}|i}.$

   (c) If $i > 0$ and $m > 1$, rank the following values in increasing order:
   $$a_{\overline{n}|i}, \quad \ddot{a}_{\overline{n}|i}, \quad a_{\overline{n}|i}^{(m)}, \quad \ddot{a}_{\overline{n}|i}^{(m)}, \quad \overline{a}_{\overline{n}|i}.$$

   (d) Assuming simple interest at rate i, find $\overline{s}_{\overline{n}|i}$.

Exercises 2.6

2.6.1 Show that if an accumulation function is multiplicative (*i.e.*, that it satisfies the principle of consistency defined by $s(t_1,t_2) \cdot s(t_2,t_3) = s(t_1, t_3)$), then the accumulated value of the continuous annuity is $s(t_0,t_e)$ times the present value, as represented in Equation (2.19).

2.6.2   (a) The force of interest $\delta_t = \frac{i}{1+it}$ corresponds to simple interest from time 0. Find expressions for $\bar{a}_{\overline{n}|}$ and $\bar{s}_{\overline{n}|}$ based on the general annuity forms given in Equation (2.19), and verify that the identity in Equation (2.19) holds in this case.

      (b) Suppose that for the annuity in part (a) the accumulation from time t_1 to time t_2 is based on simple interest starting at t_1. Thus $s(t_1, t_2) = 1 + i(t_2 - t_1)$. Find $\bar{a}_{\overline{n}|}$ and $\bar{s}_{\overline{n}|}$ in this case. Note that there is no δ_t that defines this accumulation. This case would require a $\delta_{s,t}$ denoting the force of interest at time $t > s$ based on an investment made at time s (*i.e.*, the force of interest would depend on when the investment was initiated). Note also that the identity in Equation (2.19) is not valid in this case.

2.6.3   Find the present value at time 0 of an n-year continuous annuity based on force of interest $\delta_t = p + \frac{s}{1 + re^{st}}$.

Exercises 2.7

2.7.1   A 50,000 loan made on January 1, 1990 is to be repaid over 25 years with payments on the last day of each month, beginning January 31, 1990.

      (a) If $i^{(2)} = .10$, find the amount of the monthly payment X.

      (b) Starting with the first payment, the borrower decides to pay an additional 100 per month, on top of the regular payment of X, until the loan is repaid. An additional fractional payment might be necessary one month after the last regular payment of $X + 100$. On what date will the final payment of $X + 100$ be made, and what will be the amount of the additional fractional payment?

2.7.2   A sum of 10,000 was invested on September 1, 1970 at an annual effective interest rate of 5% in order to provide an annual scholarship of 2000 every September 1 forever, starting as soon as possible. In what year will the first payment of 2000 be made? What smaller payment could be made one year earlier while still permitting the annual scholarships of 2000 thereafter? Assume that interest is credited every August 31.

2.7.3   (a) A loan of amount L is to be repaid with n periodic payments of amount K each at periodic interest rate $i > 0$, where n is even. The same loan can be repaid by $\frac{n}{2}$ payments if the periodic payment is increased to an amount larger than K. Determine whether the new payment is exactly double, more than double, or less than double the value of K.

(b) A loan of amount L at interest rate $i > 0$ is being repaid by n payments of K each. Show that if the payment is doubled to $2K$, and m is the number of doubled payments required to repay the loan, then $m < \frac{n}{2}$.

2.7.4   (a) In Example 2.10, consider a third option for the additional fractional payment. After solving for $n = 62.9019$, we could make the additional fractional payment at a point $.9019$ of the way through the 63rd month. Solve for the additional fractional payment in this case.

(b) In solving the equation $L = K \cdot a_{\overline{n}|i}$ for n, let the value of n be written as $n = t + k$, where t is an integer and k is a fraction, $0 < k < 1$. Suppose an additional fractional payment is to be made at time $n = t + k$. If an approximate value of $K \cdot k$ is used for the fractional payment, what is the error in the approximation? Show that the error is maximized at $k = \frac{1}{\delta} \cdot \ln(\frac{i}{\delta})$. Investigate the behavior of $\frac{1}{\delta} \cdot \ln(\frac{i}{\delta})$ as $i \to 0$ and as $i \to \infty$.

2.7.5   (a) In the solution for n in the equation $L = K \cdot a_{\overline{n}|i}$, find $\frac{dn}{di}$, $\frac{dn}{dK}$, and $\frac{dn}{dL}$.

(b) In the solution for n in the equation $M = J \cdot s_{\overline{n}|i}$, find $\frac{dn}{di}$, $\frac{dn}{dJ}$, and $\frac{dn}{dM}$.

2.7.6   Deposits of 500 each are made into an account on the first day of every January and July beginning on January 1, 1984.

(a) If $i^{(6)} = .06$ and interest is credited on the last day of every February, April, June, August, October and December, on what date does the account balance first exceed (i) 10,000, and (ii) 11,000?

(b) Suppose instead that $i = .04$ and interest is credited only on December 31 each year, with simple interest credited for fractions of a year. On what date should the account be closed in order that the closing balance be nearest (i) 10,000, and (ii) 11,000?

2.7.7   On the first day of each month, starting January 1, 1985, Smith deposits 100 in an account earning $i^{(12)} = .09$, with interest credited the last day of each month. In addition, Smith deposits 1000 in the account every December 31. On what day does the account first exceed 100,000?

2.7.8   On the first day of every January, April, July and October Smith deposits 100 in an account earning $i^{(4)} = .16$. He continues the deposits until he accumulates a sufficient balance to begin with-drawals of 200 every 3 months, starting 3 months after the final deposit, such that he can make twice as many withdrawals as he made deposits. On what date will he make his first withdrawal.

2.7.9   Find the smallest integer n for which deposits of 1 per period accumulate to at least 100 in each of the following cases.
(a) 20 deposits at 3% followed by n deposits at 4%.
(b) n deposits at 3% followed by n deposits at 4%.
(c) Repeat parts (a) and (b) for exact n in the case of continuous annuities. In part (a) a 20-period continuous annuity of 1 per period is followed by an n-period continuous annuity of 1 per period, and similarly for part (b).

2.7.10 Apply the following approximation methods to find n in Example 2.12.
(a) Use the binomial expansion of $(1.0075)^n$ to (i) 3 terms, and (ii) 4 terms.
(b) Take natural logarithms of both sides of the equation $(1.0075)^n = 1 + .008333n$, and use the Taylor expansion of $ln(1 + .008333n)$ to (i) 2 terms, and (ii) 3 terms.
(c) Use each of the following fixed-point iteration methods to approximate n, based on a starting value of $n_0 = 10$, and then $n_0 = 20$.
   (i) $n = \dfrac{(1.0075)^n - 1}{.008333}$ (ii) $n = \dfrac{ln(1 + .008333n)}{ln(1.0075)}$

(d) Use the Newton-Raphson iteration technique on the function
$f(n) = (1.0075)^n - 1 - .008333n.$ (See Appendix A for a review of Newton-Raphson iteration).

2.7.11 Ten annual deposits of 1000 each are made to Account A, starting on January 1, 1986. Annual deposits of 500 each are made to Account B indefinitely, also starting on January 1, 1986. Interest on both accounts is at rate $i = .05$, with interest credited every December 31. On what date will the balance for Account B first exceed the balance for Account A? Assume that the only transactions to the accounts are deposits and interest credited every December 31.

2.7.12 A loan of 10,000 is made on January 1, 1986 at interest rate $i^{(12)} = .12$. The loan calls for payments of 500 on the first day of every April, July, and October, with an additional fractional payment on the next scheduled payment date after the final regular payment of 500. Find the date and amount of the additional fractional payment.

2.7.13 A loan of 1000 is repaid with 12 annual payments of 100 each starting one year after the loan is made. The annual effective interest rate is 3.5% for the first 4 years. Find the annual effective interest rate i for the final 8 years
   (a) by linear interpolation with interest interval (i) [.02, .04] and (ii) [.02, .025],
   (b) to within .1% using the bisection method with starting interval [.02, .025], and
   (c) to within .1% using the Newton-Raphson method on an appropriately defined $f(i)$.

2.7.14 (a) Write the equation $L = a_{\overline{n}|i}$ in the form $i = \dfrac{1 - v^n}{L} = g(i)$,

   and use this as a successive approximation function to approximate i to within .10% in Exercise 2.7.13 after finding the appropriate L and n (see Appendix A on successive approximation).
   (b) Find $g'(i)$ in part (a), and show that at the actual value of i, $|g'(i)| < 1$ if $i > 0$. According to the comments in Appendix A about fixed-point iteration, this guarantees that the iteration will converge to the true value of i if the starting approximation i_0 is sufficiently close to the true value of i.

2.7.15 Write the equation $M = s_{\overline{n}|i}$ in the form $i = \dfrac{(1+i)^n - 1}{M} = g(i)$, where $i > 0$, and use this as a successive approximation function. Show that $|g'(i)| > 1$ at the true value of i, so that the iteration will not converge to i. (This follows from the comments in Appendix A.)

2.7.16 Verify that each of the following is a valid iteration function for successive approximations to i in Example 2.13. Use $i_0 = .10$ to find the next 10 successive approximations.

(a) $\;\; i \;\; = \;\; [182.1938i + 3 - 2(1+i)^{20}]^{1/8} - 1$

(b) $\;\; i \;\; = \;\; \left[\tfrac{1}{2}(182.1938i + 3 - (1+i)^8)\right]^{1/20} - 1$

(c) $\;\; i \;\; = \;\; \dfrac{2(1+i)^{20} + (1+i)^8 - 3}{182.1938}$

There are many valid iteration functions for any fixed-point iteration, some of which converge and some of which do not.

2.7.17 Show both graphically and algebraically the following results.

(a) If y is a convex function of x (*i.e.*, $y'' > 0$), and if (x_0, y_0), (x_1, y_1) are given and x_2 is between x_0 and x_1, then the interpolated value of y_2 is always larger than the exact value.

(b) If y is a concave function of x (*i.e.*, $y'' < 0$), and if (x_0, y_0), (x_1, y_1) are given and x_2 is between x_0 and x_1, then the interpolated value of y_2 is always smaller than the exact value.

Apply this to interpolation approximation for i in the case of (i) an accumulated annuity, and (ii) the present value of an annuity, and determine the bias in the interpolated interest rate.

2.7.18 Solve for i and n in terms of A and B, where $A = s_{\overline{n}|i}$ and $B = s_{\overline{n+1}|i}$.

2.7.19 (a) Let $A = a_{\overline{n}|i}$ and $B = s_{\overline{n}|i}$; express i in terms of A and B.

(b) Let $A = a_{\overline{n}|i}$ and $B = a_{\overline{2n}|i}$; express i in terms of A and B.

(c) Let $A = a_{\overline{n}|i}$ and $B = s_{\overline{2n}|i}$; express i in terms of A and B.

2.7.20 (a) Smith deposits 500 in an account on the last day of every March, June, September, and December. The account pays interest at annual rate i, credited on the last day of December, with simple interest (based on a count of months) credited for amounts on deposit for less than a full year. The first deposit is made on March 31, 1990, and the balance in the account on December 31, 1991, after deposit and interest is credited, is 4311.99. Solve algebraically for the exact value of i.

(b) Suppose that the situation is similar to that in part (a) (but at a different interest rate) and the balance in the account on December 31, 1994 is 12,490.48. Use one or more of the approximation methods to find i.

2.7.21 (a) For the equation $L = K \cdot a_{\overline{n}|i}, L, K, n > 0$, note that $L = n \cdot K$ if $i = 0$. Use (i) $\lim_{i \to \infty} a_{\overline{n}|i} = 0$, (ii) $\lim_{i \to -1} a_{\overline{n}|i} = \infty$, and (iii) $a_{\overline{n}|i}$ is a decreasing function of i to show that the equation has a unique solution for i between -1 and ∞ if L, K and n are given. Also show that $i > 0$ if $L < n \cdot K$ and $i < 0$ if $L > n \cdot K$.

(b) Derive a result similar to that in part (a) for the accumulated annuity relationship $M = J \cdot s_{\overline{n}|i}$.

(c) Derive similar results in the case of an annuity-due.

(d) Use the fact that $\delta \to -\infty$ as $i \to -1$ to derive similar results for continuous annuities.

2.7.22 Apply the Newton-Raphson method to the original $f(i)$ in Example 2.13 with various starting values i_0. If the Newton-Raphson method is applied to the function $f(i) = K \cdot a_{\overline{n}|i} - L$, then convergence to the true value of i is guaranteed with any starting value $i_0 > 0$.

2.7.23 A fund has value A at the start of a year, B at the end of the year, and interest of I earned for the year. Assuming that both interest and non-interest income accrues continuously on the fund, use the approximate relationship $\frac{i}{\delta} \approx 1 + \frac{i}{2}$ to show that the annual interest rate earned by the fund is approximately $\frac{2I}{B + A - I}$.

2.7.24 Show that the accumulated value of deposits in Example 2.13 is
$1000 \cdot s_{\overline{12}|i} \cdot (1+i)^8 + 1500 \cdot s_{\overline{8}|i} = 1000 \cdot s_{\overline{20}|i} + 500 \cdot s_{\overline{8}|i}$.

2.7.25 An insurance company offers a "capital redemption policy" whereby the policyholder pays annual premiums (in advance) of 3368.72 for 25 years, and, in return, receives a maturity (or redemption) amount of 250,000 one year after the 25th premium is paid. The insurer has determined that administrative expenses are 20% of the first premium and 10% of all remaining premiums, and these expenses are incurred at the time the premium is paid. The insurer anticipates investing the net (after expenses) premiums received at an annual effective interest rate of 12.5%. What is the insurer's accumulated profit just after the policy matures and the redemption amount of 250,000 is paid? Find the annual effective rate of return earned by the policyholder for the 25-year period.

2.7.26 Smith is negotiating to purchase a car, and he determines that he must borrow 12,000 to complete the purchase. He is offered financing at a nominal interest rate of $i^{(12)}$ with monthly payments beginning one month after the loan is made. He can repay the loan over a 2-year period (24 payments) at 592.15 per month, or over a 3-year period (36 payments) at 426.64 per month (the same interest rate in both cases). Find $i^{(12)}$ and the monthly amount payable if he were able to repay the loan over a 4-year period (still at the same interest rate).

Exercises 2.8

2.8.1   (a) Write out the terms of the series for $(Is)_{\overline{n}|i}$. Use the method of Example 2.14 to show $(Is)_{\overline{n}|i} = \dfrac{\ddot{s}_{\overline{n}|i} - n}{i}$.

(b) Use the general forms for arithmetic payment annuities in Equations (2.21) and (2.22) to derive the relationships for $(Ia)_{\overline{n}|i}$ and $(Is)_{\overline{n}|i}$ in Equation (2.23).

(c) Draw a line diagram and explain verbally why $s_{\overline{n+1}|i}$ must equal $(n+1) + i \cdot (Is)_{\overline{n}|i}$.

2.8.2 (a) If K_t is a polynomial of degree m in th variable t, show that $K_{t+1} - K_t$ is a polynomial of degree at most $m - 1$.

(b) A 15-payment annuity has annual payments of 225, 224, 221, 216, 209, 200, ..., $225 - t^2$ for $t = 0,1,2,\ldots,14$. What is the present value of this series valued one period before the first payment at $i = .08$?

(c) Show that $\displaystyle\sum_{t=1}^{n} t^2 \cdot v^t = \ddot{a}_{\overline{n}|} + 2(Ia)_{\overline{n-1}|} - n^2 v^n$.

2.8.3 Write out the terms of the series for $(Ds)_{\overline{n}|i}$ and $(Da)_{\overline{n}|i}$, and use the method of Example 2.14 to derive Equations (2.24a) and (2.24b).

2.8.4 Show that the following relationships are valid, and illustrate them using line diagrams.

(a) $(Ia)_{\overline{n}|} + (Da)_{\overline{n}|} = (n+1) \cdot a_{\overline{n}|}$

(b) $(Is)_{\overline{n}|} + (Ds)_{\overline{n}|} = (n+1) \cdot s_{\overline{n}|}$

(c) $(Ia)_{\overline{n}|} = \displaystyle\sum_{k=0}^{n-1} k \,|\, a_{\overline{n-k}|}$ and $(Is)_{\overline{n}|} = \displaystyle\sum_{k=1}^{n} s_{\overline{k}|}$

(d) $(I\ddot{a})_{\overline{n}|} = (Ia)_{\overline{n}|} + \ddot{a}_{\overline{n}|} - nv^n$

(e) $(I\ddot{s})_{\overline{n}|} = (Is)_{\overline{n}|} + \ddot{s}_{\overline{n}|} - n$

(f) $(D\ddot{a})_{\overline{n}|} = (Da)_{\overline{n}|} + n - a_{\overline{n}|}$

(g) $(D\ddot{s})_{\overline{n}|} = (Ds)_{\overline{n}|} + n(1+i)^n - s_{\overline{n}|}$

(h) $(Is)_{\overline{n}|} + (Da)_{\overline{n}|} = a_{\overline{n}|} \cdot s_{\overline{n+1}|} = \ddot{a}_{\overline{n+1}|} \cdot s_{\overline{n}|}$

(i) $(Ia)_{\overline{n+1}|} = (Ia)_{\overline{n}|} + (n+1)v^{n+1} = a_{\overline{n+1}|} + v \cdot (Ia)_{\overline{n}|}$

(j) $(Da)_{\overline{n+1}|} = n+1+v \cdot (Da)_{\overline{n}|} = a_{\overline{n+1}|} + (Da)_{\overline{n}|}$

(k) $(Is)_{\overline{n+1}|} = (1+i) \cdot (Is)_{\overline{n}|} + (n+1) = s_{\overline{n+1}|} + (Is)_{\overline{n}|}$

(l) $(Ds)_{\overline{n+1}|} = (n+1)(1+i)^n + (Ds)_{\overline{n}|} = s_{\overline{n+1}|} + (1+i) \cdot (Ds)_{\overline{n}|}$

2.8.5 Show that if $i > 0$ then $(Ia)_{\overline{\infty}|} = \dfrac{1}{i} + \dfrac{1}{i^2} = \dfrac{1}{i \cdot d} = a_{\overline{\infty}|} \cdot \ddot{a}_{\overline{\infty}|}$.
Give a verbal interpretation for the final expression.

2.8.6   Consider an increasing annuity with payments made every $\frac{1}{m}^{th}$ of a
        year for a total of n years ($n \cdot m$ payments).

        (a) $(Ia)_{\overline{n}|}^{(m)}$ denotes the present value $\frac{1}{m}^{th}$ of a year before the first
            payment of the series in which the payments in the first year
            are level at amount $\frac{1}{m}$, in the second year are level at amount
            $\frac{2}{m}$, and so on. In each subsequent year the payments are $\frac{1}{m}$
            larger than the year before, but stay level for the year. Show
            that this present value is equal to $\dfrac{\ddot{a}_{\overline{n}|} - nv^n}{i^{(m)}} = (Ia)_{\overline{n}|} \cdot \dfrac{i}{i^{(m)}}$.

        (b) $(I^{(m)}a)_{\overline{n}|}^{(m)}$ denotes the present value $\frac{1}{m}^{th}$ of a year before the
            first payment of a series with first payment $\frac{1}{m^2}$, and
            subsequent payments $\frac{1}{m^2}$ larger than the previous one. Show
            that this present value is equal to $\dfrac{\ddot{a}_{\overline{n}|}^{(m)} - nv^n}{i^{(m)}}$.

2.8.7   (a) Show that the accumulated value one period after the final
            payment of the annuity in Example 2.16 is $(1 + r)^n \cdot \ddot{s}_{\overline{n}|j}$.
        (b) Show that the present value one period before the first payment
            of the annuity in Example 2.16 is $\dfrac{1}{1 + r} \cdot a_{\overline{n}|j}$.

2.8.8   Find the present value, as of January 1, 1981, of the payments in
        Example 2.17. Find the present value (on January 1, 1981) and the
        accumulated value (on the 18th birthday) of the payments in
        Example 2.17 at the following interest ($i^{(12)}$) rates and annual rate
        of increase in the payments.
        (i)   12% interest, 9% increase in payments.
        (ii)   9% interest, 6% increase in payments.
        (iii) 6% interest, 3% increase in payments.
        (iv)   3% interest, 0% increase in payments.

2.8.9   A government provides each citizen over the age of 65 with a monthly pension payable for life. The current monthly payment is 400. The payment is indexed to inflation so that every year there is an adjustment to reflect the rate of inflation for the year (but payments within a year are level). The government proposes a cost-cutting measure whereby the payments will be "partially de-indexed," so that the payment increase will be the excess of the inflation rate over 3%. The increase is 0 if the inflation is less than 3%. As a simplified model the government regards the lifetime payments as a perpetuity. What is the present value of saving for the government if this proposal is implemented, under each of the following annual interest/inflation scenarios?
   (i) $i = .12, r = .09$ (ii) $i = .12, r = .06$ (iii) $i = .12, r = .03$
   (iv) $i = .09, r = .06$ (v) $i = .09, r = .03$ (vi) $i = .06, r = .03$

2.8.10 (a) Show that $\lim_{m \to \infty} (I^{(m)} a)_{\overline{n}|}^{(m)} = (\overline{I} \overline{a})_{\overline{n}|}$.

   (b) $\lim_{m \to \infty} (Ia)_{\overline{n}|}^{(m)}$ is denoted $(\overline{I} a)_{\overline{n}|}$. Give a verbal description of this expression.

   (c) Repeat part (c) of Exercise 2.8.1 in the continuous context; i.e., explain why $\overline{s}_{\overline{n}|}$ is equal to $n + \delta \cdot (\overline{I} \overline{s})_{\overline{n}|}$.

2.8.11 (a) Show that (i) $\frac{d}{di} a_{\overline{n}|i} = -v \cdot (Ia)_{\overline{n}|}$, (ii) $\frac{d}{di} s_{\overline{n}|i} = (Is)_{\overline{n-1}|}$,
   and (iii) $\frac{d}{d\delta} \overline{a}_{\overline{n}|i} = -(\overline{I} \overline{a})_{\overline{n}|}$.

   (b) Find an expression for $\frac{d}{dn} a_{\overline{n}|}$.

   (c) Find expressions for $\frac{d}{dn} \overline{a}_{\overline{n}|}$ and $\frac{d}{dn} \overline{s}_{\overline{n}|}$.

2.8.12 Smith is arranging a mortgage loan of 100,000 to be repaid with monthly payments over 25 years, with the first payment due one month after the loan is made. Interest is quoted at a nominal annual rate compounded semiannually of $i^{(2)}$. The loan will not be issued for several months, and the interest rate will be set at the time of the loan. Smith, in determining the sensitivity of his monthly payment to the interest rate, calculates $\frac{d}{di^{(2)}} K$, where K is the monthly payment. Find the value of this derivative for the following values of $i^{(2)}$: 21%, 13%, 10%, 5%.

2.8.13 A perpetuity-due with annual payments pays 1 now, $1 + 2 = 3$ in one year, $1 + 2 + 3 = 6$ in two years, ..., $1 + 2 + \cdots + n$ in $n - 1$ years, and so on. Show that the present value of this perpetuity-due is $\ddot{a}_{\overline{\infty}|} \cdot (I\ddot{a})_{\overline{\infty}|}$.

2.8.14 A loan of 12,000 is repaid by 36 monthly payments starting one month after the loan. The first 12 payments are $395 + X$ each, the next 12 payments are 395 each, and the final 12 payments are $395 - X$ each. If $i^{(12)} = .12$, find X.

2.8.15 Smith retires on January 1, 1984. She deposits 500,000 in an account earning annual effective interest at $i = .10$, with interest credited every December 31. Smith withdrawals $\frac{1}{19}$ of the balance in the account on January 1, 1985, $\frac{1}{18}$ of the balance on January 1, 1986, ..., $\frac{1}{2}$ of the balance on January 1, 2002, and the entire balance on January 1, 2003. Find an expression for the amount of the withdrawal on January 1, $1984 + t$, for $t = 1, 2,$ ..., 19.

2.8.16 A loan of 10,000 made on January 1, 1990 is to be repaid by monthly payments on the last date of each month starting January 31, 1990. The first payment is 1000, the second is 900, the third is 800, the fourth 700, the fifth 600, and the sixth and subsequent payments are 500 each for as long as necessary with a final smaller payment one month after the final regular payment. Find the date and the amount of the final smaller payment if $i^{(12)} = .12$.

2.8.17 On January 1 Smith deposits 100,000 in an account earning interest at rate $i^{(12)} = .09$, credited on the final day of each month.
   (a) Suppose Smith withdraws 1000 on the first day of each month starting on February 1. Smith continues the withdrawals as long as possible with a smaller withdrawal one month after the final regular withdrawal of 1000. Find the number of regular withdrawals and the date and amount of the final smaller withdrawal.

(b) Instead of level withdrawals of 1000 each, let Smith's monthly withdrawals start at 1000 on February 1, and increase by 10 each month (March 1 is 1010, April 1 is 1020, and so on). Withdrawals continue in this pattern for as long as possible with a final smaller withdrawal one month after the last regular increasing withdrawal. Find the number of regular withdrawals and the date and amount of the final smaller withdrawal.

(c) Repeat part (b) assuming that the withdrawals grow by 1% per month, so that March 1 is 1010, April 1 is 1020.10, and so on.

(d) For each of parts (a), (b), and (c) find the total amount withdrawn, and explain the relationship among the three totals.

2.8.18 On January 1, 1990 Smith deposits 500,000 in an account earning a monthly effective rate of 1%, with interest credited on the last day of each month. Withdrawals are made on the first day of each month starting February 1, 1990, with an initial withdrawal of 1000. Each subsequent withdrawal is 1% larger than the previous one, continuing in this pattern for as long as possible.

(a) When does the account finally become exhausted, and what is the amount of the last regular withdrawal?

(b) What is the maximum amount the account balance reaches during this process?

2.8.19 Smith has 100,000 with which she buys a perpetuity on January 1, 1990. Suppose that $i = .045$ and the perpetuity has annual payments beginning January 1, 1991. The first three payments are 2000 each, the next three payments are $2000(1+r)$ each, ..., increasing forever by a factor of $1+r$ every three years. What is r?

2.8.20 Each year on Smith's child's birthday Smith makes a deposit of 100 multiplied by the child's age (100 on the 1st birthday, 200 on the 2nd, and so on) to an account earning annual effective interest rate i. The final deposit is on the child's 12th birthday. The account continues to accumulate, and on the child's 18th birthday the balance is 17,177.70. Use the methods of Section 2.7 to find i.

2.8.21 For $i > 0$ and $n > 1$, show that $(Ia)_{\overline{n}|} < \left(\frac{n+1}{2}\right)a_{\overline{n}|} < (Da)_{\overline{n}|}$.

2.8.22 (a) An increasing perpetuity at annual effective interest rate i has a payment once every k years, with payment amounts 1, 2, 3, ... Show that the present value of the perpetuity at the time of the first payment is $\dfrac{1}{(i \cdot a_{\overline{k}|})^2}$.

(b) Find an expression for the present value of an increasing perpetuity-due with annual payments whose first k payments are 1 each, next k payments are 2 each, and so on, increasing in this way forever.

2.8.23 An employee serves 37 years before retiring on a pension. His initial salary was 18,000 per year and increased by 4% each year. Assume that the whole year's salary is paid at the middle of each year.

(a) If his pension is 70% of his average annual salary over his entire career, what proportion is it of his final year's salary?

(b) If the pension is 2.5% of career average salary multiplied by years of service, what is his ultimate pension?

(c) If his pension is 2.5% of his average salary over the final 10 years he worked, multiplied by his total years of service, then what is his ultimate pension?

(d) If he contributes 3% of his salary (at the time it is paid), matched by an equal contribution from his employer, to an account earning annual interest at rate $i = .06$, and the accumulated value (at the end of his 37th year of employment) is used to purchase a 20-year annuity-due with annual payments, valued at $i = .06$, find the annual payment from the annuity.

2.8.24 A $(2n-1)$-payment annuity has payments in the pattern 1, 2, ..., $n-1$, n, $n-1$, $n-2$, ..., 2, 1. Show that the present value of this annuity one payment period before the first payment is $\ddot{a}_{\overline{n}|} \cdot a_{\overline{n}|}$.

2.8.25 A general continuous annuity has rate of payment $h(t)$ at time t, $t > 0$, and had an initial discrete payment of F_0 at time 0. If the force of interest is δ and F_t denotes the accumulated value in the fund at time t, show that $\dfrac{d}{dt}F_t = \delta \cdot F_t + h(t)$.

2.8.26 Show that $\dfrac{\ddot{a}_{\overline{n}|}}{i}$ is the present value of a perpetuity-immediate whose payments increase by 1 per period for n periods, from 1 to n, and then remain level at n forever.

2.8.27 (a) If $h(t) = n - t,\ 0 \le t \le n$, in the general continuously varying annuity, the present value is denoted $(\bar{D}\bar{a})_{\overline{n}|}$. Using integration by parts, derive an expression for $(\bar{D}\bar{a})_{\overline{n}|}$. Show that $(\bar{I}\bar{a})_{\overline{n}|} + (\bar{D}\bar{a})_{\overline{n}|} = n \cdot \bar{a}_{\overline{n}|}$.

   (b) Show that $(\bar{I}\bar{a})_{\overline{n}|} = \displaystyle\int_0^n t\,|\bar{a}_{\overline{n-t}|}\,dt$ and $(\bar{D}\bar{a})_{\overline{n}|} = \displaystyle\int_0^n \bar{a}_{\overline{t}|}\,dt$.

   (c) If $h(t) = e^{\alpha t}$ and the force of interest is $\delta > \alpha$, what is the present value at $t = 0$ of (i) an n-year continuous annuity, and (ii) a continuous perpetuity?

   (d) Show that for the general forms of the present and accumulated values of a continuous annuity paying at rate $h(t)$ and with force of interest δ_t at time t, the accumulated value at time n is equal to the present value at time 0 multiplied by $\exp\left[\displaystyle\int_0^n \delta_r\,dr\right]$.

2.8.28 What series of payments is represented by the present value $A \cdot a_{\overline{n}|} + B \cdot (Da)_{\overline{n}|}$? Formulate the present value of a 25-year decreasing annuity-immediate with first payment of 100 and subsequent payments decreasing by 3 per period.

2.8.29 The first of a series of 30 annual payments is 1000 and each subsequent payment is 1% smaller than the previous one. What is the accumulated value of this series at the time of the final payment if (i) $i = .01$, (ii) $i = .05$, and (iii) $i = .10?$

2.8.30 For 100,000, Smith purchases a 20-payment annuity-immediate with annual payments. For each of the following cases, apply various methods, including the Newton-Raphson method, for finding the unknown interest rate i.

   (a) The first payment is 7000 and each subsequent payment is 750 more than the previous one.

   (b) The first payment is 7000 and each subsequent payment is 10% larger than the previous one.

2.8.31   Show in Example 2.18 that $i > 0$ if $L < \sum\limits_{s=1}^{n} K_s$, and $i < 0$ if

$L > \sum\limits_{s=1}^{n} K_s.$

2.8.32   Suppose that $K_1, K_2, \ldots, K_n$ are payments made to an account at times $0 < t_1 < t_2 < \cdots < t_n$. Show that if $L > 0$, then there is *a unique interest rate $i > -1$ for which L is the accumulated value of the series of payments at time t_n.*

2.8.33   A perpetuity pays 1 on January 1, 1990, $1 + r$ on January 1, 1991, with subsequent payments increasing by a factor of $1 + r$ each until January 1, 2000, when the payment is $(1 + r)^{10}$. From then on the annual payment remains level at $(1 + r)^{10}$. If the annual effective interest rate is $i = .10$ and $r = .12$, find the present value of the perpetuity on its starting date, January 1, 1990. Repeat the problem with r and $i = r + .02$.

2.8.34   Suppose that a series of payments at times $1, 2, 3, \cdots, n$ is represented in vector form as $\vec{P} = [P_1, P_2, \cdots, P_n]$. Suppose that effective interest rates for the n successive periods are also written in vector form as $\vec{i} = [i_1, i_2, \cdots, i_n]$, where i_t is the effective interest rate from time $t - 1$ to time t. Write a computer routine that calculates the values at time 0 and time n of the series based on the specified rates of interest.

Exercises 2.9

2.9.1   A loan is set up at periodic interest rate i, to be repaid by n periodic payments of amount K each. As the lender receives the payments, he reinvests them at interest rate j. Show that the average compound periodic rate of interest earned by the lender based on his initial outlay and his accumulated amount at time n is i', where i' is the solution of the equation $(1 + i')^n = \dfrac{s_{\overline{n}|j}}{a_{\overline{n}|i}}.$ Show also that i' is between i and j (i.e., if $j < i$ then $j < i' < i$; if $i < j$ then $i < i' < j$; if $i = j$ then $i = i' = j$).

2.9.2   Jones buys from Smith the right to receive 20 annual payments of
1000 each beginning 1 year hence.
(a) In their discussion regarding this transaction, Smith and Jones
consider three ways of determining the amount Jones must pay
to Smith. Find this amount according to each of the following
approaches.
(i) The present value at $i = .12$.
(ii) A price to yield Jones an annual return of .12   while
recovering his principal in a sinking fund earning an annual
rate of 6%.
(iii)Accumulate the payments at 6% and then find the present
value at 12% of that accumulated value.
(b) Jones calculates his annual rate of return a number of different
ways.   In case (iii) of part (a) Jones earns an annual rate of
return of 12% for the 20 years.   Find his annual "yield"
according to each of the following approaches.
(i) In part (a)(i) above, assume that Jones can reinvest the
payments at 6% per year; find Jones' average annual
compound rate of return based on the accumulated amount
after 20 years compared to his initial investment.
(ii) Using the amount invested based on the approach in (a)(ii)
as the present value of the annuity, find the unknown
interest rate (internal rate of return) using the approximation methods of Section 2.7.
(iii)Assuming that the full 1000 is deposited in the sinking
fund at 6%, find the average annual compound rate of
return over the 20 years based on the accumulated value of
the sinking fund and the initial amount invested in (a)(ii).

2.9.3   An investor is considering the purchase of an annuity of K per year
for n years, starting one year from the purchase date.   He
calculates a purchase price on each of two bases : (i) the present
value of the annuity at rate i per year, resulting in price P_1, and (ii)
the sinking fund method with annual return of i per year (same i as
in (i)), recovering the principal in a sinking fund with an
accumulation rate of j per year, resulting in price P_2.

(a) Derive the following relationships by comparing $\frac{1}{P_1}$ and $\frac{1}{P_2}$ and using the identity $\frac{1}{s_{\overline{n}|k}} + k = \frac{1}{a_{\overline{n}|k}}$.

    (i) $P_1 = P_2$ if $i = j$

    (ii) $P_1 > P_2$ if $i > j$

    (iii) $P_1 < P_2$ if $i < j$

(b) Let i' be the unknown interest rate in the solution of $P_2 = K \cdot a_{\overline{n}|i'}$. Show each of the following results.

    (i) $i' = i$ if $i = j$

    (ii) $i' > i$ if $i > j$

    (iii) $i' < i$ if $i < j$

(c) Let i'' be the solution of $P_2(1 + i'')^n = K \cdot s_{\overline{n}|j}$. Show that i'' lies between i and j. How does i'' compare with the i' found in Exercise 2.9.1?

2.9.4   Repeat part (a)(ii) of Exercise 2.9.2 for each of the following situations.

(a) Jones wishes to receive a return of 12% per year for the first 10 years and 8% per year for the final 10 years, while recovering the principal in a sinking fund earning 6% per year.

(b) Jones wishes to receive a return of 12% per year, while recovering the principal in a sinking fund earning 6% per year for the first 10 years and 4% per year for the final 10 years.

(c) Jones wishes to receive a return of 12% per year for the first 10 years and 8% for the final 10 years, while recovering the principal in a sinking fund earning 6% per year for the first 10 years and 4% per year for the final 10 years.

2.9.5   Repeat Exercises 2.9.2 and 2.9.4 if the first 10 payments are 500 each and the final 10 payments are 1500 each.

2.9.6   Repeat Example 2.20 in each of the following cases.

(a) If the equipment has a salvage value after 10 years of 10,000, find the purchase price based on the sinking fund method using the same i and j as before.

(b) Find the salvage value for which the purchase price would be 85,000 based on the sinking fund method using the same i and j as before.

2.9.7 Repeat Example 2.21 by showing that $\frac{d}{dj} P_2 > 0$.

2.9.8 (a) Show that P_2 in Example 2.21 can be written as

$$P_2 = \frac{a_{\overline{n}|j}}{1 + (i-j) \cdot a_{\overline{n}|j}}.$$

   (b) Show that L in Equation (2.31) can be written as

$$L = \frac{\sum\limits_{t=1}^{n} K_t \cdot v_j^t}{1 + (i-j) \cdot a_{\overline{n}|j}}.$$

   (c) Construct a numerical example for L in Equation (2.31) (*i.e.*, K_t's and i), such that $\frac{dL}{dj} > 0$.

2.9.9 Repeat Example 2.22 with the bond earning monthly interest at an annual rate of 12%, and the deposit account earning monthly interest at an annual rate of 6%.

2.9.10 (a) The average periodic compound yield rate earned over an n-period term on an investment of initial amount 1 that generates interest at periodic rate $i > 0$ which is reinvested at rate $j > 0$ is i', where $(1 + i')^n = 1 + i \cdot s_{\overline{n}|j}$. Show that i' lies between i and j, and that if $i = j$ then $i' = i = j$.

   (b) The average periodic compound yield rate earned over an n-period term on an annuity of 1 per period whose payments earn initial interest of i per period which is then reinvested at rate j is i', where $s_{\overline{n}|i'} = n + i \cdot (Is)_{\overline{n-1}|j}$. Show that i' lies between i and j, and that if $i = j$ then $i' = i = j$.

   (c) For each of parts (a) and (b), show that $\lim\limits_{n\to\infty} i' = j$.

2.9.11 A purchaser pays 245,000 for a mine which will be exhausted at the end of 18 years. What level annual revenue (received at the end of each year) is required in order for the purchaser to receive a 5% annual return on his investment if he can recover his principal in a sinking fund earning 3.5% per year?

2.9.12 Smith wishes to purchase an increasing annuity with 20 annual payments of 1000, 2000, 3000, ..., 20,000. Smith considers the following three methods of valuing the annuity one period before the first payment. Find the purchase price in each case.

(a) Present value method at $i = .10$.

(b) Sinking fund method, earning annual interest of 10% on the initial investment and recovering the initial investment in a sinking fund earning 6% per year. (Note that this involves *negative* sinking fund deposits for several years, which is algebraically feasible but unrealistic from a practical point of view.)

(c) Capitalizing unpaid interest each year at rate 10%: with initial investment P_0 the outstanding balance at time 1 is $P_1 = P_0(1.10) - 1000$; at time 2 it is $P_2 = P_1(1.10) - 2000$, and so on. This continues until P_t is such that the payments are large enough to support the sinking fund method with a purchase price of P_t, and Smith earns 10% per year on P_t for the remaining years while accumulating P_t in a sinking fund earning interest at 6%.

CHAPTER 3

LOAN REPAYMENT

3.1   INTRODUCTION

When a loan is being repaid by a series of payments, the total of all payments must repay the original amount of the loan (the principal) as well as pay interest on the loan. Each of the payments will pay some interest due on the loan as well as some of the outstanding principal. There are several ways in which a loan repayment scheme can be set up, each of which specifies the division of payments into interest paid and principal repaid. In this chapter we will consider various repayment schemes. The most common one is the *amortization method*, which we will consider in the next section. The amortization method of loan repayment at a specified rate of interest corresponds to setting the present value of all amounts loaned out equal to the present value of all payments made to repay the loan, with present values based on the specified loan rate.

In Section 2.7 we considered transactions for which an unknown interest rate was to be found, based on setting the present value of a series of specified payments equal to a specified loan amount. The interest rate which is the solution to this equation is called the yield rate or internal rate of return on the loan. In this chapter we will consider the determination and interpretation of yield rates on a wider class of financial transactions.

3.2   THE AMORTIZATION METHOD

The simplest example of a loan repayment is one in which a loan made at a specified point in time is to be repaid by a single payment at some later point in time. If a loan of amount L, made at time 0 with interest at rate i per period, is to be repaid by a single payment one interest period later, the amount of that single payment is $L(1+i) = L + L \cdot i$. It is clear that in this payment L represents the repayment of the original principal on the loan, and $L \cdot i$ is a payment of interest due (the interest that accrued over the period). Just before the payment is made the accumulated amount owed is $L(1+i)$, and the payment of that amount reduces the amount owed to zero. Suppose that the payment made after one period, say K_1, is somewhat less than $L(1+i)$. In this case the loan is not fully repaid by the payment of K_1, and there remains a balance owing, called the *outstanding balance* or *outstanding principal*.   The amount of the outstanding balance just after that payment is the unpaid part of the loan, so that

$$OB_1 \;=\; L(1+i) - K_1. \tag{3.1}$$

The process involved in the amortization method of loan repayment can be described by reformulating Equation (3.1) as

$$OB_1 \;=\; L(1+i) - K_1 \;=\; L - (K_1 - L \cdot i). \tag{3.2}$$

$L \cdot i$ represents the accrued interest on the original principal amount for the period. The payment of K_1 is regarded as first paying the accrued interest, $L \cdot i$, and then the remainder of the payment, $K_1 - L \cdot i$, is applied to reduce the principal, or balance owing, so that the outstanding balance that remains is equal to the initial balance owing minus the amount of principal repaid. Thus $L - (K_1 - L \cdot i) = OB_1$.

The general description of the amortization method of loan repayment is as follows. A loan of amount L at interest rate i per period will be completely repaid by a series of n successive payments, starting one period after the loan is made (*payments in arrears*), with the payments made at equally spaced intervals in amounts (in order) $K_1, K_2, \ldots, K_n$. It will be assumed that the interest period and payment period coincide, since if they do not it is easy to find the equivalent rate of interest for the payment period. We denote the initial loan amount L by OB_0, the outstanding balance at time 0. At the end of the first period the loan has accumulated, with interest, to $OB_0(1 + i)$. The payment of amount K_1 is then applied, so that the resulting outstanding balance at time 1 (just after the first payment) is $OB_1 = OB_0(1 + i) - K_1$. This relationship can also be written as $OB_1 = OB_0 - (K_1 - OB_0 \cdot i)$, where $OB_0 \cdot i = I_1$ represents the amount of *interest paid* at the end of the first period, and $K_1 - OB_0 \cdot i = K_1 - I_1 = PR_1$ represents the rest of the payment, the amount applied to reduce the outstanding balance. Thus PR_1 is the amount of *principal repaid* by the first payment. Then we have

$$OB_1 = OB_0 - (K_1 - OB_0 \cdot i) = OB_0 - (K_1 - I_1) = OB_0 - PR_1.$$

This process can now be extended to the end of the second payment period, where we have an accumulated balance of $OB_1(1 + i)$ which is then reduced by the second payment K_2, resulting in an outstanding balance just after the second payment of $OB_2 = OB_1(1 + i) - K_2$. This can be rewritten as

$$OB_2 = OB_1 - (K_2 - OB_1 \cdot i) = OB_1 - (K_2 - I_2) = OB_1 - PR_2,$$

where $I_2 = OB_1 \cdot i$ is the interest due at the end of the second period, and $PR_2 = K_2 - I_2$ is the rest of the second payment which is applied to repay principal. This process continues from one payment period to the next. Just after the tth payment there will be an outstanding balance of OB_t. During the following period this outstanding balance will accumulate with interest to $OB_t(1 + i)$, at which time the $t + 1^{st}$ payment K_{t+1} is made so that the outstanding balance is $OB_{t+1} = OB_t(1 + i) - K_{t+1}$. This can be rewritten as

$$OB_{t+1} = OB_t - (K_{t+1} - OB_t \cdot i) = OB_t - (K_{t+1} - I_{t+1}) = OB_t - PR_{t+1},$$

where $I_{t+1} = OB_t \cdot i$ is the interest due at the end of the $t + 1^{st}$ period, and $PR_{t+1} = K_{t+1} - I_{t+1}$ is the rest of the $t + 1^{st}$ payment which is applied to repay principal. This continues until the time of the nth, and final, payment, which reduces the outstanding balance to zero. That is, $OB_n = OB_{n-1}(1+i) - K_n = 0$. Therefore we see that each payment can be decomposed into a part that pays the interest that has accrued since the last payment and a part that repays some of the principal outstanding.

3.2.1 Amortization Schedule

The amortization of a loan as described above can be summarized in an *amortization schedule*, which sets out at each point in time the outstanding balance just after the payment made at that time, the interest paid, and the principal repaid. Table 3.1 presents the amortization schedule symbolically.

From Table 3.1 we see that the total amount paid during the course of repaying the loan is $K_T = \Sigma K_t$, of which $I_T = \Sigma I_t$ is the total interest paid over the course of the loan, and the total principal repaid is $K_T - I_T = \Sigma(K_t - I_t)$. In Exercise 3.2.3 you are asked to show that $K_T - I_T$ is equal to $L = OB_0$. The total amount of principal repaid during the term of the loan is simply the original loan amount. Note that I_T can be written as

$$I_T = \Sigma I_t = \Sigma(OB_{t-1} \cdot i) = i \cdot \Sigma OB_{t-1} = i[OB_0 + OB_1 + \cdots + OB_{n-1}].$$

If the final loan payment occurs at time n to completely repay the loan, then $OB_n = 0$.

TABLE 3.1

t	Payment	Interest Due	Principal Repaid	Outstanding Balance
0	—	—	—	$L = OB_0$
1	K_1	$I_1 = OB_0 \cdot i$	$PR_1 = K_1 - I_1$	$OB_1 = OB_0 - PR_1$
2	K_2	$I_2 = OB_1 \cdot i$	$PR_2 = K_2 - I_2$	$OB_2 = OB_1 - PR_2$
$\vdots$	$\vdots$	$\vdots$	$\vdots$	$\vdots$
t				OB_t
$t+1$	K_{t+1}	$I_{t+1} = OB_t \cdot i$	$PR_{t+1} = K_{t+1} - I_{t+1}$	$OB_{t+1} = OB_t - PR_{t+1}$
$\vdots$	$\vdots$	$\vdots$	$\vdots$	$\vdots$
n	K_n	$I_n = OB_{n-1} \cdot i$	$PR_n = K_n - I_n$	$OB_n = OB_{n-1} - PR_n$

$0 \cdot 01 \% / mtn$

EXAMPLE 3.1

A loan of amount 1000 at rate $i^{(12)} = .12$ is repaid by 6 monthly payments, starting one month after the loan is made. The first three payments are amount X each and the final three payments are amount $2X$ each. Construct the amortization schedule for this loan. $X' \cdot 2 \times v \cdot a$

SOLUTION

To solve for X we have $1000 = X \cdot a_{\overline{3}|.01} + 2X \cdot v^3 \cdot a_{\overline{3}|.01}$ as the equation of value, so that $X = 115.61$ to the nearest cent and $2X = 231.21$ to the nearest cent. The amortization schedule, with t measured in months, is given in Table 3.2. The exact value of OB_6 is 0, and the value of $-.01$ in the schedule is due to roundoff error which accumulates in the calculation of all quantities to the nearest cent. In practice the final payment would have been increased by 1 cent to 231.22 in order to reduce OB_6 to zero. If X and the various quantities in the schedule had been calculated with a few additional digits of accuracy, the value of OB_6 would be closer to its exact value of zero. The total amount paid on the loan is 1040.46, of which 40.47 is interest and 1000 (999.99 because of roundoff) is principal repayment. □

TABLE 3.2

t	Payment	Interest Due	Principal Repaid	Outstanding Balance
0	—	—	—	$L = OB_0 = 1000$
1	$K_1 = $ 115.61	$I_1 = OB_0 \cdot i$ = 10	$PR_1 = K_1 - I_1$ = 105.61	$OB_1 = OB_0 - PR_1$ = 894.39
2	$K_2 = $ 115.61	$I_2 = OB_1 \cdot i$ = 8.94	$PR_2 = K_2 - I_2$ = 106.67	$OB_2 = OB_1 - PR_2$ = 787.72
3	$K_3 = $ 115.61	$I_3 = OB_2 \cdot i$ = 7.88	$PR_3 = K_3 - I_3$ = 107.73	$OB_3 = OB_2 - PR_3$ = 679.99
4	$K_4 = $ 231.21	$I_4 = OB_3 \cdot i$ = 6.80	$PR_4 = K_4 - I_4$ = 224.41	$OB_4 = OB_3 - PR_4$ = 455.58
5	$K_5 = $ 231.21	$I_5 = OB_4 \cdot i$ = 4.56	$PR_5 = K_5 - I_5$ = 226.65	$OB_5 = OB_4 - PR_4$ = 228.93
6	$K_6 = $ 231.21	$I_6 = OB_5 \cdot i$ = 2.29	$PR_6 = K_6 - I_6$ = 228.92	$OB_6 = OB_5 - PR_6$ = .01
Totals	1046.46	40.47	999.99	

3.2.2 Retrospective Form of the Outstanding Balance

If we follow the amortization process from one period to the next for the general n-payment loan described in Section 3.2.1, we see that the successive outstanding balance amounts can be formulated as

$$OB_1 \; = \; OB_0(1+i) - K_1$$

$$OB_2 \; = \; OB_1(1+i) - K_2 \; = \; OB_0(1+i)^2 - K_1(1+i) - K_2$$

$$OB_3 \; = \; OB_2(1+i) - K_3 \; = \; OB_0(1+i)^3 - K_1(1+i)^2 - K_2(1+i) - K_3$$

$$\vdots$$

$$OB_t \; = \; OB_0(1+i)^t - K_1(1+i)^{t-1} - K_2(1+i)^{t-2} - \cdots - K_{t-1}(1+i) - K_t$$

$$\vdots$$

$$OB_n \; =$$
$$OB_0(1+i)^n - K_1(1+i)^{n-1} - K_2(1+i)^{n-2} - \cdots - K_{n-1}(1+i) - K_n \; = \; 0.$$

The general relationship given by

$$OB_t \; = \; OB_0(1+i)^t - K_1(1+i)^{t-1} - K_2(1+i)^{t-2} - \cdots - K_{t-1}(1+i) - K_t$$

$$(3.3)$$

is the *retrospective* method of formulating the outstanding balance of the loan just after the tth payment. The retrospective method formulates OB_t as the amount of the original loan accumulated to time t, $L(1+i)^t \; = \; OB_0(1+i)^t$, minus the accumulated value of all payments to time t, including K_t, the payment made at time t.

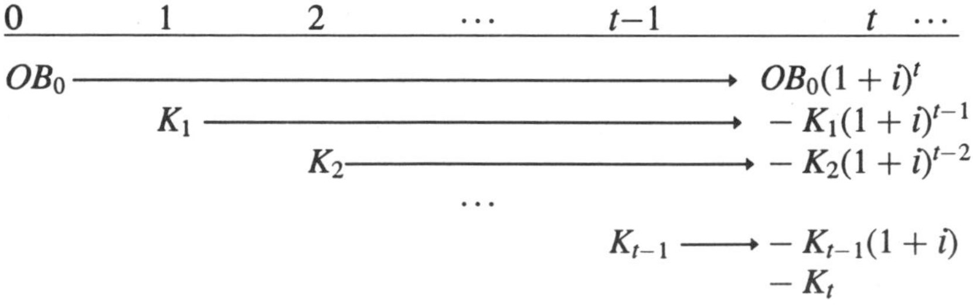

FIGURE 3.1

Applying this to Example 3.1, we see that the outstanding balance of the loan just after the third payment is

$$OB_3 = 1000(1.01)^3 - 115.61(1.01)^2 - 115.61(1.01) - 115.61$$

$$= 1000(1.01)^3 - 115.61 \cdot s_{\overline{3}|.01} = 679.99.$$

The loan is completely repaid by the nth payment, so

$$OB_n =$$

$$OB_0(1+i)^n - K_1(1+i)^{n-1} - K_2(1+i)^{n-2} - \cdots - K_{n-1}(1+i) - K_n = 0.$$

Multiplying both sides of this equation by v^n and rearranging the terms we have

$$L = OB_0 = K_1 \cdot v + K_2 \cdot v^2 + \cdots + K_n \cdot v^n. \qquad (3.4)$$

Thus it follows that under the amortization method of repaying a loan, the original loan amount is equal to the present value of the series of loan payments. In Chapter 2 there were several examples that involved the repayment of a loan. In most of these examples (see Examples 2.6, 2.10, 2.14) the loan transaction is represented by an equation of value in which the initial amount of the loan is equal to the present value of the scheduled payments. This is the most common way in which a loan transaction is set up, and, as we have just seen, it is equivalent to the amortization method of loan repayment.

3.2.3 Prospective Form of the Outstanding Balance

The general retrospective form of the outstanding balance at time t is given by Equation (3.3). If we replace OB_0 in that equation by $OB_0 = K_1 \cdot v + K_2 \cdot v^2 + \cdots + K_n \cdot v^n$, given by Equation (3.4), then Equation (3.3) is transformed into

$$OB_t = [K_1 \cdot v + K_2 \cdot v^2 + \cdots + K_t \cdot v^t + K_{t+1} \cdot v^{t+1} + \cdots + K_n \cdot v^n](1+i)^t$$
$$- K_1(1+i)^{t-1} - K_2(1+i)^{t-2} - \cdots - K_{t-1}(1+i) - K_t$$
$$= K_{t+1} \cdot v + K_{t+2} \cdot v^2 + \cdots + K_n \cdot v^{n-t}. \quad (3.5)$$

Thus we see that OB_t is equal to the present value, *at time t*, of all remaining payments from time $t+1$ onward, but not including the payment just made at time t. This is the *prospective* form of the outstanding balance, and it is algebraically equivalent to the retrospective form.

FIGURE 3.2

In Example 3.1 we can apply the prospective form to find OB_3 as $OB_3 = 231.21 \cdot v + 231.21 \cdot v^2 + 231.21 \cdot v^3 = 231.21 \cdot a_{\overline{3}|.01} = 679.98$, where the difference from the retrospective OB_3 value of 679.99 is due to roundoff error.

In the discussion of the amortization method given above, it was assumed that the interest rate on the loan remained unchanged from one period to the next. The amortization method can also be applied when the interest rate changes over time. Let i_1 denote the interest rate for the first period, which runs from time 0 to time 1, i_2 denotes the interest rate for the second period, and so on, with the interest rate for the $t+1^{st}$ period denoted by i_{t+1}. Then the amortization relationships become

$$OB_1 = OB_0 - (K_1 - OB_0 \cdot i_1) = OB_0 - (K_1 - I_1)$$
$$= OB_0 - PR_1, \quad (3.6)$$

and, in general,

$$OB_{t+1} = OB_t - (K_{t+1} - OB_t \cdot i_{t+1}) = OB_t - (K_{t+1} - I_{t+1})$$
$$= OB_t - PR_{t+1}. \quad (3.7)$$

3.2.4 Amortization of a Loan with Level Payments

A loan is typically repaid with level payments, and if this is the case the amortization schedule has a systematic form. Suppose a loan is repaid by n payments of amount 1 each, starting one payment period after the loan was made, and suppose that interest on the loan is at rate i per period. Then the original loan amount, based on the amortization method, is the present value of the payments, so that $L = OB_0 = a_{\overline{n}|i}$, and $K_1 = K_2 = \cdots = K_n = 1$. The prospective outstanding balance just after the tth payment is $OB_t = a_{\overline{n-t}|i}$, the present value of the remaining $n - t$ payments of amount 1 each. The full amortization schedule is shown in Table 3.3 on the following page.

The total amount paid during the term of the loan is $K_T = n$ (n payments of 1). The total amount of interest paid is

$$I_T = (1-v^n) + (1-v^{n-1}) + \cdots + (1-v) = n - a_{\overline{n}|},$$

and the total principal repaid is

$$K_T - I_T = n - (n - a_{\overline{n}|}) = a_{\overline{n}|} = L,$$

the original amount of the loan.

Another point to note about the amortization schedule for a loan with level payments concerns the principal repaid column. Moving down this column from time 1 to time 2 and onward, we see that $PR_2 = v^{n-1} = v^n(1 + i) = PR_1(1 + i)$, and, in general,

$$PR_t = v^{n-t+1} = v^n(1 + i)^{t-1} = PR_1(1 + i)^{t-1}.$$

This relationship involving the principal repaid amounts is valid provided the payments and the interest rate remain level. In Exercise 3.2.4 it is shown that if two successive payments on an amortized loan are equal ($K_t = K_{t+1}$) and the corresponding periodic interest rates are also equal ($i_t = i_{t+1} = i$), then $PR_{t+1} = PR_t(1 + i)$. In Example 3.1 where $K_1 = K_2 = K_3$, we expect that $PR_2 = PR_1(1 + j)$ and $PR_3 = PR_2(1 + j)$. This is easily verified since $105.61(1.01) = 106.67$ and $106.67(1.01) = 107.74$. Furthermore, since $K_4 = K_5 = K_6$, we have $PR_4(1+j) = PR_5$ and $PR_5(1+j) = PR_6$. Note that $\frac{PR_4}{PR_3} = \frac{224.41}{107.74}$ $= 2.083 \neq 1+j$, since $K_3 \neq K_4$.

TABLE 3.3

t	Pay-ment	Interest Due	Principal Repaid	Outstanding Balance
0	—	—	—	$L = OB_0 = a_{\overline{n}\rvert}$
1	$K_1 = 1$	$\begin{aligned} I_1 &= OB_0 \cdot i \\ &= i \cdot a_{\overline{n}\rvert} \\ &= 1 - v^n \end{aligned}$	$\begin{aligned} PR_1 &= K_1 - I_1 \\ &= v^n \end{aligned}$	$\begin{aligned} OB_1 &= OB_0 - PR_1 \\ &= a_{\overline{n}\rvert} - v^n \\ &= a_{\overline{n-1}\rvert} \end{aligned}$
2	$K_2 = 1$	$\begin{aligned} I_2 &= OB_1 \cdot i \\ &= i \cdot a_{\overline{n-1}\rvert} \\ &= 1 - v^{n-1} \end{aligned}$	$\begin{aligned} PR_2 &= K_2 - I_2 \\ &= v^{n-1} \end{aligned}$	$\begin{aligned} OB_2 &= OB_1 - PR_2 \\ &= a_{\overline{n-1}\rvert} - v^{n-1} \\ &= a_{\overline{n-2}\rvert} \end{aligned}$
⋮	⋮	⋮	⋮	⋮
$t-1$				$OB_{t-1} = a_{\overline{n-t+1}\rvert}$
t	$K_t = 1$	$\begin{aligned} I_t &= OB_t \cdot i \\ &= i \cdot a_{\overline{n-t+1}\rvert} \\ &= 1 - v^{n-t+1} \end{aligned}$	$\begin{aligned} PR_t &= K_t - I_t \\ &= v^{n-t+1} \end{aligned}$	$\begin{aligned} OB_t &= OB_{t-1} - PR_t \\ &= a_{\overline{n-t+1}\rvert} - v^{n-t+1} \\ &= a_{\overline{n-t}\rvert} \end{aligned}$
⋮	⋮	⋮	⋮	⋮
n	$K_n = 1$	$\begin{aligned} I_n &= OB_{n-1} \cdot i \\ &= i \cdot a_{\overline{1}\rvert} \\ &= 1 - v \end{aligned}$	$\begin{aligned} PR_n &= K_n - I_n \\ &= v \end{aligned}$	$\begin{aligned} OB_n &= OB_{n-1} - PR_n \\ &= a_{\overline{1}\rvert} - v \\ &= 0 \end{aligned}$

In Example 3.1 the interest due amounts are relatively small compared to the actual loan payments, and the excess of the payment amount over the interest due in that payment, $K_t - I_t$, is equal to the principal repaid in that payment, PR_t. It is possible that during the repayment of a loan by the amortization method, a particular payment is not large enough to cover the interest due ($K_t < I_t$), so there is a shortfall of $I_t - K_t$ in the payment of interest. In this case PR_t, the amount of principal repaid, is *negative* ($PR_t < 0$). Algebraically the new outstanding balance just after the tth

payment is $OB_t = OB_{t-1} - PR_t$, and since $PR_t < 0$ we find that $OB_t = OB_{t-1} - (K_t - I_t) = OB_{t-1} + (I_t - K_t) > OB_{t-1}$. In other words the outstanding balance *increases by the amount of unpaid interest.* The unpaid interest is *capitalized* and added to the balance still owing. For the purpose of dividing payments into interest and principal, the unpaid interest, which will accumulate as time goes on, should still be regarded as interest when payments are made at a later time. If, in Example 3.1, the loan were being repaid with monthly payments for 12 years (144 payments), with the first payment made one month after the loan is made, and for the first 6 years the 72 payments are amount Z each and for the final 6 years the 72 payments are amount $2Z$ each, then solving for Z we obtain $Z = 9.89$ (see Exercise 3.2.6). At the time of the first payment the interest due is $I_1 = 1000(.01) = 10$, but the payment made is only $K_1 = Z = 9.89$, so the principal repaid is $PR_1 = K_1 - I_1 = -.11$. There is a shortfall in the first payment of .11 in the interest due, and this .11 is *added* to the outstanding balance, resulting in $OB_1 = 1000.11$. Algebraically the calculation of OB_1 is done in the usual way: $OB_1 = OB_0(1+j) - K_1 = 1000(1.01) - 9.89 = 1000.11$, or $OB_1 = OB_0 - PR_1 = 1000 - (-.11) = 1000.11$.

Repayment by means of level payments is the most common form of repaying a loan. In such a case, as shown in Table 3.3, the amounts of principal repaid increase from one payment to the next and the amounts of interest due decrease. Occasionally a loan repayment is structured to have specified amounts of principal repaid with each payment, along with payment of interest due on the previous period's outstanding balance. This is illustrated in the following example.

EXAMPLE 3.2

A loan of 3000 at a quarterly effective interest rate of $j = .02$ is amortized by means of 12 quarterly payments, beginning one quarter after the loan is made. Each payment consists of a principal repayment of 250 plus interest due on the previous quarter's outstanding balance. Construct the amortization schedule.

SOLUTION

With an initial outstanding balance of $L = OB_0 = 3000$, we have $I_1 = 3000(.02) = 60$. Since $PR_1 = 250$, then $K_1 = I_1 + PR_1 = 310$. Then $OB_1 = OB_0 - PR_1 = 3000 - 250 = 2750$. Table 3.4, on the following page, gives the full amortization schedule, where t counts quarters.

TABLE 3.4

t	Payment	Interest Due	Principal Repaid	Outstanding Balance
0	—	—	—	$L = OB_0 = 3000$
1	$K_1 = 310$	$I_1 = OB_0 \cdot i$ $= 60$	$PR_1 = 250$	$OB_1 = OB_0 - PR_1$ $= 2750$
2	305	55	250	2500
3	300	50	250	2250
4	295	45	250	2000
5	290	40	250	1750
6	285	35	250	1750
7	280	30	250	1250
8	275	25	250	1000
9	270	20	250	750
10	265	15	250	550
11	260	10	250	250
12	255	5	250	0

The total interest paid during the course of the loan is $60 + 55 + \cdots + 5 = 390$, and the present value, at quarterly rate .02, of the payments is equal to 3000 (see Exercise 3.2.7).   □

Occasionally a loan will call for periodic payments of interest only, and a single payment of the full principal amount at the end of a specified term. Such a loan of amount L at rate i per period for n periods has interest payments of $I_1 = I_2 = \cdots = I_n = L \cdot i$, and principal payments of $PR_1 = PR_2 = \cdots = PR_{n-1} = 0$ with $PR_n = L$. The outstanding balances are $OB_0 = L$, $OB_1 = OB_0 - PR_1 = L$, $OB_2 = L, \ldots,$ $OB_{n-1} = L$, $OB_n = OB_{n-1} - PR_n = L - L = 0$. The borrower is required to make payments of interest only to the lender during the term of the loan, but then he must pay the full amount of principal at the end of the term. In this situation the borrower might accumulate the principal amount L by means of deposits into an account during the term of the loan. The deposit account is called a sinking fund, and this method of loan repayment is called the sinking fund method.

3.3   THE SINKING-FUND METHOD

The final comments of the preceding section considered the case of a loan which called for periodic payments of interest only during the term of the loan, along with repayment of the full principal amount at the end of the term.   For such a loan of amount L at periodic rate of interest i for n periods, the borrower would have to make a series of n interest payments to the lender, each of amount $L \cdot i$, along with a payment of L at time n. The borrower might offset the obligation to pay the single lump sum of amount L at time n by accumulating that amount during the term of the loan by means of n periodic deposits to an interest-bearing savings account called a *sinking fund*.   This method of loan repayment is called the *sinking-fund method.*

There is no guarantee that the rate earned in the sinking fund, say j, is the same as the periodic interest rate on the loan, i.   In a practical situation it would usually be the case that the interest rate charged by the lender is larger than the rate that can be earned in a deposit account, so that $i > j$.

A standard way of accumulating the principal amount in the sinking fund is by using level deposits.   If this is the case, then for the loan situation just described the borrower's payment would be $L \cdot i$, the interest payment to the lender, plus $\frac{L}{s_{\overline{n}|j}}$, the level sinking fund deposit, producing a total periodic outlay of $L \left[i + \frac{1}{s_{\overline{n}|j}} \right]$.   Note that if the loan were being repaid by the amortization method with n level periodic payments at the lender's rate i, the borrower's total periodic outlay would be $\frac{L}{a_{\overline{n}|i}} = L \left[i + \frac{1}{s_{\overline{n}|i}} \right]$.   Then to compare the total periodic outlays under the sinking fund and amortization methods we simply compare $\frac{1}{s_{\overline{n}|j}}$ with $\frac{1}{s_{\overline{n}|i}}$.   Since (i) $s_{\overline{n}|j} < s_{\overline{n}|i}$ if $j < i$, (ii) $s_{\overline{n}|j} = s_{\overline{n}|i}$ if $j = i$, and (iii) $s_{\overline{n}|j} > s_{\overline{n}|i}$ if $j > i$, we see that the borrower's total periodic outlay under the sinking fund method is (i) greater than, (ii) equal to, or (iii) less than the total periodic outlay under the amortization method (at rate i) if

(i) $j < i$, (ii) $j = i$, or (iii) $j > i$. As pointed out above, case (i) would be the one most likely to occur in practice. Notice also that if the lender's rate i is equal to the sinking fund rate j, the total periodic outlay required under the two methods is the same.

| EXAMPLE 3.3 |

A loan of 100,000 is to be repaid by ten annual payments beginning one year after the loan is made. The lender wants annual payments of interest only at a rate of 10% and repayment of the principal in a single lump sum at the end of 10 years. The borrower can accumulate the principal in a sinking fund earning an annual interest rate of 8%, and decides to do this by means of 10 level deposits starting one year after the loan is made.

(a) Find the borrowers total annual outlay and compare this to the level annual payment required by the amortization method at 10%. Find the annual rate of interest i' for which the amortization method at rate i' results in the same total annual outlay as the borrower pays in the sinking fund method in this example.

(b) Suppose that the lender's rate is 8% and the sinking fund rate is 10%. Repeat part (a) comparing to the amortization method at 8%.

| SOLUTION |

(a) The total annual outlay under the sinking fund method is $100,000 \left[.1 + \frac{1}{s_{\overline{10}|.08}} \right] = 16,902.95$, and the annual payment under amortization at 10% is $\frac{100,000}{a_{\overline{10}|.10}} = 16,274.54$. To find i' we have $100,000 = 16,902.95 \cdot a_{\overline{10}|i'}$. Using the Newton-Raphson method we find $i' = .1089$.

(b) The total annual outlay under the sinking fund method is $100,000 \left[.08 + \frac{1}{s_{\overline{10}|.10}} \right] = 14,274.54$, and the annual payment under amortization at 8% is $\frac{100,000}{a_{\overline{10}|.08}} = 14,902.95$. To find i' we have $100,000 = 14,274.54 \cdot a_{\overline{10}|i'}$. Using the Newton-Raphson method we find $i' = .0706$. $\qquad\qquad\square$

As deposits are made to the sinking fund, the fund balance grows toward the target value of L. For instance, in part (a) of Example 3.3, just after the fifth deposit into the sinking fund, the fund balance is $6902.95 \cdot s_{\overline{5}|.08} = 40,496.85$. This is the accumulated value after five years in the fund that will eventually pay back the principal amount. The value of the net debt outstanding after 5 years can be regarded as the initial loan amount minus the amount for repayment of principal accumulated to that point. This is $100,000 - 40,496.85 = 59,503.15$. This can be regarded as OB_5. Similarly OB_6 would be 100,000 minus the accumulated value of the sinking fund just after the sixth deposit, so $OB_6 = 100,000 - 6902.95 \cdot s_{\overline{6}|.08} = 49,360.45$. The principal repaid in the sixth year is the amount by which the value of the debt decreases, which is $PR_6 = OB_5 - OB_6 = 10,142.70$. Also in Example 3.3 we see that the amount of interest paid to the lender is $100,000(.1) = 10,000$ each year. This amount is offset by the interest earned in the sinking fund for the year. For the sixth year the amount of interest earned by the sinking fund is equal to .08 multiplied by the balance in the account at the end of the fifth year, producing $(.08)(40,496.85) = 3239.75$. Then the net interest paid for the sixth year is the amount paid to the lender minus the amount earned in the sinking fund, which is $I_6 = 10,000 - 3239.75 = 6760.25$. It then follows that $I_6 + PR_6 = 6760.25 + 10,142.70 = 16,902.95$, which is the total annual payment made by the borrower. It is possible to construct a schedule showing the principal repaid for each period (growth in the sinking fund for that period) and the net interest paid for each period (interest paid to lender for the period minus interest earned in the sinking fund that period). This is the equivalent of an amortization schedule in the context of loan repayment by the sinking fund method.

Suppose we consider a loan of amount L, repaid by the sinking fund method over n periods, with the lender receiving interest at rate i per period from the borrower and the borrower making n level deposits into a sinking fund earning interest at rate j per period. The last deposit occurs at the end of the nth period giving an accumulated amount in the sinking fund of L. The periodic sinking fund deposits are amount $\frac{L}{s_{\overline{n}|j}}$ each. Then the net amount of the debt at the end of the tth period, just after the tth deposit, is

$$OB_t = L - \frac{L}{s_{\overline{n}|j}} \cdot s_{\overline{t}|j} = L\left[1 - \frac{s_{\overline{t}|j}}{s_{\overline{n}|j}}\right], \qquad (3.8)$$

and, similarly, $OB_{t-1} = L\left[1 - \frac{s_{\overline{t-1}|j}}{s_{\overline{n}|j}}\right]$. The principal repaid in the tth period is

$$PR_t = OB_{t-1} - OB_t = L\left[\frac{s_{\overline{t}|j} - s_{\overline{t-1}|j}}{s_{\overline{n}|j}}\right] = \frac{L(1+j)^{t-1}}{s_{\overline{n}|j}}. \quad (3.9)$$

Note that if the sinking fund deposits are level, then the amount of principal repaid grows by a factor of $1+j$ per period, which is similar to the growth of PR_t in the amortization method when payments are level (see Exercise 3.3.1). The net interest paid in the tth payment is

$$I_t = L\cdot i - \frac{L\cdot s_{\overline{t-1}|j}}{s_{\overline{n}|j}}\cdot j = L\left[i - \frac{(1+j)^{t-1}-1}{s_{\overline{n}|j}}\right]. \quad (3.10)$$

Note that $I_t + PR_t = L\left[i + \frac{1}{s_{\overline{n}|j}}\right]$, the borrower's total periodic outlay.
The sinking fund method for valuing an annuity was considered in Section 2.9. Exercise 3.3.2 points out the strong relationship between this method and the sinking fund method of loan repayment described above.

3.4 YIELD RATES AND COMPARISON OF FINANCIAL TRANSACTIONS; CAPITAL BUDGETING

Methods of determining the unknown interest rate used to find the present (or accumulated) value of an annuity were considered in Chapter 2. Example 2.18 showed that if $L > 0$, and payments $K_1, K_2, \ldots, K_n$ are made at times $t_1 < t_2 < \cdots < t_n$, then there is a unique interest rate $i > -1$ (a periodic rate of interest whose effective time period is measured in the same units as the t_k's), for which L is the present value at time 0 of the given series of payments. In many circumstances this *yield rate* or *internal rate of return* on the transaction is a useful measure that helps a lender or borrower determine a preference for one transaction over another. For example suppose that 100,000 is available with which a 20-year, annual payment annuity-immediate is to be purchased. Suppose Financial Institution A offers annual payments of 11,745.96 and Financial

Institution B offers payments of 13,387.88. Clearly the purchaser would prefer Institution B, since it offers the higher payments. In terms of yield rate, we see that the annual yield on Annuity A is 10% and the yield on Annuity B is 12% using methods from Chapter 2. Using the annual yield as a measure of value, we again see that Annuity B is preferable to the purchaser.

It is possible to extend this notion of yield rate to more complex transactions. Let us consider the situation in which there are payments received of amounts $A_0, A_1, A_2, \ldots, A_n$ at times $0 = t_0 < t_1 < t_2 < \cdots < t_n$, and disbursements of amounts $B_0, B_1, B_2, \ldots, B_n$ at the same points in time, where all $A_j \geq 0$ and all $B_j \geq 0$. The net amount received at time k is $C_k = A_k - B_k$, which can be positive or negative. $A_j = 0$ if a payment of B_j is disbursed at time t_j but there is no payment received at that time. Conversely, $B_k = 0$ if there is a payment received of A_k at time t_k but no payment disbursed at that time. In the context of a transaction as in Example 2.18, $A_0 = L$ and $A_1 = A_2 = \cdots = A_n = 0$; $B_0 = 0$ and $B_1 = K_1, B_2 = K_2, \ldots, B_n = K_n$; the net amounts received are $C_0 = L$ and $C_1 = -K_1, C_2 = -K_2, \ldots, C_n = -K_n$. In general we wish to find the compound interest rate i for which the value of disbursement cashflow is equal to the value of receipt cashflow, at any point in time. The equation of value at time 0 for this general situation is

$$A_0 + A_1 \cdot v^{t_1} + A_2 \cdot v^{t_2} + \cdots + A_n \cdot v^{t_n}$$
$$= B_0 + B_1 \cdot v^{t_1} + B_2 \cdot v^{t_2} + \cdots + B_n \cdot v^{t_n}, \qquad (3.11a)$$

or, equivalently,

$$\sum_{k=0}^{n} C_k \cdot v^{t_k} = 0. \qquad (3.11b)$$

Recall that as long as compound interest is in effect, the equation of value can be set up at any time point t, and the value(s) of i for which the equation holds would be the same. The equation of value set up at time t_n is

$$C_0(1+i)^{t_n} + C_1(1+i)^{t_n-t_1} + \cdots + C_{n-1}(1+i)^{t_n-t_{n-1}} + C_n$$
$$= \sum_{k=0}^{n} C_k(1+i)^{t_n-t_k} = 0. \qquad (3.12)$$

It can be seen from Equation (3.12) that the interpretation of i as the periodic yield rate for the entire transaction involves the implicit assumption that all amounts can be reinvested at rate i at any time during the transaction. (Section 2.9 considered situations in which amounts received were reinvested at interest rates other than the original yield or valuation rate.) For either Equation (3.11b) or Equation (3.12) the problem becomes one of solving for the roots of a polynomial. The same considerations arise as in Section 2.7 regarding the solution for unknown interest rates. The solution for a yield rate usually involves the application of an approximation method. This is illustrated in the following example.

EXAMPLE 3.4

Smith buys 1000 shares of stock at 5.00 per share and pays a commission of 2%. Six months later he receives a cash dividend of .20 per share, which he immediately reinvests commission-free in shares at a price of 4.00 per share. Six months after that he buys another 500 shares at a price of 4.50 per share, along with a commission of 2%. Six months after that he receives another cash dividend of .25 per share and sells his existing shares at 5.00 per share, again paying a 2% commission. Find Smith's approximate yield rate in the form $i^{(2)}$ by means of
(a) linear interpolation using values spaced at 1%,
(b) the bisection method applied five times with initial interval [5%, 10%],
(c) four applications of the Newton-Raphson method with initial approximation (i) 6%, (ii) 10%, and (iii) 0%, and
(d) four applications of the secant method (see Appendix A) with starting approximations to $i^{(2)}$ of .05 and .10.

SOLUTION

Let time 0 represent the time of the original share purchase. Then $A_0 = 0$ and $B_0 = 5100$, the initial outlay including commission. Measuring time in 6-month intervals, we have $t = 1$ at 6 months with $A_1 = 200$ and $B_1 = 200$, since he receives and immediately reinvests the dividend of 200, buying an additional 50 shares. Then $t = 2$ is at 12 months with $A_2 = 0$ and $B_2 = 2295$ (buying an additional 500 shares for a total of 1550 shares), and $t = 3$ is at 18 months with $A_3 = 387.50 + 7595 = 7982.50$ and $B_3 = 0$ (the dividend on 1550 shares plus the proceeds from the sale of the shares after commission). The net amounts received are $C_0 = -5100$, $C_1 = 0$, $C_2 = -2295$, and $C_3 = 7982.5$, so we wish to solve the equation $-5100 - 2295 \cdot v^2 + 7982.5 \cdot v^3 = 0$, or, equivalently,

$$f(j) = 5100(1+j)^3 + 2295(1+j) - 7982.5 = 0,$$

where the v and j factors are based on 6-month effective rates so that $i^{(2)} = 2j$.

(a) With $j = .02$ we have $f(.02) = -229.4$, with $j = .03$ we have $f(.03) = -45.7$, and with $j = .04$ we have $f(.04) = 141.1$, so that $.03 < j < .04$. Applying linear interpolation on the interval from $.03$ to $.04$ produces an approximation to j of

$$.03 + (.01)\left[\frac{0 - f(.03)}{f(.04) - f(.03)}\right] = .0329,$$

so the approximation to $i^{(2)}$ is $.0658$.

(b) If $i^{(2)}$ is in the interval $[.05, .10]$ then $j = \frac{i^{(2)}}{2}$ is in the interval $[.025, .05] = [a_1, b_1]$, and the initial approximation is $p_1 = .0375$. Subsequent approximations are $p_2 = .02875$, $p_3 = .033125$, $p_4 = .0309375$, and $p_5 = .03203125$. The approximation to $i^{(2)}$ based on p_5 is $2j = .0641$.

(c) The Newton-Raphson method uses $j_{n+1} = j_n - \frac{f(j_n)}{f'(j_n)}$, where $f(j_n) = 5100(1+j_n)^3 + 2295(1+j_n) - 7982.5 = 0$ from which we find $f'(j_n) = 15{,}600(1+j_n)^2 + 2295$. With an initial $i^{(2)} = .06$, we have $j_0 = .03$. Then $j_1 = .03247$, $j_2 = .03246 = j_3 = j_4$. With initial $i^{(2)} = .10$, we have $j_0 = .05$. Then $j_1 = .03272$, $j_2 = .03246 = j_3 = j_4$. With initial $i^{(2)} = 0$, we have $j_0 = 0$. Then $j_1 = .03339$, $j_2 = .03246 = j_3 = j_4$. In all cases, four iterations of Newton-Raphson give $i^{(2)} = .0649$, the exact solution to the nearest $.01$ percent.

(d) The starting approximations to j are $p_{-1} = .025$ and $p_0 = .05$. The application of the secant method to the function $f(j)$ in part (c) results in the sequence of approximations $p_1 = .03235$, $p_2 = .03246 = p_3 = p_4$.

$\square$

The transaction in Example 3.4 has a unique solution for the yield rate since $f(j)$ in part (c) is a strictly increasing function. A solution for $i > -1$ for a transaction is called an *internal rate of return*. As mentioned above, we saw in Example 2.18 that for certain special cases there is a unique solution for i. It is possible in a more general situation that there are no real solutions for i, or that there are several real solutions for i which are greater than -1.

Descartes' *rule of signs* states that for a polynomial of the form $P(x) = C_n x^n + C_{n-1} x^{n-1} + \cdots + C_1 x + C_0$, the number of positive roots of $P(x)$ is less than or equal to the number of sign changes in the sequence $C_n, C_{n-1}, \ldots, C_1, C_0$, and the number of negative roots of $P(x)$ is less than or equal to the number of sign changes in the sequence $(-1)^n C_n$, $(-1)^{n-1} C_{n-1}, \cdots, (-1)C_1, C_0$. For the $f(j)$ in Example 3.4(c), the coefficients are $C_3 = 7928.5$, $C_2 = -2295$, $C_1 = 0$, $C_0 = -5100$, so there is at most one positive root of $P(x)$; $(-1)^3 C_3 = -7928.5$, $(-1)^2 C_2 = -2295$, $(-1)C_1 = 0$, $(-1)^0 C_0 = -5100$, so there are no negative roots.

EXAMPLE 3.5

Smith has a line of credit that allows him to make withdrawals or payments at any time. The balance may be negative, indicating the amount that he owes to the account, or positive, indicating the amount the account owes him. Balances in the account, whether positive or negative, earn interest at rate i per period. Solve for i for each of the following sets of transactions on Smith's line of credit. Assume the line of credit opened at time 0 and closed with a balance of zero just after time 2, and that the A's are withdrawals from the line of credit, and the B's are payments to the line of credit. Thus the payment of B_2 made to the line of credit clears the outstanding balance on the account.

(a) $t_1 = 1$, $t_2 = 2$, $A_0 = 0$, $A_1 = 2.3$, $A_2 = 0$, $B_0 = 1$, $B_1 = 0$, $B_2 = 1.33$.

(b) $t_1 = 1$, $t_2 = 2$, $A_0 = 0$, $A_1 = 2.3$, $A_2 = 0$, $B_0 = 1$, $B_1 = 0$, $B_2 = 1.32$.

(c) $t_1 = 1$, $t_2 = 2$, $A_0 = 0$, $A_1 = 2.3$, $A_2 = 0$, $B_0 = 1$, $B_1 = 0$, $B_2 = 1.3125$.

(d) $t_1 = 1$, $t_2 = 2$, $A_0 = 0$, $A_1 = 2.3$, $A_2 = 0$, $B_0 = 1$, $B_1 = 0$, $B_2 = 1.2825$.

SOLUTION

(a) The C_k are $C_0 = -1$, $C_1 = 2.3$, and $C_2 = -1.33$, so that the equation of value at time 0 is $-1 + 2.3 \cdot v - 1.33 \cdot v^2 = 0$. Solving this quadratic equation produces only imaginary roots for v, and thus no real roots for i.

(b) The C_k are $C_0 = -1$, $C_1 = 2.3$, $C_2 = -1.32$. The equation of value at time 2 (remember that it can be set up at any point of time) is $-(1+i)^2 + 2.3(1+i) - 1.32 = 0$, which is a quadratic equation in $1+i$. Solving the quadratic results in $i = .1$ or $.2$, so both interest rates of 10% and 20% are solutions.

(c) The C_k are $C_0 = -1$, $C_1 = 2.3$, $C_2 = -1.3125$. The equation of value at time 2 is $-(1+i)^2 + 2.3(1+i) - 1.3125 = 0$, producing $i = .05$ or .25.

(d) The C_k are $C_0 = -1$, $C_1 = 2.3$, $C_2 = -1.2825$. The equation of value at time 2 is $-(1+i)^2 + 2.3(1+i) - 1.2825 = 0$, so that $i = -.05$ or .35. ☐

For the simple annuity transaction discussed at the start of this section, it was possible to do a meaningful comparison of the two annuities by comparing their yield rates. The situations described in Example 3.5 illustrate the difficulties that can arise when solving for a yield rate on a transaction, and the limitations that occur when using only the yield rate as a measure of the relative performance of an investment. Since C_0 and C_1 are the same for all four transactions, it is easy to compare the transactions by comparing the C_2 values. We see that transaction (a) has the largest payment to pay off the line of credit at time 2, with the final payment getting progressively smaller as we consider (b), (c), and (d). Therefore to minimize his cost in repaying the line of credit, Smith would prefer (d), although this is not readily apparent by comparing the yield rates. (Note that (a) does not have a yield rate to use for comparison.)

It is possible to formulate conditions on the C_k that guarantee a unique $i > -1$ (and also a unique $i > 0$). A proof generalizing the one in Example 2.18 shows that if the C_k have only one sign change (i.e., $C_0, C_1, \ldots, C_t \geq 0$ and $C_{t+1}, C_{t+2}, \ldots, C_n \leq 0$, or vice versa), then there is a unique solution for $i > -1$. Note that the results of parts (a) and (c) of Exercise 3.4.2 guarantee a unique positive solution for i in Example 3.4.

In practice the terms of most financial transactions result in a unique yield rate. However, as pointed out with Example 3.5, problems can arise when solving for the yield rate(s) on a transaction. It is not possible to compare the relative merits of two transactions on the basis of yield rate alone if one of the transactions does not have a real-valued yield rate. Even if each of two transactions has a unique yield rate, it may not be the case that a comparison of those yields is sufficient to decide which transaction is preferable (see Exercise 3.4.10).

One alternative way of comparing transactions is by means of *interest preference rates*. It can be postulated that at a particular point in time (labeled time 0), each particular individual has an interest rate $i > -1$ that is "the payment required by that individual at time 1 in order to induce him to forgo 1 unit for one period." This would be the interest preference rate for that individual at that time. To compare two transactions whose net cashflow vectors are $C = (C_0, C_1, \ldots, C_n)$ and $C' = (C'_0, C'_1, \ldots, C'_n)$, we compare $P_i(C) = \sum_{k=0}^{n} C_k \cdot v_i^{t_k}$ with $P_i(C') = \sum_{k=0}^{n} C'_k \cdot v_i^{t_k}$. Whichever present value is larger is preferable. Note that in the transactions of Example 3.5, for any interest preference rate that exceeds -1, we have $P_i(C_a) < P_i(C_b) < P_i(C_c) < P_i(C_d)$ (see Exercise 3.4.3). The same is true for the two annuities considered at the start of this section. Exercise 3.4.10 provides an example of two transactions for which one is preferable at certain interest preference rates, and the other is preferable at other interest preference rates.

Capital budgeting refers to the process in financial management whereby criteria are set for evaluating alternative investment opportunities. Comparing investments via their internal rates of return is one of several standard capital budgeting methods. Example 3.5 and the comments following it point out the limitations of the internal rate of return to evaluate investments. The interest preference rate approach described above is another commonly used method in capital budgeting; it is also called the *net present value* method. The internal rate of return and the interest preference rate are two examples of *discounted cash-flow procedures*. There are two additional discounted cash-flow procedures commonly used in practice, the *annual capital charge* and the *profitability index*.

    (1) Annual capital charge: At a specified rate of interest i, the present value of all cash inflows is calculated at the time the project begins. Let us call this present value A. A level annual cost K is found so that $A = K \cdot a_{\overline{n}|i}$. Investment alternatives are then compared on the basis of the annual charge K.

    (2) Profitability index: At a specified rate of interest i, calculate the ratio

$$I = \frac{present\ value\ of\ cash\ inflows}{present\ value\ of\ cash\ outflows},$$

where each present value is calculated at the beginning of the project. This ratio is an index measuring the return per dollar of investment. Note that if the internal rate of return is used to find the present value, then $I = 1$.

There are several capital budgeting methods that do not make use of discounted cash-flows. Two such methods are the *payback period* and the *return on investment*.

(1) Payback period: If the investment consists of a series of cash outflows followed by a series of cash inflows (C_1, C_2,..., $C_t < 0$ and C_{t+1}, C_{t+2},..., $C_n > 0$) the payback period is the number of years required to recover the original amount invested. Thus the first k for which $-\sum_{s=1}^{t} C_s \leq \sum_{r=1}^{k} C_{t+r}$ is the payback period. A rate of return can be incorporated into the determination of the payback period. In that case, the payback period is the first k for which $-\sum_{s=1}^{t} C_s \cdot (1+i)^{t+k-s} \leq \sum_{r=1}^{k} C_{t+r} \cdot (1+i)^{k-r}$.

(2) Return on investment: The yearly cash inflows are divided by the "cost" or "book value" of the investment to calculate the annual return on the investment.

3.5 APPLICATIONS AND ILLUSTRATIONS

3.5.1 Makeham's Formula

We have seen examples of loans in which the lender receives payments of only interest each period, and then receives the full amount of principal after several periods. For a loan of this type of amount L at periodic interest rate i, with principal repaid after n periods, the sequence of payments received by the lender is $L \cdot i$, $L \cdot i$,..., $L \cdot i$, $L \cdot i + L$, where there are n terms in this sequence. Suppose the lender sells the loan to an investor, and the investor values the sequence of payments at the time the loan is made by finding the present value at periodic interest rate j. This present value is $A = L \cdot v_j^n + L \cdot i \cdot a_{\overline{n}|j}$, where the first term is the present value of the principal amount repaid at time n, and the second term is the present value of the interest payments. This present value can be written as

$$A = L \cdot v_j^n + L \cdot i \cdot a_{\overline{n}|j} = L \cdot v_j^n + L \cdot i \left(\frac{1-v_j^n}{j}\right)$$

$$= L \cdot v_j^n + \frac{i}{j}(L - L \cdot v_j^n)$$

$$= K + \frac{i}{j}(L - K), \tag{3.13}$$

where $K = L \cdot v_j^n$ is the present value of the repayment of principal. Equation (3.13) is called *Makeham's formula* for valuing the original cashflow at rate j. Note that if $j = i$, then the total present value of principal and interest payments reduces to L, the original loan.

Makeham's formula provides a useful method for valuing a loan for which there is a schedule of repayments of principal at various points in time, along with payments of interest every period on the outstanding balance. The example considered above involves a single repayment of principal, with interest payable up to and including the time of that payment of principal. Suppose that a loan of amount L is to be repaid by m payments of principal of amounts $L_1, L_2, \ldots, L_m$ to be made at times $t_1, t_2, \ldots, t_m$, so that $L_1 + L_2 + \cdots + L_m = L$, with payments of interest at rate i on the outstanding balance at the end of every period. This situation can be regarded as m separate loans, all issued at the same time and each of the type described in the previous paragraph, and is illustrated in the following figure.

0	1	2	$\cdots$	t_1	$\cdots$	t_2	$\cdots$	t_m
L_1 $\rightarrow$	$L_1 i$	$L_1 i$	$\cdots$	$L_1 i + L_1$				
L_2 $\rightarrow$	$L_2 i$	$L_2 i$	$\cdots$	$L_2 i$	$\cdots$	$L_2 i + L_2$		
$\vdots$	$\vdots$	$\vdots$		$\vdots$		$\vdots$		
L_m $\rightarrow$	$L_m i$	$L_m i$	$\cdots$	$L_m i$	$\cdots$	$L_m i$	$\cdots$	$L_m i + L_m$

$$\boxed{\text{FIGURE 3.3}}$$

The present value of the sth loan at rate of interest j per period is found from Makeham's formula to be

$$A_s = L_s \cdot v_j^{t_s} + L_s \cdot i \cdot a_{\overline{t_s}|j} = K_s + \frac{i}{j}(L_s - K_s).$$

The present value of the entire loan is then the sum of the present values of the m parts of the loan. This total present value is

$$A = \sum_{s=1}^{m} A_s = \sum_{s=1}^{m} \left[L_s \cdot v_j^{t_s} + L_s \cdot i \cdot a_{\overline{t_s}|j} \right]$$

$$= \sum_{s=1}^{m} \left[K_s + \frac{i}{j}(L_s - K_s) \right] = K + \frac{i}{j}(L - K), \quad (3.13)$$

where $K = \sum_{s=1}^{m} K_s$ and $L = \sum_{s=1}^{m} L_s$. Thus the form of the present value (at rate j) in Equation (3.13) for the cashflow represented by a loan repaid by a single principal repayment, with periodic interest at rate i, is also valid if the principal is repaid in a series of payments. However K now represents the total present value of all principal payments, $\frac{i}{j}(L - K)$ represents the present value of all interest payments, and L represents the total amount of principal. Note that Makeham's formula applies if the interest rate on the original loan remains constant throughout the course of the loan (if not, the loan would have to be broken into separate loans each at the associated interest rate), and the investor's valuation rate also remains constant for the term of the payments. The investor's valuation rate must be based on the same compounding period as are the payments of interest.

EXAMPLE 3.6

A loan of 100,000 is to be repaid with 10 annual payments of principal of 10,000 each, starting one year after the loan is made, plus monthly interest payments on the outstanding balance. The interest rate is $i^{(12)} = .12$. Two years after the loan is made (just after the second principal payment and monthly interest payment) the lender sells the loan to an investor. Find the price paid by the investor if he values the remaining payments at a nominal annual rate of interest convertible monthly of (a) .06, (b) .12, and (c) .18.

SOLUTION

(a) At the time the loan is sold, the outstanding balance is $L = 80,000$ with $m = 8$ annual principal payments of $L_1 = L_2 = \cdots = L_8 = 10,000$ and monthly interest payments at 1% per month on the outstanding balance. The present value of the principal payments is

$$K = K_1 + K_2 + \cdots + K_8 = 10,000(v^{12} + v^{24} + \cdots + v^{96})$$

$$= 10,000\left(\frac{v^{12} - v^{108}}{1 - v^{12}}\right) = 61,687.68,$$

where v is at $\frac{1}{2}\%$. The price paid by the investor is then $61,687.68 + \frac{.01}{.005}(80,000 - 61,687.68) = 98,312.33$.

(b) In this case the monthly interest rate is $j = .01$, so $K = 48,513.85$ and the investor pays $48,513.85 + \frac{.01}{.01}(80,000 - 48,513.85) = 80,000$.

(c) In this case $j = .015$, so $K = 38,878.04$ and the investor pays 66,292.68.

$\square$

3.5.2 The Yield on a Fund

Suppose that a fund of money is observed over time, and the amount in the fund at time t is $F(t)$. The fund earns interest and also receives and/or makes payments from time to time. If we wish to find the average annualized yield earned by the fund from time t_1 to time t_2 measured in years, we can formulate the yield as the internal rate of return i (in the context of Section 3.4), where

$$F(t_2) = F(t_1)(1+i)^{t_2-t_1} + \sum_t c_t(1+i)^{t_2-t} + \int_{t_1}^{t_2} \bar{c}(t)(1+i)^{t_2-t}\,dt,$$

c_t represents the net amount received ($+$) or paid out ($-$) at time t, and $\bar{c}(t)$ is the net continuous rate of payment (received or paid out) at time t.

The relationship between $F(t_1)$ and $F(t_2)$ can be more simply stated as

$$F(t_2) = F(t_1) + I_{t_1 t_2} + N_{t_1 t_2}, \tag{3.14}$$

where I represents interest earned for the period on the initial $F(t_1)$ as well as on contributions (less interest lost on withdrawals), and N represents the net amount of new money received by the fund during the period where

$$N = \sum_t c_t + \int_{t_1}^{t_2} \bar{c}(t)\,dt. \tag{3.15}$$

Suppose that the time interval from t_1 to t_2 is one year, and let us make the simplifying assumption that N is uniformly received during the course of the year. Then $F(t_2)$ is a combination of the accumulated value of $F(t_1)$ after one year and the accumulated value of a continuous one-year level annuity paying N during the year, so that $F(t_2) = F(t_1)(1+i) + N \cdot \bar{s}_{\overline{1}|i}$. Using Equation (3.14) it follows that

$$F(t_2) = F(t_1)(1+i) + [F(t_2) - F(t_1) - I] \cdot \bar{s}_{\overline{1}|i}.$$

Since $\bar{s}_{\overline{1}|i} = \int_0^1 (1+i)^s\,ds = \frac{i}{\delta}$, it is not possible to solve exactly for i. A simple approximation often used in practice is based on the trapezoidal rule for approximate integration (see Appendix A), which gives $\int_0^1 (1+i)^s ds \approx 1 + \frac{i}{2}$. With this approximation we see that

$$F(t_2) \approx F(t_1)(1+i) + [F(t_2) - F(t_1) - I]\left(1 + \frac{i}{2}\right), \qquad (3.16)$$

from which it follows that

$$i \approx \frac{2I}{F(t_1) + F(t_2) - I}. \qquad (3.17)$$

(See also Exercise 2.7.24.) In Exercise 3.5.14 we derive the approximation

$$i \approx \frac{2I}{2 \cdot \int_{t_1}^{t_2} F(t)\, dt - I}. \qquad (3.18)$$

It may be the case that $F(t)$ is changing continuously for part of the period from t_1 to t_2 (say from t_1 to t'), and there is then a significant payment (or withdrawal) at time t', with $F(t)$ again changing continuously from t' to t_2. Then $F(t)$ is piecewise continuous from t_1 to t_2. In such a case the integral in Equation (3.18) can be approximated by approximating $\int_{t_1}^{t'}$ and $\int_{t'}^{t_2}$ separately.

EXAMPLE 3.7

A large pension fund was valued at 350,000,000 on January 1, 1990. During 1990 the contributions to the fund totaled 80,000,000, benefit payments totaled 20,000,000, and the fund recorded interest income of 40,000,000. Estimate the yield on the fund for 1990 in each of the following cases.

(a) Contributions, benefit payments, and interest income occur linearly and continuously throughout the year.

(b) Benefit payments, interest income, and 20,000,000 of the contributions are uniformly spread throughout the year, but there is a lump sum contribution of 60,000,000 on September 1, 1990.

(c) Same as (b) except that there are lump sum contributions of 50,000,000 on May 1 and 10,000,000 on September 1, 1990.

SOLUTION

(a) Let January 1, 1990 be $t = 0$ and January 1, 1991 be $t = 1$. Note that $F(1) = 350 + 80 - 20 + 40 = 450$ (million). Equation (3.17) can be directly applied, producing $i \approx \dfrac{2(40)}{350 + 450 - 40} = .1053$.

(b) The lump-sum contribution is made at $t = \frac{2}{3}$. Since the part of the contributions other than the lump sum, along with the benefits and interest income, are uniformly spread over the year, then just before this lump-sum contribution the approximate value of the fund is $F_-(\frac{2}{3}) = 350 + \frac{2}{3}(80-60) - \frac{2}{3}(20) + \frac{2}{3}(40) = 376.67$. Just after the lump-sum contribution the value of the fund is $F_+(\frac{2}{3}) = 376.67 + 60 = 436.67$, and the value of the fund at the end of the year is the same as in (a), $F(1) = 450$. We can assume that $F(t)$ is linear from $t = 0$ to $t = \frac{2}{3}$ (just before the lump sum payment) and from $t = \frac{2}{3}$ (just after the lump sum payment) to $t = 1$. Based on the method described in the comments following Equation (3.18), we approximate $\int_0^1 F(t)\,dt$ by approximating each of the integrals $\int_0^{2/3} F(t)\,dt$ and $\int_{2/3}^1 F(t)\,dt$. Using the trapezoidal rule the approximate values of the integrals are $\int_0^{2/3} F(t)\,dt = \frac{2/3}{2}[350 + 376.67] = 242.22$ and $\int_{2/3}^1 F(t)\,dt = \frac{1/3}{2}[436.67 + 450] = 147.78$, so that the approximation to $\int_0^1 F(t)\,dt$ is 390. Then using Equation (3.18) we have $i \approx \dfrac{2(40)}{2(390) - 40} = .1081$.

(c) Just before the lump sum contribution at $t = \frac{1}{3}$ the fund value is $F_-(\frac{1}{3}) = 350 + \frac{1}{3}(80 - 60) - \frac{1}{3}(20) + \frac{1}{3}(40) = 363.33$, and it is $F_+(\frac{1}{3}) = 363.33 + 50 = 413.33$ just after that contribution. Just before the lump sum contribution at $t = \frac{2}{3}$ the fund value is $F_-(\frac{2}{3}) = 413.33 + \frac{1}{3}(80 - 60) - \frac{1}{3}(20) + \frac{1}{3}(40) = 426.66$, and we have $F_+(\frac{2}{3}) = 426.66 + 10 = 436.66$ just after that contribution. As in parts (a) and (b) we have $F(1) = 450$. Then

$$\int_0^1 F(t)\,dt = \int_0^{1/3} F(t)\,dt + \int_{1/3}^{2/3} F(t)\,dt + \int_{2/3}^1 F(t)\,dt.$$

Applying the trapezoidal rule to each integral as in part (b), we find $\int_0^1 F(t)\,dt = 118.89 + 140 + 147.78 = 406.66$, so that $i \approx \dfrac{2(40)}{2(406.66) - 40} = .1034$.   □

3.5.3 Time-Weighted and Money-Weighted Rates of Return

When an equation of value is formulated for a transaction in which all components (cashflow amounts and times) are known, but for which the rate of interest is not known, the *internal rate of return* for the transaction (which was defined in Section 3.4) is the annual effective interest rate which makes the equation of value true. The internal rate of return is sometimes referred to as the *money-weighted rate of return* for the transaction. This terminology is more likely to be used in the context of a transaction of one year duration, when measuring the performance of an investment fund. In this case, it is generally understood in practice that simple interest accumulation is used for time intervals of less than one year when the equation of value is being formulated.

An alternative to the money-weighted rate of return for measuring investment fund performance is the *time-weighted rate of return*. This measure of return is usually applied over a one year period in an investment fund, but it is similar in nature to the average annual effective compound rate of return that was illustrated in Example 1.5. The time-weighted rate of return for a fund over a one-year period is found by first identifying the time points at which activity takes place in the fund. These would be time points at which interest (or a capital gain) is credited, new contributions are added, or withdrawals are made. Suppose that these time points are $0 < t_1 < t_2 < \cdots < t_n = 1$. For each successive time interval $[t_{k-1}, t_k]$, a rate of return i_k (not annualized), and corresponding growth factor $G_k = 1 + i_k$ is calculated. The growth factor is found from the following formulation:

$$G_k = 1 + i_k = B_k/A_k,$$

where $A_k =$ fund value at time t_{k-1} after all transactions are completed (interest credited, deposits or withdrawals) and $B_k =$ fund value at time t_k after interest is credited but before any deposits or withdrawals occur.

The growth factors are compounded over the full one-year period to get the annual growth factor $G = G_1 \cdot G_2 \cdots G_n = (1 + i_1)(1 + i_2) \cdots (1 + i_n)$, and the time-weighted rate of interest is then i, where $G = 1 + i$. The following example illustrates the calculation of both money-weighted and time-weighted rates of return on a fund over a one-year period.

EXAMPLE 3.8

A pension fund receives contributions and pays benefits from time to time. The fund value is reported after every transaction and at year end. The details during the year 1991 are as follows:

	Date	Amount
Fund values:	1/1/91	1,000,000
	3/1/91	1,240,000
	9/1/91	1,600,000
	11/1/91	1,080,000
	1/1/92	900,000
Contributions received:	2/28/91	200,000
	8/31/91	200,000
Benefits paid:	10/31/91	500,000
	12/31/91	200,000

Find both the time-weighted and money-weighted rates of return.

SOLUTION

The fund's earned rates for various parts of the year are as follows:

1/1/91 to 2/28/91: $\dfrac{1,240,000 - 200,000 - 1,000,000}{1,000,000} = .04$

3/1/91 to 8/31/91: $\dfrac{1,600,000 - 200,000 - 1,240,000}{1,240,000} = .1290$

9/1/91 to 10/31/91: $\dfrac{1,080,000 + 500,000 - 1,600,000}{1,600,000} = -.0125$

11/1/91 to 12/31/91: $\dfrac{900,000 + 200,000 - 1,080,000}{1,080,000} = .0185$

Then the time-weighted rate of return for 1991 is

$$i_T = \quad (1.04)(1.1290)(.9875)(1.0185) - 1 = .1809.$$

The money-weighted rate of return is found by solving for i in the equation $100,000[10(1+i) + 2(1+\frac{5}{6}i) + 2(1+\frac{1}{3}i) - 5(1+\frac{1}{6}i) - 2] = 900,000$, so that $i_M = .1739$. Note that if the equation of value had been formulated using compound interest for fractions of a year, the equation would be

$100,000[10(1+i) + 2(1+i)^{5/6} + 2(1+i)^{1/3} - 5(1+i)^{1/6} - 2] = 900,000,$
which cannot be solved algebraically. Using numerical approximation methods, the solution to this equation is $i_M = .1740$ to 4 decimal places, very close to the solution of the simple interest version of the equation. □

The reader should be aware that the difference between time-weighted and money-weighted rates of return can be more pronounced than in Example 3.8 (see Exercise 3.5.16). The time-weighted rate of return is not dependent on the actual time points t_1 to t_n, but it is dependent on the successive returns i_1 to i_n in the successive periods. The money-weighted rate of return is not dependent on the successive returns i_1 to i_n but it is dependent on the times and amounts of deposits and withdrawals.

The procedure used in determining the time-weighted rate of return can be adapted to a period of time other than one year. If the fund activity time points are $0 < t_1 < t_2 < \cdots < t_n = U$ (time measured in years), then the growth factors G_k and periodic rates i_k are found in the same way as before. Then the (annual) time-weighted rate of return i_T is found from the equation $(1 + i_T)^U = G_1 \cdot G_2 \cdots G_n$, so that compounding at annual effective rate i_T for U years results in the same accumulation as the successive growth factors G_1 to G_n over the U-year period. The following example illustrates time-weighted and money-weighted rates of return over a period of time longer than one year.

| **EXAMPLE 3.9** |

Smith has made deposits of 10,000 per year to a retirement savings plan on January 1 every year from 1985 to 1990. The annual interest earned by the plan was 13%, 11%, 9%, 9%, and 10% for years 1985 to 1989 respectively. Find the money-weighted rate of return and the time-weighted rate of return for the 5-year period.

| **SOLUTION** |

Using the G_k notation above, we see that $G_1 = 1.13$, $G_2 = 1.11$, $G_3 = 1.09$, $G_4 = 1.09$, and $G_5 = 1.10$, so the time-weighted rate of return is $i_T = [(1.13)(1.11)(1.09)^2(1.10)]^{1/5} - 1 = .1039$. The value just after the final deposit is

$10,000[(1.13)(1.11)(1.09)^2(1.10) + (1.11)(1.09)^2(1.10)$
$$+ (1.09)^2(1.10) + (1.09)(1.10) + (1.10) + 1] = 76,958.37.$$
The money-weighted rate of return is i_M, the solution of $10,000 \cdot s_{\overline{6}|i_M} = 76,958.37$. Solving by Newton's method gives $i_M = .0990$. □

As can be seen from Example 3.9, the time-weighted return is similar to the geometric mean of the periodic returns without regard to the amounts actually invested in the fund. If large amounts are invested during a period of lower rates, as in Example 3.9, the internal or money-weighted rate of return will place more emphasis on the lower rates and i_M will tend to be lower than i_T. The two rates i_M and i_T are measuring quite different things. The time-weighted return regards all periods as equal (or of equal importance), whereas the money-weighted return puts more emphasis on periods in which larger amounts are invested. The time-weighted return measures the performance of the underlying investments, while the money-weighted return depends on the amounts invested as well.

3.5.4 The Merchant's Rule and The U.S. Rule

According to the *Merchant's Rule*, all amounts advanced and all loan repayments made are accumulated with simple interest until the settlement date, at which time the aggregate accumulated values of the amounts advanced must be equal to the aggregate accumulated values of the repayments made. Example 3.10 illustrates the Merchant's Rule.

| **EXAMPLE 3.10** |

Smith borrows 2000 on January 17 and makes payments of 800 each on the last day of each month, starting January 31. On March 15, he borrows an additional 2000. He continues the payments of 800 through May 31, and then pays the remainder of the obligation on June 30. What payment must be made on June 30 if the annual interest rate is 13% and the loan is based on the Merchant's Rule? (Assume a non-leap year.)

| SOLUTION |

All loan amounts and payments are accumulated with simple interest to the settlement date of June 30. Let X denote the payment required at that time. Then the equation of value is

$$2000\left[2 + (.13) \cdot \frac{164+107}{365}\right] = 800\left[5 + (.13) \cdot \frac{150+122+91+61+30}{365}\right] + X,$$

which has the solution $X = 63.68$. □

As with most transactions involving simple interest, the Merchant's Rule would not normally be used in transactions whose duration is more than one year.   Another method for calculating loan repayment is the *United States Rule*, also known as the *actuarial method*. According to this method, interest is computed each time a payment is made or an additional loan amount is disbursed.   The interest calculation is based on simple interest from the time the previous payment or additional loan disbursement was made.   The balance on the loan after the current payment is the previous balance, plus interest accrued, minus the current payment (or plus the current addition to the loan).   The following example repeats Example 3.10, solving according to the U.S. Rule.

EXAMPLE 3.11

Solve for X in Example 3.10 assuming the loan calculations are based on the U.S. method.

SOLUTION

The interest and outstanding balance calculations are summarized in the following table.

TABLE 3.5

Date	Accrued Interest	Payment	Outstanding Balance
Jan 17	—	(2000)	2000.00
Jan 31	9.97	800	1209.97
Feb 28	12.07	800	422.04
Mar 15	2.25	(2000)	2424.29
Mar 31	13.82	800	1638.11
Apr 30	17.50	800	855.61
May 31	9.45	800	65.06
Jun 30	.70	65.76	0

The payment required on June 30 is 65.76. A typical calculation made in Table 3.5 is the one for January 31. The amount of accrued interest is $2000(.13)\left(\frac{14}{365}\right) = 9.97$, so the outstanding balance is $2000 + 9.97 - 800 = 1209.97$. The U.S. Rule is essentially amortization in which the interest rate for the fraction of a year from one transaction point to the next is the corresponding fraction of the annually quoted interest rate.   □

3.5.5 Interest Preference Rates for Borrowing and Lending

In Section 3.4 the concept of an individual's interest preference rate was introduced as the rate at which that individual would value future payments. In using such a rate (i_P) for valuation, when a transaction is regarded as taking place in an account with amounts credited and debited from that account, it is implicitly assumed that over the term of the transaction the individual would receive interest credited at rate i_P when the account is in a net surplus position and pay interest at rate i_P when the account is in a net deficit position. In the context of a transaction taking place in an account by means of deposits and withdrawals, it is reasonable to extend the notion of interest preference rates somewhat further by attributing a pair of rates to the individual, one rate at which the account would pay interest when in a surplus position (i_S), and another rate at which the account would charge interest when in a deficit position (i_D). In this framework it would be possible to compare two transactions by comparing the amount (net profit) in the account at the end of each transaction.

EXAMPLE 3.12

A line of credit loan of 10,000 is to be used for investment purposes. There are two investment alternatives. The first will provide payments of 3000 each year for 10 years starting one year from now. The second will provide payments of 8000 two years and five years from now, and 7000 seven years and ten years from now. The investor plans to deposit all proceeds from the investment into the line of credit account. When there is a balance owing in the account, interest is charged at 15% per year, and when there is surplus in the account interest is credited at 9% per year. Find the account balance after 10 years for each investment alternative.

SOLUTION

Investment 1 results in the following sequence of account balances:

$t = 0$: $-10,000$ $t = 1$: $-10,000(1.15) + 3000 = -8500$
$t = 2$: -6775 $t = 3$: -4791.25 $t = 4$: -2509.94
$t = 5$: 113.57 $t = 6$: $113.57(1.09) + 3000 = 3123.79$
$t = 10$: $3123.79(1.09)^4 + 3000 \cdot s_{\overline{4}|.09} = 18,129$

Investment 2 results in the following sequence:

$t = 2$: $-10,000(1.15)^2 + 8000 = -5225$,
$t = 5$: $-5225(1.15)^3 + 8000 = 53.43$
$t = 7$: $53.43(1.09)^2 + 7000 = 7063.48$.
$t = 10$: $7063.48(1.09)^3 + 7000 = 16,147$ □

3.6 NOTES AND REFERENCES

The "double-up option" for loan repayment of Exercise 3.2.25 and the weekly repayment scheme in Exercise 3.2.45 are based on actual loan repayment options of financial institutions. These have been promoted in times of high interest rates because of the significant reduction in repayment time and interest paid. The situation in Exercise 3.2.49 in which a loan is amortized at a rate of interest higher than the lender's rate, with the difference used for an insurance premium or sales commission, is considered in detail in *Mathematics of Compound Interest*, by Butcher and Nesbitt [2].

Several books contain a discussion of conditions relating to the existence and uniqueness of yield rates for financial transactions. Discussions can be found in Butcher and Nesbitt, in *The Theory of Interest*, by Kellison [7], and also in *An Introduction to the Mathematics of Finance*, by McCutcheon and Scott [8]. The notion of interest preference rates introduced in the paper "A New Approach to the Theory of Interest" in *TSA*, Volume 32 (1980) by Promislow provides a fresh and useful alternative to yield rates as a way of comparing investments. An idea similar to that of interest preference rates is discussed in McCutcheon and Scott. Exercise 3.4.2 (c) is the statement of Theorem 3.2.2 given, but not proven, in Section 3.2 of McCutcheon and Scott.

The internal rate of return and discounted cashflow methods of capital budgeting are analyzed in considerable detail in the papers "Mathematical Analysis of Rates of Return under Certainty" and "An Analysis of Criteria for Investment and Financing Decisions under Certainty," by Teicherow, Robichek, and Montalbano, which appeared in *Management Science*, Volumes 11 and 12 (1965). The notation $F_t(k, r)$ is introduced there to denote the future value at time t of a cashflow with k as the project financing rate of interest (the rate charged when the investment is in a deficit or loan outstanding position) and r as the project investment rate (the rate earned when the investment is in a surplus position). This is similar to the pair of interest preference rates discussed in Section 3.5.5.

The paper "Axiomatic Characterization of the Time-weighted Rate of Return," by Gray and Dewar in *Management Science*, Volume 18, No. 2 (1971) argues that the time-weighted rate of return is "the only measure appropriate for measuring the performance of fund managers."

3.7 EXERCISES

Exercises 3.2

3.2.1   In Example 3.1 calculate the payment amounts to a greater degree of accuracy, such as 5 decimal places, and then recalculate the amortization table.

3.2.2   A loan of L is amortized by n level payments of amount K at rate i per period. The retrospective and prospective forms of the outstanding balance just after the tth payment are $L(1 + i)^t - K \cdot s_{\overline{t}|i}$ and $K \cdot a_{\overline{n-t}|i}$. Show that these two expressions are equal. Note that $PR_1 = K - L \cdot i$. Show that $OB_t = L(1+i)^t - K \cdot s_{\overline{t}|i} = L - PR_1 \cdot s_{\overline{t}|i}$ (see Exercise 3.2.4).

3.2.3   For the general loan of amount L that is amortized over n periods by payments $K_1, K_2, \ldots, K_n$ at interest rate i per payment period (see Table 3.1), show that $K_T - I_T = L$.

3.2.4   (a) Suppose that during the course of a loan, two successive periods have the same interest rate $(i_t = i_{t+1} = i)$. Show that $PR_{t+1} = PR_t(1+i) + K_{t+1} - K_t$. It then follows that if $K_{t+1} = K_t$ and $i_t = i_{t+1} = i$, then $PR_{t+1} = PR_t(1 + i)$.
     (b) $OB_t = L - PR_1 - PR_2 - \cdots - PR_t$. Suppose that $K_1 = K_2 = \cdots = K_t = K$ and $i_1 = i_2 = \cdots = i_t = i$. Use part (a) to show that $OB_t = L - PR_1 \cdot s_{\overline{t}|i}$.

3.2.5   A loan at rate $i^{(12)} = .12$ is repaid with 120 monthly payments starting one month after the loan. The amount of the first payment is 600 and each subsequent payment is 5 larger than the previous payment. Find the original amount of the loan. Find PR_1 and use the result of Exercise 3.2.4 to show that $PR_t = PR_1(1.01)^{t-1} + 5 \cdot s_{\overline{t-1}|i}$. Find OB_{60} prospectively, retrospectively, and by verifying that $OB_{60} = L - \sum_{k=1}^{60} PR_k$, using the form of PR_k found earlier in this exercise. Find I_{61}. Find PR_{61} using the formula above and also from $PR_{61} = K_{61} - I_{61}$, and verify that they are equal.

3.2.6 Example 3.1 is modified so that monthly payments are made for 12 years starting one month after the loan. The monthly payment is K for the first 6 years (72 payments) and $2K$ for the last 6 years (72 payments).
   (a) Find K and construct the amortization table for the first year.
   (b) Verify that the result in Exercise 3.2.4 applies here, although the PR amounts are negative during this period.
   (c) Using monthly payment amounts rounded to the nearest penny, find the amount of the final payment required at $t = 144$ to retire the debt.
   (d) Use the retrospective and prospective forms of the OB to find the outstanding balance just after 3 years ($t = 36$), 6 years ($t = 72$), and 9 years ($t = 108$).
   (e) Find the total interest paid over the course of the loan, and in each of the twelve years of the loan separately. Find the amount of principal repaid in each of the twelve years of the loan. Check that the total principal repaid equals the original loan amount.

3.2.7 Show that at quarterly interest rate $j = .02$, the total payments in Example 3.2 (*i.e.*, 310, 305, ... , 255) have present value 3000.

3.2.8 Suppose the loan in Example 3.2 is repaid by 12 level quarterly payments at rate $j = .02$. Find the total amount of interest paid over the course of the loan. This total is larger than the total in Example 3.2. Provide a non-algebraic justification for this by general reasoning.

3.2.9 A loan of amount L is to be repaid by n payments, starting one period after the loan is made, with interest at rate i per period. Two repayment schemes are considered:
   (i) level payments for the lifetime of the loan;
   (ii) each payment consists of principal repaid of $\frac{L}{n}$ plus interest on the previous outstanding balance.
   Find the total interest repaid under each scheme and show algebraically that the interest paid under scheme (i) is larger than that paid under scheme (ii). Show that for each $t = 1, 2, \ldots,$ $n - 1$, OB_t is larger under scheme (i) than under scheme (ii). Verify algebraically that L is the present value at the time of the loan, at rate of interest i per payment period, of all payments made under scheme (ii).

3.2.10 A loan of amount L is amortized according to scheme (ii) in Exercise 3.2.9.

   (a) Show that $K_t = \frac{L}{n} + L \cdot i \cdot \left(\frac{n-t+1}{n} \right)$. Use the result of Exercise 3.2.4 to show that $PR_k = \frac{L}{n}$.

   (b) Use part (a) to show that $\sum_{t=1}^{n} [1 + (n-t+1) \cdot i] \cdot v^t = n$. Give a verbal interpretation of this identity.

   (c) Show that $\sum_{t=1}^{n} [1 + (n-t) \cdot d] \cdot v^{t-1} = n$, and give a verbal interpretation.

3.2.11 A loan of amount L is being amortized by level continuous payment over n interest periods, with interest rate of i per period. The amount of payment per period is $\frac{L}{a_{\overline{n}|i}}$. Find the rate at which principal is being repaid at time t, the rate at which interest is being paid at time t, and OB_t. Find the amount of principal and interest paid in the interval from time t to time $t+1$. Show that $\frac{d^2}{dt^2} OB_t < 0$, so that the OB_t curve is concave downward.

3.2.12 (a) Plot the OB_t functions for Example 3.1 and Example 3.2.
   (b) Plot the OB_t functions for each of the two repayment schemes in Exercise 3.2.9.

3.2.13 (a) A loan of 1000 at interest of $i = .01$ per period is amortized by payments of 100 per period, starting one period after the loan, for as long as necessary, plus a final smaller payment one period after the last regular payment. Solve for the number of regular payments and the final smaller payment by constructing the amortization table (*i.e.*, do calculations from one period to the next until the OB is reduced to zero).

   (b) A deposit of 1000 is made to an account earning interest at rate $i^{(12)} = .12$, with interest credited monthly from the date of the initial deposit. Each month, just after interest is credited, a withdrawal of 100 is made. Find the number of withdrawals that will be made from the account. Set up a schedule showing the amount of interest credited to the account each period, and the balance remaining in the account.

3.2.14 (a) A loan of amount L at interest rate i per period is repaid by $n-1$ level periodic payments of K each, starting one period after the loan is made, followed by a single payment of amount B at time n to completely repay the loan. Show that the principal repaid in the tth payment $(t < n)$ is $K \cdot v^{n-t+1} + (K-B) \cdot v^{n-t} \cdot d$.

(b) Apply the result in part (a) to part (a) of Exercise 3.2.13, after finding the final payment B, to show that $PR_1 = 90$.

3.2.15 Fill in the blanks of the following amortization schedule for a loan with level 5 level payments.

t	OB_t	I_t	PR_t
0	—		
1	706.00	43.10	156.00
2	—	—	—
3	—	—	—
4	—	—	—
5	0	—	—

3.2.16 A 5-year loan made on July 1, 1989 is amortized with 60 level monthly payments starting August 1, 1989. If interest is at $i^{(12)} = .12$, find the date on which the outstanding balance first falls below one-half of the original loan amount.

3.2.17 (a) A 5-year loan is amortized with semiannual payments of 200 each, starting 6 months after the loan is made. If $PR_1 = 156.24$, find $i^{(12)}$.

(b) A loan is repaid by 48 monthly payments of 200 each. The interest paid in the first 12 payments is 983.16 and the principal repaid in the final 12 payments is 2215.86. Find $i^{(12)}$.

3.2.18 A loan of 15,000 at annual effective rate $i = .025$ is repaid by annual payments of 1000 for as long as necessary plus a smaller final payment one year after the last regular payment. The first payment is made one year after the loan. Find the t for which PR_t is most nearly equal to $4I_t$.

3.2.19 A loan is amortized by level payments every February 1, plus a smaller
final payment. The borrower notices that the interest paid in the
February 1, 1989 payment was 103.00, and the interest in the February
1, 1990 payment will be 98.00. The rate of interest on the loan is
$i = .08$.
(a) Find the principal repaid in the 1990 payment.
(b) Find the date and amount of the smaller final payment made one
year after the last regular payment.

3.2.20 Smith has two options to repay a loan at annual effective interest rate
$i > 0$ over an n-year period: (i) n level annual payments starting one
year after the loan, or (ii) $12n$ level monthly payments starting one
month after the loan.
(a) Show that on each annual anniversary of the loan, the outstanding
balance just after payment is made is the same under both options.
(b) Show that the total interest paid under scheme (i) is greater than
under scheme (ii).

3.2.21 A loan of amount L is repaid by 15 annual payments starting one year
after the loan. The first 6 payments are 500 each and the final 9
payments are 1000 each. Interest is at annual effective rate i. Show
that each of the following is a correct expression for PR_6.
(a) $500(2v^{10} - v)$
(b) $500 [1 - i (2a_{\overline{10|}} - v)]$
(c) $(500 - L \cdot i)(1 + i)^5$

3.2.22 A loan is being repaid by $2n$ level payments, starting one year after the
loan. Just after the nth payment the borrower finds that she still owes
$\frac{3}{4}$ of the original amount. What proportion of the next payment is
interest?

3.2.23 A person borrows money at $i^{(12)} = .12$ from Bank A, requiring level
payments starting one month later and continuing for a total of 15
years (180 payments). She is allowed to repay the entire balance
outstanding at any time provided she also pays a penalty of $k\%$ of the
outstanding balance at the time of repayment. At the end of 5 years
(just after the 60th payment) the borrower decides to repay the
remaining balance, and finances the repayment plus penalty with a loan
at $i^{(12)} = .09$ from Bank B. The loan from Bank B requires 10 years
of level monthly payments beginning one month later. Find the largest
value of k that makes her decision to refinance correct.

3.2.24 An amortized loan of 1000 is to be repaid with 24 monthly payments starting one month after the loan. The nominal interest rate convertible monthly is .09 for the first 18 months and .12 for the final 6 months. Construct the amortization table for this loan, and find the amount of principal repaid in the first year (first 12 payments).

3.2.25 On July 1, 1990 Smith will borrow 75,000 at rate $i^{(12)} = .12$. He has three amortization options for repayment with monthly payments starting August 1, 1990.
   (i) A standard 25-year loan with monthly payment K.
   (ii) A "double up" option, with the same monthly payment K as in (i), except that every 6th payment is $2K$. Payments continue in this pattern for as long as necessary plus a final smaller payment one month after the last regular payment.
   (iii) Constant principal of 250 per month for 25 years plus a monthly payment of interest on the previous month's outstanding balance.
   For each option find the total amount of interest paid during the lifetime of the loan, and for part (ii) find when the loan is repaid and the final smaller payment required.

3.2.26 On June 30, 1990 Smith deposits 1,000,000 in an account earning $i^{(12)} = .12$, with interest credited on the last day of each month. She makes withdrawals from the account on last day of each month (just after interest is credited) starting July 31, 1990. The first withdrawal is 2500 and each subsequent withdrawal is 2% larger than the previous one. The increasing withdrawals continue for as long as possible, with a smaller final withdrawal which exhausts the account one month after the last regular increasing withdrawal.
   (a) Find the date and amount of the final smaller withdrawal.
   (b) Find the total of all amounts withdrawn.
   (c) Find the amount of interest credited to the account from the time of the initial deposit until the account is exhausted, and also find the amount of interest credited in specific years (i) 1990, (ii) 1991, and (iii) 2000.

3.2.27 (a) For each of Examples 3.1 and 3.2 find the total present value (at the time of the loan) of the interest payments and principal payments separately.

(b) For a loan of amount L repaid by n level payments, find the total present value of the interest payments and principal payments separately.

3.2.28 A loan at $i = .05$ is to be repaid by n level annual payments of p each starting one year after the loan. The borrower misses the 5th and 6th payments. He is told that if he pays $1.16p$ for each of the remaining payments, the loan will be repaid at the originally scheduled time. Find the number of payments on the original loan. Give a verbal explanation of the equation $s_{\overline{2}|} = .16 \cdot a_{\overline{n-6}|}$ which arises in this situation.

3.2.29 A loan of amount L is repaid by n level periodic payments at rate of interest i per period. Let $I(n)$ denote the amount of interest paid over the course of the loan. Show that $I(n)$ is an increasing function of n.

3.2.30 A loan is being repaid with level payments of K every 6 months. The outstanding balances on three consecutive payment dates are $5190.72, 5084.68$, and 4973.66. Find K.

3.2.31 A loan of amount L is being repaid by n level payments of amount K each at interest rate i per period. If $t + u \le n$, show that $OB_{t+u} = OB_t \cdot (1+i)^u - K \cdot s_{\overline{u}|}$. Formulate a general version of this relationship for a loan repayment scheme with payment amounts $K_1, K_2, \ldots, K_n$.

3.2.32 Find the form of OB_t, I_t, and PR_t for each of the following loans.

(a) $L = (Ia)_{\overline{n}|i}$, with n payments $K_1 = 1$, $K_2 = 2, \ldots, K_n = n$.

(b) $L = (Da)_{\overline{n}|i}$, with n payments $K_1 = n$, $K_2 = n-1, \ldots, K_n = 1$.

3.2.33 A loan of amount L at interest rate i per period has level payments of amount K per period, starting one period after the loan, for as long as necessary plus a final smaller payment one period after the last regular payment. Show that $OB_t = \frac{K}{i} - \left(\frac{K}{i} - L\right)(1+i)^t$.

3.2.34 An estate of 1,000,000, invested at an annual interest rate of 5%, is being shared by A, B, and C. Starting 1 year after the estate is established, A receives 125,000 of principal each year for 5 years, B receives 75,000 of principal each year for 5 years, and C receives the interest each year. Find the present values of the shares of A, B, and C at 5%, and verify that their sum is 1,000,000.

3.2.35 (a) Show that a loan of amount n at interest rate i per period can be repaid by the series of n geometrically increasing payments $K_1 = (1 + i)$, $K_2 = (1 + i)^2, \ldots, K_n = (1 + i)^n$, with the first payment made one period after the loan.
(b) Show that $OB_t = (n - t)(1 + i)^t$.

3.2.36 One of the basic relationships in the n-payment amortization of a loan at rate i is $OB_{t+1} = OB_t(1+i) - K_{t+1}$. This can be rewritten as $OB_t(1+i) - OB_{t+1} = K_{t+1}$. Multiply both sides of the second relationship by v^{t+1}, and then sum both sides from $t = 0$ to $t = n - 1$ to show that the original loan amount L is equal to the present value of the n payments, $K_1, \ldots, K_n$. Show that the retrospective form of the outstanding balance at time h can be obtained by summing from $t = 0$ to $t = h - 1$ and then solving for OB_h, and the prospective form can be found by summing from $t = h$ to $t = n - 1$ and solving for OB_h.

3.2.37 (a) A loan of amount L at interest rate i per period, with equivalent force of interest δ, is repaid by means of continuous payment for n periods, at rate of payment K_t at time t, so that $L = \int_0^n K_s \cdot v^s \, ds$. Formulate prospective and retrospective forms of the outstanding balance at time t and show that $\frac{d}{dt} OB_t = \delta \cdot OB_t - K_t$.
(b) A loan being repaid continuously satisfies the differential equation $\frac{d}{dt} OB_t = \delta \cdot OB_t - X_t$. Multiply both sides by $v^t = e^{-\delta t}$. Use $\frac{d}{dt} v^t \cdot OB_t = v^t \cdot \frac{d}{dt} OB_t - \delta \cdot v^t \cdot OB_t$ to solve the differential equation using the boundary conditions $OB_0 = L$ and $OB_n = 0$.
(c) Find an expression for the amount of principal repaid and the amount of interest paid between times t_0 and t_1 on the loan in part (a).

3.2.38 A loan of 100,000 is to be repaid by monthly payments starting one month after the loan. The borrower can choose a repayment term of 15 or 30 years. For each of these terms find the total interest paid during the loan at interest rate $i^{(12)}$ of (a) .06 and (b) .12. For a loan of amount L repaid with n periodic payments at interest rate i per period, sketch the graph of I_T as a function of n and then sketch the graph as a function of i.

3.2.39 (a) A loan of 10,000 at annual effective rate $i = .08$ is to be repaid with 20 level annual payments of amount K each. At the time of the 5th payment, the borrower makes an additional payment of amount $PR_6 + PR_7 + PR_8$. The regular payments of amount K continue as usual from time 6 onward, for as long as necessary. Show that the loan will be repaid with the 17th payment, as measured from the date of the loan, and show that the amount of interest paid is $I_6 + I_7 + I_8$ less than would have been paid under the original scheme.

(b) Generalize part (a) for a loan of amount L at interest rate i to be repaid by n level payments, where, at the time of the t_0^{th} payment, the borrower makes an additional payment of $PR_{t_0+1} + PR_{t_0+2} + \cdots + PR_{t_0+m}$. Show that the loan is repaid with the $(n-m)^{th}$ payment, and the interest is $I_{t_0+1} + I_{t_0+2} + \cdots + I_{t_0+m}$ less than would have been paid under the original scheme.

3.2.40 (a) A loan of 10,000 at annual effective rate $i = .08$ is to be repaid with 20 level annual payments of amount K each. The borrower is unable to make the 6th, 7th, and 8th payments. The lender allows the payments to be missed on the condition that the loan will still be repaid on time by increasing the 9th through 20th payments to $K + X$. Show that $X = \dfrac{K \cdot s_{\overline{3|}}}{a_{\overline{12|}}}$. Find the difference in the total interest paid between this repayment scheme and the repayment scheme in which no payments are missed.

(b) Generalize the result in part (a) to a loan of amount L at interest rate i to be repaid by n level payments, where the borrower is unable to make the $(t_0 + 1)^{st}$ through $(t_0 + m)^{th}$ payment. The lender allows the payments to be missed on the condition that the loan will still be repaid on time by increasing the $(t_0 + m + 1)^{th}$ through n^{th} payments to $K + Y$. Show that $Y = \dfrac{K \cdot s_{\overline{m}|}}{a_{\overline{n-t_0-m}|}}$, and the extra interest over that paid in the original scheme is $K\left[\dfrac{(n-t_0-m) \cdot s_{\overline{m}|}}{a_{\overline{n-t_0-m}|}} - m\right]$.

3.2.41 A loan of 10,000 is to be repaid by 10 annual payments of 1000 of principal, starting one year after the loan, plus periodic payments of interest on the outstanding balance. Find the total amount of interest paid in each of the following cases.
(a) Annual interest payments at annual effective rate of interest .12550881.
(b) Semiannual interest payments at 6-month effective rate of .0609.
(c) Quarterly interest payments at 3-month effective rate of .03.
Show that at rate $i^{(4)} = .12$ the present values on the loan issue date of the interest payments in each of cases (a), (b) and (c) are equal. Explain why this is so.

3.2.42 A loan of amount L is made at interest rate i per period to be repaid by n periodic payments of amounts $K_1, K_2, \ldots, K_n$. When a payment is made, there is income tax payable at rate $r < 1$ on the interest portion of the payment; thus at the time of the tth payment the lender receives a net payment of $K_t - r \cdot I_t$. Show that the present value of the net after-tax payments received by the lender are equal to L at interest rate $i(1 - r)$.

3.2.43 A loan of amount L at rate i per period calls for payments of interest only (in arrears) for n periods, plus a single repayment of principal of amount L at the end of n periods. Show that the present value at periodic rate i of the interest and principal payments is equal to L.

3.2.44 If $L = \sum_{s=1}^{n} K_s \cdot v_i^s$, show that $OB_t = L - \sum_{s=1}^{t}(K_s - i \cdot L)(1+i)^{t-s}$.

3.2.45 (a) In times of high interest rates, lending institutions may offer some variations in repayment schemes. Suppose a loan of amount L is to be amortized with level monthly payments of K each for 25 years. The lender offers an alternate repayment plan with weekly payments, starting one week after the loan is made. The borrower is offered two choices for the payment: (i) $B_1 = \frac{K}{4}$ and (ii) $B_2 = \frac{12K}{52}$. The weekly payments continue for as long as necessary with an additional final smaller payment. Suppose that $L = 100,000$. The one-week rate j_w is $j_w = (1+i)^{7/365} - 1$, where i is the equivalent annual effective rate. For each of cases (i) and (ii) find the term of repayment and the reduction in interest paid over the course of the loan as compared to the monthly repayment scheme for each of the interest rates $i^{(12)} = .06, .12, .18,$ and $.24$.

(b) In practice, the 52nd week each year is lengthened to end on the anniversary date of the loan, with a one-day (two-day in a leap year) adjustment for interest at the end of the year. Find the addition to the outstanding balance of the loan after one year if a one-day interest adjustment is added after 52 weeks, using a one-day interest rate of $(1+i)^{1/365} - 1$.

3.2.46 Repeat Exercise 3.2.45 using $j_w = (1+i)^{1/52} - 1$.

3.2.47 Smith wishes to sell his house for $200,000$. Jones has $100,000$ available for a down payment, and can take a bank loan with monthly payments at $i^{(12)} = .15$. Smith offers to "take back" the mortgage for $100,000$ with monthly payments at $i^{(12)} = .12$, based on a 25-year amortization period, with a provision that Jones will refinance the outstanding balance of the loan elsewhere after 3 years. Jones accepts Smith's offer. Immediately after the transaction Smith sells the loan to a broker for a price that yields the broker $i^{(12)} = .15$ over the 3-year period. (The broker becomes entitled to the 3 years of monthly payments as well as the outstanding balance.) What is the net amount that Smith receives for the house?

3.2.48 (a) An amortized loan for 10,000 has interest at 8% per year on the first 5000 of outstanding balance, and 10% per year on the *OB* in excess of 5000. Suppose that annual payments are 1500 for as long as necessary. Construct the amortization table for the loan.

(b) Consider a more general amortization of a loan of amount L. The interest rate is i per period on the first L_0 of *OB* and j per period on the *OB* in excess of L_0. Suppose that $L > L_0$ and the periodic payment is level at amount K. Show by mathematical induction on the positive integers that as long as $OB_t > L_0$, the next year's outstanding balance will be

$$OB_{t+1} = L_0(1+i) \cdot s_{\overline{t+1}|j} + L(1+j)^{t+1} - L_0 \cdot \ddot{s}_{\overline{t+1}|j} - K \cdot s_{\overline{t+1}|j}$$

$$= L_0(1+i \cdot s_{\overline{t+1}|j}) + (L-L_0)(1+j)^{t+1} - K \cdot s_{\overline{t+1}|j}.$$

(c) Verify the expression in part (b) by using it in part (a) for $t = 1, 2, \ldots, 7$.

(d) Once *OB* falls below L_0, the remaining amortization is at level interest rate i. If the loan is repaid exactly at time n with level payments of amount K each, and if $t+1$ is the first time that the *OB* falls below L_0, then $OB_{t+1} = K \cdot a_{\overline{n-(t+1)}|i}$. Using part (b) for OB_{t+1} when *OB* first falls below L_0, solve for an expression for K.

(e) The expression for K in part (d) cannot be solved in its present form because the value of t is not known. In other words, it is not known for which t the inequality $OB_t > L_0 > OB_{t+1}$ is satisfied. Use the expression for OB_t and OB_{t+1} in part (b) to translate the inequality $OB_t > L_0 > OB_{t+1}$ into the inequality

$$L_0 \cdot i + \frac{L-L_0}{a_{\overline{t+1}|j}} < K < L_0 \cdot i + \frac{L-L_0}{a_{\overline{t}|j}}.$$

(f) Substitute the expression for K from part (d) into the inequality for K in part (e). In order for the level payment K to repay this loan in exactly n payments, the time $t+1$ at which OB_{t+1} first falls below L_0 must satisfy this inequality.

(g) Using the example of part (a), with $L_0 = 5000$, $L = 5000$, $i = .08$, $j = .10$, and $n = 10$, substitute values of $t = 1$, then $t = 2$, then $t = 3$, etc., until the inequality in (f) is satisfied. (For $t = 1$, the values are $3280.95 < 1504.09 < 5500$ which is false.) When the inequality is satisfied, the corresponding values of t and $t + 1$ (which are $t = 6$ and $t + 1 = 7$) are the ones for which $OB_t > L_0 > OB_{t+1}$. Now that $t + 1$ is known, it can be substituted into the expression for K in part (d) to solve for $K = 1536.64$.

(h) Using the value of K obtained in part (g) construct the amortization table for the loan.

3.2.49 A loan of 100,000 at annual effective rate 12% is to be repaid by level annual payments for 10 years. Part of each payment is an insurance premium to insure the loan against default due to the death of the borrower. In each payment the amount of the insurance premium is 2% of the previous year's outstanding balance, so the net amount of interest paid to the lender is 10% of the previous year's outstanding balance. The principal repaid in each payment is the same as in an ordinary amortization at 12%. Construct a table showing the net amount of interest and principal received in each payment, and show that the present value at $i = .10$ of the principal plus net interest payments is 100,000.

Exercises 3.3

3.3.1 (a) For Example 3.3 construct a table showing, for each t from 1 to 10, the accumulated amount in the sinking fund, the "outstanding balance" just after the sinking fund deposit, the amount of "principal repaid," and the "net amount of interest" paid.

(b) Suppose that a loan is being repaid by the sinking fund method with n level periodic deposits into a sinking fund earning interest at rate j per period. Show that for each t from 1 to n the values of OB_t and PR_t are the same as the corresponding values in an n-period level payment amortization at rate j per period. Show that if the lender's interest rate i is equal to the sinking fund rate j, then for each t the values of I_t are the same as the corresponding values in an n-period level payment amortization at rate $i = j$.

3.3.2   (a) The borrower's annual outlay in part (a) of Example 3.3 is 16,902.95. Suppose that an investor wishes to purchase a 10-payment annuity of 16,902.95, starting one year after the purchase date, and is willing to pay a price that will yield 10% per year on his investment while allowing him to recover his principal (purchase price) in a sinking fund earning 8% per year. Find the purchase price the investor will pay.

     (b) On a loan of amount L the lender receives interest only at rate i per period and a lump-sum principal repayment of amount L at the end of n periods. The borrower plans to accumulate the lump-sum payment by means of n level deposits into a sinking fund earning interest at rate j. An investor considers purchasing the right to receive the annuity formed by the series of total annual outlays (interest plus sinking fund deposit) by the borrower for the n periods. The investor will pay a price P so that he can receive a return of i per period (same as lender's rate) on his investment, while recovering his initial investment in a sinking fund earning interest at rate j (same rate as the borrower's sinking fund). Show that $P = L$. (In this situation the investor is the lender in the sense that he loans out an amount P, but the investor also plays the role of "borrower" accumulating the initial loan amount in a sinking fund.)

3.3.3   A loan is made so that the lender receives periodic payments of interest only at rate i per period for n periods plus the return of principal in a single lump-sum payment at the end of the n periods. The borrower will accumulate the principal by means of n level periodic deposits to a sinking fund earning periodic interest rate j, such that the accumulated value in the sinking fund is equal to the principal just after the nth level deposit is made. The borrower's total annual outlay is the same as if the loan were being amortized at periodic rate i'. Show that if $j < i$ then $i' > i$, and if $j > i$ then $i' < i$. An approximation to i' in terms of i and j is $i' \approx i + \frac{1}{2}(i-j)$. Compare the exact values for i' found in Example 3.3 to the approximate values found by this formula. Try various combinations of i, j and n, and compare the exact value of i' to that found by the formula.

3.3.4   The lender of a loan of 100,000 receives annual interest payments at 12% per year for 10 years, and, in addition, will receive a lump-sum repayment of the principal along with the 10th interest payment. The borrower will pay the annual interest to the lender and accumulate the 100,000 by annual deposits to an 8% sinking fund. The borrower wishes to schedule the deposits so that his total annual outlay is X for each of the first 5 years, and $2X$ for each of the final 5 years. Find X. Construct a table listing "outstanding balance," "principal repaid" and "net interest paid" for each t from 1 to 10.

3.3.5   (a) With reference to part (a) of Example 3.3, suppose the loan amount of 100,000 was not given, but rather that the borrower's total annual outlay of 16,902.95 was given. Show that the loan amount is 100,000.

       (b) A borrower's total annual outlay is K per period for n periods, including interest at rate i to the lender on a loan of L, and accumulating the principal in a sinking fund at rate j with n level periodic deposits. Solve for L in terms of K, n, i and j.

3.3.6   (a) The lender of amount L receives annual interest payments at 12% per year for 10 years, and, in addition, will receive a lump-sum repayment of the principal L along with the 10th interest payment. The borrower will pay the annual interest to the lender and accumulate the principal amount L by means of annual deposits to an 8% sinking fund. The borrower has scheduled the deposits so that his total annual outlay is 10,000 for each of the first 5 years, and 20,000 for each of the final 5 years. Find L.

       (b) Repeat part (a) under the assumption that the sinking fund earns annual interest at 8% during the first 5 years, and 10% during the second 5 years.

3.3.7   In repaying a loan of amount L, the total periodic outlay made by a borrower at time t is K_t for $t = 1, 2, \ldots, n$. The borrower pays interest on L at rate i, with the rest of the outlay going into a sinking fund earning rate j to accumulate to L at time n. Solve for L in terms of i, j, n, and the K_t's. Let X be the present value of the K_t's at rate j per period. Show that L can be written in the form $\frac{X}{Y}$, and solve for Y. Show that $Y = 1$ if $i = j$.

3.3.8   The borrower of a loan of 10,000 makes monthly interest payments to the lender at rate $i^{(12)} = .15$, and monthly deposits of 100 to a sinking fund earning $i^{(12)} = .09$. When the sinking fund reaches 10,000 the borrower will repay the principal and discharge the loan. Find the total amount paid by the borrower over the course of the loan.

3.3.9   (a) Redo part (a) of Example 3.3 if the agreement is that the lender receives annual interest payments of 5% of the loan, and a lump-sum payment of $100,000(1.05)^{10}$ at the end of 10 years.
   (b) Repeat part (a) of this exercise if the lender receives no annual interest, but only a lump-sum payment of $100,000(1.10)^{10}$ at the end of 10 years.

3.3.10 Smith can repay a loan of 250,000 in one of two ways:
   (i) 30 annual payments based on amortization at $i = .12$;
   (ii) 30 annual interest payments to the lender at rate $i = .10$, along with 30 level annual deposits to a sinking fund earning rate j.
   Find the value of j to make the schemes equivalent.

3.3.11 Show that the borrower's total outlay in Equation (3.7) can be written as $L\left[\dfrac{1}{a_{\overline{n}|i}} + \left(\dfrac{1}{s_{\overline{n}|j}} - \dfrac{1}{s_{\overline{n}|i}}\right)\right]$, and use this to compare to amortization at rate i.

3.3.12 A loan of 100,000 is to be repaid by 20 level annual payments. The lender wishes to earn 12% per year on the full loan amount and will deposit the remainder of the annual payment to a sinking fund earning 8% annually.
   (a) Find the amount of the level annual payment.
   (b) Just after receiving the 10th payment, the lender sells the remaining 10 payments. The purchaser considers two ways of valuing the remaining payments:
   (i) amortization at 10% per year, or
   (ii) earning an annual return of 12% on his investment while recovering his principal in a sinking fund earning 8%.
   Find the amount in the original lender's sinking fund at the time the remainder of the loan is sold, and in each of cases (i) and (ii) find the amount paid by the investor to the original lender.

(c) In each of cases (i) and (ii) of part (b), the original lender
    wants to calculate the average annual return (internal rate of
    return) on his investment for the 10 years. He uses two
    different approaches:
    (α) equating 100,000 to the present value (at rate i_α) of the 10
        annual payments of 12,000 plus the present value of the
        accumulated amount in the sinking fund and the proceeds
        of the sale at time 10;
    (β) equating 100,000 to the present value (at rate i_β) of the 10
        actual payments received plus the present value of the
        proceeds of the sale at time 10.
    For each of cases (i) and (ii), find i_α and i_β.

3.3.13 A loan of 100,000 is repaid on the amortization basis at $i' = .12$
    with 25 level annual payments starting one year after the loan is
    made. The lender wishes to take interest only on the loan at rate i
    per year and deposit the rest of the annual payment in a sinking
    fund earning rate j to accumulate 100,000 at the end of 25 years.
    (a) Solve for i if $j = .08; .12; .16$.
    (b) Show for a general situation of the type in part (a) that i is
        between j and i'.

3.3.14 A business currently produces 9000 units of its product each
    month, which sells for 85 per unit at the end of the month. The
    company considers an alternative process which has a startup cost
    of 1,500,000 and continuing monthly costs (on top of previous
    monthly costs) of 15,816 incurred at the end of each month. The
    alternative process will result in monthly production of 12,000
    units. The company can borrow the 1,500,000 on an interest-only
    loan at monthly rate 1.5%, with the principal repayable after 40
    months. The company can accumulate the principal in a sinking
    fund earning interest at 1% per month over the 40- month period.
    The company can reduce the selling price of the product to X per
    unit and still make a profit that is 30,000 more per month than it
    was before the new process was implemented. Find X.

Exercises 3.4

3.4.1   Repeat part (a) of Example 3.5 by setting up the equation of value at time $t_2 = 2$, and repeat part (b) by setting up the equation of value at time 0.

3.4.2   (a) Suppose there is a k between 0 and n such that either
   (i) $C_0, C_1, \ldots, C_k \leq 0$ and $C_{k+1}, C_{k+2}, \ldots, C_n \geq 0$ (*i.e.*, all the negative net cashflows precede the positive net cashflows), or
   (ii) $C_0, C_1, \ldots, C_k \geq 0$ and $C_{k+1}, C_{k+2}, \ldots, C_n \leq 0$ (*i.e.*, all the positive net cashflows precede the negative net cashflows).
   Assuming that $C_0 \neq 0$, show that there is a unique $i > -1$ for which $\sum_{s=0}^{n} C_s \cdot v^{t_s} = 0$. (Hint: show that the function

$$\sum_{s=0}^{k} C_s \cdot (1+i)^{t_k - t_s} + \sum_{k+1}^{n} C_s \cdot (1+i)^{t_k - t_s} \text{ is monotonic, either in-}$$

   creasing for all i or decreasing for all i, and check the limits as $i \to \infty$ and $i \to -1$.)
   (b) For each $t = 1, 2, \ldots, n$, define G_t to be $G_t = G_{t-1}(1+i) + C_t$, where $G_0 = C_0$. Show that $G_n = 0$ is the equation of value at time n for the sequence of net cashflows. Suppose that (i) there is at least one solution $i > -1$ for which $\sum_{s=0}^{n} C_s \cdot v^{t_s} = 0$, and (ii) at that interest rate $G_t > 0$ for all $t = 0, 1, \ldots, n-1$. Show that the solution for i is unique. (Hint: if $i' > i''$ are both solutions then $G'_n = 0 = G''_n$ for both i' and i', but $G'_t > G''_t$ for $t = 1, 2, \ldots, n$, which is a contradiction.)
   (c) Let $C_0, C_1, \ldots, C_n$ be an arbitrary sequence of net cashflows, and let $F_0 = C_0$, $F_1 = C_0 + C_1$, $F_2 = C_0 + C_1 + C_2$, ..., $F_t = C_0 + C_1 + \cdots + C_t$, ..., $F_n = C_0 + C_1 + \cdots + C_n$, so that F_t is the cumulative total net cashflow at the tth cashflow point. Suppose that both F_0 and F_n are non-zero, and that the sequence $\{F_0, F_1, \ldots, F_n\}$ has exactly one change of sign. Then there is a unique $i > 0$ for which $\sum_{s=0}^{n} C_s \cdot v^{t_s} = 0$, although there may be one or more negative roots.
   (d) Show that none of the transactions in Example 3.5 satisfy the conditions in parts (a), (b) or (c) above.

3.4.3   Show that for any $i > -1$, for the transactions in Example 3.5 we have $P_i(C_a) < P_i(C_b) < P_i(C_c) < P_i(C_d)$.

3.4.4   Smith buys an investment property for 900,000 by making a down payment of 150,000 and taking a loan for 750,000. Starting one month after the loan is made Smith must make monthly loan payments, but he also receives monthly rental payments on the property such that his net outlay per month is 1200, which is set for 2 years. In addition there are taxes of 10,000 payable 6 months after the loan is made and annually thereafter as long as Smith owns the property. Two years after the original purchase date Smith sells the property for $Y \geq 741{,}200$, out of which he must pay the balance of 741,200 on the loan.
   (a)   Show that part (a) of Exercise 3.4.2 guarantees a unique yield rate on the 2-year transaction.
   (b)   Use part (c) of Exercise 3.4.2 to find the minimum value of Y that guarantees a unique positive rate of return over the two year period.

3.4.5   Repeat Example 3.4 removing all commission expenses on the purchase and sale of shares.

3.4.6   Suppose $Y = 1{,}000{,}000$ in Exercise 3.4.4. Apply various approximation methods to find the yield rate in the form $i^{(12)}$.

3.4.7   An investment company offers a 15-year "double your money" savings plan, which requires a deposit of 10,000 at the start of each year for 15 years. At the end of 15 years each participant receives 300,000. If a participant opts out of the plan, he gets back his deposits accumulated at 4%. The company's experience shows that of 100 new participants, the numbers that opt out each year are 5 in the 1st year, 4 each in the 2nd and 3rd years, 3 each in the 4th and 5th years, 2 each in the 6th to 8th years, 1 each in the 9th to 15th years. Those that opt out are paid their accumulated deposits up to the *beginning* of the year in which they opt out. The deposits received by the company can be reinvested at annual effective rate i.
   (a)   Assuming 100 initial participants, find the company's net profit at the end of 15 years, after all plans have been settled, as a function of i, and show that it is an increasing function of i.
   (b)   What value of i gives no net profit to the company?

3.4.8 Apply part (a) of Exercise 3.4.2 to conclude that the company's net profit in Exercise 3.4.7 is positive if $i > i_0$ and negative if $i < i_0$.

3.4.9 Part (a) (ii) of Exercise 3.4.2 is solved by showing that the function
$$g(i) = \sum_{s=0}^{k} C_s \cdot (1+i)^{t_k - t_s} + \sum_{k+1}^{n} C_s \cdot (1+i)^{t_k - t_s} \text{ is monotonic.}$$ This does not necessarily imply that the function $h(i) = v^{t_k} \cdot g(i)$ is also monotonic, where $h(i)$ is the left side of the equation of value for the transaction at time 0. Suppose that $C_0 = -1$, $C_1 = -1$, $C_2 = 2$ and $C_3 = 2$.
(a) Show that $g(i)$ is a decreasing function of i.
(b) Find the value of i_0 for which the function $h(i)$ decreases for $0 < i < i_0$ and increases for $i > i_0$.

3.4.10 Transactions A and B are to be compared. Transaction A has net cashflows of $C_0^A = -5$, $C_1^A = 3.72$, $C_2^A = 0$, $C_3^A = 4$ and Transaction B has net cashflows $C_0^B = -5$, $C_1^B = 3$, $C_2^B = 1.7$, $C_3^B = 3$. Find the yield rate for each transaction to at least 6 decimal places. Show that Transaction A is preferable to B at interest preference rates less than 11.11% and at interest preference rates greater than 25%, and Transaction B is preferable at interest preference rates between 11.11% and 25%.

3.4.11 (a) A transaction has net cashflows of $C_0, C_1, C_2, \ldots, C_n$, and i_0 is a yield rate for this transaction (i.e., $\sum_{s=0}^{n} C_s \cdot v^{t_s} = 0$). Suppose now that the cashflows are "indexed to inflation" at periodic rate r, so that the transaction is modified to $C_0' = C_0$, $C_1' = C_1(1 + r)$, $C_2' = C_2(1 + r)^2$, \ldots, $C_n' = C_n(1 + r)^n$. Show that $i_0' = (1+r) \cdot i_0 + r$ is a yield rate for the new transaction.
(b) Smith can borrow 10,000 at $i = 12\%$, and repay the loan with 15 annual payments beginning one year after the loan is made. He will invest the 10,000 in equipment that will generate revenue at the end of each year for 15 years. He expects revenue of 1200 after one year, and he expects subsequent revenue to increase by an inflationary factor of $1 + r$ per year thereafter. He will apply the full amount of his annual revenue as an annual loan payment, until the loan is repaid. Find the smallest value of r that will allow repayment of the loan in 15 years.

3.4.12 When net cashflow occurs continuously, say at rate $\bar{C}(t)$ at time t, then the equation of value for a yield rate (force of interest) δ for the transaction over the period from 0 to n is

$$\int_0^n \bar{C}(t) \cdot e^{-\delta t} dt = 0.$$

If the transaction also has discrete net cashflow of amounts $C_0, C_1, \ldots, C_n$ at times $0, 1, \ldots, n$ then the overall equation of value for yield rate δ is

$$\sum_{s=0}^n C_s \cdot e^{-\delta \cdot t_s} + \int_0^n \bar{C}(t) \cdot e^{-\delta t} dt = 0.$$

(a) Suppose a company is marketing a new product. The production and marketing process involves a startup cost of 1,000,000 and continuing cost of 200,000 per year for 5 years, paid continuously. It is forecast that revenue from the product will begin one year after startup, and will continue until the end of the original 5-year production process. Revenue (which will be received continuously) is estimated to start at a rate of 500,000 per year and increase linearly (and continuously) over a two-year period to a rate of 1,000,000 per year at the end of the 3rd year, and then decrease to a rate of 200,000 per year at the end of the 5th year. Solve for the yield rate δ earned by the company over the 5-year period.

(b) Suppose that the revenue starts (after 1 year) at a rate of 400,000 per year, and increases continuously and exponentially at rate r per year, so that the rate of revenue at time t is $400,000 \cdot e^{r(t-1)}$, where t measures time in years since the start of the production process. Find the value of r necessary for this to be a "break-even" transaction, in which the yield rate is $\delta = 0$.

3.4.13 A loan of 100,000 is to be repaid by the sinking fund method over a 25-year period. The lender receives annual interest payments at rate 10% per year, and the borrower accumulates the principal by means of annual deposits in a sinking fund earning annual interest at rate 6%. After the 10th deposit to the sinking fund, the rate is increased to 8%.

(a) At the time the loan is issued, the borrower is not aware of the future interest rate change in the fund, and decides to make level annual deposits (starting one year after the loan) under the assumption that the interest rate will stay at 6% for the full 25 years. When the rate change is announced after 10 years, the borrower changes the level of future deposits so that the accumulated value will be 100,000 at the time of the 25th deposit. Find the borrower's yield rate on this transaction.

(b) Suppose that the rate change after 10 years is known by the borrower on the issue date of the loan, and he calculates a level deposit which will accumulate to 100,000 based on the 25-year schedule of interest rates. Find the borrower's yield rate in this case.

(c) From the viewpoint of the lender, suppose that he accumulates his interest income in a fund earning interest at the same rates as the borrower's sinking fund. Find the lender's yield rate on the transaction.

Exercises 3.5

3.5.1 Solve part (a) of Example 3.6 by setting up the full cashflow sequence and finding the present value. There would be 12 monthly payments of 400 each plus a payment of 10,000 with the 12th payment, followed by 12 monthly payments of 350 each plus a payment of 10,000 with the 12th payment, and so on.

3.5.2 A loan of 15,000 is to be repaid by annual payments of principal starting one year after the loan is made, plus quarterly payments of interest on the outstanding balance at a quarterly rate of 4%. Find the present value of the payments to yield an investor a quarterly rate of 3% if the principal payments are (a) 1000 per year for 15 years; (b) 1000 in the 1st year, 2000 in the 2nd year, ..., 5000 in the 5th year; (c) 5000 in the 1st year, 4000 in the 2nd year, ..., 1000 in the 5th year.

3.5.3 An amortized loan of amount $a_{\overline{n}|i}$ at rate i per period has n periodic payments of 1 each. Show that if the payments on the loan are valued at rate j per period, then the present value of the interest payments on the original loan is

$$a_{\overline{n}|j} - \frac{v_i^n - v_j^n}{j - i} \;=\; \frac{i}{j}\left(a_{\overline{n}|i} - \frac{v_i^n - v_j^n}{j - i}\right).$$

3.5.4 A loan of amount L is being repaid by n annual payments of principal of $\frac{L}{n}$ each, along with annual interest payments on the outstanding balance at rate i per year. An investor wishes to purchase this loan at the time it is issued. The investor pays a price P which provides him a yield of j per year on his investment while accumulating his initial investment in a sinking fund earning annual rate h. Show that P can be expressed in the form $\frac{Y}{X}$, where Y is the present value on the issue date of all loan (principal and interest) payments valued at rate h.

3.5.5 A home builder offers homebuyers a financing scheme whereby the buyer makes a down payment of 10% of the price at the time of purchase. At the end of each year for 5 years the buyer makes principal payments of 2% of the original purchase price, as well as monthly payments of interest on the outstanding balance at a monthly rate of $\frac{1}{2}$%. Just after the fifth annual principal payment, the full outstanding balance is due (the homebuyer will negotiate with a bank for a loan of this amount). The cost of the home to the builder is 200,000, and the builder will be selling the buyer's 5-year loan to an investor who values the loan at $i^{(12)} = .15$. What should the builder set as the purchase price of the house so as to realize a net profit of 40,000 after the sale of the loan to the investor?

3.5.6 A loan of 100,000 calls for 10 annual principal payments of 10,000 each plus quarterly interest payments on the outstanding balance at a 3-month interest rate of $2\frac{1}{2}$%. Two investors are considering the purchase of this loan on the issue date. Investor A values payments on an annual effective rate of 12%, and Investor B values payments on a monthly effective rate of 1%. Find the value of this loan to each investor.

3.5.7 (Alternative derivation of Makeham's Formula) A loan of amount L is repaid by a series of principal payments along with interest on the outstanding balance at the end of each period. If the rate of interest is i per period and the loan is valued on the issue date at a rate of j per period, denote the present value on the issue date by $A_j(i)$. Let K_j denote the present value at rate j of the principal payments. Then $A_j(i) - K_j$ is the present value (at rate j) of the interest payments. Show that (i) $\dfrac{A_j(i) - K_j}{A_j(i') - K_j} = \dfrac{i}{i'}$, and (ii) $A_j(j) = L$. Use (i) and (ii) to show that $A_j(i) = K_j + \dfrac{i}{j}(L - K_j)$.

3.5.8 A loan of 500,000 is to be repaid by 25 annual principal payments of 20,000 each, starting one year after the loan, along with quarterly interest payments on the outstanding balance at a nominal annual rate of $i^{(4)} = .10$. An investor purchases the loan just after issue. Find the nominal annual yield convertible quarterly realized by the investor if the purchase price is (a) 450,000, (b) 500,000, or (c) 550,000.

3.5.9 Using Equation (3.13), show that $A < L$ is equivalent to $j > i$, $A = L$ is equivalent to $j = i$, and $A > L$ is equivalent to $j < i$.

3.5.10 Suppose the investor in Exercise 3.5.2 is subject to a tax on all interest payments at the time they are made. Find the net present value to the investor who is subject to a tax rate of (a) 25%, (b) 40%, or (c) 60%.

3.5.11 A loan amortized at monthly effective interest rate 1% calls for monthly payments of 1000 for 25 years. Five years after the loan is issued an investor wishes to purchase the remaining 20 years of payments. The investor wishes to earn a monthly interest rate of $1\frac{1}{4}\%$. Find the amount paid by the investor if (a) he is not subject to tax on the interest portion of the payments received, and (b) he is subject to 50% tax on the interest portion (in the original amortization) of payments received ((b) can be done by finding the present value of principal payments (of the original amortization) and subtracting this from $1000 \cdot a_{\overline{240}|.0125}$ to get the present value of the full interest payments; one-half of this is then the present value of the after-tax interest payments.

3.5.12 A large pension fund has a value of 500,000,000 at the start of the
year ($t = 0$). During the year the fund receives contributions of
100,000,000, pays out benefits of 40,000,000 and has interest
income of 60,000,000. Estimate the yield rate on the fund for each
of the following circumstances:
(a) Contributions, benefits and interest are uniformly spread
throughout the year.
(b) Benefits and interest are uniformly spread throughout the year,
and the contributions are made in one lump- sum at time
(i) $t = 0$, (ii) $t = \frac{1}{4}$, (iii) $t = \frac{1}{2}$, (iv) $t = \frac{3}{4}$, or (v) $t = 1$.

3.5.13 Suppose a fund receives new money of amount N in two equal
installments, one at the beginning of the year and one at the end of
the year. Show that Equation (3.17) is an exact measure of i for
the year.

3.5.14 Recall from Chapter 1 that at force of interest δ_t, the amount of
interest earned from time t_1 to time t_2 on a fund whose amount is
$F(t)$ at time t is $I = \int_{t_1}^{t_2} F(t) \cdot \delta_t \, dt$. Show that the average force of
interest   earned   over   that   time   period   is   then
$\delta = \frac{\int_{t_1}^{t_2} F(t) \cdot \delta_t \, dt}{\int_{t_1}^{t_2} F(t) \, dt} = \frac{I}{\int_{t_1}^{t_2} F(t) \, dt}$. Suppose the time from t_1 to t_2 is
one year. The equivalent annual effective i is $i = e^\delta - 1$. Show
that for "small" values of δ, i is approximately equal to $\dfrac{\delta}{1 - \frac{\delta}{2}}$
and use this to get an approximation for i in terms of I and
$\int_{t_1}^{t_2} F(t) \, dt$. Show that using the trapezoidal rule to approximate
$\int_{t_1}^{t_2} F(t) \, dt$ results in Equation (3.17). Find an alternative
approximation to i by using Simpson's Rule for the approximate
integration of $\int_{t_1}^{t_2} F(t) \, dt$ (see Appendix A).

3.5.15 On its original issue date a mutual fund had a unit value of 10.000.
The subsequent year-end unit values for the next 5 years are
11.710, 12.694, 14.661, 14.148 and 16.836. Three investors in
the mutual fund have made annual purchases of units in the fund
for 5 years, starting on the issue date. The dollar amounts of the
purchases were as follows:

Time	0	1	2	3	4
Investor A	1000	2000	3000	4000	5000
Investor B	3000	3000	3000	3000	3000
Investor C	5000	4000	3000	2000	1000

Find the annual time-weighted rate of return earned by the fund over the 5 years, and find the annual money-weighted rates of return for each of the three investors.

3.5.16 Fund X has unit values which are 1.0 on January 1, 1991, .8 on July 1, 1991 and 1.0 on January 1, 1992. A fund manager receives contributions of 100,000 on January 1, 1991 and 100,000 on July 1, 1991 and immediately uses the entire contributions to purchase units in Fund X. Find the time-weighted and money-weighted rates of return for 1991 .

3.5.17 The details regarding fund value, contributions and withdrawals from a fund are as follows:

	Date	Amount
Fund values:	1/1/91	1,000,000
	7/1/91	1,310,000
	1/1/92	1,265,000
	7/1/92	1,540,000
	1/1/93	1,420,000
Contributions received:	6/30/91	250,000
	6/30/92	250,000
Benefits paid:	12/31/91	150,000
	12/31/92	150,000

Find the annual effective time-weighted rate of return for the two-year period of 1991 and 1992.

3.5.18 (a) A loan of 10,000 at rate $i^{(12)} = .15$ is to be repaid by 12 level monthly payments of 902.58. The lender understands that in the actual amortization table for the loan, the amounts of interest in successive payments get smaller, and the amounts of principal repaid get larger. The lender approximates the entries in the actual amortization table by assuming that the amounts of interest paid in successive payments decrease linearly in such a way that $I_1 - I_2 = I_2 - I_3 = \cdots = I_{11} - I_{12} = I_{12} - 0$. The amount of principal repaid in each payment is 902.58 minus the interest payment. Construct this approximation to the amortization table. Show that the approximate value of I_t on this basis is $\frac{13 - t}{78} \cdot I_T$, where $I_T = 831$ is the total interest paid over the course of the loan.

(b) The approximation described in (a) is called the "Rule of 78," and can be applied to any loan with level payments. Suppose a loan of amount L is repaid by n level payments of amount K each. Suppose that as an approximation to the actual amortization table, the I_t entries are assumed to decrease linearly such that $I_1 - I_2 = I_2 - I_3 = \cdots = I_{n-1} - I_n = I_n - 0$. Show that the value of I_t based on this approximation is $I_t = \frac{2(n - t + 1)}{n(n + 1)} \cdot I_T$. Construct the amortization table based on the approximate interest payments and obtain the approximation

$$\sum_{t=0}^{n-1} OB_t \approx \frac{n+1}{2} \cdot L + \frac{n-1}{6} \cdot I_T.$$

In the comments following Table 3.1 it is pointed out that for an amortization at rate i per period with n equally spaced payments

$$I_T = i \cdot \sum_{t=0}^{n-1} OB_t, \quad \text{or, equivalently,} \quad i = \frac{I_T}{\sum_{t=0}^{n-1} OB_t}. \quad \text{Use the}$$

approximation to $\sum_{t=0}^{n-1} OB_t$ to get an approximate value for the interest rate in part (a). (The reason for the name "Rule of 78" is clear in part (a) since 78 appears in the denominator of the interest payments; in general with an n-payment loan, the denominator is $1 + 2 + \cdots + n = \frac{n(n + 1)}{2}$. This approximate method of setting up the amortization table is also called the "Direct Ratio Method.")

3.5.19 Smith borrows 1000 on January 1 (of a non-leap year) at $i = .10$, and repays the loan with 5 equal payments of amount X each. The payments are made every 73 days, so that the final payment is made exactly one year after the loan was made. Calculate X based on the Merchant's Rule, and then based on the U.S. Method.

3.5.20 Suppose that a loan of amount L is made at time 0, and payments of $A_1, A_2, \ldots, A_{n-1}$ are made at times $0 < t_1 < t_2 < \cdots t_{n-1}$. Show that if $i > 0$, $A_k > 0$ for each k, and $\sum_{k=1}^{n-1} A_k < L$, then the amount A_n, required to repay the loan at time t_n, $t_n > t_{n-1}$, is larger under the U.S. Method than it is under the Merchant's Rule.

3.5.21 A corporation wishes to issue a zero-coupon bond due in 20 years with maturity value of 1,000,000 and compound annual yield rate of 9%. The corporation wants to charge the interest expense on an annualized basis and plans to use a straight-line approach (*i.e.*, the difference between the proceeds of the bond and the maturity value is divided into 20 equal parts, one part to be charged as an expense in each of the 20 years). The tax authorities insist that the "actuarial method" is the appropriate way of determining the annual interest charge (*i.e.*, the interest charge for year k is the amount of compound interest accrued on the debt in year k). For each of the first year and the 20th year, what is the interest charge under each of the two methods? In what year would the interest charges under the two methods be most nearly equal?

3.5.22 Smith has a *line of credit* with a bank, allowing loans up to a certain limit without requiring approval. Interest on the outstanding balance on the loan is based on an annual simple interest rate of 15%. Interest is charged to the account on the last day of each month, as well as the day on which the line of credit is completely repaid (the month-end balance is the accrued outstanding balance from the start of the month minus accrued payments). On January 15 Smith borrows 1000 from his line of credit, and borrows an additional 500 on March 1. Smith pays 250 on the 15th of March, April, May, June and July. What payment is required to repay the line of credit on August 15. Suppose that instead of charging interest on the last day of each month, the line of credit bases calculations on (a) the U.S. Rule, or (b) the Merchant's Rule. In each of cases (a) and (b) find the payment required on August 15.

3.5.23   Suppose the first investment in Example 3.11 pays X per year. Find the value of X for which the balance at the end of 10 years is the same as it is for the second investment.

3.5.24   Suppose Example 3.1 stated that the loan was to be repaid according to the U.S. Rule by monthly payments, starting one month after the loan, with $K_1 = K_2 = K_3 = 115.61$ and $K_4 = K_5 = 231.22$. Show that the payment K_6 required to retire the loan at time 6 is the same as in part (b). (The U.S. Rule is the same as the amortization method in that at each time a payment is made the outstanding balance is accumulated with interest from the time of the previous payment and the current payment is then subtracted.)

================================= CHAPTER 4

BONDS : PRICES AND YIELDS

4.1   INTRODUCTION

It is often necessary for corporations and governments to raise funds. Corporations have two main ways of raising funds; one is to issue *equity* by means of common (or preferred) shares of ownership which usually give the shareholder a vote in deciding the way in which the corporation is managed. The other is to issue *debt*, which is to take out a loan requiring interest payments and repayment of principal. For borrowing in the short term, the corporation might obtain a *demand loan* or a *line of credit*. For longer term borrowing it is possible to take out a loan that is amortized in the standard way, but this would usually be done only for loans of a relatively small amount. To borrow large amounts over a longer term a corporation can issue *bonds*, also called *debentures*, which are debts that call for interest payments (at a specified rate) for a stated term and the return of the principal at the end of the term. It will often be the case that the amount borrowed is too large for a single lender or investor, and the bond is divided into smaller units to allow a variety of investors to participate in the issue.

Governments generally have the option of raising funds via taxes. Governments also raise funds by borrowing, in the short term by issuing Treasury bills (see Example 1.14), and in the longer term by issuing bonds. Government *savings bonds* might not have a fixed maturity date, and can usually be redeemed at any time for the return of principal and any accrued interest.

The initial purchaser of a bond might not retain ownership for the full term to maturity, but might sell the bond to another party. There is a very active and liquid bond secondary market in which bonds are bought and sold.   Bonds are crucial components in government and corporate financing.   Through the bond market bonds also provide an important investment vehicle, and can make up large parts of pension funds and mutual funds. Bonds issued by corporations are usually backed by various corporate assets as collateral, although in recent years (the 1980's) a type of corporate bonds called *junk bonds* has been used with little or no collateral, primarily to raise funds to finance the takeover of another company.   Bonds issued by financially and politically stable governments are virtually risk-free and are a safe investment option.   There are agencies that rate the risk of default on interest and principal payment associated with a bond issuer. The purchaser of a bond will take into account the level of risk associated with the bond when determining its value.

4.2   DETERMINATION OF BOND PRICES

A bond is a contract between the issuer and the purchaser that specifies a schedule of payments that will be made by the issuer to the bondholder (purchaser).   The most common type of bond issue is the *straight-term bond*, for which the schedule of payments is similar to that of a loan with regular payments of interest plus a single payment of principal at the end of the term of the loan.   A bond specifies a *face amount* and a *bond interest rate*, also called the **coupon rate**, which are analogous to the principal amount of a loan and rate at which interest is paid.   The bond also specifies the *maturity date* or **term to maturity** during which the *coupons* (bond interest payments) are to be paid, and the *redemption amount* that is to be repaid on the maturity date.   It is generally the case that the face amount and the redemption amount on a bond are the same, and this will be assumed to be the case throughout this chapter unless specified otherwise.

For bonds issued in Canada and the United States, the coupons are nearly always paid semiannually, with the coupon rate quoted on a nominal annual basis.   (Some bonds issued in some European countries have coupons payable annually.)   Unless specified otherwise, when coupon rates are quoted in this chapter they will refer to annual rates payable semiannually, with the first coupon payable one period after the bond is issued, and with coupons payable up to and including the time at which the redemption amount is paid.   Note that bonds may be issued on a non-coupon date, in which case the first coupon is paid less than one coupon period after issue.

The following notation will be used to represent the various parameters associated with a bond:

F - The face amount (also called the *par value*) of the bond

r - the coupon rate per coupon period (six months unless otherwise specified)

C - the redemption amount on the bond (equal to F unless otherwise noted)

n - the number of coupon periods until maturity

The coupons are each of amount Fr, and the sequence of payments associated with the bond is shown in the following time diagram.

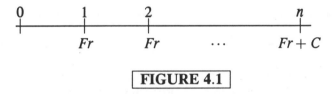

FIGURE 4.1

When an investor purchases a bond, what is being purchased is the cashflow just described. The purchase price of the bond is determined as the present value, on the purchase date, of that cashflow. There will be a number of factors that influence the rate of interest used by the purchaser to find the price of the bond. We will not explore here the relationship between economic factors and interest rates on investments. We will simply accept that "market forces" determine the interest rate used to value the bond, or in other words, to determine the purchase price. This valuation rate of interest is called the *yield rate* on the bond or the *yield to maturity*, since the rate is used to value all payments up to and including the redemption amount. Since coupons are payable semiannually, yield rates are quoted on a nominal annual basis convertible semiannually. We will use j to denote the six-month yield rate.

4.2.1 Bond Prices on Coupon Dates

It is now a straightforward matter to formulate the price of a bond on its issue date (or on any later coupon date) using the notation defined above. The price P is the present value at rate j per coupon period of the redemption amount $C = F$, plus the present value of an annuity of n coupon payments of amount Fr each, so that

$$P \; = \; C \cdot v_j^n + Fr \cdot a_{\overline{n}|j} \; = \; F \cdot v_j^n + Fr \cdot a_{\overline{n}|j}. \qquad (4.1)$$

Using the identity $v_j^n = 1 - j \cdot a_{\overline{n}|j}$, Equation (4.1) can be reformulated as

$$P \; = \; C + (Fr - Cj) \cdot a_{\overline{n}|j} \; = \; F + F(r - j) \cdot a_{\overline{n}|j}. \qquad (4.2)$$

Alternatively, writing $a_{\overline{n}|j}$ in Equation (4.1) as $a_{\overline{n}|j} = \dfrac{1 - v_j^n}{j}$, and letting the present value of the redemption amount be denoted by $K = F \cdot v_j^n$, Equation (6.1) becomes

$$P \; = \; F \cdot v_j^n + \tfrac{r}{j}(F - F \cdot v_j^n) \; = \; K + \tfrac{r}{j}(F - K). \qquad (4.3)$$

Equation (4.3) is known as *Makeham's Formula*, which is the same as Equation (3.13) with F replacing the loan amount L, and r replacing the interest rate i in Equation (3.13). Note that, as in Equation (3.13), Equation (4.3) requires r and j to be based on the same period (which for bonds is usually six months).

| EXAMPLE 4.1 |

A 10% bond with semiannual coupons has a face amount of 100,000,000 and is issued on June 18, 1990. The bond has a maturity date of June 18, 2010.

(a) Find the price of the bond on its issue date using a nominal annual yield rate $i^{(2)}$ of (i) 5%, (ii) 10%, and (iii) 15%.

(b) Find the price of the remainder of the bond on June 18, 2000, just after the coupon is paid, using the yield rates of part (a).

| SOLUTION |

(a) We have $F = C = 100{,}000{,}000$, $r = .05$, and $n = 40$. Using Equation (4.1), we see that the price of the bond is

$$P \; = \; 100{,}000{,}000 \cdot v_j^{40} + (100{,}000{,}000)(.05)a_{\overline{40}|j}.$$

With (i) $j = .025$, (ii) $j = .05$, and (iii) $j = .075$, the bond prices are (i) $P = 162{,}756{,}938$, (ii) $P = 100{,}000{,}000$, and (iii) $P = 68{,}513{,}978$.

(b) We still have $F = C = 100,000,000$ and $r = .05$, but now $n = 20$ (since there are 10 years, or 20 coupons, remaining on the bond). Using Equation (4.2), we have

$$P = 100,000,000 + 100,000,000(.05 - j)a_{\overline{20}|j}.$$

This results in prices of (i) 138,972,906, (ii) 100,000,000, and (iii) 74,513,772. □

Note that as the yield rate is increased in Example 4.1 the bond price decreases. This is due to the inverse relationship between interest rate and present value; the bond price is the present value of a stream of payments valued at the yield rate.

In the Canadian financial press bond prices are generally quoted as a value per 100 of face amount, to the nearest .001 and yield rates are quoted to the nearest .001% (one-thousandth of a percent). Thus the quoted prices in Example 4.1 would be (i) 162.757, (ii) 100.000, and (iii) 68.514 in part (a), and (i) 138.972, (ii) 100.000, and (iii) 74.514 in part (b). In the U.S. there is a variety of quotation procedures. U.S. government bond prices are quoted to the nearest $\frac{1}{32}$ per 100 of face amount, and yields are quoted to the nearest .01%. For corporate bonds, price quotations are to the nearest $\frac{1}{8}$ per 100 of face amount and *current yields* are quoted. The current yield is the coupon rate divided by the bond's price.

It is not surprising that the bond prices in (i), (ii) and (iii) decrease in both parts (a) and (b) of Example 4.1, since the present value of a series of payments decreases as the valuation rate increases. In looking at the bond price formulation of Equation (4.2) it is clear that the relative sizes of the bond price and face amount are directly related to the relative sizes of the coupon rate and yield rate. We have the relationships

$$P > F \quad \leftrightarrow \quad r > j, \tag{4.4a}$$

$$P = F \quad \leftrightarrow \quad r = j \tag{4.4b}$$

and

$$P < F \quad \leftrightarrow \quad r < j. \tag{4.4c}$$

These relationships are similar to the ones between the loan amount L and the price paid for the loan based on Makeham's Formula in Section 3.6. The terminology associated with these relationships between P and F is as follows.

(a) If $P > F$, the bond is said to be *bought at a premium*.
(b) If $P = F$, the bond is said to be *bought at par*.
(c) If $P < F$, the bond is said to be *bought at a discount*.

Equation (4.2) can be rewritten as $P - F = F(r - j) \, a_{\overline{n}|j}$. Suppose the bond is bought at a premium so that $P > F$. The rewritten version of Equation (4.2) indicates that the amount of premium in the purchase price $(P - F)$ is regarded as a loan (from the buyer to the seller) repaid at rate j by n payments of $F(r - j)$, the excess of coupon over yield.

We can also see from Equation (4.2) that if $r > j$ and the time until maturity is increased, then the bond price P increases, but if $r < j$ then P decreases as n increases. This can be seen another way. If $r > j$ then $P > F$, so that the bondholder will realize a *capital loss* of $P - F$ at time of redemption. Having the capital loss deferred would be of some value to the bondholder, so he would be willing to pay a larger P for such a bond with a later maturity date. The reverse of this argument applies if $r < j$. In any event, the level of bond yield rates would influence a bond issuer in setting the coupon rate and maturity date on a new issue, since both coupon rate and maturity date have an effect on the actual price received for the bond by the issuer.

It was pointed out earlier that it is generally the case that the face and redemption amounts of the bond are the same, so that $F = C$. In the case where they are not equal an additional parameter is defined, called the *modified coupon rate* and denoted by $g = \frac{F \cdot r}{C}$, so that $Cg = Fr$. Exercise 4.2.20 develops alternative formulations for bond prices when $C \neq F$ that are equivalent to Equations (4.1), (4.2) and (4.3). When $C = F$ the bond is said to be *redeemed at par*, when $C > F$ the bond is said to be *redeemed at a premium*, and when $C < F$ the bond is said to be *redeemed at a discount*.

4.2.2 Bond Prices between Coupon Dates

We have thus far considered only the determination of a bond's price on its issue date or at some later coupon date. In practice bonds are traded daily, and we now consider the valuation of a bond at a time between coupon dates. Let us regard the coupon period as the unit of time, and suppose that we wish to find the price P_t of a bond at time t, where $0 \leq t \leq 1$, with t measured from the last coupon payment. The value of the bond is still found as the present value at the yield rate of all future payments (coupons plus redemption). Suppose that there are n coupons remaining on the bond, including the next coupon due. At yield rate j per coupon period, the value P_1 of the bond *just after* the next coupon could be found using one of Equations (4.1), (4.2) or (4.3). Then the value of the bond at time t is the present value of the amount $P_1 + Fr$ due at time 1 (the present value of both the coupon due then and the future coupons and redemption), so that

$$P_t = v_j^{1-t}[P_1 + Fr]. \tag{4.5a}$$

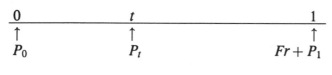

$$\boxed{\textbf{FIGURE 4.2}}$$

Alternatively, if we define P_0 to be the value of the bond just after the last coupon, then (see Exercise 4.2.15) we also have

$$P_t = P_0(1+j)^t. \tag{4.5b}$$

The value P_t given by Equations (4.5a) and (4.5b) is the actual amount of money paid for the bond at time t, and it is called the ***price-plus-accrued*** of the bond.

    In the calculation involved in Equations (4.5a) and (4.5b), the value of t is between 0 and 1 and measures the time since the last coupon was paid as a fraction of a coupon period. Given the coupon dates and the date of time t, the numerical value of t is

$$t = \frac{number\ of\ days\ since\ last\ coupon\ paid}{number\ of\ days\ in\ the\ coupon\ period}. \tag{4.6}$$

The price given by Equations (4.5a) and (4.5b), with t defined by Equation (4.6), is not the price which would be quoted for the bond in a financial newspaper. The price quoted in the financial press is called simply the *price*, and is equal to the price-plus-accrued minus the fraction of the coupon accrued to time t (throughout this section, the terms *price* and *price-plus-accrued* will have the specific meanings given here). This fractional coupon is proportional to the fractional part of the coupon period that has elapsed since the last coupon was paid, so the fractional coupon is $t \cdot Fr$. The price of the bond is then

$$Price_t \; = \; Price\text{-}plus\text{-}accrued_t \; - \; t \cdot Fr \; = \; P_0(1+j)^t \; - \; t \cdot Fr. \quad (4.7)$$

| EXAMPLE 4.2 |

For each of the yield rates (i), (ii), and (iii) in Example 4.1, find both the price-plus-accrued and quoted price on August 1, 2000. Quote the prices (to the nearest .001) per 100 of face amount.

| SOLUTION |

Using the results in part (b) of Example 4.1, we see that on the last coupon date, June 18, 2000, the value of the bond was (i) 138,972,906, (ii) 100,000,000, and (iii) 74,513,772. Using Equation (4.5b), with $t = \frac{44}{183}$, we have prices-plus-accrued of

(i) $138,972,906(1.025)^{44/183} \; = \; 139,800,445$,

(ii) $100,000,000(1.05)^{44/183} \; = \; 101,180,004$, and

(iii) $74,513,772(1.075)^{44/183} \; = \; 75,820,791$.

Per 100 of face amount these prices, to the nearest .001, are (i) 139.800, (ii) 101.180, and (iii) 75.821. The quoted prices are

(i) $139,800,445 \; - \; \frac{44}{183}(.05)(100,000,000) \; = \; 138,598,259$,

(ii) $101,180,004 \; - \; \frac{44}{183}(.05)(100,000,000) \; = \; 99,977,818$, and

(iii) $75,820,791 \; - \; \frac{44}{183}(.05)(100,000,000) \; = \; 74,618,605$.

Per 100 of face we have (i) 138.598, (ii) 99.978, and (iii) 74.618.   □

In reporting the value of assets at a particular time, a bondholder would have to assign a value to the bond at that time. This value is called the *book value* of the bond, and is usually taken as the current price of the bond valued at the original yield rate at which the bond was purchased. For accounting purposes the accrued interest since the last coupon would be considered as a separate item from the book value of the bond.

Figure 4.3 below displays the graphs of the price-plus-accrued and the price of a bond over several consecutive coupon periods. Note that the price is approximately the linear interpolation between two successive coupon dates (see Exercise 4.2.16), and the price-plus-accrued readjusts back to the price on the coupon dates.

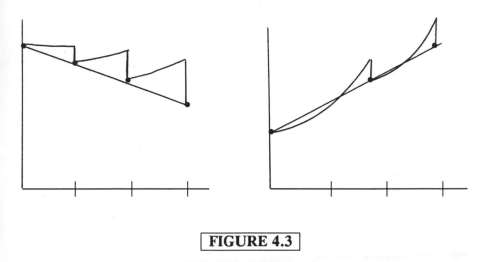

FIGURE 4.3

A bond trader would often be comparing the relative values of different bonds, and would want an equitable basis on which to compare, at a specific point in time, bonds with different calendar coupon dates. The price (see Figure 4.3) provides a smooth progression of bond values from one coupon date to the next, and it is this price that is used by bond traders to compare relative bond values. This can easily be seen if we consider a bond for which $r = j$. We see from Equation (4.2) that if $r = j$ (*i.e.*, the coupon and yield rates are equal), then on a coupon date the price of the bond would be F (*i.e.*, the bond is bought at par). However the price-plus-accrued of the bond grows from $P_0 = F$ at $t = 0$ to $P_0(1 + j)$ just before the coupon is paid at $t = 1$, and just after that coupon is paid the price drops to $P_1 = F$ (see Exercise 4.2.17). For a bond trader comparing two bonds with different coupon dates, but both with $r = j$, it would be convenient to regard both bonds as being *at par*, as they would be just after a coupon is paid. Note that in part (ii) of Example 4.2 with $r = j = .05$, the price is almost exactly the par value. Thus the price has eliminated a "distortion" caused by the accrued coupon included in the price-plus-accrued. With a more exact calculation the price would be exactly equal to the par value when $r = j$ (see Exercise 4.2.18).

The notion, introduced earlier, of a bond bought at a premium, at par, or at a discount just after a coupon is paid was based on comparing the bond price with the face amount. To describe a bond as being bought at a premium, par or discount when bought at a time between coupon dates, the comparison is made between the price and the face amount. It was pointed out that just after a coupon payment a bond is bought at a premium, par or discount according to whether $r > j$, $r = j$, or $r < j$, respectively. This relationship remains valid when comparing the price with the face amount at a time between coupon dates.

4.3   AMORTIZATION OF A BOND

For taxation and other accounting purposes, it may be necessary to determine the amount of interest received and principal returned in a bond coupon or redemption payment. This can be done by viewing the bond as standard amortized loan.

The payments made during the term of a bond can be regarded as loan payments made by the bond issuer (the borrower) to the bondholder (the lender) to repay a loan amount equal to the purchase price of the bond. The bond price is calculated as the present value of those payments (coupons plus redemption amount) at a certain yield rate (the interest rate on the loan), so the transaction can be regarded as the amortization of a loan, assuming the bondholder continues to hold the bond to the end of the term. (If the bond is sold before the end of the term, the new bondholder can regard the remaining payments on the bond as loan payments for a loan equal to the price that he paid at an interest rate equal to his yield rate.)   An amortization schedule for the bond would be constructed algebraically like the general amortization schedule in Table 4.1.

Assuming there are n coupons on the bond, the payment amounts in the schedule will be the coupon amounts Fr until the nth payment, which would be a coupon plus the redemption amount, $Fr + C$. The prospective form of the outstanding balance just after a coupon payment is the present value of all future coupons plus redemption amount, valued at the loan interest rate which is the yield rate on the bond. Thus the outstanding balance is equal to the price of the remainder of the bond valued at the original yield rate. In Section 4.2 the **book value** of the bond at a point in time was defined to be the price of the remainder of the bond, valued at the original yield rate at which the bond was purchased. Thus, just after a coupon payment, the outstanding balance is equal to the bond's book value.

For a bond of face amount F with n coupons at rate r per coupon period, bought to yield j per coupon period, the amortization schedule is given in the following table.

TABLE 4.1

k	Outstanding Balance (Book Value)	Payment	Interest Due	Principal Repaid
0	$P = F[1 + (r-j) \cdot a_{\overline{n}\rvert}]$	—	—	—
1	$F[1 + (r-j) \cdot a_{\overline{n-1}\rvert}]$	Fr	$F[j + (r-j)(1-v_j^n)]$	$F(r-j) \cdot v_j^n$
2	$F[1 + (r-j) \cdot a_{\overline{n-2}\rvert}]$	Fr	$F[j + (r-j)(1-v_j^{n-1})]$	$F(r-j) \cdot v^{n-1}$
⋮	⋮	⋮	⋮	⋮
k	$F[1 + (r-j) \cdot a_{\overline{n-k}\rvert}]$	Fr	$F[j + (r-j)(1-v_j^{n-k+1})]$	$F(r-j) \cdot v^{n-k+1}$
⋮	⋮	⋮	⋮	⋮
$n-1$	$F[1 + (r-j) \cdot a_{\overline{1}\rvert}]$	Fr	$F[j + (r-j)(1-v_j^2)]$	$F(r-j) \cdot v_j^2$
n	0	$Fr + F$	$F[j + (r-j)(1-v_j)]$	$F[1 + (r-j) \cdot v_j]$

Notice that since the coupon payments are level throughout the term of the bond, except for the final payment, the principal repaid column forms a geometric progression with ratio $1 + j$, if $r \neq j$. The following example illustrates the form of a bond amortization.

EXAMPLE 4.3

A 10% bond with face amount 10,000 matures 4 years after issue. Construct the amortization schedule for the bond over its term for nominal annual yield rates of (a) 8%, (b) 10%, and (c) 12%.

SOLUTION

(a) The entries in the amortization schedule are calculated as they were in Table 4.1, where k counts coupon periods. With a nominal yield rate of 8% the purchase price of the bond is 10,673.27. Then $I_1 = (10{,}673.27)(.04) = 426.93$, and so on. The complete schedule is shown in Table 4.2a.

TABLE 4.2a

k	Outstanding balance	Payment	Interest Due	Principal Repaid
0	10,673.27	—	—	—
1	10,600.21	500	426.93	73.07
2	10,524.22	500	424.01	75.99
3	10,445.19	500	420.97	79.03
4	10,363.00	500	417.81	82.19
5	10,277.52	500	414.52	85.48
6	10,188.62	500	411.10	88.90
7	10,096.16	500	407.54	92.46
8	0	10,500	403.85	10,096.15

Note that since $OB_7 = 10,096.16$ and $PR_8 = 10,096.15$ we should have $OB_8 = .01$. Of course $OB_8 = 0$ and the one cent discrepancy is due to rounding. The values of OB_k decrease to the redemption value as k approaches the end of the term. The entry under Principal Repaid is called **the amount for amortization of premium** for that particular period. The amortization of a bond bought at a premium is also referred to as **writing down a bond**.

(b) With a nominal yield rate of 10% the purchase price is 10,000. The schedule is shown in Table 4.2b.

TABLE 4.2b

k	Outstanding balance	Payment	Interest Due	Principal Repaid
0	10,000.00	—	—	—
1	10,000.00	500	500.00	0
2	10,000.00	500	500.00	0
3	10,000.00	500	500.00	0
4	10,000.00	500	500.00	0
5	10,000.00	500	500.00	0
6	10,000.00	500	500.00	0
7	10,000.00	500	500.00	0
8	0	10,500	500.00	10,000

(c) With a nominal yield rate of 12% the purchase price is 9379.02; the schedule is shown in Table 4.2c.

TABLE 4.2c

k	Outstanding balance	Payment	Interest Due	Principal Repaid
0	9379.02	—	—	—
1	9441.76	500	562.74	−62.74
2	9508.27	500	566.51	−66.51
3	9578.77	500	570.50	−70.50
4	9653.50	500	574.73	−74.73
5	9732.71	500	579.21	−79.21
6	9816.67	500	583.96	−83.96
7	9905.67	500	589.00	−89.00
8	0	10,500	594.34	9905.66

Round-off error again gives a value of $OB_8 = .01$, when it should be zero. Note that OB_k *increases* to the redemption amount as k approaches the end of the term. The negative of the principal repaid entry is called the *amount for accumulation of discount* when a bond is bought at a discount. This amortization is also referred to as *writing up a bond*. ☐

4.4 DETERMINATION OF THE YIELD RATE FROM THE BOND PRICE

When bonds are actually bought and sold on the bond market, the trading takes place with buyers and sellers offering "bid" and "ask" prices, respectively, with an intermediate settlement price eventually found. In Section 4.2 formulations were presented for the price of a bond, given the yield rate on the bond. In actual practice bond prices are settled first, and the corresponding yield rate is then determined and made part of the overall quotation describing the transaction. Thus the determination of the yield rate from the price becomes an unknown interest problem which can be solved by the approximation methods of Section 2.7. (The yield rate is the internal rate of return of the transaction.)

For a bond bought at a purchase price P one period before the next coupon is due, with face amount F, coupon rate r, and n coupons remaining until maturity, the yield rate j on the bond is the solution of the equation $P = F \cdot v_j^n + Fr \cdot a_{\overline{n}|j}$, or any other of our bond price formulas. If the bond is bought at time t, $0 \leq t \leq 1$, measured from the last coupon, and there are n coupons remaining, then j is the solution of the equation

$$P = [F \cdot v_j^n + Fr \cdot a_{\overline{n}|j}](1+j)^t, \tag{4.8}$$

where P is the price-plus-accrued of the bond. Note that the function $g(j) = [F \cdot v_j^n + Fr \cdot a_{\overline{n}|j}](1+j)^t$ is a decreasing function of j if $n \geq 1$, and that $\lim_{j \to -1} g(j) = +\infty$ and $\lim_{j \to \infty} g(j) = 0$ (see Exercise 4.4.1), so there is a unique yield rate j for which Equation (4.8) holds.

EXAMPLE 4.4

(a) A 20-year 8% bond of face amount 100 is quoted at a purchase price of 70.400, to the nearest .001. Find an approximation to the nominal annual yield rate using (i) linear interpolation with an interval of $\frac{1}{2}\%$, then an interval of $\frac{1}{16}\%$; (ii) the bisection method applied 5 times with a starting interval of $a_1 = 11\%$ and $b_1 = 12\%$; (iii) five iterations of the Newton-Raphson method applied to $f(j) = P - F \cdot v_j^n - Fr \cdot a_{\overline{n}|j}$ with a starting value of 0%, then a starting value of 10%.

(b) Suppose the bond in part (a) was issued on January 15, 1990, and bought by a new purchaser on April 1, 1995 for a *quoted* price of 112.225. Repeat part (a) to find the yield rate for the new purchaser.

SOLUTION

(a) (i) Since the bond is bought at a discount, the nominal annual yield rate must be larger than 8%. By trial and error it is found that at a yield rate of $i^{(2)} = .115$ the price is $P_{.115} = 72.817$, and at a yield rate of $i^{(2)} = .12$ the price is $P_{.12} = 69.907$. Performing linear interpolation over the interval from 11.5% to 12% we have $i^{(2)} = .115 + (.005)\left(\frac{70.400 - 72.817}{69.907 - 72.817}\right) = .11915$. The maximum error in this approximation is $\frac{1}{2}\%$. For interpolation over an interval of length $\frac{1}{16}\%$, we have, again by trial and error, $P_{.11875} = 70.617$ at a yield of $i^{(2)} = 11\frac{14}{16}\%$, and $P_{.119375} = 70.261$ at a yield of $i^{(2)} = 11\frac{15}{16}\%$. The interpolated value of $i^{(2)}$ is then

$.11875 + (.000625)\left(\frac{70.400-70.617}{70.261-70.617}\right) = .11913.$ The maximum error in this approximation is $\frac{1}{16}\%$.

(ii) We use the function $f(j) = 70.400 - 100 \cdot v_j^{40} - 4 \cdot a_{\overline{40}|j}$, where $j = \frac{i^{(2)}}{2}$. With a starting interval for j of $[.055, .06]$, the successive approximations are $p_1 = .0575$, $p_2 = .05875$, $p_3 = .059375$, $p_4 = .0596875$, and $p_5 = .05953125$. The approximation to $i^{(2)}$ is $2(.05953125) = .1190625$.

(iii) Newton-Raphson iteration requires a starting value j_0. Successive approximations are given by $j_{k+1} = j_k - \dfrac{f(j_k)}{f'(j_k)}$, where $f(i)$ is the function whose zero we seek. We use the given $f(j) = 70.400 - 100 \cdot v_j^{40} - 4 \cdot a_{\overline{40}|j}$, so that

$$j_{k+1} = j_k - \frac{70.400 - 100 \cdot v_{j_k}^{40} - 4 \cdot a_{\overline{40}|j_k}}{4000 \cdot v_{j_k}^{41} + 4 \cdot v_{j_k} \cdot (Ia)_{\overline{40}|j_k}}.$$

With starting value $j_0 = 0$, we have $j_1 = 0 - \dfrac{70.400 - 100 - 160}{4000 + 3280}$

$= .026044$ $\left(\text{recall that } a_{\overline{n}|j=0} = n \text{ and } (Ia)_{\overline{n}|j=0} = \dfrac{n(n+1)}{2}\right)$.

Then we find $j_2 = .047094$, $j_3 = .057020$, $j_4 = .059479$, and $j_5 = .059565$, which is the exact value of j to 6 decimal places. The value of $i^{(2)}$ is then $2j = .11913$.

(b) There are 76 days from January 15, 1995 (the time of the last coupon) until April 1, 1995. The entire coupon period from January 15, 1995 to July 15, 1995 is 181 days. The price-plus-accrued of the bond on April 1, 1995 at yield rate j per coupon period is then $P_j = [100 \cdot v_j^{30} + 4 \cdot a_{\overline{30}|j}](1+j)^{76/181}$.

(i) The price is given as 112.225, so the price-plus-accrued is $112.225 + 4 \cdot \frac{76}{181} = 113.905$. Since the price is greater than the redemption amount, we must have $i^{(2)} < .08$. By trial and error we see that $P_{.065} = 115.781$ at $i^{(2)} = .065$, and $P_{.07} = 110.787$ at $i^{(2)} = .07$. The interpolated value of $i^{(2)}$ is $.065 + (.005)\left(\frac{113.905-115.781}{110.787-115.781}\right) = .066878$. For interpolation over an interval of length $\frac{1}{16}\%$, we have $P_{.06625} = 114.503$ and $P_{.066875} = 113.871$ for yields of $i^{(2)} = 6\frac{10}{16}\%$ and $i^{(2)} = 6\frac{11}{16}\%$, respectively. The interpolated value is then $i^{(2)} = .066841$.

(ii) We use $f(j) = 113.905 - [100 \cdot v_j^{30} + 4 \cdot a_{\overline{30}|j}](1+j)^{\frac{76}{181}}$, where $j = \frac{i^{(2)}}{2}$. With a starting interval for j of $[.03, .035]$, the successive approximations are $p_1 = .0325$, $p_2 = .03375$, $p_3 = .033125$, $p_4 = .0334375$, and $p_5 = .03328125$. The approximation to $i^{(2)}$ is $2(.03328125) = .066563$.

(iii) Using the $f(j)$ from part (ii) we have $j_{k+1} = j_k - \dfrac{f(j_k)}{f'(j_k)}$, where

$$f'(j) = 100(29\tfrac{105}{181}) \cdot v_j^{30\frac{105}{181}} + 4\left[(1+j)^{\frac{76}{181}} \cdot v_j \cdot (Ia)_{\overline{30}|j} - a_{\overline{30}|j} \cdot \tfrac{76}{181} \cdot v_j^{\frac{105}{181}}\right].$$

With a starting value of $j_0 = 0$ we have $j_1 = .022253$, $j_2 = .031991$, $j_3 = .033960$, $j_4 = .033421$, and $j_5 = .033421$, which is accurate to 6 decimal places. The corresponding value of $i^{(2)}$ is $2j = .066842$.   □

The Newton-Raphson iteration method generally provides rapid convergence to the root(s) of the equation $f(x) = 0$. Suppose that $f(j)$ is defined as it was in Example 4.4, namely $f(j) = P - F \cdot v_j^n - Fr \cdot a_{\overline{n}|j}$ for a bond bought just after a coupon, and $f(j) = P - [F \cdot v_j^n - Fr \cdot a_{\overline{n}|j}](1+j)^t$ for a bond with n coupons remaining that is bought at time t since the last coupon. It can be shown that with any starting value $j_0 > -1$, the Newton-Raphson iteration will converge to the yield rate (see Exercise 4.4.1).

4.5   APPLICATIONS AND ILLUSTRATIONS

4.5.1 Serial Bonds and Makeham's Formula

A bond issue may consist of a collection of bonds with a variety of redemption dates, or redemption in installments. This might be done so that the bond issuer can stagger the redemption payments instead of having a single redemption date with one large redemption amount. Such an issue can be treated as a series of separate bonds, each with its own redemption date, and it is possible that the coupon rate differs for the various redemption dates. It may also be the case that purchasers will want different yield rates for the different maturity dates (see Section 4.5.3). Such a bond is called a *serial bond* since redemption occurs with a series of redemption payments.

Suppose that a serial bond has redemption amounts $F_1, F_2, \ldots, F_m$, to be redeemed in $n_1, n_2, \ldots, n_m$ coupon periods, respectively, and pays coupons at rates $r_1, r_2, \ldots, r_m$, respectively. Suppose also that this serial bond is purchased to yield $j_1, j_2, \ldots, j_m$, respectively, on the m pieces. Then the price of the tth piece can be formulated using any one of Equation (4.1), (4.2) or (4.3). Using Makeham's bond price formula given by Equation (4.3), the price of the tth piece is

$$P_t = K_t + \frac{r_t}{j_t}(F_t - K_t), \qquad (4.9a)$$

where $K_t = F_t \cdot v_{j_t}^{n_t}$. The price of the total serial issue would be $P = \sum_{t=1}^{m} P_t$. In the special case where the coupon rates on all pieces of the serial issue are the same ($r_1 = r_2 = \cdots = r_m = r$), and the yield rates on all pieces are also the same ($j_1 = j_2 = \cdots = j_m = j$), the total price of the issue can be written in a compact form using Makeham's Formula:

$$P = \sum_{t=1}^{m} P_t = \sum_{t=1}^{m}\left[K_t + \frac{r}{j}(F_t - K_t)\right] = K + \frac{r}{j}(F - K), \qquad (4.9b)$$

where $K = \sum_{t=1}^{m} K_t$ is the present value of all redemption amounts for the entire issue, and $F = \sum_{t=1}^{m} F_t$ is the total redemption amount for the issue.

If the series of redemptions has a systematic form, such as a level amount every period for a number of periods, then K can be conveniently formulated as the present value of the annuity formed by the series of redemption amounts. Note that Equation (4.9b) requires a uniform coupon rate and yield rate for all redemption dates in the issue.

EXAMPLE 4.5

On August 15, 1990 a corporation issues a 10% serial bond with face amount 50,000,000. The redemption is scheduled to take place as 5,000,000 every August 15 from 2000 to 2004 and 25,000,000 on August 15, 2005. Find the price of the entire issue on the issue date at a yield of $i^{(2)} = .125$.

SOLUTION

The present value of the redemption payments is

$$K = 5,000,000[v_{.0625}^{20} + v_{.0625}^{22} + v_{.0625}^{24} + v_{.0625}^{26} + v_{.0625}^{28}]$$
$$+ 25,000,000 \cdot v_{.0625}^{30} = 9,976,960.$$

Then $P = K + \frac{r}{j}(F - K)$

$$= 9,976,960 + \frac{.05}{.0625}(50,000,000 - 9,976,960) = 41,995,392. \quad \square$$

4.5.2 Callable Bonds: Optional Redemption Dates

A bond issuer may wish to add flexibility to a bond issue by specifying a range of dates during which redemption may occur, at the issuer's option. Such a bond is called a *callable bond*. From the point of view of an investor pricing the bond, a prudent approach is taken in which the investor assumes that the issuer will choose a redemption date that is to the issuer's greatest advantage, and the investor's least advantage. In order to earn a minimum yield of j, an investor will calculate the price of the bond at rate j for each of the redemption dates in the specified range, and choose the minimum of those as the purchase price. If the investor pays more than that minimum, and the issuer redeems at a point such that the price is the minimum, then the investor has "overpaid" and will earn a yield less then the minimum originally desired.

When the first optional call date arrives, the issuer will assess current market conditions and make a decision on whether to redeem the bond earlier or later in the call period. If yield rates have increased since the bond was issued, then it is in the issuer's interest to extend the term of the bond as long as possible to avoid paying a higher yield on a new bond issue. If yield rates have dropped, then it may be in the issuer's interest to redeem early, and reissue the bond at a lower yield rate thereby receiving a greater price.

EXAMPLE 4.6

(a) A 10% bond with face amount 1,000,000 is issued with the condition that redemption can take place on any coupon date between 12 and 15 years from the issue date. Find the price paid by an investor wishing a minimum yield of (i) $i^{(2)} = .12$, and (ii) $i^{(2)} = .08$.

(b) Suppose the investor pays the maximum of all prices for the range of redemption dates. Find the yield rate if the issuer chooses a redemption date corresponding to the minimum price in each of cases (i) and (ii).

(c) Suppose the investor pays the minimum of all prices for the range of redemption dates. Find the yield rate if the issuer chooses a redemption date corresponding to the maximum price in each of cases (i) and (ii).

| SOLUTION |

(a) (i) From Equation (4.2) $P = 1,000,000[1 + (.05-.06) \cdot a_{\overline{n}|.06}]$, where n is the number of coupons until redemption, $n = 24, 25, \cdots, 30$. The range of the price for this range of redemption dates is from 874,496 for redemption at $n = 24$ to 862,352 for redemption at $n = 30$. It is most prudent for the investor to offer a price of 862,352.

(ii) The range of prices is from 1,152,470 if redemption occurs after 12 years, to 1,172,920 if redemption is after 15 years. The prudent investor would pay 1,152,470.

(b) If the investor in (i) pays the maximum price of 874,496 (based on redemption at $n = 24$), and the bond is redeemed at the end of 15 years, the actual nominal yield is 11.80%. If the investor in (ii) pays 1,172,920 (based on redemption at $n = 30$), and the bond is redeemed at the end of 12 years, the actual nominal yield is 7.76%.

(c) If the investor in (i) pays 862,352 (based on 15 year redemption) and the bond is redeemed after 12 years, the actual nominal yield is 12.22%, and if the investor in (ii) pays 1,152,470 (based on 12 year redemption) and the bond is redeemed after 15 years, the actual nominal yield is 8.21%. □

Equation (4.2) shows that for a bond bought at a discount, the longer the time to redemption, the lower will be the price, with the reverse being true for a bond bought at a premium. Thus for a callable bond for which the investor desires a minimum yield rate which is larger than the coupon rate (a bond bought at a discount), the price should be based on the *latest* optional redemption date, and for a callable bond for which the investor desires a yield rate which is smaller than the coupon rate (bought at a premium), the price should be based on the *earliest* optional redemption date. If something more than the minimum price is paid, the investor runs the risk of having redemption occur at a time which is to the investor's disadvantage (as in part (b) of Example 4.6), so that the actual yield to maturity is less than the desired minimum. On the other hand, if the investor pays the minimum price and the actual redemption date is other than the one on which that minimum price is based, then the investor will earn a yield rate greater than the minimum desired (as in part (c) of Example 4.6).

Suppose a bond is bought at a discount, so that $P < F$. The sooner the bond is redeemed, the sooner the investor will realize the gain of $F - P$, so it is to the investor's disadvantage to have a later redemption date. Since the investor prices the bond assuming the redemption will occur to his greatest disadvantage, the investor assumes the latest possible redemption date. Similar reasoning in the case of a bond bought at a premium results in an investor choosing the earliest possible redemption date for calculating the price, since if $P > F$ the investor takes a loss of $F - P$ when the bond is redeemed. It is to the investor's disadvantage to have this loss come early.

When the first optional call date arrives, the bond issuer, based on market conditions and its own financial situation, will make a decision on whether or not to call (redeem) the bond prior to the maximum term. If the issuer is not in a position to redeem at an early date, under appropriate market conditions, it still might be to the issuer's advantage to redeem the bond and issue a new bond for the remaining term. As a simple illustration of this point, suppose in Example 4.6(a) that 12 years after the issue date, the yield rate on a 3-year bond is 9%. If the issuer redeems the bond and immediately issues a new 3-year bond with the same coupon and face amount, the issuer must pay 1,000,000 to the bondholder, but then receives 1,025,789 for the new 3-year bond, which is bought at a yield rate of 9%.

A callable bond might have different redemption amounts at the various optional redemption dates. It might still be possible to use some of the reasoning described above to find the minimum price for all possible redemption dates. In general, however, it may be necessary to calculate the price at several (or all) of the optional dates to find the minimum price.

EXAMPLE 4.7

A 15-year 8% bond with face amount 100 is callable (at the option of the issuer) on a coupon date. In the 10th year the bond is callable at par, in the 11th or 12th years at redemption amount 115, or in the 13th, 14th or 15th years at redemption amount 135.
(a) What price should an investor pay in order to ensure a minimum nominal annual yield to maturity of (i) 12%, and (ii) 6%?

(b) Find the investor's minimum yield if the purchase price is (i) 80, and (ii) 120.

| SOLUTION |

(a) (i) Since the yield rate is larger than the coupon rate (or modified coupon rate for any of the redemption dates), the bond will be bought at a discount. Using Equation (4.2E) from Exercise 4.2.20, we see that during any interval for which the redemption amount is level, the lowest price will occur at the latest redemption date. Thus we must compute the price at the end of 10 years, 12 years and 15 years. The corresponding prices are 77.06, 78.60 and 78.56. The lowest price corresponds to a redemption date of 10 years, which is near the earliest possible redemption date. This example indicates that the principal of pricing a bond bought at a discount by using the latest redemption date may fail when the redemption amounts are not level.

(ii) For redemption in the 10th year and the 11th or 12th years, the yield rate of .03 every six months is smaller than the modified coupon rate of .04 (for redemption in year 10) or $\frac{100(.04)}{115} = .0348$ (for redemption in years 11 or 12). The modified coupon rate is $.0296 < .03$ for redemption in the 13th to 15th years. Thus the minimum price for redemption in the 10th year occurs at the earliest redemption date, which is at $9\frac{1}{2}$ years, and the minimum price for redemption in the 11th or 12th years also occurs at the earliest date, which is at $10\frac{1}{2}$ years. Since $g < j$ in the 13th to 15th years, the minimum price occurs at the latest date, which is at 15 years. Thus we must calculate the price of the bond for redemption at $9\frac{1}{2}$ years, $10\frac{1}{2}$ years and 15 years. The prices are 114.32, 123.48, and 134.02. The price paid will be 114.32, which corresponds to the earliest possible redemption date.

(b) (i) Since the bond is bought at a discount (to the redemption value), it is to the investor's disadvantage to have the redemption at the latest date. Thus we find the yield based on redemption dates of 10 years, 12 years and 15 years. These nominal yield rates are 11.40%, 11.75 and 11.77%. The minimum yield is 11.40%.

(ii) Since the bond is bought at a premium to the redemption value in the 10th year and in the 11th and 12th years, the minimum yield to maturity occurs at the earliest redemption date for those periods, which is $9\frac{1}{2}$ years for the 10th year and $10\frac{1}{2}$ years for the 11th and

12th years. The bond is bought at a discount to the redemption amount in the 13th to 15th years, so the minimum yield occurs at the latest redemption date, which is 15 years. We find the yield based on redemption at $9\frac{1}{2}$ years, $10\frac{1}{2}$ years and 15 years. These nominal yield rates are 5.29%, 6.38% and 7.15%. The minimum is 5.29%.   □

Through the latter part of the 1980's, bonds callable at the option of the issuer became less common in the marketplace. The increased competition for funds by governments and corporations during that period produced various incentives that are occasionally added to a bond issue. One such incentive is a *retractable-extendible* feature, which gives the bondholder the option of having the bond redeemed (retracted) on a specified date, or having the redemption date extended to a specified later date. This is similar to a callable bond with the option in the hands of the bondholder rather than the bond issuer. Another incentive is to provide *warrants* with the bond. A warrant gives the bondholder the option to purchase further amounts of the bond issue at a later date at a guaranteed price (see Chapter 6).

4.5.3 Term Structure of Interest Rates and Bond Valuation

Bonds are issued with terms to maturity of just a few years to more than thirty years. The investment objectives of those investing in short-term bonds might be different from those investing in long-term bonds, and it is not unreasonable that bonds of different terms would have different yield rates. The relationship between term-to-maturity and yield-to-maturity is called the *term structure*, and can be represented graphically by a *yield curve*. The risk rating of a bond will also have an effect on the bond's yield, and it would be possible to have a yield curve for each of several different categories of bonds, graded as to risk. Government bonds form a major part of the bond market, and it might be of interest to consider the term structure related to Government issues alone. It is possible that bonds with the same term-to-maturity, but having different coupon rates, will have different yields. A yield curve can be based on yields corresponding to any fairly homogeneous class of investments. Also note that a yield curve is a representation of yields available at a specific point in time, and a yield curve for the same class of investments at some later point may be different from the current yield curve.

A *zero-coupon bond* is an investment that pays a specified maturity amount on a specified date. It can be regarded as a straight-term bond of the type described earlier in this chapter with a coupon rate of $r = 0$. A zero-coupon bond is also similar to a T-bill, except that it often has a longer term to maturity than a T-bill which is restricted to a term of no more than one year. Zero-coupon bonds are available with a wide range of terms to maturity from less than one year to thirty or more years, with fractional durations included as well. As with investments of all types, the yield rate on a zero-coupon bond will be related to general economic conditions and will depend on the term-to-maturity. A zero-coupon bond is sometimes called a *discount bond*.

The term structure for zero-coupon bonds provides an alternative way in which to value a coupon bond. If we treat each coupon and the redemption amount on a coupon bond as a separate zero-coupon bond, then the present value of each of the coupons and the redemption amount can be found separately at the corresponding spot rate of interest, with the total being the value of the entire bond. (The *spot rate* is the current market interest rate for valuing a particular type of investment, such as a zero-coupon bond; different types of investments would have different spot rates.) Since coupon bonds have coupons payable semiannually, it will be convenient to assume that the term structure measures interest rates as nominal annual rates convertible semiannually.

EXAMPLE 4.8

A 10% bond with face amount 100 matures in 7 years.

(a) Find the value of the bond based on each of the following term structures for zero-coupon bond spot rates, where $i_{0,t}$ denotes the nominal annual spot rate convertible semiannually for a t-year term zero-coupon bond.

(i) $i_{0,.5} = .075$ $\qquad$ $i_{0,1} = .0775$ $\qquad$ $i_{0,1.5} = .08$ $\qquad$ $i_{0,2} = .08$

$\qquad$ $i_{0,2.5} = .0825$ $\qquad$ $i_{0,3} = .085$ $\qquad$ $i_{0,3.5} = .085$ $\qquad$ $i_{0,4} = .09$

$\qquad$ $i_{0,4.5} = .0925$ $\qquad$ $i_{0,5} = .095$ $\qquad$ $i_{0,5.5} = .095$ $\qquad$ $i_{0,6} = .0975$

$\qquad$ $i_{0,6.5} = .10$ $\qquad$ $i_{0,7} = .1025$

(ii) $i_{0,.5} = .14$ $i_{0,1} = .1375$ $i_{0,1.5} = .135$ $i_{0,2} = .1325$

$i_{0,2.5} = .13$ $i_{0,3} = .1275$ $i_{0,3.5} = .125$ $i_{0,4} = .1225$

$i_{0,4.5} = .12$ $i_{0,5} = .1175$ $i_{0,5.5} = .115$ $i_{0,6} = .1125$

$i_{0,6.5} = .11$ $i_{0,7} = .1075$

(iii) $i_{0,.5} = .12$ $i_{0,1} = .12$ $i_{0,1.5} = .12$ $i_{0,2} = .12$

$i_{0,2.5} = .12$ $i_{0,3} = .12$ $i_{0,3.5} = .12$ $i_{0,4} = .12$

$i_{0,4.5} = .12$ $i_{0,5} = .12$ $i_{0,5.5} = .12$ $i_{0,6} = .12$

$i_{0,6.5} = .12$ $i_{0,7} = .12$

(b) For each of the bond prices found in (a), find the corresponding yield to maturity.

SOLUTION

(a) The present value of 1 due in t years at the annual t-year spot rate $i_{0,t}$ convertible semiannually is $(1 + \frac{1}{2} \cdot i_{0,t})^{-2t}$. Since each $i_{0,t}$ is nominal convertible semiannually, the total present value of all coupons and redemption amount is

(i) $5[(1.0375)^{-1} + (1.03875)^{-2} + (1.04)^{-3} + (1.04)^{-4}$

$+ (1.04125)^{-5} + (1.0425)^{-6} + (1.0425)^{-7} + (1.045)^{-8}$

$+ (.104625)^{-9} + (1.0475)^{-10} + (1.0475)^{-11} + (1.04875)^{-12}$

$+ (1.05)^{-13} + (1.05125)^{-14}] + 100(1.05125)^{-14} = 100.5097.$

(ii) $5[(1.07)^{-1} + (1.06875)^{-2} + (1.0675)^{-3} + (1.06625)^{-4}$

$+ (1.065)^{-5} + (1.06375)^{-6} + (1.0625)^{-7} + (1.06125)^{-8}$

$+ (1.06)^{-9} + (1.05875)^{-10} + (1.0575)^{-11} + (1.05625)^{-12}$

$+ (1.055)^{-13} + (1.05375)^{-14}] + 100(1.05375)^{-14} = 94.5315.$

(iii) $5 \cdot a_{\overline{14}|.06} + 100(1.06)^{-14} = 90.7050.$

(b) Using the Newton-Raphson method, we find nominal annual yield rates of (i) 9.90%, (ii) 11.15%, and (iii) 12%. It is obvious that the yield rate in (iii) must be 12%, since the price is based on a constant spot rate of 12%. $\square$

The bond market is very *liquid*, allowing investors to buy and sell bonds at any time. The bond market is usually regarded as *efficient* as well, so that information about changing conditions in the economy and in government and corporate prospects becomes widely known after being released, and is quickly factored into bond price/yield determinations. Occasionally a distortion in the market allows for an *arbitrage* opportunity, which is a risk-free opportunity for a profit. The term structures of various rates are always changing as time goes on, and bond prices are adjusted in a corresponding way. Changes in the various components of the market may not take place simultaneously, resulting in the temporary distortions mentioned above.

As an example of an arbitrage opportunity, consider the bond in Example 4.8, and assume that the current term structure is as given in case (i). The value of the bond based on the term structure is 100.51. Suppose that recent changes in the term structure of spot rates do not match exactly with recent changes in the yield to maturity of the 7-year bond. If the currently quoted price of the bond is 98 (or anything less than 100.51), an investor acting quickly can purchase the bond for 98, strip the coupons and redemption amount, and sell them immediately as separate zero-coupon bonds. (A stripped coupon becomes a zero-coupon bond itself.) The investor has an immediate risk-free profit of 2.51 per 100 of face amount transacted. Such situations are usually corrected quickly by the market forces, so that either the bond price will rise or the price of zero-coupon bonds will fall. Many bond traders have computer programs that monitor for such arbitrage opportunities, searching the market for such *strippable bonds*.

4.5.4 Bond Duration

An investor is subject to a number of risks when holding a bond, including the risk that the bond issuer will default on coupon payments and/or the redemption payment. Such risk is taken into account when pricing the bond, and investors pay lower prices and thus demand higher yields from bonds having higher possibility of default (see Exercise 4.5.17). Another risk faced by the investor is that of changes in bond values due to changes in interest rates. Even with no change in interest rates, the book value (in the amortization schedule) of a bond will change over time because of changing time until maturity.

There is no guarantee when an investor buys a bond with a certain yield to maturity that the market will continue to value that bond at that same yield for the entire term of the bond. Economic conditions may change, and rates of return demanded by investors may change, so that the market value of the bond might not always be equal to the bondholder's book value. If the market yield (or valuation) rate for the bond is higher than the bondholder's original (book) yield, then the present value of the payments represented by the bond will be less at the higher market yield rate than at the original yield rate (with the reverse occurring if the market yield is below the book yield). There is no requirement that the bondholder sell the bond before maturity, and if the bondholder keeps the bond until maturity he will realize the original book yield-to-maturity no matter what changes in interest rates occur during the term of the bond. If the bondholder sells the bond before maturity at a price other than the book value, the bondholder's return will not be the original book yield, but will be related to the market yield at the time of sale (see Exercise 4.4.5.).

The risk, volatility, or sensitivity of a bond's price to changes in the market yield rate can be quantified by the rate of change or derivative of the bond's price with respect to market yield. In general suppose L is the present value, at effective rate j per period, of a series of payments K_1, K_2, ..., K_n made at times 1, 2, ..., n, respectively. Then $L = \sum_{t=1}^{n} K_t \cdot v_j^t$. The derivative of L with respect to j is

$$\frac{dL}{dj} = \frac{dL}{d(1+j)} = -\sum_{t=1}^{n} t \cdot K_t \cdot v_j^{t+1}. \tag{4.10}$$

Equation (4.10) can be rewritten as

$$\frac{dL}{L} = \left[\frac{-\sum_{t=1}^{n} t \cdot K_t \cdot v_j^t}{L} \right] \cdot \frac{d(1+j)}{(1+j)}. \tag{4.11}$$

Equation (4.11) gives an expression for the relative volatility (per unit invested) of the present value of the cashflow with respect to a relative change in the valuation rate of interest. The quantity in brackets in Equation (4.11) is called the *duration* of the investment or cashflow. As a numerical measure, the duration can be interpreted as the approximate percentage change in the present value of the cashflow for a one percent change in $1 + j$, so that

$$\frac{\Delta L}{L} \approx -D \cdot \frac{\Delta(1+j)}{(1+j)}, \tag{4.12}$$

where D is the duration of the cashflow.

In the case of a zero-coupon bond of face amount 1 with n years to maturity, $K_n = 1$ and $K_t = 0$ for $t < n$. Using P for the price of the bond instead of L, Equation (4.11) becomes

$$\frac{dP}{P} = -\left[\frac{n \cdot v_j^n}{P}\right] \cdot \frac{d(1+j)}{(1+j)}$$

$$= -\left[\frac{n \cdot v_j^n}{v_j^n}\right] \cdot \frac{d(1+j)}{(1+j)}$$

$$= -n \cdot \frac{d(1+j)}{(1+j)}. \qquad (4.13)$$

In the case of a zero-coupon bond, the bracketed quantity in Equation (4.11) reduces to n in Equation (4.13), hence the term *duration* for the measure of relative volatility of price with respect to yield.

The duration, as defined by Equation (4.11), can be regarded as a *weighted average time to maturity*, also called the *discounted mean term*, where the weights are the present values of the cashflows at the various points in time; some investors attach real significance to the duration as an average time to maturity. In the general definition of duration given by Equation (4.11), the unit of duration measurement would be the interest rate period. This is illustrated in Example 4.9. In practice, however, duration is measured in years, even for bonds with interest on a nominal annual basis convertible semiannually.

| **EXAMPLE 4.9** |

A bond has face amount F, coupon rate r per coupon period, n coupons until maturity, and is valued at yield rate j per coupon period. Calculate the duration of the bond for all possible combinations of parameters $r = .05, .10, .15$; $n = 2, 10, 30, 60$; and $j = .05, .10, .15$.

| **SOLUTION** |

$K_t = Fr$ for $t = 1, 2, \ldots, n-1$ and $K_n = F + Fr$. Thus the duration

is $D = \dfrac{\displaystyle\sum_{t=1}^{n} t \cdot Fr \cdot v_j^t + n \cdot F \cdot v_j^n}{\displaystyle\sum_{t=1}^{n} Fr \cdot v_j^t + F \cdot v_j^n}$.   At a yield rate of 5% per coupon

period, the duration values are as shown in Table 4.3a.

TABLE 4.3a

Coupon Rate	Coupons Until Maturity			
	2	10	30	60
.05	1.952	8.108	16.141	19.876
.10	1.913	7.270	14.328	18.772
.15	1.880	6.797	13.613	18.391

At a yield rate of 10% per coupon period, the durations are given in Table 4.3b.

TABLE 4.3b

Coupon Rate	Coupons Until Maturity			
	2	10	30	60
.05	1.950	7.661	11.434	11.124
.10	1.909	6.759	10.370	10.964
.15	1.876	6.281	9.987	10.910

At a yield rate of 15% per coupon period, the durations are given in Table 4.3c.

TABLE 4.3c

Coupon Rate	Coupons Until Maturity			
	2	10	30	60
.05	1.948	7.170	8.209	7.689
.10	1.905	6.237	7.719	7.671
.15	1.870	5.772	7.551	7.665

□

The meaning of duration can be illustrated as follows. Suppose a bond of face amount 100, nominal coupon rate 10%, and 15 years to maturity is purchased at a nominal yield rate of 20%. The purchase price would be 52.87. Suppose the yield increases to 21%, a relative increase of $\frac{\Delta(1+j)}{(1+j)} = \frac{.005}{1.1} = .004545$. Then using the approximate relationship

$\frac{\Delta P}{P} \approx -D \cdot \frac{\Delta(1+j)}{(1+j)}$, where $D = 11.434$ (from Table 4.3b), we have $\frac{\Delta P}{P} \approx -11.434(.004545) = -.0520$, so that $\Delta P \approx -.0520P = -2.75$. The price of the bond at the new yield rate should be approximately $52.87 - 2.75 = 50.12$. The actual price at a nominal yield rate of 21% is 50.24. Note that for a given term-to-maturity, the duration decreases as the coupon rate increases (this is because the increased coupons shift the weighting of the overall payments to earlier time).

There is another interpretation of duration. In Example 4.9 consider the case in which the yield rate is 10%, the coupon rate is 15%, and the number of coupons to maturity is 30. The duration in this case is 9.987, approximately 10. Suppose that it is possible to reinvest coupons at the yield rate. Then the *current value*, at the time of the 10th coupon, of the entire cashflow represented by the bond is $.15s_{\overline{10}|.10} + v_{.10}^{20} + .15a_{\overline{20}|.10} = 3.816$. Suppose that just after the bond is issued, the rate at which coupons can be reinvested changes to 11% per coupon period and remains at that for the full term of the bond. Then the current value (at 11%) at the time of the 10th coupon is $.15s_{\overline{10}|.11} + v_{.11}^{20} + .15a_{\overline{20}|.11} = 3.827$. Similarly, the current value at $t = 10$ at rate 9% is 3.827.

Thus, for a small change in the rate of interest from the original yield rate, there is a relatively small change in the current value of the cashflow at the time period numerically equal to the duration. This relationship can be represented algebraically in the form $\frac{d}{di}[L(1+i)^D] = 0$, where L is the present value of the cashflow described just before Equation (4.10) and D is the duration as defined in Equation (4.11). This is verified in Exercise 4.5.14. The relationship is related to the notion of *immunization* (see Chapter 6), in that the current value of the cashflow at time $t = D$ is *immune* to, or unaffected by, small changes in the yield rate.

Suppose k separate future cashflows are under consideration, and X_j is the present value at time $t = 0$ and at interest rate i, of cashflow j. Then $X_j = c_1^{(j)} v_i + c_2^{(j)} v_i^2 + \cdots + c_n^{(j)} v_i^n$ for $j = 1, 2, \ldots, k$). According to the definition of duration given in Equation (4.11), the duration of cashflow j is $D_j = -(1+j)\left[\frac{d}{di} X_j\right]/X_j$. The duration of the aggregate present value of all k cashflows is $D = -(1+j)\left[\frac{d}{di} X\right]/X$, where $X = \sum_{j=1}^{k} X_j$. D can be reformulated as

$$D = -(1+j)\left[\frac{d}{di}X\right]/X = -(1+j)\left[\frac{d}{di}\sum X_j\right]/X$$

$$= -(1+j)\cdot\sum\frac{1}{X}\cdot\frac{d}{di}X_j$$

$$= \sum\frac{X_j}{X}\left[-(1+j)\cdot\frac{1}{X_j}\cdot\frac{d}{di}X_j\right]$$

$$= \sum\frac{X_j}{X}\cdot D_j. \tag{4.14}$$

Equation (4.14) shows that the duration of an aggregate of future cashflows is the weighted average of the durations of the individual cashflows, where the weights are the cashflow present values.

Consider a bond portfolio consisting of two bonds, each of face amount .50: (i) a 2-coupon bond with coupon rate 5%, and (ii) a 60-coupon bond with coupon rate 15%. Suppose the yield rate for short term (2-coupon) bonds is 5% per coupon period, and the yield on long (60-coupons) bonds is 15%. Since the yield rate is equal to the coupon rate for each bond, both bonds are currently valued at par, so the total value of the portfolio is 1.00. These bonds are found in Tables 4.3a and 4.3c, with durations of 1.952 and 7.665, respectively. It follows from the comments in the previous paragraph that the duration of the portfolio is $(.5)(1.952 + 7.665) = 4.81$.

Now consider a second portfolio consisting of a single bond of face amount 1, with 6 coupons and a coupon rate of 10%, valued at a yield rate of 10% per coupon period. The duration of this bond is 4.79 (see Exercise 4.5.15). Thus, the portfolios have the same value and almost the same duration at the current yield rates.

The current yield rates can be summarized in a yield curve (Figure 4.4a). Let us consider the effect on the portfolios that result from a change in the yield curve. Suppose that there is a $+1\%$ *parallel shift* in the yield curve (Figure 4.4b), so that the yield rates for all bond maturities increase by 1%. The value of the first portfolio becomes .9596, and the value of the second portfolio becomes .9577. Thus, as expected, both portfolios decrease in value by nearly the same amount as a result of a uniform (parallel) shift in the yield rate, since they have nearly the same duration. Suppose instead that the yield curve flattens slightly (Figure 4.4c), so that the yield on the 2-coupon bond increases to 6%, the yield on the 6-coupon bond stays at 10%, and the yield on the 60-coupon bond decreases to 14%. The value of the first portfolio becomes 1.026534, but the second stays at 1.00. The purpose of this discussion is to point out that although two portfolios may currently have *matched* value and duration, the effects of non-parallel shifts in the yield curve may differ from one portfolio to another.

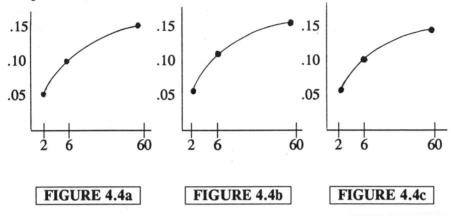

| FIGURE 4.4a | FIGURE 4.4b | FIGURE 4.4c |

It is clear that if an investor perceives that interest rates will increase, then the investor's risk of a loss in value of bond holdings is more limited with bonds of small duration, whereas if the perception is that rates will decrease, the investor's potential for gain in value of bond holdings is greater with bonds of larger duration. Duration is used to compare volatility of bond price with respect to yield rate, but would not be used in practice to actually calculate approximate changes in price as done in an earlier paragraph. There are a number of variations in the definition of duration given by Equation (4.11). See Section 4.6 for references to additional reading on duration.

4.5.5 Bond Default Risk and Premium

One issuer of a bond may not be as financially stable or secure as another. Based on various analyses of the bond issuer, such as historical performance as to default, the performance of the industry group with which the issuing company is associated, and so on, it may be possible to estimate probabilities of default. There are a number of bond-rating services which classify borrowers as to their creditworthiness, with ranks from AAA (highest) to C (lowest).

| EXAMPLE 4.10 |

Analysis of a bond with 3 years remaining until maturity indicates an estimated probability of default of .05 in any given coupon period until maturity, given that default has not yet occurred. The bond has a nominal annual coupon rate of 14%, payable semiannually, and a face amount of

100,000. If default occurs, the bond will pay no coupon for the coupon period in which it occurred, but will pay 50% of the redemption amount and no further coupons. Using expected present value, what price should an investor pay for the bond based on an annual yield of 12%, payable semiannually?

SOLUTION

With a reference point of $t = 0$ (where $t = 6$ represents the maturity date), the probabilities of default each period are as follows:

Period	Default Probability	Probability of Payment
1	.05	.95
2	$(.95)(.05)$	$(.95)^2$
3	$(.95)^2(.05)$	$(.95)^3$
4	$(.95)^3(.05)$	$(.95)^4$
5	$(.95)^4(.05)$	$(.95)^5$
6	$(.95)^5(.05)$	$(.95)^6$

We can find the total expected present value in two ways. The first approach is the find the expected payment at each of times 1 to 6 and sum them. The possible payments at time 1 are 7000 (the coupon if default doesn't take place during the first coupon period - probability .95) and 50,000 (reduced redemption if default occurred - probability .05). The expected present value is $[7000(.95) + 50,000(.05)]v$. The possible payments at time 2 are 7000 (if default hasn't occurred during the first 2 periods - probability $.95^2$), 50,000 (if default occurs in the 2nd period - probability $(.95)(.05)$) and 0 (if default occurred in the first period - probability 05), with expected present value $[7000(.95)^2 + 50,000(.95)(.05)]v^2$. Continuing in this way to time 6, we get that the total expected present value of the coupons, default payment, and redemption amount is

$$[7000(.95) + 50,000(.05)]v$$
$$+ [7000(.95)^2 + 50,000(.95)(.05)]v^2$$
$$+ [7000(.95)^3 + 50,000(.95)^2(.05)]v^3$$
$$+ [7000(.95)^4 + 50,000(.95)^3(.05)]v^4$$
$$+ [7000(.95)^5 + 50,000(.95)^4(.05)]v^5$$
$$+ [107,000(.95)^6 + 50,000(.95)^5(.05)]v^6$$
$$= 91,897.18.$$

Alternatively, we can find the total present value received for each of 7 possible events - (1) default in period 1, (2) default in period 2, ... , (6) default in period 6, (7) no default . In event (1), the total present value received is $50,000v$, with probability .05. In event (2), the total present value received is $7000v + 50,000v^2$, with probability $(.95)(.05)$. Continuing in this way leads to the same expected present value as the first approach. At the price of 91,897.18, if all coupon payments are met and the redemption amount is paid, the yield on the bond would be $i^{(2)} = .1759$. □

The difference between the *promised yield to maturity* of 17.59% and the *expected yield to maturity* of 12% in Example 4.10 is the *default premium* on the bond. The expected yield rate on a bond which has a risk of default will be larger than the yield on a government (risk-free) bond with the same coupon rate and time to maturity. The difference between this expected yield and the yield on the corresponding risk-free bond is called the *risk premium*. The total of the risk premium and the default premium on a bond is the *yield spread* for that bond.

4.6 NOTES AND REFERENCES

The reference textbook *Standard Securities Calculation Methods* defines the price of a bond bought between coupon dates to be the P_t of Equation (4.5a) minus $t \cdot Fr$, where t is calculated by Equation (4.6). That reference also suggests that bond yields be found by the Newton-Raphson method using the functional equation $f(j) = P_t - [F \cdot v_j^n + Fr \cdot a_{\overline{n}|j}] \cdot v_j^t - t \cdot Fr = 0$. The Newton-Raphson method is the routine used in some calculators having bond yield functions.

The text by Butcher and Nesbitt [2] details several numerical procedures for approximating yield rates, and provides additional references on the subject.

A more detailed discussion of the term structure and duration can be found in *Modern Portfolio Theory and Investment Analysis*, by Elton and Gruber [3]. That book also contains a discussion of *bond swaps*, in which the investor "attempts to find bonds that can be swapped for existing bonds that maintain the future cash flow pattern and yet earn immediate profit from the swap." A linear programming approach to finding appropriate bond swaps is described.

A discussion of default premium and risk premium can be found in *Investments*, by Sharpe [9].

4.7   EXERCISES

Exercises 4.2

(Unless specified otherwise, all coupon rates are nominal annual payable semiannually, all yield rates are nominal annual convertible semiannually, and bonds are valued just after a coupon has been paid.)

4.2.1   Find the prices of the following bonds, all redeemable at par, where coupons are payable semiannually and yield is nominal convertible semiannually.   Show how to compare their prices without actually calculating the numerical values.
  (a) A 10-year 100, 5% bond yielding 7.2%.
  (b) A 10-year 100, $5\frac{1}{2}$% bond yielding 7.7%.
  (c) A 12-year 100, 5% bond yielding 7.2%.
  (d) A 12-year 100, $5\frac{1}{2}$% bond yielding 7.7%.

4.2.2   An n-year 4.75% bond is selling for 95.59. An n-year 6.25% bond at the same yield would sell for 108.82. Find the yield rate.

4.2.3   A 6% bond maturing in 8 years with semiannual coupons to yield 5% convertible semiannually is to be replaced by a 5.5% bond yielding the same return. In how many years should the new bond mature? (Both bonds have the same price, yield rate and face value.)

4.2.4   Bond A has n coupons remaining at rate r_1 each, and sells to yield rate i_1 effective per coupon period. Bond B has the same face value and number of coupons remaining as Bond A, but the coupons are at rate r_2 each and the yield rate is i_2 effective per period. If $i_2 \cdot r_1 = i_1 \cdot r_2$ and $i_2 > i_1 > r_1$, which of the following statements are true?
  I.   The price of Bond B exceeds the price of Bond A.
  I.   The present value of Bond B's coupons on the purchase date exceeds the present value of Bond A's coupons.
  III. The present value of the redemption amount for Bond B exceeds the corresponding present value for Bond A.

4.2.5 Two bonds, each of face amount 100, are offered for sale at a combined price of 240. Both bonds have the same term to maturity but the coupon rate for one is twice that of the other. The difference in price of the two bonds is 24. Prices are based on a nominal annual yield rate of 3%. Find the coupon rates of the two bonds.

4.2.6 A 5% bond with face amount 1000 is redeemable in k years and is purchased for 1300. A 4% bond with the same face amount and the same redemption date as the first bond has a purchase price of 1100. The nominal annual yield rate is the same for both bonds. Find that rate.

4.2.7 Consider two bonds, each with face amount 1. One bond matures 6 months from now and carries one coupon of amount r_1. The other bond matures 1 year from now and carries two semiannual coupons of amount r_2 each. Both bonds have the same selling price to yield nominal annual $i^{(2)}$. Find a formulation for $i^{(2)}$ in terms of r_1, r_2 and constants.

4.2.8 Two bonds each carry the same number of coupons at rates r_1 and r_2 per coupon period. The first bond sells at a premium of p per unit of face amount and the second sells at a discount of q per unit of face amount. If both have the same yield rate j, express j in terms of r_1, r_2, p and q.

4.2.9 A 7% bond has a price of 79.30 and a 9% bond has a price of 93.10, both per 100 of face amount. Both are redeemable in n years and have the same yield rate. Find n.

4.2.10 When a certain type of bond matures, the bondholder is subject to a tax of 25% on the amount of discount at which he bought the bond. A 1000 bond of this type has 4% *annually* paid coupons and is redeemable at par in 10 years. No tax is paid on coupons. What price should a purchaser pay to realize an effective annual yield of 5% after taxes?

4.2.11 A bond issue carries quarterly coupons of 2% of the face amount outstanding. An investor uses Makeham's Formula to evaluate the whole outstanding issue to yield an annual effective rate of 13%. Find the value of H used in the formula $P = K + H(C-K)$.

4.2.12 A 3000 bond with *annual* coupons is selling at an annual effective yield rate equal to twice the annual coupon rate. The present value of the coupons is equal to the present value of the redemption amount. What is the selling price?

4.2.13 Smith purchases a 20-year, 8%, 1000 bond with semiannual coupons. The purchase price will give a nominal annual yield to maturity, convertible semiannually, of 10%. After the 20th coupon, Smith sells the bond. At what price did he sell the bond if his actual nominal annual yield is 10%?

4.2.14 On November 1, 1984 Smith paid 1000 for a government savings bond of face amount 1000 with annual coupons of 8%, with maturity to occur on November 1, 1996. On November 1, 1990 the government issues new savings bonds with the same maturity date of November 1, 1996, but with annual coupons of 9.5%. (Smith's bond will still pay 8%.) The government offers Smith a cash bonus of X to be paid on the maturity date if he holds his old bond until maturity. Smith can cash in his old bond on November 1, 1990 and buy a new bond for 1000. If both options yield 9.5% from November 1, 1990 to November 1, 1996, find X.

4.2.15 Show that Equations (4.5a) and (4.5b) are algebraically equivalent.

4.2.16 Show that if $(1+j)^t$ is approximated by $1+jt$, then the quoted price of a bond at time t, $0 \le t \le 1$, since the last coupon is the linearly-interpolated value at t between P_0 and P_1. (This is the linearly interpolated price exclusive of the accrued coupon.)

4.2.17 Show that $P_0(1+j) - Fr = P_1$. Then assuming that $r=j$ and $P_0 = F$, show that $P_1 = F$.

4.2.18 Suppose that a bond has semiannual coupons of amount Fr each. At six-month effective yield rate j, a continuous payment for six months equivalent to a semiannual coupon is $\bar{r} \cdot F = \frac{Fr}{\bar{s}_{\overline{1}|j}}$. Suppose that the quoted price at time t (where $0 \leq t \leq 1$ is measured since the last coupon) is redefined to be the price-plus-accrued minus $\bar{r} \cdot F \cdot \bar{s}_{\overline{t}|j}$. Show that the quoted price in part (ii) of Example 4.2 would then become exactly 100 per 100 of face amount. Show that $\bar{r} \cdot \bar{s}_{\overline{t}|j}$ is approximately equal to $t \cdot Fr$.

4.2.19 In the bond quotations of a financial newspaper, a quote was given for the price on February 20, 1990 of an 11% bond with face amount 100 maturing on April 1, 2009. The yield was quoted as 11.267%. Find the quoted price to the nearest .001.

4.2.20 Suppose the redemption amount C is not necessarily equal to the face amount F on a bond. Using $g = \frac{Fr}{C}$ as the *modified coupon rate*, show that Equations (4.1), (4.2) and (4.3) become

$$P = C \cdot v_j^n + Cg \cdot a_{\overline{n}|j}, \qquad (4.1E)$$
$$P = C + C(g-j) \cdot a_{\overline{n}|j}, \qquad (4.2E)$$

and

$$P = K + \frac{g}{j}(C-K). \qquad (4.3E)$$

Describe the relationship linking the relative sizes of P and C to the relative sizes of g and j.

4.2.21 A 1000 bond bearing coupons at annual rate 6.5%, payable semiannually, and redeemable at 1050 is bought to yield a nominal rate of 8% convertible semiannually. If the present value of the redemption amount is 210, what is the price to the nearest 10?

4.2.22 During the time when compound interest calculations were done by hand and with reference to interest tables, bond tables were constructed listing prices at issue (per 100 of face amount) of bonds with varying maturity dates, coupon rates and yield rates. Thus the bond price $P(n, r, j)$ is written as a function of n, r and j. Show that $P(n, r, j)$ is a linear function of r but not of n or j. Thus linear interpolation with respect to the coupon rate gives exact results, but linear interpolation with respect to the yield rate gives approximate results.

4.2.23 Using one of the bond price formulas given by Equation (4.1), (4.2) or (4.3), find formulations for each of the following derivatives.

(a) $\frac{\partial P}{\partial r}$, $\frac{\partial P}{\partial j}$, and $\frac{\partial P}{\partial n}$

(b) $\frac{\partial r}{\partial P}$ and $\frac{\partial n}{\partial P}$

(c) $\frac{\partial r}{\partial n}$ and $\frac{\partial n}{\partial r}$, assuming P, F and j are fixed values.

4.2.24 A company issues 1,000,000 in bonds. The prevailing yield rate on the bonds is 12%. The company considers having coupons at 8% and a maturity of 15 years. On second thought, the company decides on a maturity date of 20 years. What coupon rate must the bond issue have in order for the company to raise the same amount of revenue as it would have on the 15-year issue? Suppose the company issued the bonds with a maturity date of 10 years. What coupon rate is required to raise the same amount as under the other two issues? Relate these results to part (c) of Exercise 4.2.23.

4.2.25 On the issue date Smith buys a 20-year 12% bond with face amount 10,000. He pays a price which gives him a yield of 9%. Ten years later, just after a coupon payment, Smith sells the bond. He is given two opinions regarding the capital gain or loss incurred in the bond transaction. The first opinion states that the capital gain or loss is the difference between the price originally paid for the bond and the price at which it is sold; the second opinion states that the gain or loss is the difference between the book value of the bond and its sale price. The book value is taken as the price of the bond based on the original yield rate. For each opinion on the calculation of capital gain or loss, find each of the following:
(a) Smith's capital gain or loss if, at the time he sells the bond, the yield from the time of sale to maturity is (i) 6%, (ii) 9%, (iii) 12% , or (iv) 15%.
(b) Smith's capital gain or loss if his yield for the 10 years he held the bond is (i) 6%, (ii) 9%, (iii) 12%, or (iv) 15%.

4.2.26 Suppose $0 \leq t \leq 1$, and P_t, the price of a bond at time t coupon periods after the previous coupon, is based on the formulation described in Exercise 4.2.18. Show that $P_t \leq F$, $P_t = F$, and $P_t \geq F$ according as $r \leq j$, $r = j$, and $r \geq j$, respectively. Note that Example 4.2 shows that these equivalences might not all be valid if the price-plus-accrued is used instead of the price.

4.2.27 Find the prices of the bond in Example 4.2 using each of the following approaches.

(a) $P_t = P_0(1+j)^t - \dfrac{Fr \cdot s_{\overline{t}|j}}{s_{\overline{1}|j}}$ (See Exercise 4.2.18.)

(b) $P_t = P_0[1+t \cdot j] - t \cdot Fr$

4.2.28 (a) Suppose a bond has face (and redemption) amount F, coupon rate r per coupon period, and n coupons remaining until maturity. If the bond is purchased one period before the next coupon with a yield rate of j per coupon period, and if we define the quantity $G = \dfrac{Fr}{j}$, show that the purchase price can be written as $P = G + (F-G) \cdot v_j^n$.

(b) If the redemption amount for this bond is C, show that the purchase price is $P = G + (C-G) \cdot v_j^n$.

Exercises 4.3

4.3.1 Graph OB_k for each of the three cases in Example 4.3.
  (a) Show that for a bond bought at a premium, the graph of OB_k is concave downward.
  (b) Show that for a bond bought at a discount, the graph of OB_k is convex upward.

4.3.2 A 10% bond has face amount 10,000. For each combination of the following terms to maturity and six-month yield rates, construct the amortization table and draw the graph of OB_k: $n = 1, 5, 10, 30$; $j = .025, .05, .075$.

4.3.3 Find the total amount paid, the total interest and the total principal repaid in the amortization of Table 4.1.

4.3.4. The amortization schedule for a 100, 5% bond with semi-annual coupons yielding a nominal annual rate of $i^{(2)} = 6.6\%$ gives a value of 90.00 for the bond at the beginning of a certain 6-month period just after a coupon has been paid. What is the book value at the start of the next 6-month period?

4.3.5 A bond of face amount 100 is purchased at a premium of 36 to yield 7%. The amount for amortization of premium in the 5th coupon is 1.00. What is the term of the bond?

4.3.6 Using Table 4.1, show that the bond payments can be regarded as payments on two separate loans. The first loan is of amount F with interest only at rate j (per coupon period) for n periods, plus return of F at the end of n periods. The second loan is an amortization of $P - F$ over n periods at effective rate j (per coupon period), with payments of $F(r - j)$ per coupon period. This second loan is the amortization of premium if $P > F$.

4.3.7 A bondholder is subject to a tax of 50% on interest payments at the time interest is received, and a tax (or credit) of 25% on capital gains (or losses) when they are realized. Assume that the capital gain (or loss) on the bond is the difference between the purchase price and the sale price (or redemption amount if held to maturity), and the full amount of each coupon is regarded as interest. For each of the cases in Example 4.3, find the bond's purchase price so that the stated yield is the *after-tax* yield.

4.3.8 Suppose the redemption amount on a bond is C, not necessarily equal to the face amount F. Construct the bond's amortization table in the form of Table 4.1.

4.3.9 A 30-year bond with face amount 10,000 is bought to yield $i^{(2)} = .08$. In each of the following cases find the purchase price of the bond and the bond's coupon rate.
  (a) The final entry in the amortization schedule for accumulation of discount is 80.
  (b) The final entry in the amortization schedule for amortization of premium is 80.
  (c) The first entry in the amortization schedule for accumulation of discount is 80.
  (d) The first entry in the amortization schedule for amortization of premium is 80.

(e) The final entry in the schedule for interest due is 500.
(f) The final entry in the schedule for interest due is 400.
(g) The final entry in the schedule for interest due is 300.
(h) The first entry in the schedule for interest due is 500.
(i) The first entry in the schedule for interest due is 400.
(j) The first entry in the schedule for interest due is 300.

Exercises 4.4

4.4.1 Let $n \geq 1$, $0 \leq t \leq 1$, and $g(j) = [F \cdot v_j^n + Fr \cdot a_{\overline{n}|j}](1 + j)^t$.
  (a) Show that $g(j)$ is strictly decreasing and convex (i.e., $g'(j) < 0$ and $g''(j) > 0$).
  (b) Show that $\lim_{j \to -1} g(j) = +\infty$ and $\lim_{j \to \infty} g(j) = 0$.
  (c) Use parts (a) and (b) to show that if $P > 0$ then Equation (4.8) has a unique solution for j.
  (d) Use the results of parts (a) and (b) to provide a graphical proof that the Newton-Raphson method for the function $f(j) = P - [F \cdot v_j^n + Fr \cdot a_{\overline{n}|j}](1 + j)^t$ with starting value $j_0 = 0$, where P is the price-plus-accrued of the bond, produces a sequence $j_1, j_2, \ldots$, that converges to the exact yield rate.

4.4.2 Use part (a) of Exercise 4.4.1 to show that whenever a bond yield rate is found by linear interpolation using Equation (4.8), the interpolated yield rate is larger than the true yield rate.

4.4.3 (a) Show that bond price Equation (4.2) can be rewritten in the form $j = r - \dfrac{P-F}{F \cdot a_{\overline{n}|j}}$. Using this as the basis for the iteration $j_{n+1} = r - \dfrac{P-F}{F \cdot a_{\overline{n}|j_n}}$, with starting value $j_0 = 0$, calculate $j_1, j_2, \ldots, j_{10}$ for the bond in part (a) of Example 4.4. It can be shown that this iteration method converges to the true yield rate if $P < 2C$.
  (b) Apply the formula in part (a) to a bond bought between coupon dates, using the price for P and letting n represent the number of coupon periods to maturity, including fractions. Apply this to the bond in part (b) of Example 4.4 to find j_{10} using the starting value $j_0 = 0$. Compare j_{10} to the exact value of j.

4.4.4   A bond has face amount 100 and coupon rate 10%.
        (a) Suppose the bond is purchased for 110 just after a coupon has
            been paid.   Find the yield rate on the bond to the nearest
            .001% for each of $n = 2, 5, 10, 20, 30$ (the number of coupons
            remaining).
        (b) Repeat part (a) assuming the bond was purchased for 90.

4.4.5   For part (b) of Example 4.4, find the nominal annual yield earned
        by the original bondholder from January 15, 1990 to April 1,
        1995. Use each of the methods of Example 4.4.

4.4.6   Bonds A and B have the same face value and the same number of
        coupons remaining.   Bond A has a coupon rate of r_1 per coupon
        period and Bond B has a coupon rate of r_2 per coupon period.
        Their prices are P_1 and P_2, respectively, at the same yield rate.
        Bond C has the same face value, number of coupons and yield rate
        as the first two bonds, but Bond C has coupon rate r_3 per coupon
        period.   Express the exact price of Bond C in terms of P_1, P_2, r_1,
        r_2, and r_3.

4.4.7   It was pointed out in Section 4.2 that when a loan is amortized with
        n equally spaced (but not necessarily level) payments, the interest
        rate per period on the loan is $i = \dfrac{I_T}{OB_0 + OB_1 + \cdots + OB_{n-1}}$.
        The coupons and redemption payments of a bond can be regarded
        as payments on a loan amortized at the yield rate.   The total
        interest paid over the lifetime of a loan is the total amount of the
        payments minus the amount of the original loan.   Then, in the case
        of a bond with n coupons remaining and valued just after a coupon
        has been paid, the total interest paid over the lifetime of the bond
        is $n \cdot Fr + C - P$, where the coupons plus redemption represent
        loan payments, and the price represents the loan amount.   The
        initial outstanding balance is $OB_0 = P$, and the outstanding balance
        decreases or increases to C at time n, when the redemption amount
        is paid.
        (a) Assuming that the average OB_t is, approximately $\dfrac{P+C}{2}$, show
            that an approximation to the yield rate is

$$j = \frac{r - \dfrac{P-C}{n \cdot C}}{1 + \dfrac{P-C}{2C}}. \qquad (4.15a)$$

This approximation is called the *bond salesman's formula*.
(b) Suppose OB_t changes linearly from $OB_0 = P$ to $OB_n = C$.
Show that under this approximation $OB_t = P - t \cdot \frac{P-C}{n}$, and

$$j \approx \frac{r - \frac{P-C}{n \cdot C}}{1 + \frac{(n+1) \cdot (P-C)}{2 \cdot n \cdot C}}. \qquad (4.14b)$$

(c) Apply the formulas in parts (a) and (b) to obtain approximations of the yield rate for the bond described in part (a) of Example 4.4.

4.4.8 Use the result of Exercise 4.3.1 to reach the following conclusions regarding the yield rate approximations derived in Exercise 4.4.7.
(a) For a bond bought at a premium, the approximate yield rate is larger than the true yield rate.
(b) For a bond bought at a discount, the approximate yield rate is smaller than the true yield rate.

4.4.9 Apply the formulas in Exercise 4.4.7 to the various bonds described in Exercise 4.4.4 to find the approximate yield rates. Verify the biases in the approximations as predicted by Exercise 4.4.8 by comparing the approximate yield rates to the "exact" yield rates found in Exercise 4.4.4. Note that for bonds with shorter terms to maturity, the approximations are more accurate. Plot the outstanding balance curves for the bonds in Exercise 4.4.4 and note that the shorter the term, the closer the outstanding balance curve is to being linear. (This explains the better accuracy of the bond salesman's formula for bonds of shorter term.) The approximate formulas also lose accuracy in higher yield rate situations. As an attempt to correct the bias, the bond salesman's formula can be modified by adding $\frac{P-C}{4 \cdot n \cdot C}$ in the denominator. Apply this modified approximate formula to the bonds in Exercise 4.4.4 and to the bond bought between coupon dates in part (b) of Example 4.4, where n is taken as the number of coupon periods until maturity, including fractions.

4.4.10 (a) Calculate the Taylor polynomial of degree 1 of $\frac{1}{a_{\overline{n}|j}}$, use it in
        the relationship $j = r - \frac{P-F}{F \cdot a_{\overline{n}|j}}$, and solve for j. This results
        in the same approximation found in part (b) of Exercise 4.4.7.
        (b) Repeat part (a) with the Taylor polynomial of degree 2. Use
        this to find the approximate yield rate for the bonds in Exercise
        4.4.4.

Exercises 4.5

4.5.1   An 8% serial bond of face amount 2,000,000 issued June 15, 1990
        is to be redeemed by 10 semiannual installments of 100,000 each
        starting June 15, 1995, followed by 5 semiannual installments of
        200,000 each starting June 15, 2000. Find the price of the entire
        issue to yield $i^{(2)} = .10$.

4.5.2   A 100,000,000 serial bond issued June 1, 1986 carries a
        semiannual coupon rate of 8%. The redemption of the bond takes
        place over a 30-year period, with redemptions of 10,000,000 made
        every 3 years, starting on June 1, 1989. What is the price of this
        bond to yield $i^{(2)} = .10$?

4.5.3   Suppose the entire bond issue in Example 4.5 is purchased for
        45,000,000. Find the nominal annual yield rate.

4.5.4   An *annuity bond* has level payments (coupon plus redemption)
        every coupon period. Thus it is a serial bond, but the redemption
        amounts decrease every period. A 10-year 10% annuity bond with
        face amount 100,000 has semiannual payments of $\frac{100,000}{a_{\overline{20}|.05}}$, of
        which some would be coupon payment and some would be
        redemption payment. A purchaser wishes a yield of $i^{(2)} = .12$.
        Find the price of the bond and construct the amortization schedule
        for the first 2 years.

4.5.5   (a) Suppose that the redemption amounts are $C_1, C_2, \ldots, C_m$ (not necessarily equal to $F_1, F_2, \ldots, F_m$). Show that if $\frac{r \cdot F_t}{C_t} = g$ for all $t = 1, 2, \ldots, m$, then the price can be written as $P = K + \frac{g}{j}(C - K)$, where K is the present value of the redemption amounts at yield rate j.

   (b) Suppose $\frac{r \cdot F_t}{C_t} \neq g$ for all t. Let each C_t be written as $C_t = C_t' + C_t''$, where $\frac{r \cdot F_t}{C_t'} = g$ for each t. Show that P can now be written as $P = K + \frac{g}{j}(C' - K')$, where K is, as before, the present value of the full redemption amounts, and $C' = \sum_{t=1}^{m} C_t'$ and $K' = \sum_{t=1}^{m} C_t' \cdot v_j^{n_t}$.

   (c) Now suppose that each C_t' is taken so that $\frac{r \cdot F_t}{C_t'} = j$. Show that $P = C' + K - K'$ (see Exercise 4.2.28).

4.5.6   A 10% bond with face amount 100 is callable on any coupon date from $15\frac{1}{2}$ years after issue up to the maturity date which is 20 years from issue.
   (a) Find the price of the bond to yield a minimum nominal annual rate of (i) 12%, (ii) 10%, and (iii) 8%.
   (b) Find the minimum annual yield to maturity if the bond is purchased for (i) 80, (ii) 100, and (iii) 120.

4.5.7   Repeat Exercise 4.5.6 assuming that the bond is callable at a redemption amount of 110, including the redemption at maturity.

4.5.8   Verify that the yield rates given in the solutions of part (c) of Example 4.6 and part (b) of Example 4.7 are correct.

4.5.9   On June 15, 1990 a corporation issues an 8% bond with a face value of 1,000,000. The bond can be redeemed, at the option of the corporation, on any coupon date in 2001 or 2002 at par, on any coupon date in 2003 through 2005 for amount 1,200,000, or on any coupon date in 2006 through June 15, 2008 at redemption amount 1,300,000.
   (a) Find the price to yield a minimum nominal annual rate of (i) 10% and (ii) $6\frac{1}{2}$%.

(b) Find the minimum nominal annual yield if the bond is bought for (i) 800,000, (ii) 1,000,000, or (iii) 1,200,000.

4.5.10 Repeat Example 4.8 for (a) a bond with 8% coupons, and (b) a bond with 12% coupons.

4.5.11 Assume that the pricing of a coupon bond is consistent with its pricing based on separate coupons and redemption using the term structure of spot rates as in Example 4.8. Let $H(r,t)$ denote the current term structure for the yield to maturity of a coupon bond with coupon rate r and time t to maturity. Then $H(0,t)$ is the current term structure for zero-coupons bonds. Let $r_1 \geq r_2$.
   (a) Suppose $H(0,t)$ is a decreasing function of t for all t. Show that $H(r,t)$ is also a decreasing function of t, and $H(r_1,t) \geq H(r_2,t) \geq H(0,t)$ for any t.
   (b) Suppose $H(0,t)$ is an increasing function of t for all t. Show that $H(r,t)$ is also an increasing function of t, and $H(r_1,t) \leq H(r_2,t) \leq H(0,t)$ for any t.
   (c) Suppose $H(0,t)$ is constant for all t. Show that $H(r,t)$ is also constant and $H(r,t) = H_s(t)$ for any t.

4.5.12 Repeat Example 4.9 for parameter values $r = .04, .06, .08$; $n = 2, 10, 20, 40$; and $j = .03, .05, .07$.

4.5.13 Let $D(r,n,j)$ denote the duration of a bond of face amount F, with n coupons at rate r per coupon period, and with yield rate j. Find

(a) $\lim_{n \to \infty} D(r, n, j)$,   (b) $\lim_{n \to 0} D(r, n, j)$,   (c) $\lim_{r \to \infty} D(r, n, j)$,

(d) $\lim_{r \to 0} D(r, n, j)$,   (e) $\lim_{j \to \infty} D(r, n, j)$, and   (f) $\lim_{j \to 0} D(r, n, j)$.

4.5.14 For the cashflow with payments $K_1, K_2, \ldots, K_n$, made at times $1, 2, \ldots, n$, suppose that $L = \sum_{t=1}^{n} K_t \cdot v^t$ at rate i_0 per payment period. Show that $\frac{d}{di}[L(1 + i)^D]\big|_{i=i_0} = 0$, where D is the duration defined in Equation (4.11).

4.5.15 Suppose that the yield rate and coupon rate on an n-coupon bond are the same. Show that the duration is $\ddot{a}_{\overline{n}|}$ valued at the yield rate. Find the duration of a 6-coupon bond with coupon rate 10% per coupon period and yield rate 10%.

4.5.16 Consider a bond with continuous coupons at rate r per period and redemption amount 1 in n periods, valued at yield rate δ.

(a) Express $\frac{dL}{d\delta}$ in terms of continuous annuity symbols and the factors r, n and δ. The duration is $D = -\frac{1}{L} \cdot \frac{dL}{d\delta}$.

(b) Find an expression for $\frac{dD}{dn}$. Show that it has the same sign as $\delta + (r - \delta)\left[r(n-\bar{a}_{\overline{n}|}) + \delta\,\bar{a}_{\overline{n}|}\right]$, so that if $r \geq \delta$, then D increases with n, but if $r < \delta$, then D is increasing for $n = 0$ to $n = n_0$, and then is decreasing for $n > n_0$. This accounts for the smaller durations for the 60-coupon bonds than the 30-coupon bonds in line 1 of Table 4.3b and lines 1 and 2 of Table 4.3c.

4.5.17 A government is issuing a 5-year 15% bond with face amount 1,000,000,000. The perception in the investment community is that the government is somewhat unstable, and it is forecast that there is a 10% chance that the government will default on interest payments by the first or second years, a 20% chance of default by the third or fourth years, and a 25% chance of default (on interest and principal) by the fifth year. All probabilities are *unconditional* (measured from time 0, so that, for instance, the probability that the 7th coupon will be paid is .8)

(a) Find the price to be paid for this issue for an investor to earn yield $i^{(2)} = .18$ on the expected payments.

(b) Based on the price found in part (a), find the yield to maturity if all payments are actually made.

(c) Suppose that the risk of default on the redemption amount is only 10%, but the other default risks are as stated. Repeat parts (a) and (b).

4.5.18   It was pointed out in Section 4.2 that U.S. bond quotations are made in price increments of $\frac{1}{8}$ per 100 face amount, and in nominal yield increments of .10%. A bond of face amount 100 has n coupon periods until maturity, a coupon rate of r per coupon period, and a nominal annual yield rate of $i^{(2)}$. For each of the following sets of parameters, find the range of bond prices based on the yield rate range of $i^{(2)} \pm .0005$ (*i.e.*, calculate the bond price for yields at both ends of the range): $r = .03, .05, .07$; $n = 2, 10, 40$; $i^{(2)} = .06, .10, .14$.

4.5.19   Transform Equation (4.10) into Equation (4.11).

CHAPTER 5

THE INTEREST RATE
AS A RANDOM VARIABLE

5.1   INTRODUCTION

In earlier chapters a framework was developed for formulating an equation
of value describing a financial transaction. One of the key components in
the formulation is the interest rate (or rates) involved in the transaction.
The point of view taken has been that the interest rate in effect is known
before the transaction takes place.   In many situations this is true in
practice, such as for guaranteed investment certificates and loans with a
fixed rate of interest. The interest rate is said to be *deterministic* in that
instance. In certain other situations the rate of interest, growth or return
might not be definitely known before the transaction takes place, such as in
a variable interest rate loan where the rate is set annually (or monthly) or
in the growth of a mutual (stock market equity) fund. In these cases the
rate of interest or return may be affected by some random factors and is
said to be *stochastic*. Although stochastic interest rates are more complex
to deal with than deterministic interest rates, there is an increasing
awareness of the importance of analyzing financial transactions under the
assumption that interest rates are fluctuating in some random fashion,
governed by a specified probability distribution.   There are a number of
studies in published articles and textbooks regarding the analysis of
financial transactions when interest rates are random.   Section 5.5 lists
several references on this topic.   In this chapter we consider some
introductory concepts which relate to the rate of interest over one or more
periods as a random variable.

 It is assumed that the reader is familiar with the basic concepts of
probability, random variables, mean, variance, and so on, and these

concepts will be used throughout this chapter. Appendix B provides a review of these concepts, and Section 5.5 lists additional references on probability.

Random variables will be denoted by a tilde beneath a quantity, for example, $\underset{\sim}{X}$. Recall that for a discrete random variable $\underset{\sim}{X}$ with probability function $p(x) = Pr[\underset{\sim}{X} = x]$, the mean of $\underset{\sim}{X}$ is

$$E[\underset{\sim}{X}] = \sum_x x \cdot p(x), \tag{5.1}$$

where the sum is taken over all values of $\underset{\sim}{X}$ with nonzero probability, and for a continuous random variable with probability density function $f(x)$, the mean of $\underset{\sim}{X}$ is

$$E[\underset{\sim}{X}] = \int_{-\infty}^{\infty} x \cdot f(x) \, dx. \tag{5.2}$$

5.2   ACCUMULATED AND PRESENT VALUES

5.2.1 Accumulated Values

At an annual effective interest rate of 12.5%, an amount of 1 invested now will accumulate to 1.125 one year from now. Suppose that the annual effective interest rate for the coming year is not definitely known, but a forecasting technique has predicted that the rate will be either 10% or 15%, with both rates equally likely to occur. Thus the annual rate of interest for the coming year is a *random variable* with a two-point discrete distribution given by

$$\underset{\sim}{i} = \begin{cases} .10, & \text{with probability } .5 \\ .15, & \text{with probability } .5 \end{cases}.$$

The expected value is $E[\underset{\sim}{i}] = (.10)(.5) + (.15)(.5) = .125$, and the random growth factor for the year, $1 + \underset{\sim}{i}$, has expected value $E[1 + \underset{\sim}{i}] = 1 + E[\underset{\sim}{i}] = 1.125$. Of course the actual growth will be either 1.10 or 1.15, and both results are equally likely. The variance of $\underset{\sim}{i}$

is $Var[\underline{i}] = E[\underline{i}^2] - (E[\underline{i}])^2$. (See Appendix B for the various formulations for the variance of a random variable.) But

$$\underline{i}^2 = \begin{cases} .0100, & \text{with probability } .5 \\ .0225, & \text{with probability } .5 \text{'} \end{cases}$$

from which we find $E[\underline{i}^2] = (.01)(.5) + (.0225)(.5) = .01625$ and $Var[\underline{i}] = .01625 - (.125)^2 = .000625$. The standard deviation of $\underline{i}$ is .025, which is not surprising since the standard deviation is a measure of the average deviation of the random variable around its mean.

The distribution of $\underline{i}$ may be more complex than the one illustrated above, but it will always be true that

$$E[1 + \underline{i}] = 1 + E[\underline{i}] \tag{5.3}$$

and

$$Var[1 + \underline{i}] = Var[\underline{i}] \tag{5.4}$$

for a one-year period.

Suppose now that annual interest rates are being forecast over the two-year period beginning now, where $\underline{i}_1$ is the (random) annual rate in the first year and $\underline{i}_2$ is the rate in the second year. Assuming that whatever interest is earned in the first year is reinvested (compounded) in the second year, the (random) accumulated value at the end of two years of an initial investment of 1 made now is

$$\underline{S}(2) = (1 + \underline{i}_1)(1 + \underline{i}_2) = 1 + \underline{i}_1 + \underline{i}_2 + \underline{i}_1 \cdot \underline{i}_2. \tag{5.5}$$

Finding the expected value and variance of $\underline{S}(2)$ is more complicated than it was for a one-year accumulation, since we now have

$$E[\underline{S}(2)] = E[1 + \underline{i}_1 + \underline{i}_2 + \underline{i}_1 \cdot \underline{i}_2] = 1 + E[\underline{i}_1] + E[\underline{i}_2] + E[\underline{i}_1 \cdot \underline{i}_2].$$

In order to determine $E[\underline{i}_1 \cdot \underline{i}_2]$, and hence $E[\underline{S}(2)]$, we need to know the relationship between $\underline{i}_1$ and $\underline{i}_2$. The simplest relationship is that they are *stochastically independent* (or just *independent*). A non-rigorous interpretation of this concept is that the value that occurs for $\underline{i}_1$ in the first year has no effect on the value of $\underline{i}_2$ that occurs in the second year. The important consequence of this assumption of independence is that

$E[i_1 \cdot i_2] = E[i_1] \cdot E[i_2]$. For now we will use the simplifying assumption of independence among interest rates from year to year; at the end of this section we will consider more complex relationships among interest rates.

| EXAMPLE 5.1 |

Suppose that over a two-year period the annual effective interest rates i_1 and i_2 are independent random variables, both of which follow the distribution

$$i = \begin{cases} .10, & \text{with probability } .5 \\ .15, & \text{with probability } .5 \end{cases}$$

Find the expected value and variance of $S(2)$.

| SOLUTION |

One way to find the moments of $S(2)$ is to specify its complete distribution and apply basic principles. Since each of i_1 and i_2, and thus $1 + i_1$ and $1 + i_2$, can take on only two possible values, then the accumulated value $S(2) = (1 + i_1)(1 + i_2)$ can take on only the four possible values

$$S(2) = \begin{cases} (1.10)(1.10) = 1.21, & \text{with probability } .25 \\ (1.10)(1.15) = 1.265, & \text{with probability } .25 \\ (1.15)(1.10) = 1.265, & \text{with probability } .25 \\ (1.15)(1.15) = 1.3225, & \text{with probability } .25. \end{cases}$$

Then $E[S(2)] = (.25)[1.21 + 1.265 + 1.265 + 1.3225] = 1.265625$, and $Var[S(2)] = E[S(2)^2] - (E[S(2)])^2 = E[S(2)^2] - 1.601807$. But

$$S(2)^2 = \begin{cases} 1.4641, & \text{with probability } .25 \\ 1.600225, & \text{with probability } .25 \\ 1.600225, & \text{with probability } .25 \\ 1.74900625, & \text{with probability } .25 \end{cases},$$

so $E[S(2)^2] = 1.603389$ and $Var[S(2)] = .001582$. An alternative approach to finding the moments directly exploits the assumption of independence. If $1 + i_1$ and $1 + i_2$ are independent, then

$$E[S(2)] = E[(1+i_1)(1+i_2)] = E[1+i_1] \cdot E[1+i_2] = (E[1+i])^2.$$

Since $E[1 + \underline{i}] = 1.125$, then $E[\underline{S}(2)] = (1.125)^2 = 1.265625$, as above. The independence of $1 + \underline{i}_1$ and $1 + \underline{i}_2$ implies the independence of $(1 + \underline{i}_1)^2$ and $(1 + \underline{i}_2)^2$, so that

$$E[\underline{S}(2)^2] = E[(1 + \underline{i}_1)^2(1 + \underline{i}_2)^2] = E[(1 + \underline{i}_1)^2] \cdot E[(1 + \underline{i}_2)^2]$$
$$= (E[(1 + \underline{i})^2])^2.$$

We then find $E[(1 + \underline{i})^2] = (1.10)^2(.5) + (1.15)^2(.5) = 1.26625$, and $E[\underline{S}(2)^2] = (1.26625)^2 = 1.603389$, as above, and the variance is the same as before. □

The second method presented in Example 5.1 for finding the mean and variance of $\underline{S}(2) = (1 + \underline{i}_1)(1 + \underline{i}_2)$ in the case of independent rates of interest can be generalized to find the mean and variance of the (random) accumulated value after n periods,

$$\underline{S}(n) = (1 + \underline{i}_1)(1 + \underline{i}_2) \cdots (1 + \underline{i}_n). \tag{5.6}$$

In the general case we have

$$E[\underline{S}(n)] = E[(1 + \underline{i}_1)(1 + \underline{i}_2) \cdots (1 + \underline{i}_n)]$$
$$= E[1 + \underline{i}_1] \cdot E[1 + \underline{i}_2] \cdots E[1 + \underline{i}_n]$$
$$= (1 + E[\underline{i}_1])(1 + E[\underline{i}_2]) \cdots (1 + E[\underline{i}_n]), \tag{5.7}$$

and since $\underline{S}(n)^2 = (1 + \underline{i}_1)^2(1 + \underline{i}_2)^2 \cdots (1 + \underline{i}_n)^2$, we have

$$E[\underline{S}(n)^2] = E[(1 + \underline{i}_1)^2(1 + \underline{i}_2)^2 \cdots (1 + \underline{i}_n)^2]$$
$$= E[(1 + \underline{i}_1)^2] \cdot E[(1 + \underline{i}_2)^2] \cdots E[(1 + \underline{i}_n)^2]. \tag{5.8}$$

If $\underline{i}_1, \underline{i}_2, \ldots, i_n$ are independent and identically distributed (i.i.d.), with common distribution $\underline{i}$, then

$$E[\underline{S}(n)] = (E[1 + \underline{i}])^n = (1 + E[\underline{i}])^n \tag{5.9}$$

and

$$E[\underline{S}(n)^2] = (E[(1 + \underline{i})^2])^n. \tag{5.10}$$

Using the simpler notation $R = E[1 + \underline{i}]$ and $S = E[(1 + \underline{i})^2]$, we have

$$E[\underline{S}(n)] = R^n \qquad (5.11)$$

and

$$E[\underline{S}(n)^2] = S^n, \qquad (5.12)$$

so that

$$Var[\underline{S}(n)] = E[\underline{S}(n)^2] - (E[\underline{S}(n)])^2 = S^n - R^{2n}. \qquad (5.13)$$

| **EXAMPLE 5.2** |

Find the mean and variance of $\underline{S}(10)$ and $\underline{S}(20)$ for the distribution given in Example 5.1. Describe the complete distribution of $\underline{S}(10)$.

| **SOLUTION** |

From the discussion above we have $R = E[1 + \underline{i}] = 1.125$ and $S = E[(1 + \underline{i})^2] = 1.26625$, so $E[\underline{S}(10)] = R^{10} = (1.125)^{10} = 3.247321$ and $E[\underline{S}(20)] = R^{20} = (1.125)^{20} = 10.545094$. Furthermore

$$Var[\underline{S}(10)] = S^{10} - R^{20} = (1.26625)^{10} - (1.125)^{20} = .052190$$

and

$$Var[\underline{S}(20)] = S^{20} - R^{40} = 1.103429.$$

In each year $\underline{i}$ is either .10 or .15, so for the 10-year period $\underline{S}(10)$ can take on one of the 11 values

$$(1.10)^{10} = 2.593742$$

$$(1.10)^9(1.15) = 2.711640$$

$$(1.10)^8(1.15)^2 = 2.834896$$

$$\vdots$$

$$(1.10)(1.15)^9 = 3.869664$$

$$(1.15)^{10} = 4.045558.$$

The probabilities associated with these values come from a *binomial distribution*. In the case of $\underline{S}(10)$, let $\underline{K}$, $0 \le \underline{K} \le 10$, be the number of years during which the interest rate is .10, so that $10-\underset{\sim}{K}$ is the number of years during which the interest rate is .15. The distribution of $\underset{\sim}{K}$ is binomial, with parameters $n = 10$ and $p = .5$, so

$$Pr[\underset{\sim}{K} = k] = \binom{10}{k} \cdot (.5)^k(1 - .5)^{10-k} = \binom{10}{k} \cdot (.5)^{10} = \frac{\binom{10}{k}}{1024}.$$

Noting that $Pr[\underset{\sim}{K} = k] = Pr[\underset{\sim}{S}(10) = (1.1)^k(1.15)^{20-k}]$, we have the complete distribution of $\underset{\sim}{S}(10)$ given in the following table.

TABLE 5.1

k	$\underset{\sim}{S}(10)$	Probability	Cumulative Probability
0	2.593742	.000977	.000977
1	2.711640	.009766	.001953
2	2.834896	.043945	.054688
3	2.963755	.117188	.171875
4	3.098471	.205078	.376953
5	3.239311	.246094	.623047
6	3.386552	.205078	.828125
7	3.540486	.117188	.945313
8	3.701418	.043945	.989258
9	3.869664	.009766	.999023
10	4.045557	.000977	1.000000

The mean and variance of $\underset{\sim}{S}(10)$ can be found directly from the complete distribution of $\underset{\sim}{S}(10)$. For example

$$E[\underset{\sim}{S}(10)] = (2.593742)(.000977) + (2.711640)(.009766) + \cdots$$
$$+ (4.045557)(.000977) = 3.247321.$$
□

The complete distribution of $\underset{\sim}{S}(10)$ given in Example 5.2 can be used to determine the probabilities of more complex events involving $\underset{\sim}{S}(10)$. For example the probability that $\underset{\sim}{S}(10)$ exceeds its mean (*i.e.*, $Pr[\underset{\sim}{S}(10) > 3.247321])$ is the sum of the probabilities $Pr[\underset{\sim}{S}(10) = 3.386552] + \cdots + Pr[\underset{\sim}{S}(10) = 4.045557] = .376953$.

The interest rate distribution used in Example 5.2 allows for a straightforward determination of the complete distribution of $S(10)$, and in the same way $S(n)$ would be associated with a binomial distribution of n trials. When the distribution of the annual interest rate is more complex, or changes from period to period, the determination of the distribution of $S(n)$ becomes much more difficult, as the following two examples show.

| EXAMPLE 5.3 |

Repeat Example 5.2 when the distribution of the annual interest rate is

$$\underset{\sim}{i} = \begin{cases} .06, & \text{with probability } .2 \\ .10, & \text{with probability } .5 \\ .14, & \text{with probability } .3 \end{cases}.$$

| SOLUTION |

$E[\underset{\sim}{i}] = (.06)(.2) + (.10)(.5) + (.14)(.3) = .104$, so that $R = 1.104$. The distribution

$$(1 + \underset{\sim}{i})^2 = \begin{cases} 1.1236, & \text{with probability } .2 \\ 1.2100, & \text{with probability } .5 \\ 1.2996, & \text{with probability } .3 \end{cases}$$

gives $S = E[(1 + \underset{\sim}{i})^2] = 1.2196$. Then $E[S(10)] = R^{10} = 2.689619$, $E[S(20)] = 7.234049$, $Var[S(10)] = S^{10} - R^{20} = .046668$, and $Var[S(20)] = .667371$. The determination of the complete distribution of $S(10)$ becomes complicated. During the 10-year period let K_1 be the number of years the interest rate is .06, K_2 the number of years the interest rate is .10, and $K_3 = 10 - K_1 - K_2$ the number of years the interest rate is .14. Then K_1, K_2 and K_3 have a *multinomial distribution* (see Appendix B). In Example 5.2 there were only 11 possible outcomes for $S(10)$. In this case there are 66 possible outcomes for $S(10)$: (1) $K_1 = 10$, $K_2 = 0$, $K_3 = 0$; (2) $K_1 = 9$, $K_2 = 1$, $K_3 = 0$; (3) $K_1 = 9$, $K_2 = 0$, $K_3 = 1$; $\cdots$. (There are 66 positive integer assignments to K_1, K_2 and K_3 which add up to 10.) The general probability is given by

$$Pr[K_1 = k_1, K_2 = k_2, K_3 = k_3] = \frac{10!}{k_1! \cdot k_2! \cdot k_3!} \cdot (.2)^{k_1}(.5)^{k_2}(.3)^{k_3}.$$

For example $S(10) = 2.489523$ if $K_1 = 4, K_2 = 3$ and $K_3 = 3$, and this occurs with probability $\frac{10!}{4! \cdot 3! \cdot 3!} \cdot (.2)^4(.5)^3(.3)^3 = .022680$.   □

EXAMPLE 5.4

Annual interest rates for the next two years are assumed to have independent continuous distributions. In the first year i_1 has a uniform distribution on the interval $[.08, .12]$, and in the second year i_2 has a uniform distribution on the interval $[.06, .14]$. Find the mean, variance and probability density function of $S(2)$, and find the values of c for which $Pr[S(2) > c] = .05, .50$ and $.95$ (these would be the 95th, 50th and 5th *percentiles* of the distribution of $S(2)$).

SOLUTION

$E[S(2)] = E[1 + i_1] \cdot E[1 + i_2]$ due to the independence of i_1 and i_2. The continuous uniform distribution on $[a, b]$ has p.d.f. $f(x) = \frac{1}{b-a}$, for $a < x < b$, and mean

$$E[X] = \int_a^b x \cdot \frac{1}{b-a} \, dx = \frac{a+b}{2}.$$

Thus $E[i_1] = .10$, since i_1 has p.d.f. $\frac{1}{.12 - .08} = 25$, and $E[i_2] = .10$, since i_2 has p.d.f. $\frac{1}{.14 - .06} = 12.5$, so $E[S(2)] = (1.10)(1.10) = 1.21$. We also have $E[S(2)^2] = E[(1 + i_1)^2] \cdot E[(1 + i_2)^2]$. Since i_1 is uniformly distributed on $[.08, .12]$, it follows that $1 + i_1$ is uniformly distributed on the interval $[1.08, 1.12]$; similarly $1 + i_2$ is uniformly distributed on the interval $[1.06, 1.14]$. Then

$$Var[S(2)] = E[S(2)^2] - (E[S(2)])^2 = E[S(2)^2] - (1.21)^2.$$

But

$$E[(1 + i_1)^2] = \int_{.08}^{.12} 25(1 + i_1)^2 \, di_1 = \frac{25(1 + i_1)^3}{3} \Big|_{.08}^{.12} = 1.210133,$$

and

$$E[(1 + i_2)^2] = \int_{.06}^{.14} 12.5(1 + i_2)^2 \, di_2 = \frac{12.5(1 + i_2)^3}{3} \Big|_{.06}^{.14} = 1.210533.$$

Therefore $Var[S(2)] = (1.210133)(1.210533) - (1.21)^2 = .000807$. The problem of finding the p.d.f. of $S(2)$ is somewhat complicated. There are a number of approaches that can be taken (see the notes in Section 5.5).

Since both $1 + \underline{i}_1$ and $1 + \underline{i}_2$ have continuous distributions, then so does $\underline{S}(2)$, and the density function $g(t)$ of $\underline{S}(2)$ is $g(t) = G'(t)$, where $G(t)$ is the cumulative distribution function of $\underline{S}(2)$.

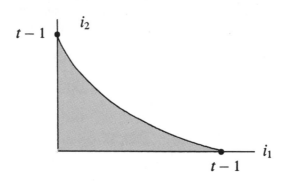

FIGURE 5.1

With reference to Figure 5.1 giving the two-dimensional region of probability for the joint distribution of $s_1 = 1 + \underline{i}_1$ and $s_2 = 1 + \underline{i}_2$, for a particular value of $t = (1 + i_1)(1 + i_2)$, $G(t)$ is equal to the probability in the shaded region, since the value of t can be obtained when $1 + i_2 = \frac{t}{(1+i_1)}$. But $G(t)$ is equal to the double integral $\int\int f(s_1, s_2)\, ds_2 ds_1$ $= \int\int (25)(12.5)\, ds_2\, ds_1$. (The joint density $f(s_1, s_2)$ of $1 + \underline{i}_1$ and $1 + \underline{i}_2$ is just the product of the individual densities, since $1 + \underline{i}_1$ and $1 + \underline{i}_2$ are independent.) Note that t ranges from a minimum of $(1.08)(1.06) = 1.1448$ to a maximum of $(1.12)(1.14) = 1.2768$. The limits of integration in the double integral depend on the range in which t lies. Figure 5.2 indicates the three regions in which t may lie, for the purpose of simplifying the limits of integration.

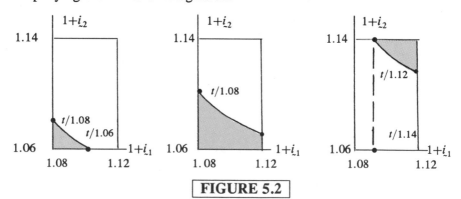

FIGURE 5.2

$$G(t) = \begin{cases} \int_{1.08}^{t/1.06} \int_{1.06}^{t/s_1} 312.5 \, ds_2 \, ds_1 & \text{for } (1.06)(1.08) \le t \le (1.06)(1.12) \\ \int_{1.08}^{1.12} \int_{1.06}^{t/s_1} 312.5 \, ds_2 \, ds_1 & \text{for } (1.06)(1.12) \le t \le (1.08)(1.14) \\ 1 - \int_{t/1.14}^{1.12} \int_{t/s_1}^{1.14} 312.5 \, ds_2 \, ds_1 & \text{for } (1.08)(1.14) \le t \le (1.12)(1.14) \end{cases}$$

Thus the c.d.f. is

$$G(t) = (312.5) \begin{cases} t \ln(t) - t[1+\ln(1.1448)] + 1.1448 & \text{if } 1.1448 \le t \le 1.1872 \\ t[\ln(1.12) - \ln(1.08)] - .0424 & \text{if } 1.1872 \le t \le 1.2312 \\ t[1+\ln(1.2768)] - t \ln(t) - 1.2736 & \text{if } 1.2312 \le t \le 1.2768 \end{cases}$$

and the p.d.f. is

$$g(t) = G'(t) = (312.5) \begin{cases} \ln(t) - \ln(1.1448) & \text{if } 1.1448 \le t \le 1.1872 \\ \ln(1.12) - \ln(1.08) & \text{if } 1.1872 \le t \le 1.2312 \\ \ln(1.2768) - \ln(t) & \text{if } .2312 \le t \le 1.2768 \end{cases}.$$

Note that $E[\underline{S}(2)]$ can be found as $\int_{1.1448}^{1.2768} t \cdot g(t) \, dt$. Since $G(t) = Pr[\underline{S}(2) \le t]$, we can find c so that $Pr[\underline{S}(2) > c] = .05, .50$ or $.95$, or, equivalently, $G(c) = .95, .50$ or $.05$. Note that $G(1.1448) = 0$, $G(1.1872) = .242396$, $G(1.2312) = .742451$, $G(1.2768) = 1$. If $G(c) = .95$, then c must lie between 1.2312 and 1.2768 such that $(312.5)\{c[1 + \ln(1.2768)] - c \ln(c) - 1.2736\} = .95$. This equation does not have an exact solution and must be solved by an approximate numerical procedure. The resulting value of c is 1.256637 (thus, there is a probability of $.05$ that $\underline{S}(2)$ is 1.2566 or more). Since $G(1.1872) = .242 \le .50 \le .742 = G(1.2312)$, the solution of $G(c) = .50$ can be found exactly as

$$(312.5)\{c[\ln(1.12) - \ln(1.08)] - .0424\} = .50,$$

which implies $c = 1.209867$. The solution of $G(c) = .05$ lies in the range $1.1448 \le c \le 1.1872$, and it too must be found by approximation; the result is $c = 1.163993$. □

Example 5.4 shows that even when $\underline{i}_1$ and $\underline{i}_2$ have very simple distributions, the distribution of $\underline{S}(2)$ and its determination can be quite complex. The distribution of $\underline{S}(n)$ usually becomes more complicated as n increases. The technique of simulation (see Appendix C), which permits an approximate description of the distribution of $S(n)$ and other random variables, could be used in such cases.

5.2.2 The Log-Normal Distribution

The discussion to this point regarding the interest rate as a random variable has focused on annual, or other periodic, rates. If the annual rate is a random variable, then so is the force of interest $\delta = ln(1 + i)$. Since $S(n) = (1 + i_1)(1 + i_2) \cdots (1 + i_n)$, it follows that

$$ln[S(n)] = ln(1+i_1) + ln(1+i_2) + \cdots + ln(1+i_n) = \delta_1 + \delta_2 + \cdots + \delta_n.$$

If δ has mean of μ_δ and variance σ_δ^2 each period, and if the δ_t's are mutually independent, then the mean of $ln[S(n)]$ is $n \cdot \mu_\delta$ and the variance of $ln[S(n)]$ is $n \cdot \sigma_\delta^2$. As a consequence of the Central Limit Theorem, if the interest rates i_t are independent and identically distributed, then as n increases $ln[S(n)]$ has a distribution that approaches a normal distribution, and can therefore be approximated by a normal distribution. In turn, if $ln[S(n)]$ is normally distributed then $S(n)$ itself is said to have a *log-normal distribution*.

| EXAMPLE 5.5 |

In the comments following Example 5.2 it is mentioned that the distribution of $S(10)$ found in that example can be used to find the exact probability $Pr[S(10) > 3.247321]$. Using the log-normal approximation for $S(10)$, find the approximate value of this probability for the distribution of i given in Example 5.2.

| SOLUTION |

The distribution of δ is

$$\delta = \begin{cases} ln\,1.10 & = .095310, \text{ with probability } .5 \\ ln\,1.15 & = .139762, \text{ with probability } .5 \end{cases}$$

so δ has a mean of $\mu_\delta = (.5)[ln(1.10) + ln(1.15)] = .117536$. Furthermore $E[\delta^2] = (.5)[(ln\,1.1)^2 + (ln\,1.15)^2] = .014309$, so $\sigma_\delta^2 = E[\delta^2] - (E[\delta])^2$ $= .00049399$. The mean of $ln[S(10)]$ is $10 \cdot \mu_\delta = 1.175361$. Since the annual interest rates (and thus the forces of interest) are independent, the variance of $ln[\underset{\sim}{S}(10)]$ is $10 \cdot \sigma_{\underset{\sim}{\varrho}}^2 = .004940$, and the standard deviation is .070284. The probability $Pr[\underset{\sim}{S}(10) > 3.247321]$ is the same as the probability $Pr[ln[\underset{\sim}{S}(10)] > ln(3.247321)] \quad = \quad Pr[ln[\underset{\sim}{S}(10)] > 1.177830]$. With the assumption that $ln[\underset{\sim}{S}(10)]$ is approximately normally distributed with mean 1.175361 and standard deviation .070284, the probability $Pr[ln[\underset{\sim}{S}(10)] > 1.177830]$ can be approximated by standardizing to the standard normal distribution; here we have

$Pr[ln[\underset{\sim}{S}(10)] > 1.177830]$

$$= Pr\left[\frac{ln[\underset{\sim}{S}(10)] - 1.175361}{.070284} > \frac{1.177830 - 1.175361}{.070284}\right]$$

$$= Pr[\underset{\sim}{Z} > .035],$$

where $\underset{\sim}{Z}$ is a normal random variable with mean 0 and variance 1. Referring to tables for the standard normal distribution we see that $Pr[\underset{\sim}{Z} > .035] = .486$. □

A number of authors have investigated the behavior of interest rates over time, and there is evidence that in some instances (and for some types of investments), the assumption that $1 + \underset{\sim}{i}$ has a distribution related to the log-normal distribution is a reasonable model of interest rate behavior.

5.2.3 Present Values

If $\underset{\sim}{i}$ is a random interest rate we can consider the present value factor $\underset{\sim}{v} = \frac{1}{1 + \underset{\sim}{i}}$ as a random variable as well. For the interest rate distribution

$$\underset{\sim}{i} = \begin{cases} .10, & \text{with probability } .5 \\ .15, & \text{with probability } .5' \end{cases}$$

the distribution of $\underset{\sim}{v}$ is

$$\underset{\sim}{v} = \begin{cases} 1/1.10 = .909091, & \text{with probability } .5 \\ 1/1.15 = .869565, & \text{with probability } .5' \end{cases}$$

Then the mean of v is given by $E[v] = (.5)\left[\frac{1}{1.10} \ \frac{1}{1.15}\right] = .889328,$

$E[v_-^2] = (.5)\left[\left(\frac{1}{1.10}\right)^2 + \left(\frac{1}{1.15}\right)^2\right] = .791295,$ and the variance of v

is $Var[v] = E[v_-^2] - (E[v])^2 = .000391.$ Note   that   although

$E[1+i] = 1.125,$ the expected value of v is $\frac{1}{1.124444} = .889328,$ and

not $\frac{1}{1.125} = .888889.$ The fact that

$$E\left[\frac{1}{1+i}\right] > \frac{1}{E[1+i]} \tag{5.14}$$

follows from *Jensen's inequality* (see Appendix B). Thus the expected present value ($E[v]$) is not the same as the present value at the expected rate of interest $\left(\frac{1}{E[1+i]}\right)$. In the deterministic setting of Chapter 1 we described $v = \frac{1}{1+i}$ as the amount that must be invested now in order to accumulate to 1 one year from now. In the stochastic setting, if we let C be the amount we must invest now in order to have an expected accumulation one year from now of 1, then $1 = C \cdot E[1+i]$, so that $C = \frac{1}{E[1+i]} \neq E[v].$ Thus the quantity $E[v]$ does not seem to have a meaningful interpretation.

The present value factor over an n-year period is given by $v_1 \cdot v_2 \cdot \cdots \cdot v_n.$ If interest rates are stochastically independent, the expected present value is $E[v_1 \cdot v_2 \cdot \cdots \cdot v_n] = E[v_1] \cdot E[v_2] \cdot \cdots \cdot E[v_n];$ if the interest rates have the same distribution in all years this expected present value is $E[v]^n$, and the variance is $E[v_-^2]^n - (E[v])^{2n}$ (see Exercise 5.2.16). We have seen that in some cases it is possible to find, with varying degrees of difficulty, the complete distribution of $S(n)$. Similar methods could be applied to obtain the distribution of $A(n) = \frac{1}{S(n)} = v_1 \cdot v_2 \cdot \cdots \cdot v_n,$ although this distribution is usually of less interest than that of $S(n)$.

5.2.4 Dependent Rates of Interest

In a realistic setting it is normally the case that there is some relationship between interest rates from one period to the next. In other words the interest rates would be stochastically dependent. This dependence usually takes the form of some sort of conditional distribution of an interest rate that depends on the value(s) of one or more previous years' interest rate(s). The following example considers a simple case.

| **EXAMPLE 5.6** |

The interest rate in year 1 has the distribution

$$i_1 = \begin{cases} .06, & \text{with probability .5} \\ .12, & \text{with probability .5} \end{cases}.$$

The interest rate in year 2 is also a random variable, but one which is dependent on i_1. i_2 has the distribution

$$i_2 = \begin{cases} i_1 - .04, & \text{with probability .5} \\ i_1 + .04, & \text{with probability .5} \end{cases}.$$

Find the expected value and variance of $S(2)$.

| SOLUTION |

Each possible value of i_1 has two corresponding possible values of i_2. If i_1 is .06 then i_2 is either .02 or .10, and if i_1 is .12 then i_2 is either .08 or .16. This results in four possible values for $S(2)$. The distribution of $S(2)$ is

$$S(2) = \begin{cases} (1.06)(1.02) = 1.0812, & \text{with probability .25} \\ (1.06)(1.10) = 1.166, & \text{with probability .25} \\ (1.12)(1.08) = 1.2096, & \text{with probability .25} \\ (1.12)(1.16) = 1.2992, & \text{with probability .25} \end{cases}.$$

The expected value and variance of $S(2)$ can be found directly from the distribution.

$$E[S(2)] = (.25)[1.0812 + 1.166 + 1.2096 + 1.2992] = 1.189,$$

$$E[S(2)^2] = (.25)[(1.0812)^2 + (1.166)^2 + (1.2096)^2 + (1.2992)^2]$$
$$= 1.41990056,$$

and $Var[S(2)] = 1.41990056 - (1.189)^2 = .00617596$. ☐

Situations involving dependent interest rates can become complex quite quickly (see Exercises 5.2.20 and 5.2.21). There is a systematic way of finding the mean, variance, and other moments of the accumulated value and present value random functions $\underline{S}(n)$ and $\underline{A}(n)$, respectively, when interest rates are random (and not necessarily independent). Suppose that $\underline{\delta}_t = ln(1 + \underline{i}_t)$ is the force of interest in year t. Then $\underline{S}(n) = (1 + \underline{i}_1)(1 + \underline{i}_2)\cdots(1 + \underline{i}_n)$, and $ln[\underline{S}(n)] = \underline{\delta}_1 + \underline{\delta}_2 + \cdots + \underline{\delta}_n$. We define the random variable $\underline{\Delta}(n)$ to be $ln[\underline{S}(n)]$. Then

$$E[\underline{S}(n)] = E[e^{ln\underline{S}(n)}] = E[e^{\underline{\Delta}(n)}] = M_{\Delta(n)}(1), \qquad (5.15)$$

where $M_{\Delta(n)}(t)$ is the *moment generating function* of the random variable $\underline{\Delta}(n)$, and

$$Var[\underline{S}(n)] = M_{\Delta(n)}(2) - [M_{\Delta(n)}(1)]^2. \qquad (5.16)$$

The expected value of $\underline{A}(n)$ is

$$E[\underline{A}(n)] = M_{\Delta(n)}(-1) \qquad (5.17)$$

and the variance is

$$Var[\underline{Z}(n)] = M_{\Delta(n)}(-2) - [M_{\Delta(n)}(-1)]^2. \qquad (5.18)$$

For certain assumptions regarding the distributions of the $\underline{\delta}_t$'s, the moment generating function of $\underline{\Delta}(n)$ may be relatively straight-forward to formulate and calculate.

5.3   ANNUITIES

5.3.1 Accumulated Values

An *n*-period accumulated annuity-immediate at periodic interest rate i can be formulated as $s_{\overline{n}|} = 1 + (1+i) + (1+i)^2 + \cdots + (1+i)^{n-1}$. If the interest rates change from year to year then the accumulated value of the annuity is

$$1 + (1+i_n) + (1+i_n)(1+i_{n-1}) + \cdots + (1+i_n)(1+i_{n-1})\cdots(1+i_2),$$

since the first payment is made at the end of the first year. The corresponding formulations for an accumulated annuity-due are $\ddot{s}_{\overline{n}|} = (1+i) + (1+i)^2 + \cdots + (1+i)^{n-1} + (1+i)^n$ if the interest rate is constant, and

$$(1+i_n) + (1+i_n)(1+i_{n-1}) + \cdots$$
$$+ (1+i_n)(1+i_{n-1})\cdots(1+i_2) + (1+i_n)(1+i_{n-1})\cdots(1+i_2)(1+i_1)$$

if the interest rates change from year to year.

If interest rates are assumed to be random from year to year, then the accumulated values for the annuity-immediate and annuity-due are also random variables, given by

$$\underline{s}_{\overline{n}|} = 1 + (1+\underline{i}_n) + (1+\underline{i}_n)(1+\underline{i}_{n-1})$$
$$+ \cdots + (1+\underline{i}_n)(1+\underline{i}_{n-1})\cdots(1+\underline{i}_2) \qquad (5.19)$$

and

$$\underline{\ddot{s}}_{\overline{n}|} = (1+\underline{i}_n) + (1+\underline{i}_n)(1+\underline{i}_{n-1}) + \cdots + (1+\underline{i}_n)(1+\underline{i}_{n-1})\cdots(1+\underline{i}_2)$$
$$+ (1+\underline{i}_n)(1+\underline{i}_{n-1})\cdots(1+\underline{i}_2)(1+\underline{i}_1), \qquad (5.20)$$

respectively. These accumulated values are random variables in the context of anticipating at time 0 what the accumulated value will be at time n.

If we have independence of interest rates from year to year, and the same distribution of $\underline{i}_t$ for each year (or simply the same expected interest rate $E[\underline{i}_t] = \overline{i}$ each year), then

$$E[\underline{s}_{\overline{n}|}] = s_{\overline{n}|\overline{i}} \qquad (5.21)$$

and

$$E[\underline{\ddot{s}}_{\overline{n}|}] = \ddot{s}_{\overline{n}|\overline{i}}, \qquad (5.22)$$

since in each case the expected values of the individual terms reduce to the form $E[(1+\underline{i}_n)(1+\underline{i}_{n-1})\cdots(1+\underline{i}_{n-t})] = (1+\overline{i})^{t+1}$ for $t = 0, 1, 2, \ldots, n-1$.

| EXAMPLE 5.7 |

Suppose that annual interest rates are independent random variables with distribution

$$\underline{i} = \begin{cases} .10, & \text{with probability } .5 \\ .15, & \text{with probability } .5 \end{cases}$$

Describe the distributions of $\underline{s}_{\overline{n}|}$ and $\underline{\ddot{s}}_{\overline{n}|}$ for $n = 2$, and find the mean and variance of each. Do the same for $n = 5$ and $n = 10$.

| SOLUTION |

$\underline{s}_{\overline{2}|} = 1 + (1+\underline{i}_2)$, which is equal to 2.1 or 2.15 with equal probability of .5. Thus $\underline{s}_{\overline{2}|}$ has mean $(.5)(2.1 + 2.15) = 2.125$, which is $s_{\overline{2}|\,i=.125}$ as indicated above, and variance

$$(.5)[(2.1 - 2.125)^2 + (2.15 - 2.125)^2] = .000625.$$

$\underline{\ddot{s}}_{\overline{2}|}$ can take on one of four values, each with probability .25, based on the two possible values for each of $\underline{i}_1$ and $\underline{i}_2$, as shown in the following table.

| TABLE 5.2 |

$\underline{i}_1$	$\underline{i}_2$	$\underline{\ddot{s}}_{\overline{2}|}$
.10	.10	2.31
.15	.10	2.365
.140	.15	2.415
.15	.15	2.4725

Then the expected value is

$$E[\underline{\ddot{s}}_{\overline{2}|}] = (.25)[2.31 + 2.365 + 2.415 + 2.4725] = 2.390625 = \ddot{s}_{\overline{2}|\,i=.125}.$$

The variance is

$$(.25)[(2.31 - 2.390625)^2 + \cdots + (2.4725 - 2.390625)^2] = .00361367.$$

For $n = 5$ tables similar to Table 5.2 can be created for $\underline{s}_{\overline{5}|}$ and $\underline{\ddot{s}}_{\overline{5}|}$. These tables will have $2^4 = 16$ entries, reflecting the 16 possible combinations of the values of $\underline{i}_2, \underline{i}_3, \underline{i}_4$ and $\underline{i}_5$ for $\underline{s}_{\overline{5}|}$, and $2^5 = 32$ entries for the 32 possible combinations of values for $i_1, i_2, i_3, i_4,$ and i_5 for $\ddot{s}_{\overline{5}|}$. Note that for the annuity-immediate i_1 becomes irrelevant. The expected values and variances can be found from these tables (see Exercises 5.3.3 and 5.3.4). The same comments apply to the case $n = 10$, except that now there are $2^9 = 512$ possible values for $s_{\overline{10}|}$, since there are 2^9 combinations of values for $i_2, \ldots, i_9, i_{10}$, each equally likely, and $2^{10} = 1024$ possible values for $\ddot{s}_{\overline{10}|}$. $\qquad\qquad\qquad\qquad\qquad\qquad\qquad\qquad\qquad\qquad\qquad\square$

The complications that arise when describing the distribution of accumulated values as the interest rate distribution becomes more complex were seen in the previous section. Fortunately it is not necessary to have the complete distributions of $s_{\overline{n}|}$ or $\ddot{s}_{\overline{n}|}$ in order to determine their variances. There is a formulation for the variance of an accumulated annuity, when interest rates are independent from one period to another, which follows from a result in the theory of probability. Exercise 5.3.2 provides a step-by-step proof of the following theorem. (References for this result are provided in Section 5.5.)

$\boxed{\text{THEOREM}}$ Suppose that $r_1, r_2, \ldots, r_n$ are independent random variables with common mean $E[r_t] = A$ and common second moment $E[r_t^2] = B$. Let Z be the random variable

$$Z = r_1 + r_1 \cdot r_2 + r_1 \cdot r_2 \cdot r_3 + \cdots + r_1 \cdot r_2 \cdot r_3 \cdots \cdots r_n.$$

Then $E[Z] = A + A^2 + A^3 + \cdots + A^n = \dfrac{A - A^{n+1}}{1 - A}$ and

$$Var[Z] =$$

$$\left(\frac{B^{n+1} - B}{B - 1}\right)\left(\frac{B + A}{B - A}\right) - \left(\frac{A^{n+1} - A}{A - 1}\right)\left(\frac{2B}{B - A}\right) - \left(\frac{A^{n+1} - A}{A - 1}\right)^2.$$

$$\nabla$$

We apply this theorem to find the variance of an n-period accumulated annuity-due of 1 per period for which $E[1 + i_t]$ and $E[(1 + i_t)^2]$ do not change as t changes. Let $r_1 = 1 + i_n,\ r_2 = 1 + i_{n-1},\ r_3 = 1 + i_{n-2},$ $\ldots, r_{n-1} = 1 + i_2,\ r_n = 1 + i.$ With this definition of the r_t's the value of Z in the theorem is

$$\ddot{s}_{\overline{n}|} = (1 + i_n) + (1 + i_n)(1 + i_{n-1}) + \cdots + (1 + i_n)(1 + i_{n-1}) \cdots (1 + i_2)$$

$$+ (1 + i_n)(1 + i_{n-1}) \cdots (1 + i_2)(1 + i_1)$$

$$= r_1 + r_1 \cdot r_2 + r_1 \cdot r_2 \cdot r_3 + \cdots + r_1 \cdot r_2 \cdot r_3 \cdots \cdots r_n.$$

Since $r_t = 1 + i_{n-t+1}$ we have $E[r_t] = R = 1 + E[i] = 1 + \bar{i}$, in the notation defined earlier, and $E[r_t^2] = S = E[(1+i)^2]$. Then according to the theorem

$$Var[\ddot{s}_{\overline{n}|}] = \left(\frac{S^{n+1}-S}{S-1}\right)\left(\frac{S+R}{S-R}\right) - \left(\frac{R^{n+1}-R}{R-1}\right)\left(\frac{2S}{S-R}\right) - \left(\frac{R^{n+1}-R}{R-1}\right)^2.$$

$$(5.23)$$

Note that $\dfrac{R^{n+1}-R}{R-1}$ is equal to $\ddot{s}_{\overline{n}|}$ at interest rate $E[i]$, and $\dfrac{S^{n+1}-S}{S-1}$ is equal to $\ddot{s}_{\overline{n}|}$ at interest rate $E[(1+i)^2] - 1$.

To find the variance of the n-period accumulated annuity-immediate $s_{\overline{n}|}$, recall the identity $s_{\overline{n}|} = 1 + \ddot{s}_{\overline{n-1}|}$ in the non-random case (see part (b) of Exercise 2.4.1). A similar identity holds in the random case, namely $s_{\overline{n}|} = 1 + \ddot{s}_{\overline{n-1}|}$, where the $n-1$ payment annuity-due starts at time $t = 1$ and continues until time $t = n - 1$, and is based on interest rates $i_2, i_3, \ldots, i_n$. Then

$$Var\left[s_{\overline{n}|}\right] = Var\left[1 + \ddot{s}_{\overline{n-1}|}\right] = Var\left[\ddot{s}_{\overline{n-1}|}\right]. \qquad (5.24)$$

| EXAMPLE 5.8 |

For the distribution of i in Example 5.7, find the variances of $s_{\overline{n}|}$ and $\ddot{s}_{\overline{n}|}$ for $n = 2, 5$ and 10. Apply Chebyshev's rule to find approximate 75% and 89% intervals for $s_{\overline{n}|}$ and $\ddot{s}_{\overline{n}|}$ about their means.

| SOLUTION |

We first find $R = 1 + E[i] = 1.125$ and $S = E[(1+i)^2] = 1.126625$. Using Equations (5.23) and (5.24) we see that

$$Var[s_{\overline{2}|}] = Var[\ddot{s}_{\overline{1}|}]$$

$$= \left(\frac{S^2-S}{S-1}\right)\left(\frac{S+R}{S-R}\right) - \left(\frac{R^2-R}{R-1}\right)\left(\frac{2S}{S-R}\right) - \left(\frac{R^2-R}{R-1}\right)^2$$

$$= .000625.$$

(Note that $\ddot{s}_{\overline{1}|} = 1 + i$, so $Var[\ddot{s}_{\overline{1}|}] = Var[1 + i] = .000625$.) We also have

$$Var[\ddot{s}_{\overline{2}|}] =$$

$$\left(\frac{S^3-S}{S-1}\right)\left(\frac{S+R}{S-R}\right) - \left(\frac{R^3-R}{R-1}\right)\left(\frac{2S}{S-R}\right) - \left(\frac{R^3-R}{R-1}\right)^2 = .003614.$$

Similarly we find $Var[\underline{s}_{\overline{5}|}] = Var[\underline{\ddot{s}}_{\overline{4}|}] = .029379$, $Var[\underline{\ddot{s}}_{\overline{5}|}] = .062932$, $Var[\underline{s}_{\overline{10}|}] = Var[\underline{\ddot{s}}_{\overline{9}|}] = .619221$, and $Var[\underline{\ddot{s}}_{\overline{10}|}] = .986107$.

Chebyshev's rule (see Exercise 5.2.9) states that, for any random variable $\underline{W}$, we have the probability relationship

$$Pr[\,|\,\underline{W} - \mu_{\underline{W}}| < k \cdot \sigma_{\underline{W}}] \geq 1 - \frac{1}{k^2}.$$

Thus at $k = 2$ we have the interval $(\mu_{\underline{W}} - 2 \cdot \sigma_{\underline{W}}, \mu_{\underline{W}} + 2 \cdot \sigma_{\underline{W}})$, and at least 75% of the distribution of $\underline{W}$ lies inside the interval. With $k = 3$ the interval $(\mu_{\underline{W}} - 3 \cdot \sigma_{\underline{W}}, \mu_{\underline{W}} + 3 \cdot \sigma_{\underline{W}})$ includes at least $\frac{8}{9} = 89\%$ of the distribution. The intervals are given in the following table.

TABLE 5.3

	75%	89%
$\ddot{s}_{\overline{2}|}$	$(2.270, 2.511)$	$(2.210, 2.571)$
$\ddot{s}_{\overline{5}|}$	$(6.717, 7.720)$	$(6.466, 7.971)$
$\ddot{s}_{\overline{10}|}$	$(18.240, 22.212)$	$(17.247, 23.205)$

$\square$

It must be kept in mind that Chebyshev's rule says that the probability that $\ddot{s}_{\overline{2}|}$ lies in the interval $(2.270, 2.511)$ is *at least* 75%, and may be more. In fact the exact probability is 100%, since $\ddot{s}_{\overline{2}|}$ must be between $\ddot{s}_{\overline{2}|.10} = 2.31$ and $\ddot{s}_{\overline{2}|.15} = 2.4725$ (see Exercise 5.3.5). Note also that as n increases, the standard deviation of $\underline{s}_{\overline{n}|}$ or $\underline{\ddot{s}}_{\overline{n}|}$ becomes a larger fraction of the expected value.

EXAMPLE 5.9

Smith opens an individual retirement account and will make 10 level annual deposits. The annual return on the account is either .10 or .15, each with 50% probability (as in Example 5.7), and the returns from year to year are assumed to be independent of one another. Smith wishes to determine the level annual deposit needed (as of when the account is opened and the first deposit is made) in order to have a 95% probability that the accumulated value in the account is at least \$100,000 one year after the 10th deposit. Smith approximates the distribution of $\ddot{s}_{\overline{10}|}$ by assuming it is normal with mean $\ddot{s}_{\overline{10}|.125} = 20.226$ and variance .986107 (as found in Example 5.8). What level annual deposit does Smith make? What is Smith's expected accumulation one year after the 10th deposit with this deposit amount?

SOLUTION

With a deposit of amount D, the accumulated amount one year after the 10th deposit is $D \cdot \ddot{s}_{\overline{10}|}$. We wish to solve for D from the probability relationship $P[D \cdot \ddot{s}_{\overline{10}|} > 100{,}000] = .95$. This can be written as

$$P\left[\ddot{s}_{\overline{10}|} > \frac{100{,}000}{D}\right] = P\left[\frac{\ddot{s}_{\overline{10}|} - 20.226}{\sqrt{.986107}} > \frac{\frac{100{,}000}{D} - 20.226}{\sqrt{.986107}}\right] = .95.$$

Using the normal approximation, we see that $\dfrac{\frac{100{,}000}{D} - 20.226}{\sqrt{.986107}}$ must be

equal to the 5th percentile of the standard normal distribution, which is -1.645. Solving for D results in $D = 5378.52$. Smith's expected accumulation with this deposit is $5378.52 \cdot \ddot{s}_{\overline{10}|.125} = 108{,}786$.   □

5.3.2 Annuity Present Values

Under the assumption of random interest rates per period, the present value of an n-period annuity-immediate of 1 per period would be

$$a_{\overline{n}|} = \underline{v}_1 + \underline{v}_1 \cdot \underline{v}_2 + \underline{v}_1 \cdot \underline{v}_2 \cdot \underline{v}_3 + \cdots + \underline{v}_1 \cdot \underline{v}_2 \cdot \cdots \cdot \underline{v}_{n-1}$$
$$+ \underline{v}_1 \cdot \underline{v}_2 \cdot \cdots \cdot \underline{v}_{n-1} \cdot \underline{v}_n.$$

Assuming independent and identically distributed interest rates from one period to another, the expected value of $a_{\overline{n}|}$ is

$$\begin{aligned} E[a_{\overline{n}|}] &= E[\underline{v}] + (E[\underline{v}])^2 + (E[\underline{v}])^3 + \cdots + (E[\underline{v}])^n \\ &= \bar{v} + \bar{v}^2 + \bar{v}^3 + \cdots + \bar{v}^n, \end{aligned} \qquad (5.25)$$

where $\bar{v}$ is used to denote $E[\underline{v}]$. This geometric sum simplifies to $E[\underline{a}_{\overline{n}|}] = \frac{\bar{v} - \bar{v}^{n+1}}{1 - \bar{v}}$ (see Exercise 5.3.8), which is the usual present value of an annuity-immediate at a deterministic rate of interest whose present value factor is $\bar{v}$.

A similar formulation results for the present value of an n-period annuity-due when interest rates are random each period. The present value is

$$\ddot{\underline{a}}_{\overline{n}|} = 1 + \underline{v}_1 + \underline{v}_1 \cdot \underline{v}_2 + \underline{v}_1 \cdot \underline{v}_2 \cdot \underline{v}_3 + \cdots + \underline{v}_1 \cdot \underline{v}_2 \cdots \cdot \underline{v}_{n-1} = 1 + \underline{a}_{\overline{n-1}|}.$$

If interest rates are independent and identically distributed then

$$E[\ddot{\underline{a}}_{\overline{n}|}] = 1 + \bar{v} + \bar{v}^2 + \cdots + \underline{v}^{n-1} = \frac{1 - \bar{v}^n}{1 - \bar{v}}. \qquad (5.26)$$

The theorem stated earlier can also be applied to find the variance of $\underline{a}_{\overline{n}|}$ when interest rates are independent and the $\underline{v}_t$'s all have the same mean and variance. If the $\underline{i}_t$'s are independent then so are the $\underline{v}_t$'s, and letting $\underline{r}_t = \underline{v}_t$ we have $\underline{Z} = \underline{a}_{\overline{n}|}$ as defined in the theorem. With $A = E[\underline{v}]$ and $B = E[\underline{v}^2]$, the formulation in the theorem gives the variance of $\underline{a}_{\overline{n}|}$. To find the variance of the present value of an annuity-due, we note that $\ddot{\underline{a}}_{\overline{n}|} = 1 + \underline{a}_{\overline{n-1}|}$ so that

$$Var[\ddot{\underline{a}}_{\overline{n}|}] = Var[\underline{a}_{\overline{n-1}|}]. \qquad (5.27)$$

Note that, as in the deterministic interest rate case, the identity $\underline{s}_{\overline{n}|} = (1 + \underline{i}_1)(1 + \underline{i}_2) \cdots (1 + \underline{i}_n) \cdot \underline{a}_{\overline{n}|}$ is valid in the random interest rate case. In Exercise 5.3.9 it is shown that $E[\underline{s}_{\overline{n}|}]$ is *not* equal to $E[(1 + \underline{i}_1)(1 + \underline{i}_2) \cdots (1 + \underline{i}_n)] \cdot E[\underline{a}_{\overline{n}|}] = (1 + \bar{i})^n \cdot E[\underline{a}_{\overline{n}|}]$.

| EXAMPLE 5.10 |

For the interest rate distribution of Example 5.7, show that $E[\underline{s}_{\overline{5}|}]$ is not equal to $E[(1 + \underline{i}_1)(1 + \underline{i}_2) \cdots (1 + \underline{i}_5)] \cdot E[\underline{a}_{\overline{5}|}]$.

| SOLUTION |

$E[\underline{s}_{\overline{5}|}] = s_{\overline{5}|.125} = 6.416260$, $E[(1 + \underline{i}_1)(1 + \underline{i}_2) \cdots (1 + \underline{i}_5)] = 1.802032$,

and $E[\underline{a}_{\overline{5}|}] = \frac{\bar{v} - \bar{v}^6}{1 - \bar{v}} = 3.565437$, where $\bar{v} = E[\underline{v}] = .889328$. Then $E[(1 + \underline{i}_1)(1 + \underline{i}_2) \cdots (1 + \underline{i}_5)] \cdot E[\underline{a}_{\overline{5}|}] = 6.425033 \neq E[\underline{s}_{\overline{5}|}]$. □

5.3.3 Variable Interest Rate Loans

The earlier sections of this Chapter were concerned with analyzing accumulations (and present values) of payments involving interest rates that fluctuated randomly from one period to the next according to some probability distribution. Many financial institutions offer *variable interest rate loans*, in which the payment amount is determined in advance, based on an assumed rate of interest but with the understanding that interest rates will fluctuate in the future and payments may need to be adjusted accordingly. The amortization of a variable interest rate loan takes place in the usual way, with the exception that the rate of interest applied each period fluctuates randomly, usually tied to some benchmark interest rate in the economy such as the institution's prime lending rate or the rate on a specified government security. In addition, the payment may be adjusted at certain times, with the new payment based on the current outstanding balance and a new rate of interest. Some of the methods developed earlier in this chapter can be applied to the situation of a variable interest rate loan. Viewed from the time when the loan is issued, all of the future entries in the amortization table will be random variables, such as OB_t, PR_t and I_t.

EXAMPLE 5.11

A loan of 100,000 is being repaid over 25 years by monthly payments starting one month after the loan is made. The loan is a variable rate loan, and the lender assumes that monthly interest rates will follow the distribution

$$j = \begin{cases} .0075, & \text{with probability } .5 \\ .0125, & \text{with probability } .5 \end{cases}$$

over the 25-year period and that rates are independent from month to month. The lender calculates the monthly payment based on an average monthly rate of 1.0% for the 25-year period. The payment will remain fixed for one year, and will then be readjusted.

(a) Find the expected value and variance of OB_{12}, the (random) outstanding balance after 12 months, and the probability that OB_{12} is less than or equal to its expected value.

(b) The lender decides, for a measure of security, to calculate the monthly payment on the basis of a 1.1% monthly rate. Use a computer to find the expected value and variance of OB_{12} in this case, and the probability that OB_{12} is less than or equal to the expected value in part (a).

| SOLUTION |

(a) With a 1.0% monthly interest rate, the monthly payment is
$$\frac{100,000}{a_{\overline{300}|.01}} = 1053.22.$$

$$OB_{12} = 100,000(1 + \underline{i}_1)(1 + \underline{i}_2) \cdots (1 + \underline{i}_{12}) - 1053.22 \cdot \underline{s}_{\overline{12}|},$$

and its expected value is

$$
\begin{aligned}
E[\,OB_{12}] &= E0[100,000(1+\underline{i}_1)(1+\underline{i}_2) \cdots (1+\underline{i}_{12}) - 1053.22 \cdot \underline{s}_{\overline{12}|}] \\
&= 100,000(1+\overline{i})^{12} - 1053.22 \cdot s_{\overline{12}|\overline{i}} = 99,324.98,
\end{aligned}
$$

where $\overline{i} = .01$. The variance of OB_{12} can be found as

$Var\,[OB_{12}]$
$$
\begin{aligned}
&= Var\,[100,000(1+\underline{i}_1)(1+\underline{i}_2) \cdots (1+\underline{i}_{12}) - 1053.22 \cdot \underline{s}_{\overline{12}|}] \\
&= (100,000)^2 \cdot Var\,[(1+\underline{i}_1)(1+\underline{i}_2) \cdots (1+\underline{i}_{12})] \\
&\quad + (1053.22)^2 \cdot Var\,[\underline{s}_{\overline{12}|}] \\
&\quad - 2(100,000)(1053.22) \cdot Cov[(1+\underline{i}_1)(1+\underline{i}_2) \cdots (1+\underline{i}_{12}), \underline{s}_{\overline{12}|}].
\end{aligned}
$$

From Equation (5.13) we have

$$Var[(1 + \underline{i}_1)(1 + \underline{i}_2) \cdots (1 + \underline{i}_{12})] = S^{12} - R^{24},$$

where $R = E[1 + \underline{i}] = 1.01$ and

$$S = E[(1 + \underline{i})^2] = (.5)(1.0075)^2 + (.5)(1.0125)^2 = 1.02010625.$$

Therefore $Var[(1 + \underline{i}_1)(1 + \underline{i}_2) \cdots (1 + \underline{i}_{12})] = .000093356$. Also, from Equations (5.23) and (5.24) we have

$Var[\underline{s}_{\overline{12}|}]$

$$= \left(\frac{S^{12} - S}{S - 1}\right)\left(\frac{S + R}{S - R}\right) - \left(\frac{R^{12} - R}{R - 1}\right)\left(\frac{2S}{S - R}\right) - \left(\frac{R^{12} - R}{R - 1}\right)^2,$$

where R and S are given above. Therefore $Var[s_{\overline{12}|}] = .0035787$. To find the covariance term note that $s_{\overline{12}|}$ is equal to

$$1 + (1+\underline{i}_{12}) + (1+\underline{i}_{11})(1+\underline{i}_{12}) + \cdots + (1+\underline{i}_2)\cdots(1+\underline{i}_{12}),$$

and thus the covariance of $(1 + \underline{i}_1)(1 + \underline{i}_2)\cdots(1 + \underline{i}_{12})$ with $s_{\overline{12}|}$ is equal to

$Cov[(1+\underline{i}_1)(1+\underline{i}_2)\cdots(1+\underline{i}_{12}), 1]$
$\qquad + Cov[(1+\underline{i}_1)(1+\underline{i}_2)\cdots(1+\underline{i}_{12}), (1+\underline{i}_{12})]$
$\qquad\quad + \cdots + Cov[(1+\underline{i}_1)(1+\underline{i}_2)\cdots(1+\underline{i}_{12}),(1+\underline{i}_{11})(1+\underline{i}_{12})]$
$\qquad\qquad + Cov[(1+\underline{i}_1)(1+\underline{i}_2)\cdots(1+\underline{i}_{12}), (1+\underline{i}_2)\cdots(1+\underline{i}_{12})].$

Using the identity $Cov[\underline{X}, \underline{Y}] = E[\underline{X}\cdot\underline{Y}] - E[\underline{X}]\cdot E[\underline{Y}]$, we have
$Cov[(1 + \underline{i}_1)(1 + \underline{i}_2)\cdots(1 + \underline{i}_{12}), s_{\overline{12}|}]$

$$= 0 + [R^{11}\cdot S - R^{13}] + [R^{10}\cdot S^2 - R^{14}] + \cdots + [R\cdot S^{11} - R^{23}]$$

$$= .00049188.$$

Therefore the variance of OB_{12} is

$$(100,000)^2(.000093356) + (1053.22)^2(.0035787)$$

$$- 2(100,000)(1053.22)(.00049188) = 833,918,$$

and the standard deviation is $\sqrt{833,918} = 913$. The probability $Pr[OB_{12} \le 99,324.98]$ is found by using a computer routine that calculates the distribution of OB_{12}; there are $2^{12} = 4096$ points in the distribution, one of two interest rates for each of the 12 months. This probability is $\frac{2077}{4096} = .507$.

(b) At 1.1% per month the payment is $\frac{100,000}{a_{\overline{300}|.011}} = 1142.92$, and the expected outstanding balance after one year is

$$E[OB_{12}] = E[100,000(1 + \underline{i}_1)(1 + \underline{i}_2)\cdots(1 + \underline{i}_{12}) - 1142.92\cdot s_{\overline{12}|}]$$

$$= 98,187.40 = 100,000(1 + \overline{i})^{12} - 1142.92\cdot s_{\overline{12}|i}.$$

The variance of OB_{12} is

$$(100,000)^2(.000093356) + (1142.92)^2(.0035787)$$
$$- (100,000)(1142.92)(.00049188) = 825,799,$$

with standard deviation 909. $\square$

5.4 CONTINUOUS STOCHASTIC INTEREST RATE MODELS

To this point in this chapter we have considered accumulation (and present value) assuming interest accrues at specified (discrete) points in time. Interest is random in period 1 with random rate i_1, in period 2 with random rate i_2, etc., and the accumulated value of an initial amount of 1 after n periods is the random variable $S(n) = (1+i_1)(1+i_2)\cdots(1+i_n)$. In Chapter 1 we considered a continuous non-random accumulation in which $S(n)$ was expressed in terms of the force of interest, $S(n) = exp(\int_0^n \delta_t \, dt)$. Now we formulate continuous accumulation using random interest rates.

A "stochastic process" or "random process" refers to a collection of random variables that may (usually are) or may not be related to one another. A discrete stochastic process is a finite (or countably infinite) collection of random variables that is often described in the form X_0, X_1, $X_2, \ldots$ (where the subscripts usually refer to successive points in time). An example of a discrete stochastic process is any of the series of annual interest rates that occurred in examples in sections 5.2 or 5.3 (for instance, the sequence $i_1, i_2, \ldots, i_{10}$ in Example 5.2, or its corresponding accumulation sequence $S(1), S(2), \ldots, S(10)$).

A continuous stochastic process is one for which there is a random variable X_t for each real number $t \geq 0$ (it is true that in Example 5.10 there is an $S(t)$ for each real $t \geq 0$, but if $0 \leq t < 1$, then $S(t) = 1$, and if $1 \leq t < 2$, then $S(t) = S(1)$, etc., since it is understood that no interest is credited at fractional parts of a year, thus, this really is a discrete stochastic process). Interest can be modeled to accrue continuously in a random fashion resulting in a stochastic process of accumulated values, $\{S(t): t \geq 0\}$. We describe here the continuous stochastic process of Brownian motion and some of its properties, and apply the process to investment growth.

The *Brownian motion stochastic process* was defined in the early 19th century to describe the seemingly random motion of small particles suspended in a fluid. Brownian motion is a stochastic process $\{ X(t): t \geq 0 \}$ with the following properties.

(1) Every increment $X(t+s) - X(s)$ is normally distributed with mean 0 and variance $\sigma^2 \cdot t$, where σ^2 is fixed.
(2) For any pair of disjoint time intervals $[t_1, t_2]$ and $[t_3, t_4]$ (*i.e.*, either $t_2 \leq t_3$ or $t_4 \leq t_1$), the increments $X(t_2) - X(t_1)$ and $X(t_4) - X(t_3)$ are independent. It is also usually assumed that $X(0) = 0$, as the starting point for the process.

Brownian motion can be regarded as the limit (as $m \to \infty$) of a *random walk process* $\left\{ X(t): t = 0, \frac{1}{m}, \frac{2}{m}, \dots \right\}$, where all increments $X\left(\frac{k}{m}\right) - X\left(\frac{k-1}{m}\right)$ are independent of one another and each is a two-point distribution with outcomes $\pm \frac{\sigma}{\sqrt{m}}$, each with probability .5. A probability relationship concerning the Brownian motion process that can be applied to the analysis of investment accumulation is the following, for $a \geq 0$:

$P[X(t) \geq a$ for some t between 0 and $T]$

$$= P\{ \max_{0 \leq t \leq T} X(t) \geq a \}$$

$$= P\{ \min_{0 \leq t \leq T} X(t) \leq -a \} = \frac{2}{\sigma \sqrt{2\pi T}} \cdot \int_a^\infty \exp\left(-\frac{t^2}{2\sigma^2 T} \right) dt$$

$$= 2 \cdot \Phi\left(-\frac{a}{\sigma \sqrt{T}} \right) \qquad (5.28)$$

where Φ is the c.d.f. of the standard normal distribution. This probability can also be written in the form (using change of variable $u = Ta^2/t^2$)

$$\frac{a}{\sigma \sqrt{2\pi}} \cdot \int_0^T u^{-3/2} \cdot \exp\left(-\frac{a^2}{2\sigma^2 u} \right) du.$$

The following example shows how the theory of Brownian motion can be applied to investment accumulation.

EXAMPLE 5.12

Suppose that an equity fund pays periodic dividends, and that the unit value of the equity fund (minus dividends) is a stochastic process $\{S(t): t \geq 0\}$ such that the related process $\{ln[S(t)]: t \geq 0\}$ is Brownian motion, with $\sigma^2 = .04$. Assume that the fund's unit value is 1 at time 0.
(a) Find the probability that the unit value of the fund will be greater than 1.25 at time $m = 5$.
(b) Find the probability that the unit value will be greater than or equal to 1.25 at some time between time 0 and time 5.

SOLUTION

(a) $W = ln[S(5)] - ln[S(0)] = ln[S(5)]$ has a normal distribution with mean 0 and variance $\sigma^2 \cdot m = .2$.

$$P\{S(5) \geq 1.25\} = P\{ln[S(5)] \geq ln(1.25)\} = P\{W \geq .2231\} = .31.$$

(b) The fund's unit value can be viewed as the stochastic process $\{S(t): t \geq 0\}$, where $S(t) = exp[X(t)]$. Thus, $ln[S(n)] = X(t)$ is a Brownian motion process. We are to find the probability

$$P[S(t) \geq 1.25 \text{ for some } t \text{ between 0 and 5}]$$

$$= P\left[\max_{0 \leq t \leq 5} S(t) \geq 1.25\right] = P\left[\max_{0 \leq t \leq 5} X(t) \geq ln(1.25)\right].$$

According to Equation (5.28) above, this probability is

$$2 \cdot \Phi\left(-\frac{ln(1.25)}{(.2) \cdot \sqrt{5}}\right) = 2 \cdot \Phi(-.50) = .62,$$

where $a = ln(1.25)$, $\sigma = .2$, and $m = 5$.   □

The graph below illustrates a possible sample path for Brownian motion.

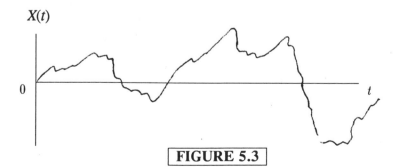

$X(t)$

0

t

FIGURE 5.3

The assumption that $ln[\underline{S}(t)] = \underline{X}(t)$ is a standard Brownian motion process is somewhat restrictive, since it requires that for any s, $\underline{X}(s)$ has mean 0. The implication is then that the underlying (random) force of interest, $\underline{\delta}_t$, also has a mean of 0 for each t. Thus, this is not an appropriate model for more typical interest accumulation or investment growth, which has a generally positive (but perhaps random) force of interest. The Brownian motion process described above can be modified to take into account a positive force of interest.

We can define a Brownian motion process with *drift* μ. This process is defined in the same way as the original Brownian motion, except that $\underline{X}(t+s) - \underline{X}(s)$ now has a mean of $\mu \cdot t$ (instead of a mean of 0 in the original definition). This drift will take into account a (usually) positive average force of interest when the model is applied to investment accumulation.

When the Brownian motion process has a drift μ, the probability formulation corresponding to Equation (5.28) becomes more complicated. Equation 5.29 which follows is a version of the *Bachelier-Levy formula*. If $a > 0$ and $b \geq 0$, then

$$P\{\underline{X}(t) \geq a + b \cdot t \text{ for some } t \leq T\}$$

$$= \Phi\left[\frac{-a \cdot T^{-1/2} + (\mu-b)T^{1/2}}{\sigma}\right]$$

$$+ e^{2a(\mu-b)/\sigma^2} \cdot \Phi\left[\frac{-a \cdot T^{-1/2} - (\mu-b)T^{1/2}}{\sigma}\right]. \qquad (5.29)$$

The following example illustrates the Brownian motion with drift process applied to an investment accumulation.

EXAMPLE 5.13

Suppose that the stochastic process of accumulated values for a certain investment, $\{\underline{S}(t): t \geq 0\}$, is such that the corresponding process $\{\underline{X}(t): t \geq 0\}$ is Brownian motion with drift $\mu = .08$ and $\sigma^2 = .04$, where $\underline{X}(t) = ln[\underline{S}(t)]$.

(a) Calculate the probabilities $P\{\max_{0 \leq t \leq n} \underline{S}(t) \geq c\}$ in each of the following
    cases: $n = 5, 10,$ and 20; and $c = 1.25, 1.50,$ and 2.

(b) Calculate the probability that $\underline{S}(t)$ rises above $(1.25)e^{.08t}$ at some point $0 \leq t \leq n$, for $n = 5, 10,$ and 20.

SOLUTION

(a) For $n = 5$ and $c = 1.25$, the parameters in Equation (5.29) are $a = \ln(1.25) = .2231$, $T = 5$, $\mu = .08$, $b = 0$, $\sigma = 2$. This probability is $P = \Phi(.395) + e^{.893} \cdot \Phi(-1.393) = .853$, and the others are:

$n = 5, c = 1.50 \rightarrow P = .677$	$n = 5, c = 2 \rightarrow P = .372$
$n = 10, c = 1.25 \rightarrow P = .948$	$n = 10, c = 1.50 \rightarrow P = .877$
$n = 10, c = 2 \rightarrow P = .713$	$n = 20, c = 1.25 \rightarrow P = .989$
$n = 20, c = 1.50 \rightarrow P = .972$	$n = 20, c = 2 \rightarrow P = .928$

(b) Note that since $b = \mu$, $X(t) - .08t$ becomes a Brownian motion without drift, so that Equation (5.28) can be applied. If Equation (5.29) is applied, the result is the same since $\mu - b = 0$; in either case the probability reduces to $2 \cdot \Phi\left(-\dfrac{a \cdot m^{-1/2}}{\sigma}\right)$. For $n = 5$, the probability is

$$P\{X(t) \geq \ln(1.25) + .08t \text{ for some } t \text{ between } 0 \text{ and } 5\}$$

$$= 2 \cdot \Phi(-.49896) = .618.$$

For $n = 10$ the probability is .724, and for $n = 20$ it is .803.   □

In Exercise 5.4.2 you are asked to show that for a stochastic process $Y(t)$ with drift μ and $a > 0$ and $b \geq 0$,

$$P\{Y(t) \leq -a - b \cdot t \text{ for some } t \leq T\}$$

$$= P\{-Y(t) \geq a + b \cdot t \text{ for some } t \leq T\}$$

$$= \Phi\left[\frac{-a \cdot T^{-1/2} - (\mu + b) \cdot T^{1/2}}{\sigma}\right]$$

$$+ e^{-2a(\mu+b)/\sigma^2} \cdot \Phi\left[\frac{-a \cdot T^{-1/2} + (\mu+b) \cdot T^{1/2}}{\sigma}\right]. \tag{5.30}$$

Note that Equation (5.29) reduces to Equation (5.28) if $b = \mu = 0$.

EXAMPLE 5.14

Consider the same stochastic process as in Example 5.13.

(a) Calculate the probabilities $P\{\min_{0 \leq t \leq n} S(t) \leq c\}$ in each of the following cases: $n = 5, 10,$ and 20; $c = .75$ and $c = .50$.

(b) Calculate the probability that $\underline{S}(t)$ falls below $(.75)e^{.06t}$ at some point $0 \leq t \leq n$, for $n = 5$, 10, and 20.

| SOLUTION |

As in Example 5.13 we consider the process $\{\underline{X}(t): t \geq 0\}$.

(a) For $n = 5$, $c = .75$, the values in Equation (5.30) are $a = -\ln(.75)$, $T = 5$, $\mu = .08$, $b = 0$, and $\sigma = .2$. The probability is $P = \Phi(-1.53770) + e^{-1.15073} \cdot \Phi(.25115) = .252$. The other probabilities are: $n = 10$, $c = .75 \rightarrow .293$; $n = 20$, $c = .75 \rightarrow .311$; $n = 5$, $c = .50 \rightarrow .023$; $n = 10$, $c = .50 \rightarrow .045$; $n = 20$, $c = .50 \rightarrow .058$. Note that the limit of P as $n \rightarrow \infty$ is $e^{-2a(\mu+b)/\sigma^2}$ (see Exercise 5.4.3). This is the probability that $\underline{S}(t)$ falls below c at some point in the future. For $c = .75$, this probability is .316, and for $c = .50$ it is .0625.

(b) $P\{\underline{S}(t) \leq (.75)e^{.06t}$ for some $t \leq n\}$

$$= P\{\ln[\underline{S}(t)] \leq \ln[(.75)e^{.06t}] \text{ for some } t \leq n\}$$

$$= P\{\underline{X}(t) - .06t \leq \ln(.75) \text{ for some } t \leq n\}.$$

$\underline{X}(t) - .06t$ becomes a Brownian motion with drift $\mu = .02$ and variance $\sigma^2 = .04$, so we can now apply Equation (5.30) with $a = -\ln(.75)$ and $b = 0$. For $n = 5$, the probability is .446, for $n = 10$ the probability is .554, and for $n = 20$ the probability is .633. ☐

5.5   NOTES AND REFERENCES

Stochastic models of interest rates have been analyzed in a number of articles, notably the paper "Rates of Return as Random Variables," by Boyle, *Journal of Risk and Insurance*, Volume 43 (1976), and the two articles "Stochastic Modeling of Interest Rates with Application to Life Contingencies, I & II," by Panjer and Bellhouse, *Journal of Risk and Insurance*, Volume 47 (1980), as well as the work by McCutcheon and Scott [8]. The Panjer-Bellhouse articles discuss empirical justification for various interest rate models, and also develop the moment generating function method for the mean and variance of $\underline{S}(n)$ discussed in Section 5.2.4.

There are many good references for probability and mathematical statistics at the introductory and intermediate level. *Introductory*

Probability Theory and its Applications, Volumes I and II, by Feller [4], are highly regarded texts. The proof of the theorem in Section 5.3 can be found there. Others include *Introduction to Mathematical Statistics*, by Hogg and Craig [6], and the two-volume set *Introduction to Probability Theory* and *Introduction to Statistical Theory*, by Hoel, Port, and Stone [5].

The standard way of finding the distribution of a transformation of continuous random variables, such as that of $\underline{S}(2) = (1 + \underline{i}_1)(1 + \underline{i}_2)$, is the *Jacobian method* (see Appendix B.) In the special case where the transformation is a sum or product of random variables, the *convolution method* may be used to analyze the distribution of the sum or product.

5.6   EXERCISES

Exercises 5.2

5.2.1   Smith invests 1000 in a mutual fund on January 1, 1990.   Smith estimates the growth for the fund in 1990 to be 20%, with probability .80, or -5%, with probability .20.

(a) Find the expected accumulated value of Smith's fund on December 31, 1990.

(b) Find the variance (as calculated on January 1, 1990) of the accumulated value on December 31, 1990.

(c) Smith estimates that the fund's growth rate in 1991 will be 30%, with probability .60, or -8%, with probability .40, independent of the growth rate in 1990.   Repeat parts (a) and (b) (as calculated on January 1, 1990) for the December 31, 1991 accumulated value.

(d) Based on the assumed growth distributions for 1990 and 1991, what is the probability that Smith will have annual average growth of at least 15% for the two-year period?

5.2.2   Effective annual interest rates for the next two years are assumed to be independent random variables i_1 and i_2. i_1 has a continuous uniform distribution on the interval $[.06, .16]$ and i_2 has a continuous uniform distribution on $[.12, .22]$. Let k be the (random) average annual interest rate for the two-year period $\Big(i.e.,$

$$1 + k = \sqrt{(1 + i_1)(1 + i_2)}\Big).$$

(a) Find $E[k]$.
(b) Find the probability $Pr[S(2) > (1.16)^2]$, where $S(2) = (1 + k)^2 = (1 + i_1)(1 + i_2)$.

5.2.3   Annual effective interest rates will be random in years 1 and 2, following a uniform distribution between 6% and 12%. In years 3 and 4 the rates will be uniformly distributed between 5% and 15%. Find $Var[S(4)]$.

5.2.4   The annual effective interest rates in various years are assumed to be mutually independent. In each year the interest rate i has a normal distribution with mean .08 and variance .0009. Find the mean and variance of $S(20)$.

5.2.5   Suppose that over a 30-year period annual effective interest rates are random, independent and identically distributed according to the distribution $i = \begin{cases} .05, & \text{with probability } .60 \\ .20, & \text{with probability } .40 \end{cases}$.

(a) Calculate and plot the probability function and cumulative distribution function for $S(10)$, $S(20)$ and $S(30)$.
(b) For $n = 10, 20$ and 30, and $c = .10, .50, .90, 1, 1.10$ and 1.50, find the probability $Pr[S(n) > c \cdot E[S(n)]]$ by (i) using the exact distribution of $S(n)$; (ii) assuming $S(n)$ is normal; (iii) assuming that $1 + i_t$ has a log-normal distribution for each t, so that $S(n)$ also has a log-normal distribution.

5.2.6   Write a computer routine to calculate the 66 outcomes for $S(10)$ in Example 5.3. Draw the histogram for $S(10)$. Do the same for $S(20)$.

5.2.7 Repeat Example 5.4 assuming that both i_1 and i_2 are uniformly distributed on $[.08, .12]$. Try to repeat Example 5.4 with $n = 3, 5$ or 10.

5.2.8 Solve for the values of c in Example 5.4 by the Newton-Raphson method.

5.2.9 Chebyshev's Rule states that for a random variable X with finite mean μ and finite variance σ^2, for any $k > 0$ we have $Pr[|X - \mu| < k \cdot \sigma] \geq 1 - \frac{1}{k^2}$. Apply Chebyshev's Rule to $X = S(n)$ for $n = 10, 20$ and 30 and $k = 2, 3$ and 4 for the distribution in Exercise 5.2.5, and compare the resulting intervals to exact intervals that can be obtained using the exact distribution of $S(n)$.

5.2.10 Suppose that δ has a normal distribution with mean μ and variance σ^2.
(a) Express the mean and variance of $1 + i$ in terms of μ and σ.
(b) Express σ^2 and μ in terms of $E[i]$ and $Var[i]$.

5.2.11 For the random interest rate i, denote $E[i]$ by j and $Var[i]$ by s^2. Assuming independence of rates, show that $E[S(n)] = (1 + j)^n$ and $Var[S(n)] = (1 + 2j + j^2 + s^2)^n - (1 + j)^{2n}$.

5.2.12 Find the mean and variance of $A(n) = v_1 \cdot v_2 \cdots \cdot v_n$ for $n = 10, 20$ and 30 by (a) using the interest rate distribution in Exercise 5.2.5; (b) assuming δ has a normal distribution with mean $.125$ and variance $.0005625$.

5.2.13 P is the amount that must be invested now in order to accumulate to $1,000,000$ in n years, assuming annual interest rates are independent and follow the distribution in Exercise 5.2.5. P is found in each of two different ways:
(i) P_1 is the value of P for which the expected value of accumulated profit (the excess of accumulated value of P over $1,000,000$) is zero at time n.
(ii) P_2 is the value of P for which the expected net present value (the excess of P over the present value of $1,000,000$) is zero at time 0.
Find P_1, P_2 and the standard deviations of accumulated profit and net present value for $n = 10, 20$ and 30.

5.2.14 An amount of 1 is invested for 10 years. The interest rate earned by the investment for the 10-year period will be either 5% for all 10 years, or 10% for all 10 years, or 15% for all 10 years. Each of the three possible cases is equally likely. Find the expected value and variance of the accumulated value at the end of 10 years. Suppose the interest rates may be different from year to year, but again for a particular year the rate is either 5%, 10% or 15%. Assuming independent interest rates from year to year, find the expected value and variance of the accumulated value.

5.2.15 If $\underline{i}$ is a random interest rate, show that $Var[\underline{d}] = Var[\underline{v}]$.

5.2.16 Suppose that interest rates from year to year are mutually independent.
(a) Show that $Var[\underline{A}(n)] = (E[\underline{v}^2])^n - (E[\underline{v}])^{2n}$.
(b) Show that $\lim_{n\to\infty} Var[\underline{A}(n)] = 0$.
(c) Find the value of n which maximizes $Var[\underline{A}(n)]$.

(d) Show that $\lim_{n\to\infty} \dfrac{\sqrt{Var[\underline{A}(n)]}}{E[\underline{A}(n)]} = +\infty$.

5.2.17 (a) Find the covariance between
$\underline{S}(10) = (1+\underline{i}_1)(1+\underline{i}_2)\cdots(1+\underline{i}_{10})$ and
$\underline{S}(20) = (1+\underline{i}_1)(1+\underline{i}_2)\cdots(1+\underline{i}_{10})\cdots(1+\underline{i}_{20})$.
(b) Find the covariance between $\underline{S}(n)$ and $\underline{S}(m)$, where $n < m$.

5.2.18 Denote $E[\underline{i}]$ by $\bar{i}$ and denote $E[\underline{v}]$ by $\bar{v}$. Let $i_{\bar{v}}$ be the rate of interest whose present value factor is $\bar{v}$ (i.e., $\frac{1}{1+i_{\bar{v}}} = \bar{v}$). Show that $i_{\bar{v}} < \bar{i}$.

5.2.19 Show that $E[\underline{S}(n)] = M_{\Delta(n)}(1)$ and
$Var[\underline{S}(n)] = M_{\Delta(n)}(2) - [M_{\Delta(n)}(1)]^2$.

5.2.20 Suppose that $i_1 = \begin{cases} .08, & \text{with probability } 1/3 \\ .10, & \text{with probability } 1/3, \\ .12, & \text{with probability } 1/3 \end{cases}$

and in subsequent years the interest rate distribution is

$i_t = \begin{cases} i_{t-1} - .02, & \text{with probability } 1/3 \\ i_{t-1}, & \text{with probability } 1/3. \\ i_{t-1} + .02, & \text{with probability } 1/3 \end{cases}$

Find the expected value and variance of $S(n)$ for $n = 2, 3$ and 5.

5.2.21 i_1 has a continuous uniform distribution between 6% and 12%. If the actual interest rate in year 1 is i_1, then the distribution of i_2 is continuous and uniform between $i_1 - .04$ and $i_1 + .04$. Find the mean and variance of $S(2)$.

Exercises 5.3

5.3.1 Assuming independent interest rates from year to year, find the expected value and variance of $s_{\overline{n}|}$ and $a_{\overline{n}|}$ for $n = 20$ and 30 for each of the following interest rate distributions :

(a) $i = \begin{cases} .10, & \text{with probability } .50 \\ .15, & \text{with probability } .50 \end{cases}$

(b) $i = \begin{cases} .05, & \text{with probability } .50 \\ .20, & \text{with probability } .50 \end{cases}$

(c) i has a uniform distribution on the interval $(.05, .20)$.

5.3.2 (a) The covariance between the random variables U and V is $Cov[U, V] = E[(U - \mu_U)(V - \mu_V)]$, which can be readily shown to be equal to $E[U \cdot V] - E[U] \cdot E[V]$. For random variables U and $V_1, V_2, \dots, V_n$, show that the covariance between U and $\sum_{t=1}^{n} V_t$ is

$$Cov\left[\underset{\sim}{U}, \sum_{t=1}^{n} \underset{\sim}{V}_t\right] = \sum_{t=1}^{n} Cov[\underset{\sim}{U}, \underset{\sim}{V}_t].$$

For random variables $\underset{\sim}{U}_1, \ldots, \underset{\sim}{U}_m$ and $\underset{\sim}{V}_1, \ldots, \underset{\sim}{V}_n$, show that the covariance between $\sum_{s=1}^{m} \underset{\sim}{U}_s$ and $\sum_{t=1}^{n} \underset{\sim}{V}_t$ is

$$Cov\left[\sum_{s=1}^{m} \underset{\sim}{U}_s, \sum_{t=1}^{n} \underset{\sim}{V}_t\right] = \sum_{s=1}^{m}\sum_{t=1}^{n} Cov[\underset{\sim}{U}_s, \underset{\sim}{V}_t].$$

(b) Suppose that $\underset{\sim}{r}_1, \underset{\sim}{r}_2, \ldots, \underset{\sim}{r}_n$ are independent random variables with $E[\underset{\sim}{r}_k] = A$ and $E[\underset{\sim}{r}_k^2] = B$ for each k. Let $\underset{\sim}{U}_t = \underset{\sim}{r}_1 \cdot \underset{\sim}{r}_2 \cdot \cdots \cdot \underset{\sim}{r}_t$. Show that if $s < t$ then

$$Cov[\underset{\sim}{U}_s, \underset{\sim}{U}_t] = B^s \cdot A^{t-s} - A^{s+t},$$

if $s > t$ then

$$Cov[\underset{\sim}{U}_s, \underset{\sim}{U}_t] = B^t \cdot A^{s-t} - A^{s+t},$$

and if $s = t$ then

$$Cov[\underset{\sim}{U}_s, \underset{\sim}{U}_t] = Cov[\underset{\sim}{U}_s, \underset{\sim}{U}_s] = Var[\underset{\sim}{U}_s]$$

$$= B^s - A^{s+s} = B^s - A^{2s}.$$

(c) Let
$$\underset{\sim}{Z} = \underset{\sim}{r}_1 + \underset{\sim}{r}_1 \cdot \underset{\sim}{r}_2 + \cdots + \underset{\sim}{r}_1 \cdot \underset{\sim}{r}_2 \cdot \cdots \cdot \underset{\sim}{r}_n$$
$$= \underset{\sim}{U}_1 + \underset{\sim}{U}_2 + \cdots + \underset{\sim}{U}_n.$$

For any random variable $\underset{\sim}{W}$, $Var[\underset{\sim}{W}] = Cov[\underset{\sim}{W}, \underset{\sim}{W}]$, so
$$Var[\underset{\sim}{Z}] = Cov\left[\sum_{t=1}^{n} \underset{\sim}{U}_t, \sum_{t=1}^{n} \underset{\sim}{U}_t\right].$$
Use the results of part (a) to show that $Var[\underset{\sim}{Z}]$ can be written as $\sum_{s=1}^{n}\sum_{t=1}^{n} Cov[\underset{\sim}{U}_s, \underset{\sim}{U}_t]$. Break the double summation into the two components $\sum_{s=1}^{n}\sum_{t=1}^{n} = \sum_{s=1}^{n}\sum_{t=1}^{s} + \sum_{s=1}^{n}\sum_{t=s+1}^{n}$. In the first sum on the right side of the equation $s \geq t$, and in the second

sum $s < t$. Use the result of part (b) to show that the variance of Z can be written as

$$\sum_{s=1}^{n}\sum_{t=1}^{s} B^t \cdot A^{s-t} + \sum_{s=1}^{n}\sum_{t=s+1}^{n} B^s \cdot A^{t-s} - \sum_{s=1}^{n}\sum_{t=1}^{n} A^{s+t}.$$

Simplify these summations and show that they can be put into the form given for the variance of Z in the theorem stated in Section 5.3.

5.3.3 Find the variance of $\ddot{s}_{\overline{10|}}$ for each of the following distributions:

(i) $i = \begin{cases} .10, & \text{with probability } .50 \\ .15, & \text{with probability } .50 \end{cases}$

(ii) $i = \begin{cases} .05, & \text{with probability } .50 \\ .20, & \text{with probability } .50 \end{cases}$

In each case approximate the probabilities $Pr[\ddot{s}_{\overline{10|}} \le 18]$, $Pr[\ddot{s}_{\overline{10|}} \le 19]$ and $Pr[\ddot{s}_{\overline{10|}} \le E[\ddot{s}_{\overline{10|}}]]$ based on the assumption that (a) $\ddot{s}_{\overline{10|}}$ has a normal distribution, and (b) $\ddot{s}_{\overline{10|}}$ has a log-normal distribution (see Exercise 5.2.10).

5.3.4 Write a computer routine (BASIC or FORTRAN) that enumerates all $2^{10} = 1024$ possible 10-year sequences of interest rates and calculates the corresponding values of $\ddot{s}_{\overline{10|}}$ for the distributions in Exercise 5.3.3. Incorporate into the program the ability to determine the number of values of $\ddot{s}_{\overline{10|}}$ that are less than n, thereby obtaining the exact values of the probabilities in Exercise 5.3.3.

5.3.5 Find the exact probabilities associated with the intervals in Table 5.3 in Example 5.8 for $n = 5$ and $n = 10$.

5.3.6 Suppose that annual effective interest rates are independent and identically distributed with a continuous uniform distribution between 9% and 15%. Let W denote the (random) accumulated value 10 years after the final payment of a 10-payment annuity of 1 per year. Find the mean and variance of W.

5.3.7 (a) If interest rates are $i_1, i_2, \cdots, i_n, i_{n+1}$ in $n+1$ successive years, show that the relationship between the $(n+1)$-payment accumulated annuity-due and the n-payment accumulated annuity-due is $\ddot{s}_{\overline{n+1}|} = (1 + i_{n+1})(1 + \ddot{s}_{\overline{n}|})$. If rates are random with common mean and variance, show that
$$\ddot{\underline{s}}_{\overline{n+1}|} = (1 + \underline{i}_{n+1})(1 + \ddot{\underline{s}}_{\overline{n}|}).$$

(b) If interest rates are independent, show that $E[\ddot{\underline{s}}_{\overline{n+1}|}] = E[1 + \underline{i}_{n+1}] \cdot (1 + E[\ddot{\underline{s}}_{\overline{n}|}])$.

(c) Show that
$$(\ddot{\underline{s}}_{\overline{n+1}|})^2 = (1 + \underline{i}_{n+1})^2 \cdot (1 + \ddot{\underline{s}}_{\overline{n}|})^2$$
$$= (1 + 2 \cdot \underline{i}_{n+1} + \underline{i}_{n+1}^2)(1 + 2 \cdot \ddot{\underline{s}}_{\overline{n}|} + (\ddot{\underline{s}}_{\overline{n}|})^2).$$

(d) Using notation $E[\underline{i}] = \overline{i}$, $E[\ddot{\underline{s}}_{\overline{n}|}] = \mu_n$, $E[(\ddot{\underline{s}}_{\overline{n}|})^2] = m_n$, and $Var[\underline{i}] = s^2$, show that the expected value of the equation in part (c) can be written as
$$m_{n+1} = (1 + 2 \cdot \overline{i} + \overline{i}^2 + s^2)(1 + 2 \cdot \mu_n + m_n).$$

Thus there is a recursive way to calculate successive values of m_{n+1}. The variance of $\ddot{\underline{s}}_{\overline{k}|}$ can then be written as $Var[\ddot{\underline{s}}_{\overline{k}|}] = m_k - \mu_k^2$.

5.3.8 Show that $E[\underline{a}_{\overline{n}|}]$ can be written as $a_{\overline{n}|}$ at interest rate i_v (see Exercise 5.2.18).

5.3.9 Show that $\dfrac{E[\underline{s}_{\overline{n}|}]}{E[\underline{a}_{\overline{n}|}]} < E\left[\dfrac{\underline{s}_{\overline{n}|}}{\underline{a}_{\overline{n}|}}\right]$.

5.3.10 For part (a) of Example 5.11, find the expected amount of interest paid and principal repaid in the first year. Show that the variance of the interest paid in the first year is equal to the variance of $\underline{OB}_{12}$.

Exercises 5.4

5.4.1   (a) Use Equation (5.28) to show that for the stochastic accumulation $\underline{S}(t)$ for which $ln[\underline{S}(t)]$ is a Brownian motion (where $S(0) = 1$) and $k > 0$,

$$P\{\underline{S}(t) \geq k \text{ for some } t \leq n\} \ = \ 2 \cdot P\{\underline{S}(n) \geq k\}.$$

(b) Show that the limit as $n \to \infty$ of the probability in (a) is 1.

5.4.2   Use Equation (5.29), which is valid for negative drift μ, to derive Equation (5.30).

5.4.3   Show that as $n \to \infty$, the limit of P in Example 5.13(a) is $e^{-2a(\mu+b)/\upsilon^2}$.

5.4.4   Repeat Examples 5.12, 5.13, and 5.14 with a variance of (i) $\sigma^2 = .0004$ and (ii) $\sigma^2 = 40$.

5.4.5   Repeat Example 5.12(a) with 1.25 replaced by each of the following.

(i) $(1.25)e^{.06t}$

(ii) $(1.25)e^{.1t}$

CHAPTER 6

TOPICS IN FINANCE AND INVESTMENT

6.1   INTRODUCTION

In this chapter we consider topics that are related to investment and finance. In Chapter 4 we looked at bonds in some detail. Bonds are one of several investments available to an investor, and in this chapter we look at other investment-related vehicles including stocks, options and futures, and foreign exchange.   Options and futures are examples of a class of investments known as *derivatives*.   A "derivative" in the context of investments, is an investment vehicle whose value is *derived* from the value of some other investment. The value of an option derives from the value of the underlying stock or security that the option holder has a right to buy or sell. The value of a futures contract derives from the underlying commodity or security that the futures contract holder has contracted to buy or sell.

We also consider a topic of considerable importance in investment planning, the idea of asset-liability matching. We introduce the basic ideas involved in *Redington immunization*, a process which attempts to eliminate the risk of changes in the valuation interest rate to the value of an asset-liability portfolio.

6.2   SPOT RATES, FORWARD RATES OF INTEREST, AND INTEREST RATE SWAPS

In investment terminology, a *spot interest rate* or *spot rate* is an interest rate on an investment or loan that is available now and effective from now until some specified future time. A commonly used benchmark for the short-term spot rate is the *LIBOR* rate. LIBOR stands for the "London InterBank Overnight Rate," a rate that refers to one-day lending. This is an example of a *floating rate*, a rate of interest which fluctuates from day to day. Another notion that arises in an investment context is a *forward rate*. This refers to an interest rate that will be available for a certain period of time (usually one year) beginning a specified amount of time from now. The forward rate for a one-year loan to be made one year from now refers to a transaction that is arranged now, with the loan to be made in one year and repaid in two years at the specified forward rate. Forward rates are usually not quoted explicitly, but can be determined implicitly when related to certain types of investments.

A typical way of calculating a forward interest rate is through the use of zero-coupon bonds (also called *pure-discount bonds*). Zero-coupon bonds, introduced in Chapter 4, are investments that pay a specified maturity amount on a specified date. They are bought at a price that represents their present value at an agreed-upon yield rate that is usually calculated and quoted on an annual effective basis. The following example illustrates the way in which a forward interest rate can be found from the yield rates on zero-coupon bonds.

EXAMPLE 6.1

Yield rates to maturity for zero-coupon bonds are currently quoted at annual effective interest rates of 8% for a one-year maturity, 9% for a two-year maturity, and 10% for a three-year maturity. Calculate the current prices for three bonds with maturity values of 1000 each and maturity dates 1, 2 and 3 years from now. Calculate the annual effective forward rate for year two and the annual effective forward rate for year three implied by current yields of these bonds.

SOLUTION

Let the bond prices be labeled P_1, P_2, and P_3 for the one-year, two-year and three-year maturities, respectively. Then $P_1 = 925.93$, $P_2 = 841.68$ and $P_3 = 751.31$. We wish to find the forward rate for year two corresponding to these bonds. This can be done if we assume that an individual can sell as well as buy these zero-coupon bonds, and if we assume that these bonds can be bought and sold in fractional denominations (*i.e.*, it is not necessary to buy or sell in integral multiples of 1000). Suppose an individual sells a two-year 1000 bond for 841.68, and with the proceeds she buys a one-year bond. The one-year bond yields 8%, the bond will mature in one year for $841.68(1.08) = 909.01$ (or, equivalently, with the 841.68 she can buy a bond with maturity value $\frac{841.68}{925.93} \times 1000 = 909.01$). Thus she has arranged a transaction in which she receives 909.01 one year from now and pays 1000 two years from now. The implied interest rate on this one-year loan starting one year from now is $\frac{1000}{909.01} - 1 = .1001$, or 10.01%. Note that an equivalent way of calculating this forward rate is $\frac{(1.09)^2}{1.08} - 1$, and, in general, the forward rate effective in the second year would be $\frac{(1+j_2)^2}{(1+j_1)} - 1$, where j_1 is the yield rate on the one-year investment and j_2 is the annual yield rate on the two-year investment. In a similar way, the forward rate in effect two years from now is $\frac{(1+j_3)^3}{(1+j_2)^2} - 1$ $= \frac{(1.10)^3}{(1.09)^2} - 1 = .1202$. Exercise 6.2.1 looks at forward interest rates in more detail. □

A spot rate for a term of t years is denoted $i_{0,t}$, so the present value of a zero-coupon bond due in t years is $(1 + i_{0,t})^{-t}$. The forward rate for the tth year from now is denoted $i_{t-1,t}$ and is given by

$$i_{t-1,t} = \frac{(1 + i_{0,t})^t}{(1 + i_{0,t-1})^{t-1}} - 1, \tag{6.1}$$

so that the accumulated value of 1 in n years is

$$(1 + i_{0,1})(1 + i_{1,2}) \cdots (1 + i_{n-1,n})$$

$$= (1 + i_{0,1}) \cdot \frac{(1 + i_{0,2})^2}{(1 + i_{0,1})} \cdot \cdots \cdot \frac{(1 + i_{0,n})^n}{(1 + i_{0,n-1})^{n-1}}$$

$$= (1 + i_{0,n})^n. \tag{6.2}$$

An **interest rate swap** is a contractual agreement between two parties to exchange a series of payments for a stated period of time. Interest rate swaps may be implemented for a number of reasons. An interest rate swap can be used to convert floating-rate (short-term) liability into fixed-rate liability or vice-versa. A swap can also change the risk characteristics of assets or liabilities that are associated with the swap.

As an example of an interest rate swap, consider two borrowers, A and B. Borrower A has a high credit rating, and can borrow in the the fixed-rate market (medium to long-term bond market) at a rate of 8%, or in the floating-rate market (short-term or spot market) at 6%. Borrower B has a medium credit rating and can borrow in the fixed-rate market at 9% or in the floating-rate market at 6.5%. Borrower A wishes to borrow in the floating-rate market and B wishes to borrow the same amount in the fixed-rate market. The two borrowers construct the following swap. A borrows in the fixed-rate market at 8% and loans the funds to B at a rate of 8.5%. B borrows in the floating-rate market at 6.5% and loans the funds to A at 6.25%. The net effect for borrower A is that borrower A pays 8% on the fixed-rate loan, receives 8.5% from B and pays 6.25% to B, for a net payment rate of 5.75%. The net effect for borrower B is that B pays 6.5% on the floating-rate loan, receives 6.25% from A and pays 8.5% to A, for a a net payment rate of 8.75%. A's net payment rate of 5.75% is .25% below the floating rate that A would pay directly, and B's net payment rate of 8.75% is .25% below the fixed-rate that B would pay directly. What allows this arrangement to be made is that the differential between fixed and floating rates for A is not the same as that for B, and the two borrowers are able to take advantage of that by taking *parallel loans* (or *back-to-back loans*) and swapping them.

The practice of interest rate swapping began in the late 1970's. It has grown incredibly quickly since that time. An estimate of 1992 activity in interest rate and currency swaps is 5 trillion dollars (US), and an estimate of the same activity in 1995 is 18 trillion dollars. Currency swaps may involve two borrowers who exchange loans in different currencies (and, perhaps, at different rates). The example just given is quite elementary compared to some of the more sophisticated interest rate swaps that can be made. A swap is an example of an investment derivative. The following few sections of Chapter 6 consider some other widely used investments and related derivatives.

6.3   STOCKS AND OPTIONS

6.3.1 Stock Valuation

Shares of common stock represent ownership in a corporation, entitling the stockholder to certain privileges including the right to vote on matters regarding the management of the corporation. In addition the common stock owner, from time to time, receives *dividends* that reflect a share of the profit earned by the corporation.

Among the many factors affecting the price of a stock are the nature of the company's business, the quality of the company's management, current economic conditions, and forecasts of future conditions as they relate to the company's current and prospective profitability. An investor in stock would be looking for a return on that investment in the form of future dividends and share price increases. For an investor with a long-term outlook, intending to hold the stock indefinitely, the price (or value) of the stock might be regarded as the present value of future dividends expected to be paid on the stock. If d_t denotes the expected dividend payable at the end of the tth year (with time measured from the purchase date of the stock), and i is the (long-term) annual rate of valuation for this investment, then according to the *dividend discount model for valuing stocks*, the price of the stock can be valued as

$$P = \sum_{t=1}^{\infty} \frac{d_t}{(1+i)^t}. \qquad (6.3a)$$

A more general formulation would use separate valuation rates each year, so that

$$P = \frac{d_1}{(1+i_1)} + \frac{d_2}{(1+i_1)(1+i_2)} + \cdots. \qquad (6.3b)$$

Using the spot rate $i_{0,t}$ for discounting a payment due at time t results in

$$P = \frac{d_1}{(1+i_{0,1})} + \frac{d_2}{(1+i_{0,2})^2} + \cdots. \qquad (6.3c)$$

Stocks are bought by investors who anticipate gains from dividends and increases in share prices. An investor who believes the share price of a stock will fall over a period of time can *sell short* the stock (sell something he does not own) at the current price and cover the short sale (buy the stock) at a later date when (he hopes) the stock can be purchased at a lower price. In practice, the investment dealer will often take the other side of the position in the short sale, meaning that the investment dealer is owed the shares by the short seller, with the understanding that the short seller will eventually purchase the stock and give it to the dealer. If the stock pays a dividend while in a short position, the short seller must pay the dividend amount to the investment dealer, or the amount is deducted from the margin account. When an investor is a short seller of stock, the investment dealer who executes the transaction will usually require a certain amount of *margin* to be paid by the short seller. This margin may be up to 50% of the value of the stock sold in the short sale, and it is held in an account administered by the investment dealer. The equity in the short seller's margin account is regularly updated when there are movements in the stock price. If the stock price increases, the short seller may be required to add to the margin account to maintain a minimum margin level. The following example illustrates this.

EXAMPLE 6.2

The current price of a share of stock in Corporation XYZ is 50. Smith short sells 1000 shares of XYZ stock. Smith's investment dealer charges a commission of 2% of the value of stock purchased or sold short and also requires that Smith open a margin account for the short sale. While Smith is "short the stock," the margin account must maintain a balance of at least 40% of the value of the stock. Thus, when the short sale is initiated, Smith must deposit 20,000 into the margin account, and pay the investment dealer a commission of 1000.

(a) Suppose that the stock price drops to 40, at which time Smith "covers the short sale." If the commission on the stock purchase is deducted from the margin account, find the equity in the account after the short sale is covered.

(b) Repeat part (a) if the price rises to 60. Suppose that the price rises to 60 but Smith does not wish to cover the short sale yet. Find the amount Smith must add to the margin account to maintain the required balance of 40% of the stock value.

(c) Suppose that the stock pays a dividend of 2 per share while the short sale is in effect. Find the least amount by which the share price must drop in order that Smith not get a "margin call" to add to the margin account to maintain the 40% minimum balance.

| SOLUTION |

(a) When Smith sells the stock short, Smith is owed 70,000 (the 50,000 sale price of the stock and the 20,000 in the margin account) and owes 1000 shares of stock. At a price of 40, the cost of purchasing the stock is 40,000 plus 800 in commission. Smith's equity after the transaction is then $70,000 - 40,800 = 29,200$. Smith's overall gain is 9,200 minus the initial 1000 commission on the short sale, for a net gain, after commissions, of 8200. Smith's gain could also have been found as $1000 \times (50 - 40) - \text{commission} = 10,000 - 1800 = 8200$.

(b) Smith must now have a margin account balance of $.40 \times 60,000 = 24,000$, and so must add 4000 to the margin account.

(c) Smith's account has 2000 deducted to pay for dividends, leaving a balance of 18,000. In order for the account to be at least 40% of the stock value, it must be the case that $18,000 \geq .40 \times 1000 \times P$. Thus, $P \leq 45$, so that the stock must drop in value by at least 5 in order to avoid a margin call. □

A stock will have a certain amount of risk associated with it. The stock's price will be related to the level of prices in the stock market as a whole, so that part of the risk, called the *market risk* (or *systematic risk*), for an individual stock will be related to general factors that affect the overall economy. In addition, because of the specific nature of the stock's industry group and the position of the issuing corporation in that industry, there will be *non-market risk* or *diversifiable risk*. Diversifiable risk can be managed by carefully choosing the mix of stocks in the overall portfolio. If an investor's portfolio exactly matches the portfolio used to measure overall market performance, such as the portfolio used for the Dow Jones index or the Standard & Poor's index, then the risk of the portfolio will be entirely market risk as measured by the standard portfolio. The market and non-market risks are generally assumed to be independent. The valuation rate (or sequence of rates) used in price formulas (6.3) for a specific stock may be related to the risk classification of that stock.

The relationship between the rate of return on a stock over a period of time and the average return on the entire stock market (represented by a broad market portfolio such as Standard and Poor's 500 index) during the same period is represented by the stock's *characteristic line*, given by

$$\underset{\sim}{R}_s = \alpha_s + \beta_s \cdot \underset{\sim}{R}_m + \underset{\sim}{e}_s, \tag{6.4}$$

where $\underline{R}_s$ is the (random) return on the stock for the period under consideration, α_s is the part of the stock's return not related to the market, β_s is the expected change in R_s, given a change of 1 unit in the market return R_m, $\underline{R}_m$ is the (random) return on the entire market for the period, and $\underline{e}_s$ is a random variable (with mean 0) measuring the non-market risk (usually assumed to be independent of R_m).

The factor β_s is called the *beta* of the stock, and measures the volatility of the stock's return in relation to the return on the entire market (see Exercise 6.3.2). The larger the beta for a stock, the larger the expected return and the larger the risk (standard deviation of return). These parameters change over time; estimates of α_s and β_s can be obtained using statistical regression based on historical data.

Taking the expected value of both sides of Equation (6.4) results in

$$\bar{R}_s = \alpha_s + \beta_s \cdot \bar{R}_m. \tag{6.5}$$

Under reasonable assumptions regarding investor behavior, this relationship can be written as the *capital asset pricing model*

$$\bar{R}_s = R_f + \beta_s(\bar{R}_m - R_f). \tag{6.6}$$

In Equation (6.6) R_f denotes the risk-free rate of return available, as measured by an appropriate government security. We do not derive this model in this text; Section 6.7 provides references for further reading in this area, and in portfolio analysis in general.

6.3.2 Options

An option, in the financial sense, is a contract conveying a right to buy or sell designated securities or commodities at a specified price during a stipulated period. The specified price mentioned in this definition is called the option's *striking price* or *exercise price*. A *call option* gives the holder the right to buy (or call away) a specified amount of the underlying security from the option seller (writer), and a *put option* gives the holder the right to sell (or put) a specified amount of the underlying security to the option seller. An *American option* allows the right to buy or sell to be exercised any time up to the expiration date, and a *European option* allows the option to be exercised only on the expiration date.

As time goes on, new option contracts on a particular security are introduced on a regular basis; when this occurs there are generally several contract types set up with striking prices varying from somewhat below to somewhat above the market price at the time the option is introduced. The contracts are set up with striking prices at increments appropriate to the underlying security. For example, if the underlying stock price is 30, options may be issued with strike prices of 25, 30 or 35. New options also will be introduced so that exercise dates of up to one year in the future are always available. When option values are quoted in a financial publication, the expiration date is given as a particular month, but it is understood that there is a specific day in that month when the option expires (usually the 2nd or 3rd Saturday). There will always be two parties to an options contract, the purchaser of the option and the writer of the option. For a call option, as indicated above, the purchaser has the right to buy stock at the strike price by a certain date. In exchange for receiving a payment for the writing the option, the writer of the call option has the obligation to provide to the option purchaser the stock at the strike price, if the option purchaser exercises the option. Similar comments apply to put options.

Suppose that on January 15 an investor obtains a call option to purchase 1 share of XYZ Corporation before July 20 at a price of 50 per share. An investor holding such an option would exercise it only if the share price goes above 50, since the investor could then exercise the option and buy at 50 and immediately sell at the higher current price. If XYZ Corporation has a share price of 55 on January 15, the value of the option on that date is at least its *intrinsic value* of 5, this intrinsic value being the excess, if any, of the share price over the strike price (for a call option). The intrinsic value can also be regarded as the immediate return that the option holder could realize by exercising the option and buying a share at 50 and selling it at 55 (transaction costs such as commissions excluded). There is also a possibility that the stock price will increase above 55 before July 20. This suggests that the value of the option is more than the intrinsic value of 5. There is also a *time value* or *time premium* included in the value of the option which takes into account the possible increase in the price of the underlying security before the expiration date. A call option whose striking price is less than the market price of the underlying security is said to be *in-the-money*. If XYZ Corporation has a price of 45 per share on January 15, then the option is *out-of-the-money* and has no intrinsic value. An out-of-the-money option will still have a time value, since it is still possible for the share price to rise sufficiently before the expiration date to put it in-the-money. It is possible that the option will stay out-of-the-money until the expiration date, in which case it will expire without having been exercised, and the original cost of the option to the option purchaser is lost, whereas the writer of the option made a gain. A similar analysis can be applied to put options.

The actual price paid for an option depends on the perceptions of investors regarding the behavior of the underlying stock's price prior to the option's expiration date. It is clear that as time moves closer to the expiration date, the value of a call option approaches the limit $max [0, CP - SP]$, where CP is the current price of the stock and SP is the striking price of the option. Note also that there is a lower limit to the potential loss on the transaction, namely the amount paid for the option. This loss occurs if the option expires unexercised. The potential profit does not have an upper limit since it depends on the level to which the stock's price can rise. For the writer of the call there is a limit to the profit, namely the price received for the sale of the call. If the holder exercises the option, the call writer is obliged to buy the stock on the market (or use existing inventory of that stock) and sell to the holder of the call. There is no limit to the call writer's potential liability, since there is no limit on the potential price of the stock that the call writer will have to buy in order to cover the call. There are a wide variety of investment strategies such as *spreads* and *straddles* that involve the purchase or writing of options in combination with purchase or (short) sale of the underlying stock (see Exercise 6.3.4).

Since the introduction of *"exchange-traded options"* in 1973, a considerable amount of research has been done into the valuation of options. In order to determine the value of an option on an underlying security, a combination of selling (or buying) the option and buying (or selling) an appropriate amount of the security is made that forms a *riskless hedge* that provides the same return as would be realized over the same period when investing at the *risk-free rate of return*, the rate of return available on essentially risk-free government securities. The way in which such a riskless hedge is constructed can best be seen in an elementary illustration in which, on the expiration date, the price of the underlying security will be one of two possible values. This is called the *binomial model*.

Suppose that a stock has a current price of 100, and at the end of the current period the stock's price will be either 110 or 90. Suppose that the stock has a call option on it to purchase at a striking price of 105 at the end of the period. If an investor sells a call option on one share, the value of the option at the end of the period will be $110 - 105 = 5$ on the expiration date, if the stock's price is then 110. The holder of the option can buy the stock for 105 and sell for 110. The purchaser will allow the option to expire unexercised if the stock's price is 90, so the value of the option in this case is 0 on the expiration date. Suppose that at the same time the investor sells the option on one share, he also purchases $\frac{1}{4}$ share of the stock for $\frac{1}{4}(100) = 25$. Let us denote by P_0 the value of the option to purchase one share at the start of the period. The net amount invested by the investor is $25 - P_0$, the amount paid for the $\frac{1}{4}$-share of stock minus the amount received from the sale of the option. At the end of the period, the net value of the combined investment is $27.50 - 5 = 22.50$ if the stock price goes to 110 (the value of the stock minus the cost of fulfilling the obligation to the option holder), and the net value is $22.50 - 0 = 22.50$ if the stock price goes to 90. Thus, the net value of the investment at the end of the period is 22.50 no matter what the stock price is. This is a riskless hedge in that the value of the investment at the end of the period will be 22.50 with certainty. In order to determine the price of the option at the start of the period, this riskless investment should be equivalent to a riskless investment in a government security over the same period. Suppose that the risk-free rate of return for the period is 1%. In order for the investment to be equivalent to a risk-free investment in the government security, we must have $(25 - P_0)(1.01) = 22.50$, so that $P_0 = 2.7228$.

In the general binomial model for stock price movement, suppose the current stock price is S_0, and suppose that at the end of the current period the stock price will be either S_1^+ or S_1^-, where $S_1^+ > S_1^-$. Suppose there is a call option on the stock with a striking price of S_p. The value of the option at the end of the period is either P_1^+ or P_1^-, depending on whether the stock price is S_1^+ or S_1^-. It is possible to create a riskless hedge by selling a call option on one share of stock at the same time as purchasing h shares of stock, where $h = \dfrac{P_1^+ - P_1^-}{S_1^+ - S_1^-}$ is called the *hedge ratio*.

The net amount invested at the start of the period is $h \cdot S_0 - P_0$, and the value of the investment at the end of the period is $h \cdot S_1^+ - P_1^+ = h \cdot S_1^- - P_1^-$, whether the stock price goes to S_1^+ or S_1^-. If the risk-free rate of return is r for the period, then

$$(h \cdot S_0 - P_0)(1 + r) = h \cdot S_1^+ - P_1^+ = h \cdot S_1^- - P_1^-.$$

Since h, S_0, S_1^+, S_1^-, P_1^+, P_1^- and r are known, it is possible to solve for P_0.

This binomial model for stock prices and option valuation can be extended to a two-period scenario in which the stock price S_0 moves to one of two prices S_1^+ or S_1^- at the end of the first period. For each price at the end of period 1 there are two possible prices to which the stock can move at the end of period 2, which may be different for S_1^+ and S_1^-. This generalization can be continued to more than two consecutive periods. The period can be shortened and the number of periods, n, can be increased, allowing a limiting case in which, as $n \to \infty$, the stock price becomes a continuous stochastic process.

The limiting case described in the previous paragraph is the *Black-Scholes option pricing formula*. The formula assumes that the stock pays no dividends prior to expiry of the option, and that $\{ln[S_t] \,|\, 0 \le t \le n\}$ forms a Brownian motion process (see Section 5.4) with variance σ^2 per unit time period, where S_t is the stock price at time t. (It is possible to adjust the formulation to account for dividends.) This assumption regarding the behavior of the stock's price can be more simply described by saying that the continuously compounded annual rate of return on the stock has a normal distribution with variance σ^2; in practice, σ^2 is estimated as a sample variance based on historical data for the stock. The following parameters are also required for the valuation formula:

δ - the risk-free force of interest
P_0 - the current price of the stock
E - the exercise price of the option
n - the time (in years) until expiry of the option

The Black-Scholes formula gives the price of the option at the current time as

$$P = P_0 \cdot \Phi(d_1) - E \cdot e^{-n\delta} \cdot \Phi(d_2), \qquad (6.7)$$

where

$$d_1 = \frac{ln(P_0/E) + \left(\delta + \frac{1}{2}\sigma^2\right) \cdot n}{\sigma\sqrt{n}}, \qquad (6.8a)$$

$$d_2 = \frac{ln(P_0/E) + \left(\delta - \frac{1}{2}\sigma^2\right) \cdot n}{\sigma\sqrt{n}}, \qquad (6.8b)$$

and $\Phi(x)$ is the cumulative distribution function of the standard normal distribution.

| **EXAMPLE 6.3** |

The price on January 15 of a share of XYZ stock is 50. Use the Black-Scholes option pricing formula to find the value on January 15 of an option to buy 1 share of XYZ, with an expiration date of July 20, and with an exercise price of (a) 45, (b) 50, and (c) 55. Assume the risk-free force of interest is .08, and the continuously compounded rate of return on the stock has a standard deviation of $\sigma = .03$.

| **SOLUTION** |

$P_0 = 50$, $\quad n = \frac{186}{365} = .5096$, $\quad \delta = .08$, $\quad \sigma^2 = .0009$, $\quad e^{-n\delta} = .9601$.
(a) $E = 45$ so $d_1 = 6.8341$ and $d_2 = 6.8127$, implying $\Phi(d_1)$ $= \Phi(d_2) = 1.0000$, implying an option price of $50(1) - 45(.9601)(1) =$ 6.7955; (b) $E = 50$ so $d_1 = 1.9143$ and $d_2 = 1.8929$, implying $\Phi(d_1) = .9722$ and $\Phi(d_2) = .9708$, implying an option price of $50(.9722) - 50(.9601)(.9708) = 2.0067$; (c) $E = 55$ so $d_1 = -2.5362$ and $d_2 = -2.5576$, implying $\Phi(d_1) = .0056$ and $\Phi(d_2) = .00527$, implying an option price of $50(.0056) - 55(.9601)(.00527) = .0017$. $\square$

Options are available on a variety of financial instruments, including government Treasury Bonds (both long and short term) and foreign currency contracts. Options provide the investor with a certain amount of *leverage* in the investment. On a call option, the option price (or *premium*) on an in-the-money option will fluctuate in tandem, more or less, with the price of the underlying security. Thus the option investor can make the same numerical gain as the holder of the underlying security, but the premium paid by the option investor is, typically, considerably less than the price of the underlying security. The call option buyer's potential loss is limited to the original cost of the option.

As mentioned at the start of the chapter, options are one example of the class of investments known as derivative investments or derivatives. The value of a derivative investment is derived from or tied to the value of some underlying investment – the option value is completely dependent upon the value of the underlying stock. The previous paragraph indicated that the value of an option is generally a fraction of the value of the underlying stock but may be subject to similar price changes. From Example 6.3 we see that the Black-Scholes price of the call option with strike price 50 is 2.01. If the stock price rises to 55 by the expiration date, the option value rises to 5, which is 150% increase, while the stock itself has risen from 50 to 55 – a 10% increase. On the other hand, if the stock prices drops to 45 at the expiration date, the call option has a value of 0, which is a 100% loss of the investment in the option, while the stock has had a 10% decrease in value. The call option is generally considerably more risky than the underlying stock, and this is a feature of most derivative investments.   Small percentage changes in the underlying investment can result in large percentage changes in the related derivative investment.

Another type of derivative investment that provides considerable leverage and risk is the futures contract. This is considered in the next section.

6.4   FUTURES AND FORWARD CONTRACTS

A *forward contract* is an agreement to conduct a specified transaction at a specified date in the future. Suppose the 90-day forward exchange rate between Canadian dollars and U.S. dollars is 1 Cdn. $\equiv$ .835 U.S.   Then a 90-day forward contract signed on January 15 for the purchase by party A of 100,000 Cdn. from party B 90 days hence would specify that A will pay B 83,500 U.S. on April 15 in return for 100,000 Cdn.   A forward contract provides a way of "locking-in" a sale or purchase price to be paid or received at a specified future date.   Such a contract might be used as a *hedge* against an adverse change (between the time the contract is signed and the future date at which the transaction is to take place) in the value of the goods to be purchased or sold.   The forward contract guarantees the price to be paid on that future date regardless of the actual value of the goods on that future date.   It is also possible to use a forward contract as an investment in a speculative way.   Party A above may anticipate an increase in value over the next 90 days of the Canadian currency with respect to the U.S. currency.   On April 15 , if the value of the Canadian dollar is .86 U.S. then *A* will pay B 83,500 U.S. for 100,000 Cdn., and immediately exchange the 100,000 Cdn. for 86,000 U.S. at the April 15 exchange rate.   A loss will occur to the speculator (party A) if the value of the Canadian dollar drops below .835 U.S. on April 15.

It is usually the intention of the original parties to a forward contract to actually take part in the transaction specified for the future date, although it is possible for one of the parties to sell his side of the contract to a third party. For both hedging and speculation on future changes in value of a particular financial instrument or commodity, *futures contracts* are much more widely used than forward contracts. A futures contract is similar in many respects to a forward contract. One of the differences is that in setting up a forward contract, there is no restriction regarding the goods to be exchanged or the future date on which the transaction will take place, whereas futures contracts are restricted to a (reasonably broad) group of financial instruments and commodities, and they expire on specific days (such as the second Friday of the expiry month) in various months. The existence of centralized facilities (such as the Chicago Board of Trade and International Monetary Market) for the trading of futures contracts and standardization of the contracts has led to a highly liquid and efficient market in futures contracts. A few examples of goods on which futures contracts are traded are the following.

(1) Japanese yen, with a standard contract size of 12.5 million yen.
(2) U.S. Treasury Bonds, for 15 years paying 8%, with a standard contract size of 100,000.
(3) 30-day Interest Rate Future, with a standard contract size of 5,000,000. Interest rate futures are based on an underlying government Treasury bill or corporate investment certificate with an appropriate term to maturity.
(4) Pork Bellies, with a standard contract size of 40,000 pounds.

Another distinction between a futures contract and a forward contract is that with a forward contract there is generally no exchange of goods and money until the future transaction date, whereas with a futures contract the purchaser must place a fraction of the cost of the goods with an intermediary and give assurances that the remainder of the purchase price will be paid when required. Usually 5-10% of the contract value is paid to a futures broker, with the rest of the contract amount owed *on margin*. Futures investments tend to be highly leveraged and very risky.

Suppose a 6-month forward contract to purchase 100,000 Canadian dollars is bought on January 15 with a price of .85 U.S. per Canadian dollar to be paid on July 15. The exchange of funds relating to this contract will not take place until July 15. On January 15 a 6-month futures contract for 100,000 Canadian dollars may also be valued at .85 U.S. per Canadian dollar, but the purchaser will have to pay a *margin* of 4250 to 8500 U.S. (5% - 10% of the contract value) plus a broker commission on the purchase date. If the purchaser holds the futures contract until the expiration or delivery date, then he must pay the remaining 76,500 to 80,750 U.S. (85,000 minus the original margin paid). A futures contract provides considerable leverage and risk, since changes in the contract value are reflected directly in the equity that the contract holder has with the broker or investment dealer. If, a short time after the contract is issued, the Canadian dollar rises to .88 U.S. then the contract value is 88,000 U.S. and the contract holder's equity rises 3000 above the original margin. Thus a relatively small change in the value of the underlying commodity can have effects which are proportionally much larger on the equity of the contract holder. If the value of the Canadian dollar drops any significant amount, the futures broker may require an additional margin payment to maintain a minimum level of equity for the futures contract holder. Suppose that a minimum 5% margin is required for the Canadian dollar futures contract just mentioned. The purchaser of the futures contract would pay 4250 U.S. to open the contract. If the Canadian dollar drops in value to 82 cents U.S., then the value of the contract has fallen by 3000 U.S., and the investor's equity has dropped to 1250 U.S. In order to maintain the minimum 5% margin, the investor would have to deposit $.05 \times 82,000 - 1250 = 2850$ to maintain the account (otherwise the investment dealer will close out the account, selling the futures contract for 82,000 and charging the 3000 loss to the investor's margin account). In order to maintain order in the futures market, there is a limit on the amount by which the value of a contract can change in a given day.

As mentioned above, the purchaser of a forward contract will usually proceed with the purchase of the goods at the specified date in the future. The holder of a futures contract usually does not intend to hold the contract until maturity, but rather hopes to gain from a hedged or speculative position by selling the contract before expiration.

The purchaser of a futures contract may be attempting to hedge a position. For example, a company may have a substantial investment in bonds or other interest-sensitive securities. The risk of adverse interest rate changes affecting the value of these securities may be reduced by the purchase (or sale) of an appropriately related futures contract. This is illustrated in the following example.

EXAMPLE 6.4

The holder of a 1,000,000 12% bond with a maturity of 25 years wishes to hedge the position by selling an appropriate number of 100,000 15-year 8% Treasury bond futures contracts. The bondholder's objective is to neutralize the effect of a small change in interest (yield or valuation) rate on the current value of his holding. Suppose the current yield on the 25-year bond is 10% and the current yield on 15-year Treasury bonds is

9.5%, and that small changes in yield on the two bonds are numerically equal. Find the number of 100,000 T-bond futures contracts that must be sold by the bondholder to create the hedge.

| SOLUTION |

Let $P(i^{(2)})$ denote the price of the 25-year bond at yield rate $i^{(2)}$, and let $j = \frac{i^{(2)}}{2}$. Then

$$\frac{d}{d\,i^{(2)}} P(i^{(2)}) = 1{,}000{,}000 \cdot \frac{1}{2} \cdot \frac{d}{dj} \left[v_j^{50} + .06 \cdot a_{\overline{50}|j} \right]$$

$$= 500{,}000 \left[-50 v_j^{51} + .06(-v_j)(Ia)_{\overline{50}|j} \right].$$

With $i^{(2)} = .10$, we have $j = .05$ and $\frac{d}{d\,i^{(2)}} P(i^{(2)}) = -10{,}538{,}299$, or a decrease in value of 105,383 for an increase of 1% in $i^{(2)}$. Let $Q(i^{(2)})$ denote the price of a 15-year 8% 100,000 Treasury bond at yield rate $i^{(2)}$, and let $j = \frac{i^{(2)}}{2}$. Then

$$100{,}000 \cdot \frac{1}{2} \cdot \frac{d}{dj} \left[v_j^{30} + .04 \cdot a_{\overline{30}|j} \right]$$

$$= \frac{d}{d\,i^{(2)}} Q(i^{(2)}) = 50{,}000 \left[-30 v_j^{31} + .04(-v_j)(Ia)_{\overline{30}|j} \right].$$

With $i^{(2)} = .095$ we have $j = .0475$ and $\frac{d}{d\,i^{(2)}} Q(i^{(2)}) = -722{,}316$. In order to hedge the bond position, the required number of T-bond contracts to sell is $\frac{10{,}538{,}299}{722{,}316} = 14.6$. If interest rates increase, the reduction in the value of the 25-year bond is offset by the increase in value of the futures contracts. □

As another example of a hedge consider a bondholder, whose bonds will mature in six months, who plans to reinvest the proceeds in a new bond issue at that time. The price of the new purchase can be locked in now by purchasing a six-month futures contract on a bond similar to that which will be purchased. The locked-in price is the one reflected in the value of the futures contract when it is purchased. Any changes in yield over the six months will change the ultimate cost of the bonds to be purchased in six months, but if the futures contract is equivalent to the bonds to be bought, then the changes in the value of the futures contract will cancel those in the actual bond price.

It is often the case that the futures contract purchaser has no intention of taking delivery (or the contract seller has no intention of making delivery) at the termination of the contract. The purchaser of the contract may be interested in it as an investment, hoping that the value of the underlying commodity or security will increase, so that the contract can be sold to another purchaser at a higher price before the delivery date.

Financial practice is always evolving, and new types of financial instruments appear from time to time (with some types occasionally disappearing). In the previous section, mention was made of the various securities on which options can be purchased - options are also available on a variety of futures contracts. In the mid 1990's investment derivatives have attained a certain glamour and notoriety. As a result of highly risky investing in derivatives, a few companies (centuries old Baring's Investment Bank of England for example) and at least one local government (Orange County in California) have faced serious losses or even bankruptcy.

6.5   FOREIGN CURRENCY EXCHANGE RATES

Corporations involved in international trade scheduled to receive delayed payment in various foreign currencies, but whose expenditures are mainly in their own country's currency, are concerned with the fluctuation of exchange rates among the currencies.   There are a number of ways to protect against adverse fluctuations in exchange rates, including the use of *foreign currency futures* and forward markets for currency exchange as discussed in Section 6.4.   Forward rate contracts can be established for periods as short as one month or as long as 10 years into the future.

The economic factors that determine the relationships among foreign currencies are very complex.   One important factor is the relationship between interest rates in the various countries.   The following example gives a simple illustration of the effect of interest on the exchange rate between currencies of different countries.

EXAMPLE 6.5

According to today's spot exchange rate between the Canadian and U.S. currencies, 1 Cdn. is equivalent to .85 U.S. Suppose interest rates for the coming year are 6% in Canada and 3% in the U.S. What should be the one-year forward exchange rate between the values of the two currencies in order that the relationship between the currencies remains unchanged with regard to borrowing and lending for one year?

| SOLUTION |

One year from now 1.06 Cdn. will be required to repay a loan of 1 Cdn. now. Similarly, one year from now $.85 \times 1.03 = .8755$ U.S. will be required to repay a loan of .85 U.S. now. In order to maintain a market balance between the currencies, one year from now 1.06 Cdn. should be equivalent to .8755 U.S., or 1 Cdn. should be equivalent to $\frac{.8755}{1.06} = .8259$ U.S. dollars. □

The situation in Example 6.4 can be generalized as follows. Suppose the spot exchange rate today between currencies A and B is that 1 unit of currency A is equivalent to C_s units of currency B. Let the annual interest rate on currency A (in the country with that currency) be i_A and the annual interest rate on currency B be i_B. In order to balance two one-year loans in the respective currencies, the relationship between the currencies one year from now should be $1 + i_A$ units of currency A equivalent to $C_s(1 + i_B)$ units of currency B, or one unit of currency A equivalent to

$$C_f = \frac{C_s(1 + i_B)}{1 + i_A}, \tag{6.9}$$

where C_f is the one-year forward rate of exchange.

The relationship between the spot and forward rates of exchange can also be explained in terms of the inflation rates in the respective currencies. If the real (inflation-adjusted) rates of interest over the following year are the same in the two currencies, then $i_A^{real} = \frac{i_A - r_A}{1 + r_A} = i_B^{real} = \frac{i_B - r_B}{1 + r_B}$, where r_A and r_B are the annual inflation rates in currencies A and B. Then

$$1 + i_A^{real} = \frac{1 + i_A}{1 + r_A} = 1 + i_B^{real} = \frac{1 + i_B}{1 + r_B},$$

so $\frac{1 + i_B}{1 + i_A} = \frac{1 + r_B}{1 + r_A}$, and therefore

$$C_f = \frac{C_s(1 + i_B)}{1 + i_A} = \frac{C_s(1 + r_B)}{1 + r_A}. \tag{6.10}$$

This relationship can be explained as follows: if one unit of currency A is now worth C_s units of currency B, then to maintain the same balance of purchasing power between the currencies one year from now, $1 + r_A$ units of currency A should have the same value as $C_s(1 + r_B)$ units of currency B, which is the relationship of Equation (6.10).

Using the approximation $\frac{1+x}{1+y} \approx 1+x-y$, Equation (6.9) becomes $C_s(1 + i_B - i_A) \approx C_f$, or

$$\frac{C_f - C_s}{C_s} \approx i_B - i_A. \tag{6.11}$$

The relationship in Equation (6.11) is called the *interest rate parity theorem*, which states that the percentage difference between the spot and forward exchange rates is approximately equal to the difference between the interest rates on the two currencies.

The relationships in Equations (6.9), (6.10), and (6.11) are quite simplistic, and do not account for all of the dynamics affecting exchange rates. For instance, a typical way in which a country supports its currency is by increasing the rate of interest on government securities. The reasoning behind this is that as the rate of return increases in the country's currency, there will be more foreign demand for that currency in order to invest at the higher rate, and the demand for the currency will increase its value in terms of other currencies. However if we increase i_A in Equation (6.9) while keeping i_B unchanged, the ratio C_f/C_s must decrease. It is not clear whether this occurs because of a decrease in C_f or because of an increase in C_s. The most likely scenario is that both C_f and C_s increase, but C_s increases proportionally more than C_f since the increased rate i_A may change (decrease) before the forward exchange could take place.

6.6   ASSET-LIABILITY MATCHING; IMMUNIZATION

In the course of conducting business, an enterprise will make commitments involving future income and outgo of capital. To maintain a viable (and profitable) position, the company will make investments so that funds will be available to provide for outgoing payments as they come due. Projected at time 0, the net outgoing payment at time $t > 0$ represents the company's *liability due* (or *outgo*) L_t at time t. The funds available from investment income and investments maturing at time t to cover that liability represent the company's *asset income* (or *proceeds*) A_t at time t. If the company can arrange its investments so that asset income exactly covers liability due at each point in time, so that $A_t = L_t$ for all t, then the projected asset income and liabilities due are said to be *exactly matched*. Asset-liability matching is generally considered from the point of view of asset income and liability due cash flows occurring at discrete (usually equally spaced) points of time, $t = 0, 1, 2, \ldots$. It is also possible to consider continuous models of asset-liability matching, where A_t is the *rate* of asset income and L_t is the *rate* of liability due at time t.

| **EXAMPLE 6.6** |

A small company terminating its operations has decided to provide each of its three employees with a severance package that pays 10,000 per year (at the end of each year) up to and including age 65, plus a lump sum payment of 100,000 at age 65. The three employees are now exact ages 50, 53 and 55. The company determines that the payments due under this package can be met by the income and maturities generated by three 100,000 face amount 10% annual coupon bonds with maturities of 10, 12, and 15 years. Determine the cost to the company to fund the severance package if the bonds have (annual effective) yield rates of 10% for the 10-year bond, 11% for the 12-year bond and 12% for the 15-year bond.

| SOLUTION |

Applying any of the bond price formulas from Chapter 4 gives prices of 100,000 for the 10-year bond, 93,507.64 for the 12-year bond and 86,378.27 for the 15-year bond, for a total cost of 279,885.91. With the purchase of these bonds, the company's liabilities to the three employees are exactly matched. ☐

As a variation on Example 6.6 suppose there are bonds available with a variety of coupon rates and maturity dates (including, perhaps, zero-coupon bonds). The company might have several alternative combinations of investments whose asset income flows match the liabilities. Linear programming can be used to find the minimum cost combination of investments which matches asset flow to liability flow (see Exercise 6.6.1).

It may not always be possible to obtain an exact match between projected asset income and liabilities due. However, with a reasonable assumption as to the interest rate, i_0, used to accrue the differences $A_t - L_t$ from one period to the next during the term of the asset-liability flow, it may be possible to have a match of assets and liabilities in the sense that the present values of the asset income flow and liability due flow are matched at rate i_0. That is

$$PV_A(i_0) = \sum A_t v_{i_0}^t = \sum L_t v_{i_0}^t = PV_L(i_0). \qquad (6.12)$$

It is implicit in Equation (6.12) that from time t to time $t+1$, the difference $A_t - L_t$ will accrue at interest rate i_0 for the period, whether $A_t - L_t$ is positive or negative. (This assumes that lending and borrowing can both be done at rate i_0.) If the asset/liability flow is exactly matched then Equation (6.12) holds for *any* rate i_0. Without exact matching, there is the risk that if the rate for accrual of $A_t - L_t$ deviates from i_0 to i, the asset income flow will not be sufficient to balance the liabilities due, so that $PV_A(i) < PV_L(i)$. F.M. Redington (see Section 6.7) developed a theory of *immunization* for an asset/liability flow. According to this theory, with a careful structuring of asset income in relation to liabilities due, small deviations in the interest rate from i_0 to i result in $PV_A(i) > PV_L(i)$, for both $i > i_0$ and $i < i_0$.

The basic theory of immunization is as follows. Suppose asset income has been allocated so as to balance liabilities due at interest rate i_0 according to Equation (6.12). Suppose this allocation of asset income also satisfies the conditions

$$\left. \frac{d}{di} PV_A(i) \right|_{i_0} = \left. \frac{d}{di} PV_L(i) \right|_{i_0} \qquad (6.13)$$

and

$$\left. \frac{d^2}{di^2} PV_A(i) \right|_{i_0} > \left. \frac{d^2}{di^2} PV_L(i) \right|_{i_0}. \qquad (6.14)$$

If we define the function $h(i)$ to be

$$h(i) = PV_A(i) - PV_L(i), \qquad (6.15)$$

then $h(i_0) = h'(i_0) = 0$ (from Equations (6.12) and (6.13)), and $h''(i_0) > 0$ (from Equation (6.14)), so $h(i)$ has a *relative minimum* at i_0. In other words, for some interval around i_0, say $I = (i_l, i_u)$, if $i \in I$ then $h(i) > h(i_0) = 0$, or, equivalently, $PV_A(i) > PV_L(i)$. With the asset/liability flow immunized in this way, a *small change* in the interest rate from i_0 to i

results in a *surplus* position in the sense that there is an excess of the present value of asset income over liabilities due when valued at the new rate *i*. The change in the interest must be small enough so that *i* stays within the interval *I*. This immunization of the portfolio against small changes in *i* is called *Redington immunization*.

In Exercise 6.6.3 it is shown that Equation (6.13) is equivalent to

$$\sum t \cdot A_t \cdot v^t_{i_0} = \sum t \cdot L_t \cdot v^t_{i_0}, \tag{6.16}$$

and if Equation (6.13) is true then Equation (6.14) is equivalent to

$$\sum t^2 \cdot A_t \cdot v^t_{i_0} > \sum t^2 \cdot L_t \cdot v^t_{i_0}. \tag{6.17}$$

It follows from Equation (6.13) that $PV_A(i)$ and $PV_L(i)$ have the same volatility with respect to interest rates. It is not surprising, then, that a consequence of the conditions for immunization given by Equations (6.12) and (6.13) is that at interest rate i_0, the assets and liabilities have the same *duration*. (The concept of duration of a cashflow was discussed in Section 4.5.4.) Let us denote by $D(i_0)$ this common duration of assets and liabilities at rate i_0.

If the conditions in Equations (6.12) and (6.13) are met, and since $D(i_0)$ is a time constant (the weighted average time to maturity or discounted mean term of the A_t's or L_t's), it follows that Equation (6.17) is equivalent to

$$\sum [t - D(i_0)]^2 \cdot A_t \cdot v^t_{i_0} > \sum [t - D(i_0)]^2 \cdot L_t \cdot v^t_{i_0}. \tag{6.18}$$

Therefore if Equations (6.12) and (6.13) are met, the asset/liability match is immunized if the asset income flow is more dispersed or widely spread (in time) about $D(i_0)$ than the liabilities due. The liability cashflow in Example 6.6 is used in the following example to illustrate how the conditions for immunization might be met.

EXAMPLE 6.7

To immunize the liabilities due in the severance package described in Example 6.5, the company purchases an investment portfolio consisting of two zero-coupon bonds, due at times t_1 and t_2 (measured from the starting date of the severance package), both having a yield to maturity of 10%. For each of the following pairs t_1 and t_2, determine the amounts of each zero-coupon bond that must be purchased and whether or not the overall asset/liability portfolio is in an immunized position: (a) $t_1 = 0$, $t_2 = 15$; (b) $t_1 = 6$, $t_2 = 12$;   (c) $t_1 = 2$, $t_2 = 14$.

SOLUTION

Let X be the amount of zero-coupon bond purchased with maturity at t_1 and Y the amount with maturity at t_2.   In order to satisfy Equation (6.12) we must have $X \cdot v^{t_1}_{.10} + Y \cdot v^{t_2}_{.10} = \Sigma L_t \cdot v^t_{.10} = 300,000$ and in order to satisfy Equation (6.13) we must have

$$t_1 \cdot X \cdot v^{t_1}_{.10} + t_2 \cdot Y \cdot v^{t_2}_{.10} = \Sigma t \cdot L_t \cdot v^t_{.10}$$
$$= 30,000v + 2(30,000)v^2 + 3(30,000)v^3 + \cdots = 2,262,077.228.$$

Solving these two equations for X and Y, we obtain the values

(a) $X = 149,194.85$, $Y = 629,950.53$;
(b) $X = 395,035.30$, $Y = 241,699.38$; and
(c) $X = 195,407.21$, $Y = 525,977.96$.

The third immunization condition, Equation (6.14), requires that

$$t_1^2 \cdot X \cdot v^{t_1}_{.10} + t_2^2 \cdot Y \cdot v^{t_2}_{.10} > \Sigma t^2 \cdot L_t \cdot v^t_{.10}$$
$$= 30,000v + 2^2(30,000)v^2 + 3^2(30,000)v^3 + \cdots =$$
27,709,878.

In case (a) the left hand side is 33,931,158, so this portfolio is immunized. In case (b) the left hand side is 19,117,390, so small changes in the interest rate away from 10% will make the present value of assets less than the present value of liabilities.   In case (c) the left side is 27,793,236, so the portfolio is again immunized.   □

In Exercise 6.6.4 you are asked to show that in case (a) of Example 6.7 the portfolio is actually *fully immunized*. That is, $\Sigma t \cdot A_t \cdot v^t > \Sigma t \cdot L_t \cdot v^t$ for *any* $i > 0$, whereas in case (c) $h(i)$ has a relative minimum at $i_0 = .10$, but $\Sigma t \cdot A_t \cdot v^t < \Sigma t \cdot L_t \cdot v^t$ for sufficiently large values of i. Thus, in case (c), a loss may occur if the change in interest is large enough so that i lies outside of the interval I. Thus, in case (c), the portfolio satisfies the conditions of Redington immunization at $i = .10$, but the portfolio is not fully immunized. The graphs of $h(i)$ for cases (a) and (c) of Example 6.6 are shown in Figure 6.1 (not to scale).

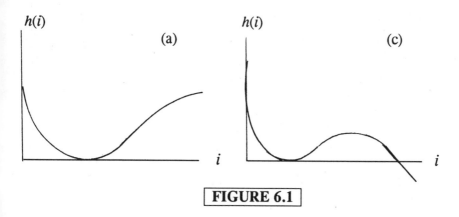

$$\boxed{\textbf{FIGURE 6.1}}$$

As time goes on, changes in interest rates may occur. This consideration, along with changing times until liabilities are due and asset income is received, may require that the asset portfolio be updated to maintain an immunized position.

We now investigate further the concept of *full immunization* defined above. Suppose liabilities due consist of a single liability of amount L_s at time $s \geq 0$. Suppose also that L_s, s, $0 \leq t_1 \leq s$, $t_2 \geq s$, and A_{t_1} and A_{t_2} satisfy Equations (6.12) and (6.13) at interest rate i_0 per unit time. Then

$$A_{t_1} \cdot v_{i_0}^{t_1} + A_{t_2} \cdot v_{i_0}^{t_2} = L_s \cdot v_{i_0}^{s} \qquad (6.19)$$

and

$$t_1 \cdot A_{t_1} \cdot v_{i_0}^{t_1} + t_2 \cdot A_{t_2} \cdot v_{i_0}^{t_2} = s \cdot L_s \cdot v_{i_0}^{s}. \qquad (6.20)$$

To simplify notation we define $a = s - t_1$ and $b = t_2 - s$. As before, the function $h(i) = PV_A(i) - PV_L(i)$ will be the present value of asset minus liability flow, valued at interest rate i. With some algebraic manipulation (see Exercise 6.6.5) $h(i)$ can be formulated as

$$h(i) = v_i^s \cdot A_{t_1} (1+i_0)^a \left[\left(\frac{1+i}{1+i_0} \right)^a + \frac{a}{b} \left(\frac{1+i}{1+i_0} \right)^{-b} - \left(1 + \frac{a}{b} \right) \right]$$

$$= v_i^s \cdot A_{t_1} \cdot g(i).$$

$$(6.21)$$

We see that $g(i_0) = 0$ and $g'(i) = a\left(\frac{1+i}{1+i_0}\right)^{-1}\left[\left(\frac{1+i}{1+i_0}\right)^a - \left(\frac{1+i}{1+i_0}\right)^{-b}\right]$.

Since $a \geq 0$ and $b \geq 0$, it follows that $g'(i) \geq 0$ if $i \geq i_0$, and $g'(i) \leq 0$ if $i \leq i_0$. Therefore $h(i) \geq 0$ for all i, and the asset/liability flow is fully immunized against changes in interest rates of any size.

This full immunization of a single liability due can be seen from another point of view. In Chapter 4 we saw that the duration of a single amount payable at time t in the future is simply equal to t. It then follows from Equation (6.18) that any allocation of asset income involving two or more non-zero A_t's that satisfies Equations (6.16) and (6.17) will result in full immunization, since the right hand side of (6.18) is zero for a single liability due but the left hand side will exceed zero.

EXAMPLE 6.8

Use the method of full immunization outlined in Equations (6.19), (6.20) and (6.21) to find the values of A_0 and A_{15} that immunize $L_{12} = 120,000$ in Example 6.5, assuming $i_0 = .10$, $t_1 = 0$, $t_2 = 15$ and $s = 12$.

SOLUTION

We wish to solve the two equations

$$A_0 \cdot v_{.10}^0 + A_{15} \cdot v_{.10}^{15} = 120{,}000 \cdot v_{.10}^{12} = 38{,}235.70$$

and

$$0 \cdot A_0 \cdot v_{.10}^0 + 15 \cdot A_{15} \cdot v_{.10}^{15} = 12(120{,}000 \cdot v_{.10}^{12}) = 458{,}828.38.$$

The solution is $A_0 = 8193.36$ and $A_{15} = 125{,}494.29$. Note that $h(0) = 13{,}687.65$, $h(.10) = 0$, $\lim_{i \to \infty} h(i) = 8193.37$, and $h(i)$ is decreasing for $0 \leq i < .10$ and increasing for $i > .10$. If the interest valuation rate were to drop to 0 from $i_0 = .10$, a profit of 13,687.65 could be made, since some of the assets could be sold while still maintaining sufficient assets to cover liabilities at the new interest rate of 0.   □

Assuming s, L_s, and i_0 are known, Equations (6.19) and (6.20) involve the unknown quantities A_{t_1}, A_{t_2}, t_1 and t_2. In general, given any two of these four quantities, there will be a unique solution for the other two so as to fully immunize the portfolio. (Cases may arise in which one of the A's or t's is negative, or there may be infinitely many or no solutions; see Exercise 6.6.8.) In Exercise 6.6.7 it is shown that if each of the liabilities due in Example 6.6 is fully immunized (at $i = .10$) according to the method above, using $t_1 = 0$ and $t_2 = 15$, then the total asset income allocated for all liabilities combined is the same as in part (a) of Example 6.7.

The methods developed in this section can be applied to continuous asset/liability flows, with integration of payments replacing summation. When formulating immunization relationships, it is sometimes more convenient to represent present and accumulated values in terms of force of interest rather than effective annual rate of interest.

In discussing Redington immunization and full immunization, there have been the following two implicit assumptions.
(1) The *term structure* of interest rates is constant or *flat*.
(2) When interest rate changes occur, the change is the same throughout the term structure. In other words, there is a *parallel shift* in the term structure.

These implicit assumptions have been reflected in the examples. In practice it is not common to find a flat yield curve, and shifts in the term structure are usually not parallel, so that it may not be possible to fully immunize a portfolio (arbitrage opportunities do not survive long in the marketplace). Suppose in Example 6.7 the 10% interest rate becomes 11% for the 12-year term and 11.1% for the 15 year term. Then the present value of the asset flow is $8193.36 + 125,494.29 \cdot v_{.111}^{15} = 34,070.31$ while the present value of the liabilities is $120,000 \cdot v_{.11}^{12} = 34,300.90$. The portfolio is not immunized against this almost parallel shift in the yield curve. The theory of immunization has been extended to situations involving term structures that are not flat and shifts in the term structure that are not parallel, and even stochastic models of the term structure.

6.7 NOTES AND REFERENCES

There are a number of good references for topics in finance and portfolio analysis. Discussions of the capital asset pricing model, the binomial model, and the Black-Scholes option pricing model can be found in *Investments*, by Sharpe [9], and in *Modern Portfolio Theory and Investment Analysis*, by Elton and Gruber [3]. The Black-Scholes formula was developed in "The Pricing of Options and Corporate Liabilities," by Black and Scholes, *Journal of Political Economy*, (May/June 1973). A good introduction to interest rate and currency swaps can be found in "Interest

Rate and Currency Swaps" by R. Dattatreya, S. Venkatesh and V. Venkatesh.

Practical information on the nature of options and futures is available from trading exchanges such as the Chicago Board Options Exchange and the Chicago Board of Trade.

The early development of immunization theory can be found in the paper "Review of the Principles of Life Office Valuations," by Redington, *Journal of the Institute of Actuaries*, Volume 8 (1952). A discussion of full immunization can be found in Chapter 10 of *An Introduction to the Mathematics of Finance*, by McCutcheon and Scott [8].

6.8   EXERCISES

Exercises 6.2

6.2.1   Let $i_{0,1}$, $i_{0,2}$, $i_{0,3}$, ..., $i_{0,n}$ be the annual effective rates of return for zero-coupon bonds with maturities of 1 year, 2 years, 3 years, ..., n years, respectively. Let $i_{1,2}$, $i_{2,3}$, ..., $i_{n-1,n}$ be the corresponding annual forward rates for year 2, year 3, ..., year n, respectively.
   (a) Find an expression for $i_{k-1,k}$ in terms of the $i_{0,t}$'s.
   (b) Show that $(1 + i_{0,1})(1 + i_{1,2}) \cdots (1 + i_{k-1,k}) = (1 + i_{0,k})^k$ for $k = 1, 2, \ldots, n$.
   (c) Show that $\dfrac{d}{di_{0,k}} i_{k-1,k} > 0$ and $\dfrac{d}{di_{0,k-1}} i_{k-1,k} < 0$.
   (d) Show that if $i_{0,k} > i_{0,k-1}$, then $i_{k-1,k} > i_{0,k}$.

6.2.2   Consider the following two yield curves (representing perhaps annual yields on two different classes of zero-coupon bonds), based on the notation of Exercise 6.2.1:   (i) $i_{0,k} = .09 + .001k$; (ii) $i_{0,k} = .09 + .002k - .0001k^2$, both for $k = 1, 2, \ldots, 10$. For each of these yield curves, calculate the corresponding forward rates of interest for years 2 to 10, and plot the forward rates on a graph along with a plot of the yield curve. Note that since both yield curves are increasing, part (d) of Exercise 6.2.1 guarantees that the graph of the forward rates will lie above the graph of the corresponding yield curve. Note that for yield curve (ii), although the yield curve is increasing, the corresponding forward rates do not form an increasing sequence.

6.2.3 Let $H_s(t)$ denote the term structure or yield curve of spot rates, so that $H_s(t)$ is the annual effective yield rate for a zero-coupon bond maturing in t years. Let $H_f(t)$ denote the term structure of forward rates, so that $H_f(t)$ is the forward rate in effect in the tth year from now (from time $t-1$ to t).
   (a) Prove each of the following relationships between $H_s(t)$ and $H_f(t)$.
      (i) If $H_s(t)$ is increasing, then $H_s(t) \leq H_f(t)$.
      (ii) If $H_s(t)$ is decreasing, then $H_s(t) \quad H_f(t)$.
   (b) (i) Construct an increasing yield curve $H_s(t)$ for which $H_f(t)$ is decreasing for $t \quad 2$.
      (ii) Construct a decreasing yield curve $H_s(t)$ for which $H_f(t)$ is increasing for $t \quad 2$.

Exercises 6.3

6.3.1 Stock of the XYZ Corporation is expected to pay annual dividends in the years to come. The next dividend will be of amount 1.00 and is due one year from now. Dividends are expected to grow at the rate of 5% per year. A prospective purchaser plans to hold the stock for 10 years. The purchaser uses an annual effective interest rate of 15% for valuation purposes.
   (a) If the purchaser anticipates a stock price of 50.00 (excluding dividend) when he sells 10 years from now, what value will he put on the stock now?
   (b) Suppose the purchaser is willing to pay 20.00 now for the stock. What stock price is implied 10 years from now?

6.3.2 Use Equation (6.4) to show that under the assumption that $\tilde{R}_m$ and $\tilde{e}_s$ are independent, the covariance between $\tilde{R}_s$ and $\tilde{R}_m$ is $\beta_s \cdot \text{Var}(\tilde{R}_m)$.

6.3.3 The stock of XYZ Corporation is currently valued at 25 per share. An annual dividend has just been paid and the next dividend is expected to be 2 with each subsequent dividend $1+r$ times the previous one. The valuation is based on an annual interest rate of 12%. What value of r is implied? Suppose the dividends are payable quarterly with the next one due in exactly one quarter. For the next four quarters the dividend will be .50 each quarter. Every year (after every 4 quarters) the dividend is increased by a factor of $1+s$. If the stock is now valued at 25 based on a nominal annual interest rate of $i^{(4)} = .12$, what value of s is implied?

6.3.4   On January 15 the share price of XYZ Corporation stock is 100, and the value of a July 20 call at 110 is 1, the value of a July 20 call at 90 is 15, the value of a July 20 put at 110 is 14, and the value of a July 20 put at 90 is 1.50. For each of the following strategies, determine the profit on the transaction, after exercising the option or letting it expire, whichever is more profitable, as a function of the share price (excluding commissions and interest).

(a) On January 15 buy a call at 110 and sell the stock after exercising the option.
(b) On January 15 buy the stock and sell a call at 110.
(c) On January 15 buy a call at 110 and sell a call at 90.
(d) On January 15 buy a call at 90 and sell a call at 110.
(e) On January 15 buy a put at 90 and buy a call at 110.
(f) On January 15 buy a put at 110 and buy a call at 90.
(g) On January 15 sell a put at 90 and sell a call at 90.

6.3.5   Repeat Example 6.3 (a) if the stock price on January 15 is 45, and (b) if the stock price on January 15 is 55.

6.3.6   Keeping all other parameters fixed, sketch the graph of the option price according to the Black-Scholes formula as a function of (a) P_0, (b) E, (c) n, (d) δ, and (e) σ.

Exercises 6.5

6.5.1   (a) Smith has 10,000 U.S. dollars. He can buy Canadian dollars today at the exchange rate of 1 U.S. = 1.38 Cdn., or he can sign a forward contract guaranteeing him an exchange rate of 1 U.S. = 1.42 Cdn. one year from now. If he exchanges his U.S dollars for Canadian dollars today, he can earn interest at effective annual rate 9% on his Canadian dollars. Alternatively, he can sign the forward exchange rate contract and invest his 10,000 U.S. at effective annual rate i, exchanging his U.S. dollars for Canadian dollars next year. If he ends up with the same amount of Canadian funds in one year either way, what is i?

(b) Suppose Smith has just signed the forward contract. Later in the day the Canadian interest rate increases from 9% to 10%, but the U.S. interest rate remains at i. What spot rate of exchange would Smith now regard as fair, assuming again that he would end up in one year with same amount of Canadian funds?

Exercises 6.6

6.6.1   Liabilities of 1 each are due at the ends of periods 1 and 2. There
are three securities available to produce asset income to cover these
liabilities, as follows:
(i) A bond due at the end of period 1 with coupon at rate .01 per
period, valued at a periodic yield of 14%;
(ii) A bond due at the end of period 2 with coupon rate .02 per
period, valued at a periodic yield of 15%;
(iii) A bond due at the end of period 2 with coupon rate .20 per
period, valued at a periodic yield of 14.95%.
Determine the cost of the portfolio that exactly-matches asset
income to liabilities due using (a) bonds (i) and (ii) only, and (b)
bonds (i) and (iii) only. (c) Show that the combination of securities
in (b) minimizes the cost of all exact-matching portfolios made up
of a combination of the three securities. Note that the minimum
cost exact-matching portfolio does not use the highest yielding
security in this case.

6.6.2   In order to match asset income to the liabilities in Example 6.6 so
that $PV_A(.10) = PV_L(.10)$, a level annual payment annuity-
immediate with n payments is purchased to provide the asset
income flow. For each of $n = 5, 15, 50, 100$, find the required
annual payment and calculate both $\Sigma t \cdot A_t \cdot v'_{10}$ and $\Sigma t^2 \cdot A_t \cdot v'_{10}$.
Which value of n provides the nearest match to the relation
$\Sigma t \cdot A_t \cdot v'_{10} = \Sigma t \cdot L_t \cdot v'_{10}$?   Solve for the exact value of n for
which $\Sigma t \cdot A_t \cdot v'_{10} = \Sigma t \cdot L_t \cdot v'_{10}$. Determine whether this provides Redington immunization for the portfolio.

6.6.3   (a) Show that Equation (6.13) is equivalent to Equation (6.16).
(b) Show that if Equation (6.13) is true, then Equation (6.14) is
equivalent to Equation (6.17).

6.6.4   (a) Consider the function $h'(i)$ for the portfolio of assets and
liabilities in part (a) of Example 6.7. Use one of the methods
of Section 3.4 (such as the *rule of signs* of Exercise 3.4.2) to
show that $h'(i) = 0$ has only one solution for $i \quad 0$. (This
unique solution is $i = .10$.) Note that $h(0) > 0$, $h(.10) = 0$,
$h'(.10) = 0$ and $\lim_{i\to\infty} h(i) = 149,195$.   Use these facts to
conclude that $h(i)$ has its overall minimum at $i = .10$.

    (b) Show that for (very) large values of i, $h(i) < 0$ for the portfolio of assets and liabilities in part (c) of Example 6.7. (Try increasing values of i, such as 200%, 400%, and so on.)

6.6.5   (a) Multiply Equation (6.19) by s and subtract Equation (6.20) to show that $a \cdot A_{t_1} \cdot v_{i_0}^{t_1} = b \cdot A_{t_2} \cdot v_{i_0}^{t_2}$.
    (b) Use part (a) to solve for L_s in terms of A_{t_1}, a, b and v_{i_0}.
    (c) Use parts (a) and (b) to write $h(i)$ as given in Equation (6.21).

6.6.6   For each of parts (a), (b), and (c) of Example 6.7, determine $h(i)$ for $i = .03, .08, .12$ and $.20$.

6.6.7   For each of the liabilities due in Example 6.6 find the values of A_0 and A_{15} at $i = .10$, according to the method of full immunization described in Section 6.6. Find the total of all A_0's and the total of all A_{15}'s separately, and show that this gives the same asset income as that found in part (a) of Example 6.7.

6.6.8   Let $i_0 > 0$, $L_s > 0$ and s be given. Show that in each of the following cases there is a unique solution for the unknown quantities in Equations (6.19) and (6.20), with the solution consisting of positive numbers.
    (a) $t_1 \leq s$ and $t_2 \geq s$, with t_1 and t_2 given
    (b) $t_2 \geq s$ and A_{t_2} satisfying $A_{t_2} \cdot v_{i_0}^{t_2-s} \leq \frac{s}{t_2} \cdot L_s$, with t_2 and A_{t_2} given
    (c) $t_1 \leq s$ and A_{t_1} satisfying $A_{t_1}(1 + i_0)^{t_2-s} \leq L_s$, with t_1 and A_{t_1} given
    (d) $t_2 \geq s$ and $A_{t_1} \leq L_s$, with t_2 and A_{t_1} given

6.6.9   A liability of 1 is due at time 10. An attempt is made to fully immunize this liability at $i_0 = .10$ by means of two zero-coupon bonds of amounts A_{t_1} and A_{t_2} due at times t_1 and t_2, respectively. In each of the following cases, solve for the two missing quantities out of A_{t_1}, A_{t_2}, t_1, t_2, given the other two.
    (a) $t_1 = 5$, $t_2 = 15$
    (b) (i) $t_1 = 5$, $A_{t_1} = .40$
        (ii) $t_1 = 5$, $A_{t_1} = .70$ (no solution for $t_2 \geq 10$)
    (c) (i) $t_1 = 5$, $A_{t_2} = .90$ (two solutions for $t_2 \geq 10$)
        (ii) $t_1 = 5$, $A_{t_2} = 1.5$ (one solution for $t_2 \geq 10$)
        (iii) $t_1 = 5$, $A_{t_2} = .75$ (no solutions for $t_2 \geq 10$)

(d) (i) $t_2 = 15$, $A_{t_1} = .80$
(ii) $t_2 = 15$, $A_{t_1} = 1.1$ (no solution for $A_{t_2} \geq 0$, $0 \leq t_1 \leq 10$)
(iii) $t_2 = 15$, $A_{t_1} = .01$ (no solution for $0 \leq t_1 \leq 10$)
(e) (i) $t_2 = 15$, $A_{t_2} = .80$
(ii) $t_2 = 15$, $A_{t_2} = 1.5$ (no solution for $t_1 \geq 0$)
(f) $A_{t_1} = .40$, $A_{t_2} = .90$

6.6.10 A financial institution has taken over the business of another company. One of the acquired liabilities is a capital redemption policy that obligates the payment of 1,000,000 by the institution to the policyholder in exactly 12 years, and requires the policyholder to make annual premium payments (at the start of each of the remaining 12 years) of 15,000. Out of the assets of the acquired company, the financial institution wants to allocate a single asset income payment A_{t_0} to be made at time t_0 so that, along with the asset income represented by the premiums payable by the policyholder, the capital redemption policy will be fully immunized at the current interest rate of 10%. Find t_0 and the asset income amount A_{t_0} that must be allocated, and show that this fully immunizes the policy.

APPROXIMATION METHODS

A.1   LINEAR INTERPOLATION

Given x_1, x_2, $f(x_1)$ and $f(x_2)$, the estimate of $f(x_0)$ on the basis of linear interpolation is

$$f(x_0) \approx f(x_1) + [f(x_2) - f(x_1)] \cdot \left[\frac{x_0 - x_1}{x_2 - x_1} \right] \qquad (A.1)$$

This follows from setting equal the ratios of altitude to base in the similar triangles in Figure A.1 below.   Linear interpolation approximates the function $f(x)$ as a straight line based on the function values at points x_1 and x_2.

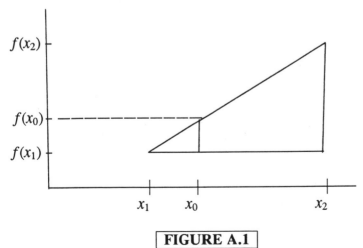

$$\boxed{\textbf{FIGURE A.1}}$$

A.2   SOLUTIONS OF EQUATIONS IN ONE VARIABLE

A.2.1 Bisection Algorithm

If f is continuous on the interval $[a,b]$ and $f(a) \cdot f(b) < 0$, so that one of $f(a)$, $f(b)$ is positive and one is negative, then $f(x)$ has at least one root p, where $f(p) = 0$, on $[a,b]$.   Let $a_1 = a$ and $b_1 = b$ and $p_1 = \frac{a_1 + b_1}{2}$. Since one of $f(a_1), f(b_1)$ is positive and one is negative, pick the one whose sign is opposite to the sign of $f(p_1)$. If $f(a_1)$ and $f(p_1)$ have opposite signs, then let $a_2 = a_1$ and $b_2 = p_1$, and $p_2 = \frac{a_2 + b_2}{2}$. If $f(p_1)$ and $f(b_1)$ have opposite signs, then let $a_2 = p_1$ and $b_2 = b_1$, and repeat the process.   At stage n, with $f(a_n)$ and $f(b_n)$ having opposite signs, let $p_n = \frac{a_n + b_n}{2}$. Then $f(p_n)$ and one of $f(a_n)$ and $f(b_n)$ will have opposite signs, so p_n and one of a_n, b_n will become a_{n+1} and b_{n+1}, and so on.   At each stage, the root of $f(x)$ is trapped in the interval $[a_n, b_n]$, so the absolute error $|e_n| = |p_n - p|$ in the nth approximation is no larger than $\frac{b_n - a_n}{2}$. But since the width of each successive interval $[a_n, b_n]$ is half the previous interval $[a_{n-1}, b_{n-1}]$, the bound on the error in the nth approximations is

$$|e_n| \leq \left| \frac{b_n - a_n}{2} \right| = \left(\frac{1}{2} \right)^2 \cdot |b_{n-1} - a_{n-1}| = \cdots$$

$$= \left(\frac{1}{2} \right)^n \cdot |b_1 - a_1| = \frac{b - a}{2^n}.$$
$$\text{(A.2)}$$

EXAMPLE A.1

Apply 5 iterations of the bisection method to find an approximate root of $x^3 - 3x + 1 = 0$ on the interval $[0, 1]$.

SOLUTION

$f(x)$ is a polynomial, and is continuous at all values of x. We have $a_1 = 0$, $f(a_1) = f(0) = 1 > 0$, $b_1 = 1$,   and $f(b_1) = f(1) = -1 < 0$,   so that $f(a_1) \cdot f(b_1) < 0$. $p_1 = \frac{0 + 1}{2} = .5$, and $f(p_1) = -0.375 < 0$, so that $a_2 = 0$ and $b_2 = .5$. Then $p_2 = \frac{0 + .5}{2} = 0.25$. The process of obtaining successive approximations is represented in the following table, with $+$ or $-$ indicating the sign of the corresponding function value.

n	a_n	b_n	p_n	$f(p_n)$
1	0(+)	1(−)	.5	−
2	0(+)	.5(−)	.25	+
3	.25(+)	.5(−)	.375	−
4	.25(+)	.375(−)	.3125	+
5	.3125(+)	.375(+)	.34375	

TABLE A.1

Then the approximation to the root is $p_5 = .34375$. □

The exact value of the root in Example A.1 is .347296, to 6 decimal places, so the absolute error in the approximate value $p_5 = .34375$ is $|.347296 - .34375| = .003546$, which is less than $\frac{1-0}{2^5} = .03125$, as guaranteed by the error bound in Equation (A.2).

A.2.2 Fixed Point Iteration

The point p is called a fixed point of the function $g(x)$ if $g(p) = p$. With a starting approximation p_0, the sequence $\{p_n\}_{n=0}^{\infty}$ can be constructed as $p_1 = g(p_0)$, $p_2 = g(p_1), \cdots, p_{n+1} = g(p_n), \cdots$. This is called fixed point iteration or functional iteration. The resulting sequence may or may not converge to the fixed point p. If $|g'(p)| < 1$ and if the starting value p_0 is close enough to p, then the iteration will converge to p. This convergence is called *linear* or *first order* convergence. If $|g'(p)| > 1$ then the iteration will not converge to p for any starting value, other than p itself. If $|g'(p)| = 1$ then the iteration may or may not converge. If $g'(p) = 0$, then the iteration will converge rapidly to p; this is called *quadratic* or *second order* convergence.

Fixed point iteration can be used to solve the equation $f(x) = 0$ by translating the equation into the fixed point form $g(x) = x$. The solution(s) of the original equation $f(x) = 0$ are the same as the solutions of the fixed point equation $g(x) = x$. In general the translation may be done in very many ways, but not all of the fixed point translations result in a fixed point sequence that converges to the root. Each of the following are equivalent fixed point forms for $x^3 - 3x + 1 = 0$.

(i) $\dfrac{x^3 + 1}{3} = x$ (ii) $\dfrac{3x - 1}{x^2} = x$ (iii) $(3x - 1)^{1/3} = x$

With a starting value of $p_0 = .5$, the three fixed point functions give the following sequences of approximations.

(i)   .5, .375, .3509, .3477, .3473, .3473
(ii)   .5, -2.0, 1.75, -1.3878, 2.6810, $-.9799, \cdots$
(iii) .5, $-.7937$, 1.5009, -1.5187, 1.7712, -1.6278, 1.8053, -1.6406

The first iteration converges rapidly to the root at .347296. The second iteration does not appear to converge. Neither does the third, although the consecutive negative numbers in this iteration may be converging to -1.8794, which is also a root of the original equation.

A.2.3 The Newton-Raphson Method

The Newton-Raphson fixed point function used to find the solution of $f(x) = 0$ is $g(x) = x - \dfrac{f(x)}{f'(x)}$, so the sequence of approximations is of the form $x_0, x_1, \cdots$, where

$$x_{n+1} = g(x_n) = x_n - \frac{f(x_n)}{f'(x_n)}. \tag{A.3}$$

In most cases, the Newton-Raphson method will result in quadratic convergence. This method has a graphical interpretation, illustrated in Figure A.2. Given the approximation x_n, the successive approximation x_{n+1} is the x-intercept of the tangent line to the curve $f(x)$ at the point $(x_n, f(x_n))$.

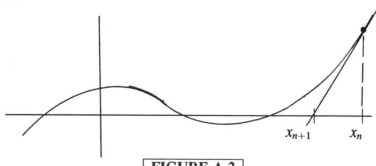

$$x_{n+1} \qquad x_n$$

FIGURE A.2

The Newton-Raphson method applied to $f(x) = x^3 - 3x + 1 = 0$ has the fixed point function $g(x) = x - \dfrac{x^3 - 3x + 1}{3x^2 - 3} = \dfrac{2x^3 - 1}{3x^2 - 3}$. With a starting value of $x_0 = 0$, the sequence of approximations is 0, .3333, .3472, .3473, accurate to 8 decimal places on the 4th iteration. With a starting value of $x_0 = 2$, the resulting sequence is 2, 1.6667, 1.5486, 1.5324, 1.5321, which also a root of $f(x) = 0$.

A.2.4 The Secant Method

The secant method is a modification to Newton-Raphson, which is used when f' is not known. With two approximations to p, say p_{n-2} and p_{n-1}, an approximation to $f'(p_{n-1})$ is the slope of the line between the points $(p_{n-2}, f(p_{n-2}))$ and $(p_{n-1}, f(p_{n-1}))$, so that $f'(p_{n-1}) \approx \dfrac{f(p_{n-1}) - f(p_{n-2})}{p_{n-1} - p_{n-2}}$. Then

$$p_n = p_{n-1} - \frac{f(p_{n-1})}{f'(p_{n-1})} \approx p_{n-1} - \frac{f(p_{n-1})}{\dfrac{f(p_{n-1}) - f(p_{n-2})}{p_{n-1} - p_{n-2}}}$$

$$= p_{n-1} - \frac{f(p_{n-1}) \cdot (p_{n-1} - p_{n-2})}{f(p_{n-1}) - f(p_{n-2})}. \qquad (A.4)$$

A.3 APPROXIMATE INTEGRATION

A.3.1 The Trapezoidal Rule

The trapezoidal rule approximation is

$$\int_a^b f(x)\, dx \approx \frac{b-a}{2} [f(a) + f(b)], \qquad (A.5)$$

with error term $-\dfrac{h^3}{12} \cdot f''(\xi)$, where $h = b - a$ and ξ is between a and b. It is illustrated in Figure A.3.

A.3.2 The Midpoint Rule

The midpoint rule approximation is

$$\int_a^b f(x)\,dx \;\approx\; (b-a)\cdot f\!\left(\tfrac{a+b}{2}\right), \qquad\qquad (\text{A.7})$$

which is the interval width multiplied by the functional value at the midpoint of the interval. The error in the approximation is $\frac{h^3}{3}\cdot f''(\xi)$, where $h = \frac{b-a}{2}$ is half the width of the interval, and ξ is some point between a and b. It is illustrated in Figure A.4.

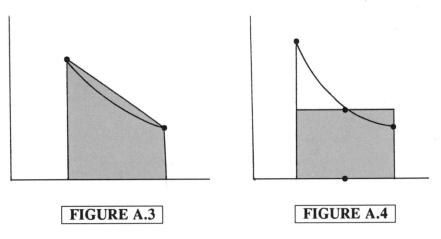

| FIGURE A.3 | FIGURE A.4 |

A.3.3 Simpson's Rule

If x_0, x_1 and x_2 are equally spaced points with $x_2 - x_1 = x_1 - x_0 = h$, then Simpson's rule approximation is

$$\int_{x_0}^{x_2} f(x)\,dx \;\approx\; \tfrac{h}{3}\,[f(x_0) + 4f(x_1) + f(x_2)], \qquad\qquad (\text{A.8})$$

with error term $-\frac{h^5}{90}\cdot f^{(4)}(\xi)$ where, ξ is in the interval $[x_0, x_2]$.

REVIEW OF PROBABILITY

B.1 RULES OF PROBABILITY

1. Conditional probability of event B given event A
   a. Requires $P[A] > 0$
   b. $P[B \mid A] = \dfrac{P[A \cap B]}{P[A]}$

2. Independent events A and B
   a. Must satisfy $P[A \cap B] = P[A] \cdot P[B]$
   b. Also called stochastically independent or statistically independent

3. Mutually independent events $A_1, A_2, \cdots, A_n$ must satisfy
$$P[A_1 \cap A_2 \cap \cdots \cap A_n] = P[A_1] \cdot P[A_2] \cdots P[A_n] = \prod_{i=1}^{n} P[A_i]$$

4. $P[A \cap B] = P[B \mid A] \cdot P[A] = P[A \mid B] \cdot P[B]$, for any events A and B

5. $P[A' \mid B] = 1 - P[A \mid B]$

B.2 RANDOM VARIABLES AND PROBABILITY DISTRIBUTIONS

1. For a continuous random variable, the probability $P[a < X < b]$ is defined to be $\int_a^b f(x)\,dx$, where the probability density function $f(x)$ must satisfy

a. $f(x) \geq 0$ for all x
b. $\int_{-\infty}^{\infty} f(x)\, dx = 1$

2. Cumulative distribution function (c.d.f.)
   a. Also called distribution function (d.f.)
   b. $F(x) = P[X \leq x]$
   c. For a discrete random variable with probability function $f(x)$, $F(x) = \sum\{f(w) : w \leq x\}$; in this case $F(x)$ is a "step function," with jump (or step) increases at each point with non-zero probability, then remaining constant until the next jump
   d. If X has a continuous distribution with p.d.f. $f(x)$, then $F(x) = \int_{-\infty}^{x} f(t)\, dt$ is a continuous, differentiable, non-decreasing function such that $F'(x) = f(x)$

3. Expected value of a random variable X
   a. Denoted $E[X]$, or μ_X, or μ
   b. $\sum_x x f(x)$ if X is discrete
   c. $\int_{-\infty}^{\infty} x f(x)\, dx$ if X is continuous
   d. Also called the mean of X, or expectation of X

4. Expectation of $h(x)$
   a. $\sum_x h(x) \cdot f(x)$ if X is discrete
   b. $\int_{-\infty}^{\infty} h(x) \cdot f(x)\, dx$ if X is continuous

5. Variance of a random variable X
   a. Denoted $Var[X]$, σ_X^2 or σ^2
   b. Defined to be $E[(X - \mu_X)^2]$
   c. Never negative, and is 0 only if the random variable is actually a constant (not random at all)
   d. The standard deviation of X
      (1) Denoted σ_X
      (2) Defined to be $+\sqrt{Var[X]}$

6. Moment generating function of a random variable X
   a. Denoted $M_X(t)$, $m_X(t)$, $M(t)$ or $m(t)$
   b. Defined to be $E[e^{tX}]$
   c. It is always true that $M_X(0) = 1$

7. $100p^{th}$ percentile of the distribution of X
   a. Defined for $0 < p < 1$
   b. Also called the quantile of order p
   c. Defined to be any number c_p such that both $P[X \le c_p] \ge p$ and $P[X \ge c_p] \ge 1 - p$ are true
   d. Such a value c_p may not be unique
   e. If $p = .5$, then $c_p = c_{.5}$ is called a *median of X*

8. For any constants a_1, a_2 and b and functions h_1 and h_2,

   $$E[a_1 \cdot h_1(X) + a_2 \cdot h_2(X) + b] = a_1 \cdot E[h_1(X)] + a_2 \cdot E[h_2(X)] + b$$

9. Jensen's inequality
   a. States that if $\dfrac{d^2}{dx^2} h(x) \ge 0$, then $E[h(X)] \ge h\left(E[X]\right)$
   b. The inequality reverses if the second derivative of h is negative

10. The variance of X can be written as
    a. $Var[X] = E[(X - \mu_X)^2] = E[X^2] - \mu_X^2 = E[X^2] - \left(E[X]\right)^2$

11. If a and b are constants then $Var[a \cdot X + b] = a^2 \cdot Var[X]$

12. Chebyshev's inequality: if X is a random variable with mean μ_X and standard deviation σ_X, then $P[|X - \mu_X| > r \cdot \sigma_X] \le \dfrac{1}{r^2}$, for any $r > 0$

B.3 FREQUENTLY USED PROBABILITY DISTRIBIUTIONS

1. Discrete uniform distribution on N points

   a. $f(x) = \dfrac{1}{N}$ for $x = 1, 2, \cdots, N$, and $f(x) = 0$ otherwise
   b. $E[X] = \dfrac{N+1}{2}$

   c. $Var[X] = \dfrac{N^2 - 1}{12}$

   d. $M_X(t) = \displaystyle\sum_{j=1}^{N} \dfrac{e^{jt}}{N}$ for any real t

2. **Binomial with parameters *n* and *p***

    a. *X* is the number of successes in *n* independent trials, where the probability of a success on each separate trial is *p*

    b. $f(x) = \binom{n}{x} \cdot p^x \cdot (1-p)^{n-x}$ for $x = 0, 1, 2, \cdots, n$

    c. $E[X] = n \cdot p$

    d. $Var[X] = n \cdot p \cdot (1-p)$

    e. $M_X(t) = (1 - p + p \cdot e^t)^n$

    f. If $n = 1$, this distribution is also called the Bernoulli distribution

3. **Poisson with parameter $\lambda > 0$**

    a. $f(x) = \frac{e^{-\lambda} \cdot \lambda^x}{x!}$ for $x = 0, 1, 2, \cdots$, and $f(x) = 0$ otherwise

    b. $E[X] = \lambda$

    c. $Var[X] = \lambda$

    d. $M_X(t) = e^{\lambda(e^t - 1)}$

4. **Continuous uniform distribution on (a, b)**

    a. $f(x) = \frac{1}{b-a}$ for $a < x < b$, and $f(x) = 0$ otherwise

    b. $E[X] = \frac{a+b}{2}$

    c. $Var[X] = \frac{(b-a)^2}{12}$

    d. $M_X(t) = \frac{e^{bt} - e^{at}}{(b-a) \cdot t}$ for any real t

5. **Normal with parameters μ (mean) and σ^2 (variance)**

    a. $f(x) = \frac{1}{\sigma \cdot \sqrt{2\pi}} \cdot e^{-(x-\mu)^2/2\sigma^2}$ for $-\infty < x < \infty$

    b. $E[X] = \mu$

    c. $Var[X] = \sigma^2$

    d. $M_X(t) = exp\left[\mu + \frac{\sigma^2 \cdot t^2}{2}\right]$

e. Special case of $\mu = 0$ and $\sigma^2 = 1$
   (1) Called the standard normal distribution
   (2) $f(x)$ is denoted $\phi(x)$, and $F(x)$ is denoted $\Phi(x)$

6. Exponential with mean $\frac{1}{\lambda}$
   a. $f(x) = \lambda \cdot e^{-\lambda x}$ for $x > 0$, and $f(x) = 0$ otherwise
   b. $E[X] = \frac{1}{\lambda}$
   c. $Var[X] = \frac{1}{\lambda^2}$
   d. $M_X(t) = \frac{\lambda}{\lambda - t}$ for $t < \lambda$

B.4 JOINT, MARGINAL AND CONDITIONAL DISTRIBUTIONS

1. Expectation of a function of joint random variables
   a. Denoted $E[h(X, Y)]$
   b. $\sum\sum h(x, y) \cdot f(x, y)$ if X and Y are discrete
   c. $\int\int h(x, y) \cdot f(x, y) \, dy \, dx$ if X and Y are continuous
   d. Can be extended to a function of n jointly distributed random variables, $E[h(X_1, X_2, \cdots, X_n)]$

2. Marginal distribution of a random variable X
   a. Denoted $f(x)$ or $f_X(x)$ or $f_1(x)$
   b. If X and Y are jointly distributed, then $f_X(x)$ is defined by
      (1) $f_X(x) = \sum_y f(x, y)$ if Y is discrete
      (2) $f_X(x) = \int_{-\infty}^{\infty} f(x, y) \, dy$ if Y is continuous

3. Independence of random variables X and Y
   a. If the joint c.d.f. of X and Y can be factored as $F(x, y) = F_X(x) \cdot F_Y(y)$, then X and Y are independent
   b. If the p.d.f. factors as $f(x, y) = f_X(x) \cdot f_Y(y)$, then X and Y are usually (but not always) independent

4. Conditional distribution of Y given $X = x$

    a. Defined by $f_{Y|X}(y \mid x) = \frac{f(x, y)}{f_X(x)}$ if $f_X(x) \neq 0$

    b. Can be extended to distributions with more than two variables

    c. The conditional expectation is defined by $E[Y \mid X = x] = \int_{-\infty}^{\infty} y \cdot f(y \mid x) \, dy$, or $\sum_y y \cdot f(y \mid x)$

5. Covariance of random variables X and Y: if X and Y have mean values μ_X and μ_Y respectively, and joint density function $f(x, y)$, the covariance of X and Y is defined by $Cov[X, Y] = E[(X - \mu_X)(Y - \mu_Y)] = E[XY] - \mu_X \cdot \mu_Y = \int \int x y f(x, y) \, dy \, dx - \mu_X \cdot \mu_Y$

6. Correlation of random variables X and Y

    a. Denoted $\rho(X, Y)$ or ρ_{XY}

    b. Defined by $\frac{Cov[X, Y]}{\sigma_X \cdot \sigma_Y}$, where σ_X and σ_Y are the standard deviations of X and Y, respectively

    c. If $\rho_{XY} = 0$, then X and Y are uncorrelated

    d. If $E[Y \mid X = x]$ is a linear function of x, then $E[Y \mid X = x] = \mu_Y + \rho_{XY} \cdot \frac{\sigma_Y}{\sigma_X} \cdot (x - \mu_X)$; the conditional variance of Y given $X = x$ is $Var[Y \mid X] = k(X)$, where $E[k(X)] = \sigma_Y^2 \cdot (1 - \rho_{XY}^2)$

7. $Cov[X, Y] = E[X \cdot Y] - \mu_X \cdot \mu_Y = E[X \cdot Y] - E[X] \cdot E[Y]$; if X and Y are independent, then $E[X \cdot Y] = E[X] \cdot E[Y]$, so $Cov[X, Y] = 0$

8. $-1 \leq \rho_{XY} \leq 1$ for any jointly distributed X and Y

9. $Var[X + Y]$

    $$= E[(X + Y)^2] - (E[X + Y])^2$$
    $$= E[X^2 + 2XY + Y^2] - (E[X] + E[Y])^2$$
    $$= E[X^2] + E[2XY] + E[Y^2] - (E[X])^2 - 2E[X]E[Y] - (E[Y])^2$$
    $$= Var[X] + Var[Y] + 2 \cdot Cov[X, Y]$$

10. If X and Y are independent
    a. $Var[X + Y] = Var[X] + Var[Y]$
    b. $Var[aX + bY] = a^2 Var[X] + b^2 Var[Y] + 2ab \cdot Cov[X, Y]$

11. Multinomial distribution with parameters $n, p_1, p_2, \cdots, p_k$
    a. $0 \le p_i \le 1$ for all $i = 1, 2, \cdots, k$, and $p_1 + p_2 + \cdots + p_k = 1$
    b. $f(x_1, x_2, \cdots, x_k) = \dfrac{n!}{x_1! \cdot x_2! \cdots x_k!} \cdot p_1^{x_1} \cdot p_2^{x_2} \cdots p_k^{x_k}$
    c. $E[X_i] = n \cdot p_i$
    d. $Var[X_i] = n \cdot p_i \cdot (1 - p_i)$
    e. $Cov[X_i, X_j] = -n \cdot p_i \cdot p_j$

B.5 TRANSFORMATIONS OF RANDOM VARIABLES

1. Distribution of a function of a continuous random variable X
    a. Let $Y = u(X)$, where u has an inverse function v
    b. p.d.f. of Y is $g(y) = f_X[v(y)] \cdot \left| \frac{d}{dy} v(y) \right|$
    c. c.d.f. of Y is $G(y) = F_X[v(y)]$

2. Distribution of a transformation of continuous variables X_1, X_2
    a. Let X_1 and X_2 have joint p.d.f. $f(x_1, x_2)$
    b. Let $Y_1 = u_1(x_1, x_2)$ and $Y_2 = u_2(x_1, x_2)$, where u_1 and u_2 form a one-to-one transformation with inverse functions v_1 and v_2
    c. The p.d.f. of the joint distribution of Y_1 and Y_2 is
       $g(y_1, y_2) = f[v_1(y_1, y_2), v_2(y_1, y_2)] \cdot |J|$
    d. J is called the *Jacobian* of the transformation
    e. J is the determinant of the matrix $\begin{bmatrix} \dfrac{\partial v_1}{\partial y_1} & \dfrac{\partial v_1}{\partial y_2} \\ \dfrac{\partial v_2}{\partial y_1} & \dfrac{\partial v_2}{\partial y_2} \end{bmatrix}$

3. Distribution of $X_1 + X_2$

   a. If X_1 and X_2 are discrete with joint probability function $f(x_1, x_2)$

      (1) The joint probability of $Y_1 = X_1 + X_2$ and $Y_2 = X_2$ is $g(y_1, y_2) = f(y_1 - y_2, y_2)$

      (2) The marginal probability function of $Y_1 = X_1 + X_2$ is
$$g_{Y_1}(y_1) = \sum_{y_2} g(y_1, y_2)$$

   b. If X_1 and X_2 are continuous with joint p.d.f. $f(x_1, x_2)$, then the joint p.d.f. of $Y_1 = X_1 + X_2$ and $Y_2 = X_2$ is $g(y_1, y_2) = f(y_1 - y_2, y_2)$

   c. $E[X_1 + X_2] = E[X_1] + E[X_2]$

   d. $Var[X_1 + X_2] = Var[X_1] + Var[X_2] + 2Cov[X_1, X_2]$

   e. Convolution method

      (1) If X_1 and X_2 have continuous p.d.f.'s $f_1(x_1)$ and $f_2(x_2)$, then
$$g(y) = \int_{-\infty}^{\infty} f_1(y - z) \cdot f_2(z)\, dz = \int_{-\infty}^{\infty} f_2(y - z) \cdot f_1(z)\, dz$$

      (2) For discrete random variables, summation replaces integration

4. Distribution of $\sum_{i=1}^{n} X_i$

   a. $E[\sum X_i] = \sum E[X_i]$

   b. $Var[\sum X_i] = \sum Var[X_i] + 2\sum\sum_{j<k} Cov[X_j, X_k]$

   c. If the X_i's are mutually independent

      (1) $Var[\sum X_i] = \sum Var[X_i]$

      (2) $M_Y(t) = M_{X_1}(t) \cdot M_{X_2}(t) \cdots M_{X_n}(t) = \prod_{i=1}^{n} M_{X_i}(t)$,

      where $Y = \sum X_i$

5. If $a_1, a_2, \cdots, a_n$ and $b_1, b_2, \cdots, b_m$ are constants and $X_1, X_2, \cdots, X_n$ and $Y_1, Y_2, \cdots, Y_m$ are random variables, then
$$Cov\left[\sum_{i=1}^{n} a_i X_i, \sum_{j=1}^{m} b_j Y_j\right] = \sum_{i=1}^{n} \sum_{j=1}^{m} a_i b_j\, Cov[X_i, Y_j]$$

6. If X and Y have a bivariate normal distribution with means μ_X and μ_Y, variances σ_X^2 and σ_Y^2, and coefficient of correlation ρ, then $X + Y$ has a normal distribution with mean $\mu_X + \mu_Y$ and variance $\sigma_X^2 + \sigma_Y^2 + 2\rho\sigma_X\sigma_Y$

SIMULATION

In Chapter 5 we developed formulas for the mean and variance of accumulation and present value functions and accumulated and present values of annuities if interest rates are random and independent from one period to the next. We also saw that complications quickly arose in trying to describe the distributions of these functions. Furthermore, when interest rates are not independent, Equations (5.13) and (5.23) for expected value and variance do not apply.

When it is too difficult to describe and analyze the precise distribution of a random variable, it is sometimes possible to obtain information about the distribution by using the technique of *simulation* of the random variable. The simulation of a random variable refers to imitating or reproducing the behavior of the random variable without actually performing the experiment upon which the random variable is based. Simulation is usually performed using numbers produced by a *random number generator*.

As a simple example, suppose a random number generator was available to generate integers from 1 to 6, with each integer being equally likely to occur (*i.e.*, each with probability 1/6), and independent of the previous results. The generated integers could be used to simulate the outcomes of successive throws of a single fair die with the numbers 1 to 6 on the six faces of the die. Most computers have a random number generating algorithm that generates successive numbers that are independent and uniformly distributed on the interval [0, 1], usually to 8 or more digits. These are referred to as *pseudo-random numbers*, since they are generated from a predetermined numerical algorithm and are not truly random (in the sense of "unpredictable"). However careful choice of the algorithm can produce successive numbers that behave, for practical statistical purposes, like independent uniform numbers on the interval [0, 1]. It is these pseudo-random uniform [0, 1] numbers that are used to simulate random variables.

C.1   SIMULATION OF A DISCRETE RANDOM VARIABLE

The crucial requirement in simulating a random variable is to ensure that the simulated values behave statistically and probabilistically like the random variable that is being simulated. In the simulation of a discrete random variable, this involves partitioning [0, 1] into subintervals whose sizes are equal to the probabilities of the various outcomes of the random variable being simulated. In throwing a fair six-sided die, for example, each face has a probability of $1/6 = .166667$ of turning up. We can partition [0,1] into the subintervals $0 \leq u \leq .166667$, $.166667 < u \leq .333333$, $.333333 < u \leq .500000$, $.500000 < u \leq .666667$, $.666667 < u \leq .833333$, $.833333 < u \leq 1.000000$ and simulate a throw of 1 if the pseudo-random number u is in the first interval, a 2 if it is in the second interval, and so on. Note that in general there are infinitely many valid ways of partitioning the interval [0, 1] to create a simulation of a discrete random variable. The probabilities of the simulated throws are each 1/6 (to within the 6th decimal place), so the simulated observations are statistically equivalent to the outcomes that would occur if a die were actually thrown.

The first step in performing a simulation is to establish the relationship between the generated pseudo-random uniform [0, 1] numbers and the outcomes of the random variable being simulated. As pointed out above, [0, 1] is partitioned into disjoint subintervals whose lengths are equal to the probabilities of the outcomes of the random variable. Suppose that X is a discrete random variable with c.d.f. $F(x)$ and outcomes $x_1 < x_2 < \cdots < x_k$ (such that $F(x_1) < F(x_2) < \cdots < F(x_k)$), and corresponding probabilities $p_1, p_2, \ldots, p_k$, where $\sum_{t=1}^{k} p_t = 1$. We partition [0, 1] into the subintervals

$$[0, F(x_1)], \ [F(x_1), F(x_2)], \ \cdots, \ [F(x_{k-1}), F(x_k)].$$

Note that

$$F(x_1) = p_1, \ F(x_2) = p_1 + p_2, \ \cdots, \ F(x_k) = p_1 + p_2 + \cdots + p_k,$$

and the interval $[F(x_{t-1}), F(x_t)]$ has length p_t. (In general, we would partition $[0, 1]$ into any k disjoint subintervals, with lengths $p_1, p_2, \ldots, p_k$.) If the generated pseudo-random uniform $[0, 1]$ value falls in the first interval the simulated value of X is x_1, if it falls in the second interval the simulated value is x_2, and so on. It is clear that the probability of uniform $[0, 1]$ u falling in the first interval is equal to p_1, the interval width. Furthermore, the probability of u falling in the interval

$$F(x_{j-1}) = \sum_{t=1}^{j-1} p_t < u \le \sum_{t=1}^{j} p_t = F(x_j)$$

is $p_j = F(x_j) - F(x_{j-1})$, the interval width. Thus the probability of simulating an X-value of x_j is equal to p_j, and the simulation is a true representation (statistically and probabilistically) of the distribution of X.

The following example illustrates how the simulation method described above can be applied to investigate the distributions of compound interest functions (accumulated values, present values, or annuities) when the interest rates in any given year are governed by a discrete distribution.

EXAMPLE C.1

The interest rate in each year has the distribution

$$i = \begin{cases} .10, & \text{with probability } .50 \\ .15, & \text{with probability } .50' \end{cases}$$

and interest rates are independent from year to year. Use the following 10 independent uniform $[0,1]$ values to simulate a sample occurrence of $S(10)$. Use the same uniform values to simulate a sample occurrence of $\ddot{s}_{\overline{10}|}$ and $s_{\overline{10}|}$. The uniform random numbers are .765, .931, .835, .355, .232, .117, .446, .708, .908, .432.

SOLUTION

We will simulate i_t for each t from 1 to 10. Since in each year i is either 10% or 15%, each with .5 probability, an appropriate simulation procedure is $i = .10$ if $0 \le u \le .500$ and $i = .15$ if $.500 < u \le 1.00$. Then the 10 successive simulated interest rates are $i_1 = .15$, $i_2 = .15$, $i_3 = .15$,

$i_4 = .10$, $i_5 = .10$, $i_6 = .10$, $i_7 = .10$, $i_8 = .15$, $i_9 = .15$ and $i_{10} = .10$.

The resulting value of $S(10)$ is $\prod_{t=1}^{10}(1 + i_t) = 3.239$, the value of $\ddot{s}_{\overline{10}|}$ is

$$(1+i_{10}) + (1+i_9)(1+i_{10}) + \cdots + (1+i_1)(1+i_2)\cdots(1+i_{10}) = 19.752,$$

and the value of $s_{\overline{10}|}$ is

$$1 + (1+i_{10}) + (1+i_9)(1+i_{10}) + \cdots + (1+i_2)\cdots(1+i_{10}) = 17.513.$$

Note that we could have used i_1 through i_9 to calculate $s_{\overline{10}|}$; although the numerical value would be different from that obtained using i_2 through i_{10}, it would also be a valid simulation.   □

   In a practical application the simulation is repeated a large number of times to get a large sample of the behavior of the random variable being simulated. In the case of Example 5.8, each simulation of $S(10)$, $\ddot{s}_{\overline{10}|}$ and $s_{\overline{10}|}$ requires a series of 10 uniform [0, 1] random values. In Example 5.2 the complete distribution of $S(10)$, an 11-point discrete random variable, was found. The distribution of $\ddot{s}_{\overline{10}|}$ is discrete with $2^{10} = 1024$ points, and is much more cumbersome to describe.
   The following tables outline the results of performing first 100 simulations, then 1000, then 10,000 and finally 100,000 simulations of the random variables $S(10)$ and $\ddot{s}_{\overline{10}|}$. For the simulation of $S(10)$, Table C.1 shows how many of the simulated values were equal to each of the 11 possible values $x_1, x_2, \ldots, x_{11}$ (see Example 5.2) of $S(10)$, along with the exact probabilities. The range of $\ddot{s}_{\overline{10}|}$ is from $\ddot{s}_{\overline{10}|.10} = 17.5312$ to $\ddot{s}_{\overline{10}|.15} = 23.3493$. For the simulation of $\ddot{s}_{\overline{10}|}$, Table C.2 shows how many of the simulated values are in each of 10 subintervals that break the full range of $\ddot{s}_{\overline{10}|}$ into equal pieces of length $\frac{23.3493 - 17.5312}{10} = .5818$; the subintervals are [17.5312, 18.1130], [18.1130, 18.6948], \ldots, [22.7675, 23.3493]. Then a simulated value falling in the first subinterval is denoted x_1, one falling in the second subinterval is x_2, and so on.

TABLE C.1

Number of simulations	Number of simulations resulting in										
	x_1	x_2	x_3	x_4	x_5	x_6	x_7	x_8	x_9	x_{10}	x_{11}
100	0	2	2	14	20	26	25	8	2	1	0
1,000	1	7	46	125	209	252	210	107	29	13	1
10,000	10	85	438	1144	2081	2511	2068	1166	409	79	9
100,000	100	959	4392	11624	20665	24548	20610	11671	4460	880	91

k	Exact Probability for Outcome x_k	k	Exact Probability for Outcome x_k
1	.000977	6	.246094
2	.009766	7	.205078
3	.043945	8	.117188
4	.117188	9	.043945
5	.205078	10	.009766
		11	.000977

For computational purposes in the simulation of $\ddot{s}_{\overline{10}|}$, for each sequence of interest rates $i_1, i_2, \ldots, i_{10}$ the numerical value of $\ddot{s}_{\overline{10}|}$ is found from the iterative loop $\ddot{s}_{\overline{t}|} = (1 + \ddot{s}_{\overline{t-1}|})(1 + i_t)$, for $t = 1, 2, \cdots, 10$.

TABLE C.2

Number of simulations	Number of simulations resulting in									
	x_1	x_2	x_3	x_4	x_5	x_6	x_7	x_8	x_9	x_{10}
100	1	4	11	23	25	19	9	4	3	1
1,000	10	59	125	193	219	205	109	52	21	7
10,000	99	463	1193	1920	2288	1957	1223	596	213	48
100,000	1032	4788	11910	18908	22632	19446	12220	6273	2265	526

k	Exact Probability for Outcome x_k	k	Exact Probability for Outcome x_k
1	.0107	6	.1934
2	.0467	7	.1250
3	.1182	8	.0615
4	.1904	9	.0225
5	.2246	10	.0059

The results of the simulation can be used to approximate probabilities. For $\underline{S}(10)$, the probability $Pr[\underline{S}(10) = x_4 = 3.0985]$ is approximated by .1144 based on the simulation of 10,000 trials, and by .1162 based on 100,000 simulated trials. The exact value is .1172.

An indication of the accuracy and reliability of a simulation can be seen by calculating sample means and sample variances and comparing them with the exact values (see Section C.3). For $\underline{S}(10)$ the exact mean is $(1.125)^{10} = 3.247321$. The simulation of 100 trials gives a sample mean of 3.241934, 1000 trials gives 3.246150, 10,000 trials gives 3.247746, and 100,000 trials gives 3.247290. The exact variance of $\underline{S}(10)$ is .052190 (see Equation (5.13)), and the sample variances obtained by the simulations are .054229 for 100 trials, .050162 for 1000 trials, .054071 for 10,000 trials, and .052781 for 100,000 trials. The exact mean of $\ddot{\underline{s}}_{\overline{10|}}$ is 20.225889, and the simulated sample means are 20.238507 for 100 trials, 20.206612 for 1000 trials, 20.225090 for 10,000 trials, and 20.225584 for 100,000 trials. The exact variance of $\ddot{\underline{s}}_{\overline{10|}}$ (see the Theorem in Section 5.3) is .986107, and the simulated sample variances are 1.066023 for 100 trials, .969215 for 1000 trials, 1.015488 for 10,000 trials, and .991989 for 100,000 trials.

In the cases of $\underline{S}(10)$ and $\ddot{\underline{s}}_{\overline{10|}}$ it was not difficult to find the exact values of the probabilities, but in other situations it may be very tedious or impossible to find exact probabilities. Suppose we wish to analyze the behavior of $\ddot{\underline{s}}_{\overline{30|}}$ when annual interest rates have the independent two-point distribution given in Example C.1. The actual distribution of $\ddot{\underline{s}}_{\overline{30|}}$ has $2^{30} = 1{,}073{,}741{,}824$ outcomes, each with the same probability. It would be possible, but very tedious, to describe the complete distribution of $\ddot{\underline{s}}_{\overline{30|}}$, although it would not be difficult to write a computer program that calculated and stored all the possible outcomes. The minimum possible value of $\ddot{\underline{s}}_{\overline{30|}}$ is $\ddot{s}_{\overline{30|}.10} = 180.9434$, and the maximum possible value is $\ddot{s}_{\overline{30|}.15} = 478.2197$. As an example we can approximate the probability $Pr[\ddot{\underline{s}}_{\overline{30|}} \leq 300]$ by simulation using 10,000 trials, by calculating the proportion of trials that result in a value of $\ddot{s}_{\overline{30}|}$ less than or equal to 300. The following table lists the results of 10 separate simulations of 10,000 trials each, giving the number of simulated values of $\ddot{s}_{\overline{30}|}$ that were less than 300.

TABLE C.3

Simulation Number									
1	2	3	4	5	6	7	8	9	10
5277	5350	5260	5275	5306	5312	5323	5299	5307	5260

Each of the simulations gives an approximate probability. Using all ten simulations together, 52,969 trials out of 100,000 resulted in values of $\ddot{s}_{\overline{30}|}$ less than 300, giving an approximate probability of .52969. (See Section C.3 for a discussion of the accuracy of this estimate of the probability.)

We have seen that when interest rates from one period to the next are independent and have a common mean, then the expected value of an accumulated amount is simply the accumulated amount valued at the common expected rate of interest per period, although the evaluation of exact probabilities related to the distribution, such as $Pr[\ddot{s}_{\overline{30}|} \leq 300]$, may be difficult. The following example involves a discrete interest rate distribution for which there is a dependence among the interest rates from year to year. Such distributions usually result in accumulated values and annuities that have quite complex distributions and are more easily approximated by simulation.

EXAMPLE C.2

Suppose the interest rate distribution is $\quad \underline{i}_1 = \begin{cases} .09, & \text{with probability } .30 \\ .10, & \text{with probability } .40 \\ .11, & \text{with probability } .30 \end{cases}$

in the first year, and in subsequent years the distribution is

$$\underline{i}_{t+1} = \begin{cases} i_t - .01, & \text{with probability } .30 \\ i_t, & \text{with probability } .40. \\ i_t + .01, & \text{with probability } .30 \end{cases}$$

Apply the method of simulation to find estimates for the mean and variance of $\underline{S}(10)$ and $\ddot{s}_{\overline{10}|}$.

SOLUTION

The simulation procedure can be

$$i_1 = \begin{cases} .09, & \text{if} \quad u \le .30. \\ .10, & \text{if} \quad .30 < u \le .70 \\ .11, & \text{if} \quad .70 < u \le 1.0 \end{cases}$$

for i_1 and

$$i_{t+1} = \begin{cases} i_t - .01, & \text{if} \quad u \le .30 \\ i_t, & \text{if} \quad .30 < u \le .70 \\ i_t + .01, & \text{if} \quad .70 < u \le 1.0 \end{cases}$$

for subsequent i_{t+1}, where u is a random uniform number on $[0, 1]$. For each sequence of $u_1, u_2, \ldots, u_{10}$, we have a simulated sequence of interest rates based on the given simulation procedure. Generation of 100,000 sequences of 10 random numbers each results in a simulation of 100,000 trials of 10-year interest rate sequences, and thus 100,000 simulated values of $S(10)$ and $\ddot{s}_{\overline{10|}}$. Separate simulations of 10,000 and 100,000 trials were performed; the resulting sample means and variances of $S(10)$ and $\ddot{s}_{\overline{10|}}$ for both simulations are given in the following table.

TABLE C.4

	Simulation with 10,000 Trials		Simulation with 100,000 Trials	
	Sample Mean	Sample Variance	Sample Mean	Sample Variance
$S(10)$	2.6088	.1327	2.6141	.1298
$\ddot{s}_{\overline{10|}}$	17.5841	3.2624	17.6122	3.0942

□

Note that as t increases, so does the range of i_t; i_2 can take on any of the values .08, .09, .10, .11 or .12, i_3 takes on values from .07 through .13, ..., and i_{10} takes on values from 0 through .20. It can be shown that for each t, $E[i_t] = .10$. However the mean of $S(10)$ is *not* simply $(1.10)^{10} = 2.5937$, and the mean of $\ddot{s}_{\overline{10|}}$ is *not* simply $\ddot{s}_{\overline{10|}.10} = 17.5312$, as would be the case if the i_t's were independent with common mean. The exact mean and variance of $S(10)$ are 2.615011 and .130799, and for $\ddot{s}_{\overline{10|}}$ they are 17.616609 and 3.2239788, respectively.

C.2 SIMULATION OF A CONTINUOUS RANDOM VARIABLE

A continuous random variable X has an associated probability density function (p.d.f.) $f(x)$ which must satisfy the two conditions (i) $f(x) \geq 0$ for all x, and (ii) $\int_{-\infty}^{\infty} f(x)\, dx = 1$. Probabilities related to X are found by integrating the p.d.f. over the appropriate region; for example

$$Pr[a \leq X \leq b] = \int_{a}^{b} f(x)\, dx. \qquad (C.1)$$

(Note that the inequality in the probability may be strict or not, and the integral and probability value will remain the same.)

The cumulative distribution function (c.d.f.) of X is denoted $F(x)$ and is given by

$$F(x) = Pr[X \leq x] = \int_{-\infty}^{x} f(t)\, dt. \qquad (C.2)$$

The c.d.f. of a continuous random variable must satisfy the conditions (i) $F(x)$ is non-decreasing, (ii) $\lim_{x \to \infty} F(x) = 1$, (iii) $\lim_{x \to -\infty} F(x) = 0$, and (iv) $F(x)$ is continuous and differentiable, with $F'(x) = f(x)$. The graph of a typical c.d.f. is shown in Figure C.1. $F(x)$ will be strictly increasing, except in regions where $f(x) = 0$.

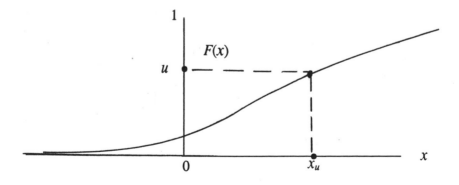

FIGURE C.1

One method of simulating a continuous random variable is the *inversion method*, which involves the use of the c.d.f. Suppose that X is a continuous random variable with c.d.f. $F(x)$. Given a random number u from the uniform distribution on $[0, 1]$, find the smallest x_u for which the equation $F(x_u) = u$ is satisfied. This value x_u is sometimes denoted $F^{-1}(u)$; it can be seen from the graph in Figure C.1 above that x_u is the inverse value to u under the function F, explaining the name "inversion method." Since $F(x)$ increases from 0 to 1 as x goes from $-\infty$ to ∞, and since $0 \le u \le 1$, there must be some point at which $F(x)$ first reaches u. This is x_u and is simply the solution of the equation $F(x_u) = u$. It can be shown (see Exercise 5.4.7) that if u is chosen randomly from a uniform distribution on $[0, 1]$, then x_u behaves statistically like a random observation from the distribution of X, with c.d.f. $F(x)$. The following example illustrates this method.

| EXAMPLE C.3 |

The distribution of X has p.d.f. $f(x) = 1250(x - .08)$ if $.08 \le x \le .12$, and $f(x) = 0$ otherwise. Given the random uniform $[0, 1]$ value $u = .716$, what is the simulated value of X using the inversion method?

| SOLUTION |

We wish to find the x_u for which $F(x_u) = u = .716$. We must first find $F(x) = \int_{-\infty}^{x} f(t)\, dt$. If $x \le .08$ then $F(x) = 0$ since $f(t) = 0$ for all $t < .08$. If $.08 \le x \le .12$ then

$$F(x) = \int_{.08}^{x} 1250(t - .08)\, dt = 625(t - .08)^2 \Big|_{.08}^{x} = 625(x - .08)^2.$$

If $x \ge .12$ then $F(x) = 1$, since all the density of X has been reached by $x = .12$. Thus x_u is the solution of the equation $625(x_u - .08)^2 = .716$, giving $x_u = .1138$. (Note that .0462 is also a solution of the equation, based on the negative square root of $.716/625$, but this root is ignored since it is less than .08.)   □

Example C.2 considered a discrete model of interest rates that were dependent from year to year. The following example involves a model of dependent continuous interest rates.

| EXAMPLE C.4 |

Over a 20-year period the interest rate i_t in year t for $t = 2, \ldots, 20$ has a continuous distribution on the interval $[c_t - .02, c_t + .02]$ with density function $f(i_t) = 1250(i_t - c_t + .02)$ if $c_t - .02 \leq i_t \leq c_t + .02$, and $f(i_t) = 0$ otherwise, where $c_t = .10 + k(i_{t-1} - .10)$. The distribution of i_1 has density function $f(x) = 1250(x - .08)$ if $.08 \leq x \leq .12$, and $f(x) = 0$ otherwise. Estimate the mean and variance of each of $S(20)$ and $\ddot{s}_{\overline{20|}}$ by means of simulation separately for $k = 0, .25, .50, .75$ and 1.

| SOLUTION |

The distribution of i_1 is the same as that of X in Example C.3, and the distributions of the other i_t's are similar to that of X; i_t is distributed on a different interval, but the form of the p.d.f. is the same. The simulation method described in Example C.1 can be adapted to simulating the i_t's in this case. Given independent random uniform $[0, 1]$ values $u_1, u_2, \ldots, u_{20}$, we first simulate i_1 by $i_1 = .08 + \frac{\sqrt{u_1}}{25}$, so that $c_2 = .10 + k(i_1 - .10)$. Then we simulate i_2 by $i_2 = c_2 - .02 + \frac{\sqrt{u_2}}{25}$, and continue in this manner to $c_{20} = .10 + k(i_{19} - .10)$ and $i_{20} = c_{20} - .02 + \frac{\sqrt{u_{20}}}{25}$. Once the i_t's are simulated, the values of $S(20)$ and $\ddot{s}_{\overline{20|}}$ can be calculated. Table C.5 below describes the results of a simulation of 100,000 trials for each of the values of k. (Note that for $k = .75$ and $k = 1$ it is possible for i_t to drift into negative values; such a situation might not be acceptable from a practical point of view and the model might have to be modified to eliminate the possibility of negative interest rates.)

| TABLE C.5 |

k	Simulated Mean		Simulated Variance	
	$S(20)$	$\ddot{s}_{\overline{20|}}$	$S(20)$	$\ddot{s}_{\overline{20|}}$
0	7.5918	63.3884	.0842	3.6691
.25	7.8836	70.2760	.1541	6.6430
.50	8.4737	74.1740	.3785	16.0420
.75	10.1850	85.8683	1.7697	73.3736
1	24.8501	188.1098	109.8352	4476.9537

□

We have seen that the normal distribution often plays a role in modeling interest rate distributions (see Section 5.2). If the force of interest δ has a normal distribution, then $1 + i$ has a distribution which is log-normal since $\ln(1 + \underline{i}) = \underline{\delta}$. The normal distribution may be simulated by the inversion method described above, but there is an alternative simulation method that is easier to apply. This alternative is called the *polar method*.

Once a standard normal value z has been simulated, it is easy to transform it into a simulation of a normal distribution with mean μ and variance σ^2 using the transformation $x = \sigma \cdot z + \mu$.

A model involving the normal distribution which is often used to model interest rates is the *autoregressive model*. An autoregressive model assumes that the current random interest rate depends on a fixed average rate of interest (say μ_i), one or more of the previous periods' interest rates, and a normally distributed random component. The *order* of the autoregressive model is the number of previous period interest rates upon which the current rates depend. The general form of an autoregressive model of order 1 would be

$$\underline{i}_t = \mu_i + k(\underline{i}_{t-1} - \mu_i) + \underline{e}_t, \qquad (C.3)$$

where $\underline{e}_t$ is the normally distributed random component, usually with mean 0 and variance σ_e^2. Thus, given the value of i_{t-1} that occurred at the last period, the random variable $\underline{i}_t$ is normal with mean $\mu_i + k(i_{t-1} - \mu_i)$ and variance σ_e^2. Additional assumptions regarding this model are (i) $\underline{e}_t$ is independent of all "previous" $\underline{e}$'s (*i.e.*, $\underline{e}_{t-1}, \underline{e}_{t-2}, \ldots$), and (ii) $|k| < 1$. Research into autoregressive interest rate models has shown that such models allow for convenient analysis of accumulated amount and annuity random variables, and such models are often reasonable representations of actual interest rate series.

EXAMPLE C.5

Smith makes monthly deposits of 1 each for 3 years. The bank credits interest monthly, with the rate adjusted every month. Smith has been following interest rate movements for a while, and formulates the model $\underline{i}_t^{(12)} = .09 + .5(i_{t-1}^{(12)} - .09) + \underline{e}_t$, where t is measured in months and $\underline{e}_t$ is normally distributed with mean 0 and standard deviation .01. $\underline{e}_t$ is assumed to be independent of all previous $\underline{e}$'s. Assuming that $i_0^{(12)}$, the nominal annual interest rate for the month prior to Smith's first deposit, was .09, use simulation to estimate the mean and variance of the accumulated value of Smith's deposits one month after the final deposit.

SOLUTION

We apply the inversion method to generate the 36 independent values e_1, $e_2, \ldots, e_{36}$. These are then used to simulate $i_1^{(12)} = .09 + e_1$, $i_2^{(12)} = .09 + .5\left(i_1^{(12)} - .09\right) + e_2, \ldots, \quad i_{36}^{(12)} = .09 + .5(i_{35}^{(12)} - .09) + e_{36}$, as one sequence of nominal interest rates. The monthly interest rate earned is $\frac{i_t^{(12)}}{12}$, so that the accumulated value of the deposits is

$$\left[\left[\cdots\left[\left[\left(1 + \frac{i_1^{(12)}}{12}\right) + 1\right]\left(1 + \frac{i_2^{(12)}}{12}\right) + 1\right]\cdots\right] + 1\right]\left(1 + \frac{i_{36}^{(12)}}{12}\right).$$

A simulation of 10,000 trials (10,000 sequences of 36 nominal rates each) results in a sample mean of 41.4652 and a sample variance of .05284. Note that every month the expected rate of interest is $i^{(12)} = .09$, and $\ddot{s}_{\overline{36}|.0075} = 41.4614$. However, because of the dependence of each i_t on the previous i's, it is *not* true that $E[\ddot{s}_{\overline{36}|}] = \ddot{s}_{\overline{36}|.0075}$. (Recall that the identity $E[\ddot{s}_{\overline{n}|}] = \ddot{s}_{\overline{n}|i}$ is true only in the case of independent periodic rates of interest.) □

C.3 SAMPLE SIZE AND CONFIDENCE INTERVALS

When a random sample is taken from a distribution, it is possible to use the sample to formulate an approximate confidence interval for the mean of the distribution. Suppose that X has mean μ and variance σ^2. If the random sample $x_1, x_2, \ldots, x_k$ is taken from the distribution of X, then an approximate 95% confidence interval for μ is

$$\left(\bar{x} - \frac{1.96\sigma}{\sqrt{k}}, \bar{x} + \frac{1.96\sigma}{\sqrt{k}}\right). \tag{C.4}$$

For a 99% confidence interval, replace 1.96 with 2.58. (As before, these are the 97.5 and 99.5 percentiles of the standard normal distribution.) If σ is unknown and k is "large enough," then the sample standard deviation s

is used as an estimate of σ. Recall that $s^2 = \frac{1}{k-1} \cdot \sum_{i=1}^{k}(x_i - \bar{x})^2$ is the sample variance.

In the context of a simulation, k would be the number of simulated trials. The following example illustrates the construction of confidence intervals based on the sample obtained in a simulation.

| **EXAMPLE C.6** |

The discussion following Example C.1 gives the sample mean and sample variance for simulations of $\underline{S}(10)$ and $\ddot{s}_{\overline{10|}}$ for several different numbers of trials, when

$$\underline{i} = \begin{cases} .10, & \text{with probability .50} \\ .15, & \text{with probability .50} \end{cases}$$

and interest rates are independent from year to year. Use that information to find the corresponding 95% and 99% confidence intervals for the means of $\underline{S}(10)$ and $\ddot{s}_{\overline{10|}}$ if (a) the exact σ is used, and (b) the sample standard deviation s is used.

| **SOLUTION** |

For $\underline{S}(10)$ we saw that the sample mean for 100 simulations was 3.2419, the exact variance was $\sigma^2 = .052190$, and the sample variance was $s^2 = .054229$. Using the exact variance the 95% interval will be $3.2419 \pm 1.96 \cdot \sqrt{\frac{.052190}{100}} = (3.1971, 3.2867)$; using the sample variance the interval will be $3.2419 \pm 1.96 \cdot \sqrt{\frac{.054229}{100}} = (3.1963, 3.2875)$. Table C.6a gives the intervals for $\underline{S}(10)$ using the exact standard deviation, and Table C.6b gives the corresponding intervals using the sample standard deviation.

| **TABLE C.6a** |

Sample Size (No. of Simulations)	95% interval for $\underline{S}(10)$	99% interval for $\underline{S}(10)$
100	(3.1971, 3.2867)	(3.1834, 3.3004)
1,000	(3.2320, 3.2604)	(3.2277, 3.2647)
10,000	(3.2432, 3.2522)	(3.2419, 3.2535)
100,000	(3.2459, 3.2487)	(3.2455, 3.2491)

TABLE C.6b		
Sample Size (No. of Simulations)	95% interval for $\underline{S}(10)$	99% interval for $\underline{S}(10)$
100	(3.1963 , 3.2875)	(3.1823 , 3.3015)
1,000	(3.2318 , 3.2606)	(3.2273 , 3.2651)
10,000	(3.2431 , 3.2523)	(3.2417 , 3.2537)
100,000	(3.2459 , 3.2487)	(3.2454 , 3.2492)

The same approach can be taken for $\ddot{s}_{\overline{10|}}$, which has an exact variance of .986107 and sample means and variances listed after Example 5.8. Intervals for $\ddot{s}_{\overline{10|}}$ using the exact standard deviation are given in Table C.7a, and those using the sample standard deviation are given in Table C.7b.

TABLE C.7a		
Sample Size (No. of Simulations)	95% interval for $\ddot{s}_{\overline{10|}}$	99% interval for $\ddot{s}_{\overline{10|}}$
100	(20.044 , 20.433)	(19.984 , 20.493)
1,000	(20.145 , 20.268)	(20.126 , 20.287)
10,000	(20.206 , 20.245)	(20.200 , 20.251)
100,000	(20.219 , 20.232)	(20.218 , 20.234)

TABLE C.7b		
Sample Size (No. of Simulations)	95% interval for $\ddot{s}_{\overline{10|}}$	99% interval for $\ddot{s}_{\overline{10|}}$
100	(20.036 , 20.441	(19.974 , 20.503)
1,000	(20.146 , 20.268)	(20.127 , 20.286)
10,000	(20.205 , 20.245)	(20.199 , 20.251)
100,000	(20.219 , 20.232)	(20.218 , 20.234)

□

Note that for both $\underline{S}(10)$ and $\underline{\ddot{s}}_{\overline{10}|}$ in Example C.4, as the sample size increases the width of the confidence interval tends to decrease, producing a more accurate interval estimate for the mean of the distribution. Since the width of the 95% interval is $2 \times 1.96 \times \sqrt{\frac{\sigma \text{ or } s}{k}}$, where k is the sample size, it is possible to find the number of simulations required for an approximate interval of a specified accuracy. (If σ is not known the sample value s from an initial sample can be used.)

Just before Example C.2 simulation was used to estimate the probability $Pr[\underline{\ddot{s}}_{\overline{30}|} \leq 300]$ when annual interest rates were independent and either .10 or .15, each with probability .50. When estimating a proportion p, by counting the number of "successes" j in a series of n trials and calculating the sample proportion $\hat{p} = j/n$, it is possible to formulate a confidence interval for the proportion p. An approximate 95% confidence interval for p based on the sample value $\hat{p}$ is

$$CI = \hat{p} \pm 1.96 \cdot \sqrt{\frac{\hat{p}(1-\hat{p})}{n}}; \qquad (C.5)$$

intervals of different percent confidence are found by replacing the 1.96 value. For the problem of finding $Pr[\underline{\ddot{s}}_{\overline{30}|} \leq 300]$, the probability is estimated in the simulation by j/n, where j is the number of trials resulting in a value of $\underline{\ddot{s}}_{\overline{30}|}$ less than 300 and n is the total number of trials. 5277 of the first 10,000 trials resulted in a value of $\underline{\ddot{s}}_{\overline{30}|}$ less than 300, so the estimate of the probability based on 10,000 trials is $\hat{p} = .5277$, and the approximate 95% confidence interval for $Pr[\underline{\ddot{s}}_{\overline{30}|} \leq 300]$ is $.5277 \pm 1.96 \cdot \sqrt{\frac{.5277(1-.5277)}{10,000}} = (.5179, .5374)$. When all 100,000 trials are used, the estimate becomes $\hat{p} = .52969$, and the approximate 95% interval becomes $.52969 \pm 1.96 \cdot \sqrt{\frac{.52969(1-.52969)}{100,000}} = (.52660, .53278)$.

For proportions it is also possible to determine the sample size n necessary to obtain a confidence interval of a specified width. Since $\hat{p}$ is always between 0 and 1, the quantity $\hat{p}(1 - \hat{p})$ is never larger than .25. In order to ensure an approximate 95% confidence interval of width no greater than w, we must choose n large enough so that $1.96 \times \sqrt{\frac{.25}{n}} \leq w$.

Exercises 1.2

1.2.1 $i \leq .04$

1.2.2 12.04%, -21.57%

1.2.3   (a) 278.93

1.2.4   (a) $X = 1 + j_1 t_1$ (b) $X = \dfrac{1 + it}{1 + j_2(t - t_1)}$

       (e)

j_1	X	j_2
.03	1.0073	.1807
.08	1.0195	.1530
.13	1.0317	.1260
.18	1.0439	.0996
.23	1.0561	.0738

1.2.5   224.5 days, or August 12 or 13

1.2.6 $i = 1.0735$, $i = .6759$,   913.32,   451 days

1.2.7   (a) $i \leq .4069$ (b) $i \leq \left(\dfrac{j}{1-j}\right) \cdot \left(\dfrac{365}{n-m}\right)$

1.2.9   (a) (i) 1.07   (ii)   1.06

1.2.10 (a) $\dfrac{3a + b}{2} < c$ (b) 720   (c) $a + b - c$

1.2.11 (a) 3500   (b) 3700.61   (c) 3714.87   (d) 3722.16

1.2.12 (a) $(1.0075)^{67/17} = 1.0299 < 1.03$;
$(1.0075)^{68/17} = (1.0075)^4 = 1.0303$
(b) $(1.015)^{67/17} = 1.0604 > 1.06$

1.2.16 .8853

1.2.17 (a) 10.25%

Exercises 1.3

1.3.1   (b) At focal time t,
$$P_0(1 + it) = P_s[1 + i(t - s)] = K \rightarrow \frac{P_0(1 + it)}{1 + i(t - s)} = P_s$$
At focal time 0,
$$P_0 = \frac{K}{1 + it}, \quad \frac{P_s}{1 + is} = \frac{K}{1 + it} \rightarrow P_0(1 + is) = P_s$$

(c) (a) $P_0 = 909.09$, $P_{1/2} = 953.46$
(b) Focal time t, $P_0 = 909.09$, $P_{1/2} = 952.38$
Focal time 0, $P_0 = 909.09$, $P_{1/2} = 954.55$

1.3.2   (a) $B_1 = B_0(1 + i) + \displaystyle\sum_{k=1}^{n} a_k[1 + i(1 - t_k)]$

$= B_0 + \displaystyle\sum_{k=1}^{n} a_k + \left[B_0 + \sum_{k=1}^{n} a_k(1 - t_k) \right] \cdot i$

$\dfrac{B_0 t_1 + (B_0 + a_1)(t_2 - t_1) + (B_0 + a_1 + a_2)(t_3 - t_2) + \cdots + (B_0 + a_1 + a_2 + \cdots + a_n)(1 - t_n)}{t_1 + (t_2 - t_1) + (t_3 - t_2) + \cdots + (1 - t_n)}$

$= B_0 + a_1(1 - t_1) + a_2(1 - t_2) + \cdots + a_n(1 - t_n)$

$= B_0 + \displaystyle\sum_{k=1}^{n} a_k(1 - t_k)$.

1.3.3   1492.00

1.3.4 $X = 4997$

1.3.5 $X = 379.48$

1.3.6   903.98

1.3.7   1-month rate of .01 $\rightarrow X = 67.98$
3-month rate if .03 $\rightarrow X = 67.57$

1.3.8 $j < k$

1.3.9 $i = 26.92\%$

1.3.10 $1000 \cdot v^3_{.06} \cdot v^4_{.07} \cdot v^3_{.09} = 494.62$

1.3.11   (a) 1,607,391   (b) 1,747,114   (c) 1,795,551

1.3.12 $j = .0389$

1.3.13   12.68

1.3.14   (a) $\frac{d}{di}(1+i)^n = n(1+i)^{n-1}$ (b) $\frac{d}{di} v^n = -nv^{n+1}$

(c) $\frac{d}{dn}(1+i)^n = (1+i)^n \ln(1+i)$ (d) $\frac{d}{dn} v^n = -v^n \ln(1+i)$

1.3.15   (a) 13,150   (b) 13,160.27
(c) 13,150.76   (d) 13,161.12

1.3.16   (a) P.V. $= \dfrac{1}{1 + i(1-t)}$ (b) P.V. $= \dfrac{1}{(1+i)^{1-t}}$

(c) $\dfrac{1}{1+i} \cdot [1 + it]$

1.3.18   (a) $i = .0769$ (b) i is smaller than that in (a)

1.3.19   75,686

1.3.20 $1000(1+i)^2 + 1092 = 2000(1+i)$, which gives no real roots

Exercises 1.4

1.4.1 $m = 4$; nominal rate of 16% cannot accumulate to an effective rate of more than 17.35%

1.4.3   (b) .1080

1.4.4 $m = \frac{365}{45} = 8.1111$, $i = .104495$

1.4.5   (a) $i^{(.5)} = 105$, $i^{(.25)} = .116025$

$i^{(.1)} = .159374$, $i^{(.01)} = 137.796$

(b) $i = .0954$,   .0878,   .0718,   .0472

(c) $\lim_{m \to 0} f(m) = 1$, $\lim_{m \to 0} g(m) = \infty$

1.4.6   (a) 414.64 (b) 409.30 (c) 407.94

1.4.7 $i^{(365)} \geq .144670$

1.4.8 $-.007479$

1.4.9   Binomial expansion: $i = \left(1 + \frac{i^{(m)}}{m}\right)^m - 1$

$$= \left[1 + m \cdot \frac{i^{(m)}}{m} + \frac{m(m-1)}{2} \cdot \left(\frac{i^{(m)}}{m}\right)^2 + \frac{m(m-1)(m-2)}{3!} \cdot \left(\frac{i^{(m)}}{m}\right)^3 + \cdots\right] - 1$$

1.4.10   .1365

Exercises 1.5

1.5.4   (a) Discount from $t = 1$ to $t = \frac{1}{2}$ is $(.50)(1)$, Discount from $t = \frac{1}{2}$ to $t = 0$ is $(.50)(.50) = .25$
(b) $d^{(m)} \leq m$

1.5.6   .1154

1.5.7   (b) $d = \frac{i}{1+i} = i[1 - i + i^2 - i^3 + i^4 - \cdots]$

1.5.8 (a) True; (b) True; (c) True; (d) False; (e) True; (f) True; (g) False

1.5.10 (a) $d = .1 \rightarrow d^{(.5)} = .095, d^{(.25)} = .085975, d^{(.1)} = .065132,$
        $d^{(.01)} = .010000$

      (b) $d^{(.5)} = .1 \rightarrow d = .105573, d^{(.25)} = .1 \rightarrow d = .119888,$
        $d^{(.1)} = .1 \rightarrow d = 1; d^{(.01)} = .1$ has no meaning since $d^{(m)}$ must
        be $\leq m$

1.5.11 1 month effective interest $= .009902$, discount $= .009805$
       2 month effective interest $= .019901$, discount $= .019513$
       3 month effective interest $= .03$, discount $= .029126$
       4 month effective interest $= .040199$, discount $= .038645$
       6 month effective interest $= .0609$, discount $= .057404$
       1 year effective interest $= .125509$, discount $= .111513$

1.5.12 $1 + k < \left(1 + \frac{k}{2}\right)^2 < \left(1 - \frac{k}{2}\right)^{-2} < (1-k)^{-1}$

1.5.13 $i^{(m)} - d^{(m)} = \frac{i^{(m)} d^{(m)}}{m}$

1.5.14 (a) $i = \frac{365}{n}\left[\frac{1}{1 - d \cdot \frac{n}{365}} - 1\right] = \frac{d}{1 - d \cdot \frac{n}{365}}$; as n increases, i
        increases
      (b) $t = 1 \rightarrow d = .099099, t = .50 \rightarrow d = .104265, t = \frac{1}{12} \rightarrow$
        $d = .109001$

1.5.15 .1287

1.5.16 $i = .0909$

1.5.18 .0976

1.5.20 (a) $m = 6$ (b) $d = .1377$

1.5.21 $j = .0436$

1.5.22 (a) 5187.84   (b) 5191.68   (c) 5204.52   (d) 5200

1.5.23 (a) $P = 95{,}250.52$

   (b) $\dfrac{dP}{di} = -45{,}239.03$ if $i = .10$, $\quad \Delta P \approx -45.24$

   (c) $\dfrac{dP}{di} = -23{,}733.34$ if $i = .10$; as T-bill approaches maturity, volatility goes to 0

1.5.24 Smith: annual effective rate of .1701
            annual simple interest rate of $= .1587$
         Brown: annual effective rate of .0653
            annual simple interest rate of .0647

1.5.26 (a) $d = .1515$

1.5.27 $\dfrac{i^{(m)} - d^{(m)}}{i^{(m)}d^{(m)}} = \dfrac{1}{d^{(m)}} - \dfrac{1}{i^{(m)}} = \dfrac{1}{m}$

1.5.28 (a) $\dfrac{d}{di^{(m)}} d^{(m)} = \dfrac{1}{\left(1 + \frac{i^{(m)}}{m}\right)^2}$ (b) $\dfrac{d}{dd} i = \dfrac{1}{(1-d)^2}$

Exercises 1.6

1.6.1 (a) $\dfrac{S(t + \frac{1}{m}) - S(t)}{S(t + \frac{1}{m})}$

   (b) $d^{(m)} = m \cdot \dfrac{S(t + \frac{1}{m}) - S(t)}{S(t + \frac{1}{m})} = \dfrac{S(t + \frac{1}{m}) - S(t)}{\frac{1}{m} \cdot S(t + \frac{1}{m})}$

   (c) $\lim\limits_{m \to \infty} d^{(m)} \dfrac{S'(t)}{S(t)}$

1.6.2 (a) 328.77   (b) 328.82

1.6.3 (a) $d^{(2)} = \delta - \dfrac{\delta^2}{4} + \dfrac{\delta^3}{24} - \dfrac{\delta^4}{192} + \cdots$

   (b) $d^{(m)}\delta - \dfrac{\delta^2}{2m} + \dfrac{\delta^3}{6m^2} - \dfrac{\delta^4}{24m^3} + \cdots,$

   $i^{(m)} = \delta + \dfrac{\delta^2}{2m} + \dfrac{\delta^3}{6m^2} + \dfrac{\delta^4}{24m^3} + \cdots$

   $\dfrac{i^{(m)} + d^{(m)}}{2} = \delta + \dfrac{\delta^3}{6m^2} + \cdots$

(c) $\delta = d^{(2)} + \dfrac{(d^{(2)})^2}{4} + \dfrac{(d^{(2)})^3}{12} + \dfrac{(d^{(2)})^4}{32} + \cdots$

1.6.5 (a) 4150.62 (b) 3951.27 (c) 4051.90

1.6.6 .06825

1.6.8 (a) 1044.73

(b) For $0 < t \le \frac{1}{4}$, $S(t) = 1000[1 + (.08)t]$

for $\frac{1}{4} \le t \le \frac{1}{2}$, $S(t) = 1000(1.02)[1 + (.08)(t - \frac{1}{4})]$

for $\frac{1}{2} \le t \le \frac{3}{4}$, $S(t) = 1000(1.02)^2[1 + (.08)(t - \frac{1}{2})]$

for $\frac{3}{4} \le t \le 1$, $S(t) = 1000(1.02)^3[1 + (.08)(t - \frac{3}{4})]$

1.6.9 (a) $i = .1008$

(b) $i_1 = .091629$, $i_2 = .099509$, $i_3 = .102751$

$i_4 = .104532$, $i_5 = .105659$

(c) 821.00

1.6.12 1215

1.6.13 $i' > 2i$, $d' < 2d$

1.6.15 (a) $i = .10$, $i^{(12)} = .0957$, $i^{(2)} = .0976$, $d = .0909$, $d^{(12)} = .0949$,
$\delta = .0953$

(b) $i = .1047$, $i^{(12)} = .1$, $i^{(2)} = .1021$, $d = .0948$, $d^{(12)} = .0992$,
$\delta = .0996$

(c) $i = .1025$, $i^{(12)} = .0980$, $i^{(2)} = .1$, $d = .0930$, $d^{(12)} = .0972$,
$\delta = .0976$

(d) $i = .1111$, $i^{(12)} = .1058$, $i^{(2)} = .1082$, $d = .1$, $d^{(12)} = .1049$,
$\delta = .1054$

(e) $i = .1056$, $i^{(12)} = .1008$, $i^{(2)} = .1030$, $d = .0955$, $d^{(12)} = .1$,
$\delta = .1004$

(f) $i = .1080$, $i^{(12)} = .1030$, $i^{(2)} = .1053$, $d = .0975$, $d^{(12)} = .1$
$\delta = .1026$

(g) $i = .1052, i^{(12)} = .1004, i^{(2)} = .1025, d = .0952, d^{(12)} = .0996,$
$\delta = .1$

1.6.16 $\dfrac{d}{dt}\,\delta_t = \dfrac{d}{dt}\,\dfrac{S'(t)}{S(t)} = \dfrac{S(t)S''(t) - [S'(t)]^2}{[S(t)]^2}$

1.6.17 $S(t) = S_1(t) \cdot S_2(t)$

1.6.18 $S(t) = exp\left[\dfrac{(1+t)^{-k+1} - 1}{-k+1} \cdot ln(B)\right]$

1.6.19 $\dfrac{d}{d\delta}\,i = \dfrac{d}{d\delta}\,(e^\delta - 1) = e^\delta,\ \dfrac{d}{d\delta}\,d = \dfrac{d}{d\delta}\,(1 - e^{-\delta}) = e^{-\delta}$

$\dfrac{d}{d\delta}\,i^{(m)} = \dfrac{d}{d\delta}\,m(e^{\delta/m} - 1) = e^{\delta/m}$

$\dfrac{d}{d\delta}\,d^{(m)} = \dfrac{d}{d\delta}\,m(1 - e^{-\delta/m}) = e^{-\delta/m}$

Exercises 1.7

1.7.1 (a) $i_{real} = -.043478$
       (b) Net gain is 5,000 (in year-end dollars)

1.7.2 $-.0309$

1.7.3 (b) The real growth in taxes paid will be 1.015873 (1.59%) and the real growth in ATI is .990476 $= 1 - .009524$

1.7.5 $i = .070175$

1.7.6 One year from now, 1000 U.S. $\equiv$ 1382.43 Cdn., or equivalently, .7233 U.S. $\equiv$ 1 Cdn.

1.7.8 (a) Real after tax rate of return on standard term deposit is
       $\dfrac{i(1 - t_x) - r}{1 + r}$ and on inflation-adjusted term deposit is
       $\dfrac{r + i'(1+r)(1-t_x) - r}{1 + r}$.
       (b) If $i' = .02$ and $r = .12$, then i equals (i) .1424   (ii) .1824
       (iii) .2224   (iv) .3224

Exercises 2.2

2.2.2 3665.12,   36.65

2.2.3 (a) 2328.82

2.2.4 (a) 10.4622,   10.5098,   10.5576,   10.6057,   10.6541,   10.7027,
10.9497,   11.4639,   12.0061,   12.5779,   15.9374,   20.3037,
25.9587,   33.2529,   113.3301,   1023

(b) $\dfrac{d}{di} s_{\overline{n}|i} = (n-1)(1+i)^{n-2} + (n-2)(1+i)^{n-3} + \cdots + 2(1+i) + 1$

$\dfrac{d^2}{di^2} s_{\overline{n}|i} = (n-1)(n-2)(1+i)^{n-3} + (n-2)(n-3)(1+i)^{n-4} + \cdots$

$+ 3 \cdot 2(1+i) + 2, \quad \dfrac{d^{n-1}}{di^{n-1}} s_{\overline{n}|i} = (n-1)!$

$\dfrac{d^n}{di^n} s_{\overline{n}|i} = 0$

(c) 10.5103, 10.5151

Follows from the convexity of $s_{\overline{n}|i}$ as function of i

(d) 10.5084, 15.9968

2.2.6 (a) $(1+i)^n = 2$, $i = .014286$, $s_{\overline{3n}|i} = 490$

(b) $v^n = \dfrac{1}{(1+i)^n}$

(c) .1355, -2.1630 (discard negative root)

2.2.7 640.72

2.2.8 (a) A.V. $= R\left(1 + \dfrac{i}{n}\right)^n - k \cdot s_{\overline{n}|i} = R(1+j)$, where j is the
effective annual earned rate

(b) (i) $n = 12$ (ii) $n = 3$ (iii) $n = 1$

2.2.9 $11S - 10$

2.2.10 $I_t = (1+i)^{t-1} - 1$

2.2.12 $n = 15 \rightarrow P = 14.53$; $n = 20 \rightarrow P = 17.19$; $n = 25 \rightarrow 20.75$

Exercises 2.3

2.3.1   An investment of amount 1 is equal to the present value of the return of principal in n years plus the present value of the interest generated over the n years.

2.3.3   (a) 2802.37

2.3.5   (a) 9.4713, 9.4207, 9.3704, 9.3207, 9.2712, 9.2222, 8.9826, 8.5302, 8.1109, 7.7217, 6.1446, 5.0188, 4.1925, 3.5705, 1.8896, .9990

   (b) $\dfrac{d}{di} a_{\overline{n}|i} = -v^2 - 2v^3 - \cdots - (n-1)v^n - nv^{n+1}$

   $\dfrac{d^2}{di^2} a_{\overline{n}|i}$

   $= -3 \cdot 2v^3 - 4 \cdot 3v^4 - \cdots - n(n-1)v^{n+1} - (n+1)nv^{n+2}$

   (c) 9.4215, 9.1214

   Follows from the convexity of $a_{\overline{n}|i}$ as function of i

   (d) 9.4205, 6.1182

2.3.7 $P_1 = 1050$, $P_2 = 537.80$, $P_3 = 367.21$, $P_4 = 282.01$, $P_5 = 230.97$ $P_{10} = 129.50$, $P_{15} = 96.34$, $P_{20} = 80.24$, $P_{25} = 70.95$, $P_{50} = 54.78$, $P_{100} = 50.38$, $P_{200} = 50.00$, $P_{500} = P_{1000} = 50.00$

2.3.8 $\dfrac{d}{dn} s_{\overline{n}|i} = \dfrac{d}{dn} \dfrac{(1+i)^n - 1}{i} = \dfrac{(1+i)^n \ln(1+i)}{i}$

   $\dfrac{d}{dn} a_{\overline{n}|i} = \dfrac{d}{dn} \dfrac{1 - v^n}{i} = \dfrac{v^n \ln(1+i)}{i}$

2.3.11   (a) $K = 1079.68$

2.3.12 $\displaystyle\lim_{i \to 0} \dfrac{s_{\overline{n}|i}}{s_{\overline{m}|i}} = \lim_{i \to 0} \dfrac{a_{\overline{n}|i}}{a_{\overline{m}|i}} = \dfrac{n}{m}$

   If $n < m$, then $\displaystyle\lim_{i \to \infty} \dfrac{(1+i)^n - 1}{(1+i)^m - 1} = \lim_{i \to \infty} \dfrac{n}{m(1+i)^{m-n}} = 0$

   If $m < n$, then $\displaystyle\lim_{i \to \infty} \dfrac{(1+i)^n - 1}{(1+i)^m - 1} = \lim_{i \to \infty} \dfrac{n(1+i)^{n-m}}{m} = \infty$

2.3.13 $X = 573.76$, $Y = 449.54$

2.3.14 $a_{\overline{10}|} = 7.7748$, $s_{\overline{10}|}a_{\overline{10}|} = S(10) = (1.12)^{\sqrt{10}} = 1.4310$

2.3.15 7.3729

2.3.16 17th month

2.3.17 $Y = 19,788.47$

2.3.18 109,926

2.3.19 $v^n = .6180$

Exercises 2.4

2.4.3 $X = 294.84 = \dfrac{308.11}{1.045}$

2.4.4 (a) For $t > n$, $v^t \cdot s_{\overline{n}|} = v^{t-n} \cdot v^n \cdot s_{\overline{n}|} = v^{t-n} \cdot a_{\overline{n}|}$

(b) For $t > n$, $(1 + i)^t \cdot a_{\overline{n}|} = (1 + i)^{t-n} \cdot (1 + i)^n \cdot a_{\overline{n}|}$
$$= (1 + i)^{t-n} \cdot s_{\overline{n}|}$$

2.4.5 $i = .1539$

2.4.6 (a) 16.1409, $s_{\overline{n}|i} = \ddot{a}_{\overline{n}|}$ evaluated at $d = -i$

(b) $s_{\overline{-n}|i} = -a_{\overline{n}|i}$

2.4.7 (a) $v_i \cdot [1 + v_j] \cdot \dfrac{1}{1 - v_j \cdot v_i}$ (b) (i) $\dfrac{v + 2v^2}{1 - v^2}$ (ii) $\dfrac{1 + 2v}{1 - v^2}$

Exercises 2.5

2.5.1 (a) $i = (1 + j)^m - 1$, $(1 + i) = (1 + j)^m$, $v_i = v_j^m$

(b) $s_{\overline{n}|i} = \dfrac{(1 + i)^n - 1}{i} = \dfrac{[(1 + j)^m]^n - 1}{(1 + j)^m - 1}$

$\ddot{s}_{\overline{n}|i} = \dfrac{(1 + i)^n - 1}{1 - v_i} = \dfrac{[(1 + j)^m]^n - 1}{1 - v_j^m}$

(c) $s_{\overline{n}|i} = \dfrac{[(1+j)^m]^n - 1}{(1+j)^m - 1} = \dfrac{([(1+j)^m]^n - 1)\big/ i}{((1+j)^m - 1)\big/ i} = \dfrac{s_{\overline{m\cdot n}|j}}{s_{\overline{m}|j}}$

(e) $1 + i = e^{\delta} \rightarrow s_{\overline{n}|i} = \dfrac{(1+i)^n - 1}{i} = \dfrac{e^{n\delta} - 1}{e^{\delta} - 1}$

(f) $a_{\overline{\infty}|i} = \dfrac{1}{i} = \dfrac{1}{(1+j)^m - 1} = \dfrac{a_{\overline{\infty}|j}}{s_{\overline{m}|j}}, \quad \ddot{a}_{\overline{\infty}|i} = \dfrac{1}{d} = \dfrac{1}{1 - v_j^m} = \dfrac{a_{\overline{\infty}|j}}{a_{\overline{m}|j}}$

2.5.2   In all cases, j represents the 2-year effective rate of interest
(a) 10,123.81   (b) 6235.03   (c) 67,895.89
(d) 75,168.66   (e) 11,743.76

2.5.3   (a) $s_{\overline{m}|j} = \dfrac{(1+j)^m - 1}{j} = \dfrac{(1+j)^{m_0 + t} - 1}{j}$

$= \dfrac{(1+j)^{m_0 + t} - (1+j)^t + (1+j)^t - 1}{j}$

$= (1+j)^t \cdot \dfrac{(1+j)^{m_0} - 1}{j} + \dfrac{(1+j)^t - 1}{j}$

$= (1+j)^t \cdot s_{\overline{m_0}|j} + s_{\overline{t}|j}$

(c) Accumuated value is $100 s_{\overline{10}|.075}(1.075)^{1/2} + 50 = 1516.80$

$100 s_{\overline{10.5}|.075} = 100 \dfrac{(1.075)^{10.5} - 1}{.075} = 1515.90$

2.5.4 $1 + i = (1+j)^m, \ 1 + j = (1+i)^{1/m}, \ v_i = v_j^m, \ v_j = v_i^{1/m}$

(a) $\dfrac{1}{m} \cdot s_{\overline{n\cdot m}|j} = \dfrac{1}{m} \cdot \dfrac{(1+j)^{n\cdot m} - 1}{j} = \dfrac{1}{m} \cdot \dfrac{(1+i)^n - 1}{(1+i)^{1/m} - 1}$

(b) $\dfrac{1}{m} \cdot a_{\overline{n\cdot m}|j} = \dfrac{1}{m} \cdot \dfrac{1 - v_j^{n\cdot m}}{j} = \dfrac{1}{m} \cdot \dfrac{1 - v_i^n}{(1+i)^{1/m} - 1}$

(c) $\dfrac{1}{m} \cdot \ddot{s}_{\overline{n\cdot m}|j} = \dfrac{1}{m} \cdot \dfrac{(1+j)^{n\cdot m} - 1}{d_j} = \dfrac{1}{1 - v_j} = \dfrac{1}{m} \cdot \dfrac{(1+i)^n - 1}{1 - v_i^{1/m}}$

(d) $\dfrac{1}{m} \cdot s_{\overline{n \cdot m}|j} = \cdot \dfrac{(1+i)^n - 1}{m[(1+i)^{1/m} - 1]} = \dfrac{(1+i)^n - 1}{i^{(m)}}$

$$= \dfrac{(1+i)^n - 1}{i} \cdot \dfrac{i}{i^{(m)}} = s_{\overline{n}|i} \cdot \dfrac{i}{i^{(m)}}$$

$\dfrac{1}{m} \cdot \ddot{a}_{\overline{n \cdot m}|j} = \dfrac{1}{m} \dfrac{1 - v_j^{n \cdot m}}{d_j} = \dfrac{1 - v_j}{1 - v_i^n} = \dfrac{1 - v_i^n}{m[1 - v_i^{1/m}]} = \dfrac{1 - v_i^m}{d^{(m)}}$

$$= \dfrac{1 - v_i^m}{d_i} \dfrac{d}{d^{(m)}} = \ddot{a}_{\overline{n}|j} \cdot \dfrac{d}{d^{(m)}}$$

(h) Exact:
      10.00   9.5146 8.8519 7.8971 6.4213 4.5641 2.3828
Approximate:
      10.00   9.5147 8.8523 7.8987 6.4262 4.5768 2.4157

2.5.5   The 2-month effective rate is j
    (a) $25a_{\overline{36}|j} = 150a_{\overline{6}|.06}^{(6)} = 755.83$ where $j = (1.015)^{1/3} - 1$
    (b) $25v_j^4\, a_{\overline{36}|j} = 50v_{.02}^2\, a_{\overline{18}|.02}^{(2)} = 724.08$ where $j = (1.02)^{1/2} - 1$
    (c) $25v_j^3\, a_{\overline{36}|j} = 730.92$ where $j = (1.015)^{2/3} - 1$
    (d) $25(1+j)s_{\overline{36}|j} = 1092.02$ where $j = (.97)^{-1/3} - 1$
    (e) $25(1+j)^6 s_{\overline{36}|j} = 1144.57$ where $j = e^{.01} - 1$

2.5.6 $Y = \dfrac{100d^{(12)}}{12d^{(4)}}$

2.5.10 (a) $s_{\overline{1}|}^{(m)} = 1 + i \cdot \dfrac{m-1}{2m}$ (b) $a_{\overline{1}|}^{(m)} = 1 - d \cdot \dfrac{m+1}{2m}$

2.5.11 (c) $a_{\overline{n}|i} < a_{\overline{n}|i}^{(m)} < \bar{a}_{\overline{n}|i} < \ddot{a}_{\overline{n}|i}^{(m)} < \ddot{a}_{\overline{n}|i}$ (d) $\bar{s}_{\overline{n}|i} = 1 + \dfrac{i}{2}$

Exercises 2.6

2.6.2 (a) $\bar{s}_{\overline{n}|} = \int_0^n e^{\int_t^n \delta_r\, dr}\, dt,\quad \bar{a}_{\overline{n}|} = \int_0^n e^{-\int_0^t \delta_r\, dr}\, dt$
    (b) $\bar{s}_{\overline{n}|} = n\left(1 + \dfrac{in}{2}\right),\quad \bar{a}_{\overline{n}|} = dt = \dfrac{ln(1 + in)}{i}$

2.6.3 $\bar{a}_{\overline{n}|} = \dfrac{1 - e^{-pn}}{p} + \dfrac{1 - e^{-(p+s)n}}{r(p+s)}$

Exercises 2.7

2.7.1 $X = 447.24$ (b) December 31, 2003, 290.30

2.7.2   1161.36

2.7.3   (a) $K' \le 2K$

2.7.4   (a) 90.15   (b) $K \cdot \left[\frac{(1+i)^k - 1}{i} - k \right]$

2.7.5   (a) $\dfrac{dn}{di} = \dfrac{\left[\frac{\delta \cdot L}{K - LiK} + v \cdot ln(1 - \frac{Li}{K}) \right]}{\delta^2}$

$\dfrac{dn}{dK} = \dfrac{-Li}{\delta K(K - Li)}, \quad \dfrac{dn}{dL} = \dfrac{i}{\delta(K - Li)}$

(b) $\dfrac{dn}{di} = \dfrac{\left[\frac{\delta \cdot M}{J + Mi} - v \cdot ln(1 + \frac{Mi}{J}) \right]}{\delta^2}$

$\dfrac{dn}{dJ} = \dfrac{-Mi}{\delta J(J + Mi)}, \quad \dfrac{dM}{dn} = \dfrac{i}{\delta(J + Mi)}$

2.7.6   (a) (i) July 1, 1991   (ii) February 28, 1992
        (b) (i) January 10, 1992   (ii) January 1, 1993

2.7.7   April 30, 2003

2.7.8   26 deposits

2.7.9   (a) 23   (b) 22   (c) (a) $n = 22.0896$ (b) $n = 21.117$

2.7.10 (a) 3-terms - $n \ge 30.63$; 4-terms - $n \ge 28.8$
        (b) 2 terms - $n = 24.8$; 3 terms - $n = 29.7$
        (c) (i) $n_0 = 10, n_1 = 9.31, n_2 = 8.65 , \ldots$
             $n_0 = 20, n_1 = 19.34, n_2 = 18.66$
        (ii) $n_0 = 10, n_1 = 10.71, n_2 = 11.44 , \ldots, n_{50} = 28.41$
             $n_{75} = 28.66, n_{100} = 28.68$
             $n_0 = 20, n_1 = 20.63, n_2 = 21.23 , \ldots$

(d) $n_0 = 10, n_1 = -10.43, \ldots, n_0 = 20, n_1 = 35.95$
$n_2 = 29.99, n_3 = 28.74, n_4 = 28.68$

2.7.11 January 1, 2016

2.7.12 $X = 490.85$ on April 1, 1999

2.7.13 (a) (i) .022200   (ii) .022098
(b) With $f(i) = a_{\overline{8}|i} - 7.260287$, we have $f(.02) > 0 > f(.025)$
Then $f(.0225) < 0 < f(.02), f(.0225) < 0 < f(.02125) \rightarrow$
$i = .021875$ is within .001
(c) $i = .02207882$

2.7.14 (a) With $i_0 = .02$, we have $i_1 = .020180$, $i_2 = .020345$
$i_3 = .020497$, $i_4 = .020637$, $i_5 = .020765$, $i_6 = .020883$
$i_7 = .020990$, $i_8 = .021089$, $i_9 = .021179$, $i_{10} = .021261$
$i_{11} = .021336, i_{12} = .021404, i_{13} = .021466, \ldots$

2.7.16 (a) $i_0 = .10, i_1 = .292002, i_2$ does not exist
(b) $i_1 = .119367, i_2 = .128099, i_3 = .131620, \ldots$
(c) $i_1 = .069149, i_2 = .034713, \ldots$

2.7.18 $i = \dfrac{B - A - 1}{A}$

2.7.19 (a) $i = \dfrac{1}{A} - \dfrac{1}{B}$ (b) $i = \dfrac{1}{A} - \dfrac{B - A}{A^2}$
(c) $v^{2n} \cdot B = a_{\overline{2n}|} = A(1 + v^n) \rightarrow B(v^n)^2 - A \cdot v^n - A = 0$
$\rightarrow$ solve quadratic for v^n in terms of B and A then substitute
into $A = \dfrac{1 - v^n}{i}$ to solve for i (the quadratic has one positive
and negative root)

2.7.20 (a) $i = .0875$
(b) By interpolation at 1% intervals we find that i is between .09
and .10; interpolated value is .094

2.7.25 $i = .076$

Exercises 2.8

2.8.2 1508

2.8.8 (i) p.v. = 3875.57, a.v. = 33,247.03
(ii) p.v. = 3992.96, a.v. = 20,055.21
(iii) p.v. = 4091.73, a.v. = 12,016.45
(iv) p.v. = 4168.59, a.v. = 7148.51

2.8.9 (i) p.v. before deindexing = 168,620,
p.v. after deindexing = 84,310
(ii) p.v. before deindexing = 84,310,
p.v. after deindexing = 56,207
(iii)p.v. before deindexing = 56,207,
p.v. after deindexing = 42,155
(iv) p.v. before deindexing = 166,497,
p.v. after deindexing = 83,249
(v) p.v. before deindexing = 83,249,
p.v. after deindexing = 55,499
(vi) p.v. before deindexing = 164,354,
p.v. after deindexing = 82,117

2.8.12 $i^{(2)} = .21 \rightarrow \frac{d}{d\,i^{(2)}} K = 7459.13$
(or 74.59 per 1% increase in $i^{(2)}$)
$i^{(2)} = .13 \rightarrow \frac{d}{d\,i^{(2)}} K = 7101.66$
(or 71.02 per 1% increase in $i^{(2)}$)

2.8.14 $X = 44.98$

2.8.15 $\dfrac{500,000(1+i)^t}{19}$

2.8.16 $n = 19$, $X = 428.27$

2.8.17 (a) $n = 185.5$, $X = 532.46$ (b) $n = 99$, $X = 761.19$
(c) $n = 90$, $X = 37.95$
(d) Total withdrawn: (a) 185,532 (b) 148,271 (c) 144,901. The more rapidly the payments increase, the more quickly th' account is exhausted and the smaller the total withdrawn

2.8.18 (a) $n = 505$ (b) 5,569,741

2.8.19 $r = .0784$

2.8.20 $i \approx .08197$ by interpolation (exact value is .0820)

2.8.22 (b) $\dfrac{\ddot{a}_{\overline{k}|}}{(i \cdot a_{\overline{k}|})^2}$

2.8.23 (a) $27,823 = (.38)(73,871)$ (b) 36,766
(c) 57,639   (d) $X = 19,874$

2.8.28 $25a_{\overline{25}|} + 3(Da)_{\overline{25}|}$

2.8.29 (i) 30,407   (ii) 59,704   (iii) 151,906

2.8.30 (a) $i = .1014$ (b) $i = .1266$

2.8.33 p.v. $= 24.03$

Exercises 2.9

2.9.2 (a) (i) 7469.44   (ii) 6794.19   (iii) 3813.44
(b) (i) $i = .0830$ (ii) $i = .1368$ (iii) $i = .0885$

2.9.4 (a) $P = 7527.17$ (b) $P = 6590.70$ (c) $P = 7326.47$

2.9.6 (a) $P = 80,898$ (b) $S = 18,311$

2.9.9 $i^{(12)} = .1169$

2.9.11 $R = 22,250$

Exercises 3.2

3.2.1 $X = 115.60737$, $OB_1 = 894.3926$, $OB_2 = 787.7292$
$OB_3 = 679.9991$, $OB_4 = 455.5844$, $OB_5 = 228.9255$, $OB_6 = 0$

3.2.5 $L = 58{,}490.89$, $PR_1 = 15.09$, $OB_{60} = 46{,}424$, $I_{61} = 464.24$,
        $PR_{61} = 435.76$

3.2.6   (a) $K = 9.89\,(9.888857)$, $OB_{1mo} = 1000.11$, $OB_{2mo} = 1000.22$,
             $\ldots$, $OB_{12mo} = 1001.41$

        (d) $OB_{3yr} = 1004.79$, $OB_{6yr} = 1011.64$, $OB_{9yr} = 595.46$

        (e) $I_T = K \cdot (72 + 144) - 1000 = 1135.99$

             Interest in 1st year is 120.08,

             Principal repaid in 1st year is -1.41

3.2.8   Quarterly payment is 283.68, total interest paid is 404.15

3.2.9   (i) Total interest paid is $\dfrac{n \cdot L}{a_{\overline{n}|i}} - L$

        (ii) Total interest paid is
             $$L \cdot i \cdot [1 + \tfrac{n-1}{n} + \tfrac{n-2}{n} + \cdots + \tfrac{2}{n} + \tfrac{1}{n}] = L \cdot i \cdot \tfrac{n+1}{2}$$

3.2.13 (a) $OB_{10} = 58.40$
             Smaller payment at time 11 is 58.98

3.2.15

Year (t)	OB_t	I_t	PR_t
0	862		
1	706.00	43.10	156.00
2	542.20	35.30	163.80
3	370.21	27.11	171.99
4	189.62	18.51	180.59
5	0	9.48	189.62

3.2.16 $t = 35$ is June 1, 1992

3.2.17 (a) $i^{(12)} = .0495$ (b) $i^{(12)} = .15$

3.2.18 $t = 11$

3.2.19 (a) 67.50   (b) Final smaller payment is on February 1, 2001
                            of amount 109.54

3.2.22 $\frac{2}{3}$

3.2.23 $k \leq .1326$

3.2.24 Principal repaid in the first year is 478.75

3.2.25 (i) total interest $= 161,976$
  (ii) final smaller payment $= 734.49$ on October 1, 2004 , total interest $= 82,139$
  (iii) 112,875

3.2.26 (a) February 28, 2004, 22,418.47
  (b) 3,050,520
  (c) 2,050,520

3.2.27 (a) 4.1 - p.v. of int. $= 39.33$, p.v. of princ. $= 960.67$
  4.2 - p.v. of int. $= 356.16$, p.v. of princ. $= 2643.84$
  (b) p.v. of int. $= L\left[1 - \dfrac{nv^{n+1}}{a_{\overline{n}|}}\right]$, p.v. of princ. $= L \cdot \dfrac{nv^{n+1}}{a_{\overline{n}|}}$

3.2.28 $n = 27$

3.2.30 $K = 349.81$

3.2.33 (a) $OB_t = t \cdot a_{\overline{n-t}|i} + (Ia)_{\overline{n-t}|i}$,
  $I_t = t - 1 - n \cdot v^{n-t+1} + \ddot{a}_{\overline{n-t+1}|i}$, $PR_t = t - I_t$
  (b) $OB_t = (Da)_{\overline{n-t}|i}$, $I_t = n - t + 1 - a_{\overline{n-t+1}|i}$,
  $PR_t = n - t + 1 - I_t$

3.2.35 A - 541,184.58, B - 324,710.75, C - 134,104.67

3.2.38 (a) $OB_t = \displaystyle\int_t^n K_s \cdot v^{s-t}\, ds$ (prospective)

  $= L(1 + i)^t - \displaystyle\int_0^t K_s \cdot (1 + i)^{t-s}\, ds$ (retrospective)

  (c) $PR_{t_0 \to t_1} = OB_{t_0} - OB_{t_1}$, $I_{t_0 \to t_1} = \displaystyle\int_t^n K_s\, ds - PR_{t_0 \to t_1}$

3.2.39 (a) 15 yrs. - $I_t = 51,894.23$, 30 yrs. - $I_t = 115,838.19$
  (b) 15 yrs. - $I_t = 116,302.25$, 30 yrs. - $I_t = 270,300.53$

3.2.41 (a) Difference in interest is $K\left[\dfrac{12s_{\overline{3}|}}{a_{\overline{12}|}} - 3\right]$

3.2.42 (a) 6902.98   (b) 6699   (c) 6600

3.2.46 (a) $i^{(12)} = .06$: Monthly - $I_t = 93,290$
        (i) $I_t = 75,649$ (20 *yrs.* 50 *weeks*)

3.2.47 192,858

3.2.48 (a)

t	OB	PR	I
0	10,000	—	—
1	9400	600	900
2	8740	660	840
3	8014	726	774
4	7215.4	798.6	701.4
5	6336.94	878.46	621.54
6	5370.63	966.31	533.69
7	4307.69	1062.94	437.06
8	3152.31	1155.38	341.62
9	1904.49	1247.82	252.18
10	556.85	1347.64	152.36
11	0	556.85	44.55

Exercises 3.3

3.3.1 (a)

t	AV	OB	I	PR
1	6902.95	93,097.95	10,000	6902.95
2	14,358.13	85,641.87	9447.76	7455.18

3.3.2 (a) 100,000

3.3.4 $X = 13,454.36$

3.3.5 (b) $L = \dfrac{K \cdot s_{\overline{n}|j}}{1 + i \cdot s_{\overline{n}|j}}$

3.3.6 (a) $L = 94{,}274.53$ (b) 96,505.60

3.3.7 $L = \dfrac{\Sigma K_t \cdot v_j^t}{v_j^n + i \cdot s_{\overline{n}|_j}}$

3.3.8   16,856.67

3.3.9 (a) Total annual outlay $= 16{,}244.17$, $i' = .099566$
     (b) Total annual outlay $= 17{,}904.47$, $i' = .122837$

3.3.10 $j = .021322$

3.3.12 (a) 14,185.22
     (b) Amount in Sinking Fund at time loan is sold $= 31{,}656.34$
         (i)   87,162.04   (ii) 75,042.37
     (c) (i) $i_\alpha = .130206$, $i_\beta = .135051$
         (ii) $i_\alpha = .123749$, $i_\beta = .128183$

3.3.13 $j = .08 \rightarrow i = .113821$, $j = .12 \rightarrow i = .12$, $j = .16 \rightarrow$
     $i = .123487$

3.3.14 $X = 71.98$

Exercises 3.4

3.4.4 (b) $Y \geq 938{,}800$

3.4.5 $j = .049301$

3.4.9 $i_0 = 516.2\%$

3.4.10 $i_A = .253304$, $i_B = .253280$

3.4.11 (b) $r > .0388$

3.4.12 (b) $r = .1077$

3.4.13 (a) .10601   (b) .10508   (c) lender's yield $= .08617$

Exercises 3.5

3.5.2   (a) 17,795   (b) 16,723   (c) 16,165

3.5.4 $P = \dfrac{Y}{v_h^n + j \cdot a_{\overline{n}|j}}$

3.5.5   330,117

3.5.6 A - 94,343 B - 92,120

3.5.8   (a) .1169   (b) .10   (c) .0858

3.5.10   (a) at tax rate 25% 4.5.2 (a) 15,000, (b) 15,000, (c) 15,000
         (b) at tax rate 40% 4.5.2 (a) 13,323

3.5.11   (a) 75,942.28
         (b) 46,188.00

3.5.12   (a) .1132   (b) (i) .1034 (ii) .1081 (iii) .1132

3.5.15   Money-weighted return: A - .1049, B - .1036, C - .1029
         Time-weighted return: .1098 for A, B and C

3.5.16   Time-weighted return: 0
         Money-weighted return: .1689

3.5.17   .0910

3.5.19   Merchant's Rule: $X = 211.54$, U.S. Rule: $X = 212.16$

3.5.21   Straight-line: 41,078.46 each year,
         Actuarial: 16,058.78 in first year, 82,568.81 in 20th year

3.5.22   August 15th pmt. $= 328$, U.S. rule pmt. $= 328$,
         Merchant's Rule pmt. $= 324$

3.5.23   2882

Exercises 4.2

4.2.1   (a) 84.5069   (b) 84.8501   (c) 82.5199   (d) 82.9678

4.2.2 $i^{(2)} = .0525$

4.2.3 $21\frac{1}{2}$ years

4.2.4   I. False   II. True   III. False

4.2.5   Coupon rates are .0225 and .045

4.2.6 $i^{(2)} = .035$

4.2.7 $i^{(2)} = \dfrac{4r_2 - 2r_1}{1 + r_1 - r_2}$

4.2.8 $\dfrac{q \cdot r_1 + p \cdot r_2}{q + p}$

4.2.9   12 years

4.2.10 908.78

4.2.11 $H = .6446$

4.2.12 2000

4.2.13 875.38

4.2.14 $X = 114.28$

4.2.19 97.900

4.2.21 1076.67

4.2.23 (a) $\dfrac{\partial P}{\partial r} = F \cdot a_{\overline{n}|j}, \quad \dfrac{\partial P}{\partial j} = F \cdot \left[-n \cdot v_j^{n+1} - r \cdot v \cdot (Ia)_{\overline{n}|j} \right]$

$\dfrac{\partial P}{\partial n} = \dfrac{F \cdot (r - j) \cdot \delta \cdot v_j^n}{j}$

4.2.24 20-year issue requires (annual) coupon rate of .0834

4.2.25 (a) (i)   First opinion - gain of 1703.00
                    second opinion - 2512.05
        (b) (i)   First opinion - loss of 5836.05
                    second opinion - loss of 5027.01

4.2.27 (a) (i) 138,609,509   (b) (i) 138,606,077

Exercises 4.3

4.3.2 $n = 5, j = .025$

t	K_t	I_t	PR_t	OB_t
1	500	279.04	220.96	10,940.49
2	500	273.51	226.49	10,714.01
3	500	267.85	232.15	10,481.86
4	500	262.05	237.95	10,243.90
5	10,500	256.10	10,243.90	0

$n = 5, j = .075$

t	K_t	I_t	PR_t	OB_t
1	500	674.14	− 174.14	9,162.67
2	500	687.20	− 187.20	9,349.89
3	500	701.24	− 201.24	9,551.11
4	500	716.33	− 216.33	9,767.44
5	10,500	732.56	9,767.44	0

4.3.3 Total paid $= F + n \cdot F \cdot r$
        Total principal repaid $= P = F + F(r - j)a_{\overline{n}|j}$
        Total interest paid $= n \cdot F \cdot r - F(r - j)a_{\overline{n}|j12}$

4.3.4 90.47

4.3.5 13 years or 26 coupon periods

4.3.7 (a) 8764

4.3.9 (a) 8117.73, .06336 (b) 11,882.27, .09664 (c) cannot occur
(d) 29,039.25, .2483

Exercises 4.4

4.4.3 (b) $j_{10} = .032603$

4.4.4 (a) $n = 2$, $i^{(2)} = 0$; $n = 5$, $i^{(2)} = .056544$
$n = 10$, $i^{(2)} = .075610$; $n = 20$, $i^{(2)} = .084959$
$n = 30$, $i^{(2)} = .087875$
(b) $n = 2$, $i^{(2)} = .216517$; $n = 5$, $i^{(2)} = .149393$
$n = 10$, $i^{(2)} = .127669$; $n = 20$, $i^{(2)} = .117242$
$n = 30$, $i^{(2)} = .114072$

4.4.6 $P_C = P_1 + \frac{r_3 - r_1}{r_2 - r_1} \cdot (P_2 - P_1)$

4.4.7 (c) from (a) - $j = .055634$ ($i^{(2)} = .111268$)
from (b) - $j = .055876$ ($i^{(2)} = .111753$)

Exercises 4.5

4.5.1 1,768,084

4.5.2 85,565,872

4.5.3 11.5%

4.5.6 (a) (i) 84.95 (ii) 100.00 (iii) 117.59
(b) (i) 12.8% (ii) 10.0% (iii) 8.13%

4.5.10 (a) (i) 90.34 (ii) 85.23 (iii) 81.41
(b) (i) 110.68 (ii) 104.14 (iii) 100.00

4.5.13 (a) $\frac{1}{d}$ (b) 1 (if $n = 1$) (c) $\frac{(Ia)_{\overline{n}|}}{a_{\overline{n}|}}$ (d) n (e) 1
(f) $\frac{\frac{(n+1)}{2} \cdot r + n}{nr + 1}$

4.5.15   4.79

4.5.16   (a) $L = r \cdot \bar{a}_{\overline{n}|} + e^{-n\delta} \quad \rightarrow \quad \frac{dL}{d\delta} = -r(\bar{I}\bar{a})_{\overline{n}|} - ne^{-n\delta}$

4.5.17   (a) 722,854,822   (b) 25.0%   (c) 786,216,443,   22.3%

Exercises 5.2

5.2.1   (a) 1150   (b) 10,000   (c) 59,358.16   (d) .48

5.2.2   (a) $E[\underset{\sim}{k}] = .1394$
        (b) .174

5.2.3   .0039

5.2.4   mean $= 4.6610$, variance $= .3377$

5.2.10   (a) $E[1 + \underset{\sim}{i}] = E[e^{\underset{\sim}{\delta}}] = e^{.5\sigma^2 + \mu}$

(this the moment generating function of $\underset{\sim}{\delta}$ at $t = 1$: $M_{\underset{\sim}{\delta}}(1)$)

$Var[1 + \underset{\sim}{i}] = E[e^{2\underset{\sim}{\delta}}] - \left(E[e^{\underset{\sim}{\delta}}]\right)^2 = e^{.5\sigma^2(4) + \mu(2)} - e^{\sigma^2 + 2\mu}$

$= e^{\sigma^2 + 2\mu} \cdot (e^{\sigma^2} - 1)$

(b) $E[\underset{\sim}{i}] = e^{.5\sigma^2 + \mu} - 1$ and

$Var[\underset{\sim}{i}] = Var[1 + \underset{\sim}{i}] = e^{\sigma^2 + \mu} \cdot (e^{\sigma^2} - 1)$

$\rightarrow \quad \dfrac{Var[1 + \underset{\sim}{i}]}{\left(1 + E[\underset{\sim}{i}]\right)^2} = (e^{\sigma^2} - 1)$

$\rightarrow \quad \sigma^2 = \ln\left[1 + \dfrac{Var[1 + \underset{\sim}{i}]}{\left(1 + E[\underset{\sim}{i}]\right)^2}\right], \quad \mu = \ln(1 + E[\underset{\sim}{i}]) - \dfrac{\sigma^2}{2}$

5.2.12   (a) $\bar{v} = (.6)(1.05)^{-1} + (.4)(1.2)^{-1} = .904762$
        $E[\underset{\sim}{A}(10)] = \bar{v}^{10} = .367573$
        $E[\underset{\sim}{A}(20)] = \bar{v}^{20} = .135110, \quad E[\underset{\sim}{A}(30)] = \bar{v}^{30} = .049663$
        $E[\underset{\sim}{v}^2] = (.6)(1.05)^{-2} + (.4)(1.2)^{-2} = .821995$
        $Var[\underset{\sim}{A}(10)] = (E[\underset{\sim}{v}^2])^{10} - (\bar{v}^{10})^2 = .005720$
        $Var[\underset{\sim}{A}(20)] = .001578, \quad Var[\underset{\sim}{A}(30)] = \bar{v}^{30} = .000327$

(b) $\underline{\delta}$ is normal with $\mu = .125$ and $\sigma^2 = .0005625$

$$\bar{v} = E[\underline{v}] = E[e^{-\underline{\delta}}] = M_{\underline{\delta}}(-1)$$
$$= e^{.5(.0005625)(-1)^2+(.125)(-1)} = .882745$$
$$E[\underline{v}^2] = E[e^{-2\underline{\delta}}] = M_{\underline{\delta}}(-2)$$
$$= e^{.5(.0005625)(-2)^2+(.125)(-2)} = .779677$$
$$E[\underline{A}(10)] = \bar{v}^{10} = .287312, \quad E[\underline{A}(20)] = \bar{v}^{20} = .082548$$
$$E[\underline{A}(30)] = \bar{v}^{30} = .023717$$
$$Var[\underline{A}(10)] = (E[\underline{v}^2])^{10} - (\bar{v}^{10})^2 = .000466$$
$$Var[\underline{A}(20)] = .000077, \quad Var[\underline{A}(30)] = \bar{v}^{30} = .000010$$

5.2.13 $n = 10$: (i) $P_1 \cdot (1.125)^{10} = 1,000,000 \rightarrow P_1 = 307,946.15$

$$Var[accumulated\ profit] = Var[P_1 \cdot \underline{S}(10) - 1,000,000]$$
$$= (P_1)^2 \cdot Var[\underline{S}(10)] = 34,177,305,570, \quad SD = 184,871$$

(ii) $P_2 = 1,000,000 \cdot \bar{v}^{10} = 367,572.54$

$$Var[present\ value] = (P_2)^2 \cdot Var[\underline{A}(10)] = 772,826,757,$$
$$SD = 27,800$$

5.2.14 The accumulated value $\underline{S}$, is either $(1.05)^{10}$, $(1.1)^{10}$ or $(1.15)^{10}$, each with probability $\frac{1}{3}$. The expected accumulated value is
$$E[\underline{S}] = \frac{1}{3} \cdot [(1.05)^{10} + (1.1)^{10} + (1.15)^{10}] = 2.7561.$$

The variance of $\underline{S}$ is $E[\underline{S}^2] - (E[\underline{S}])^2$
$$= \frac{1}{3} \cdot [(1.05)^{20} + (1.1)^{20} + (1.15)^{20}] - (2.7561)^2 = .9866.$$

If rates can change from year to year then $E[1 + \underline{i}] = 1.1$
$$E[(1 + \underline{i})^2] = 1.211667 \text{ and } E[\underline{S}(10)] = (1.1)^{10} = 2.5937$$
$$Var[\underline{S}(10)] = (1.211667)^{10} - (1.1)^{20} = .093242$$

5.2.17 (a) $Cov[\underline{S}(10), \underline{S}(20)]$
$$= E[\underline{S}(10) \cdot \underline{S}(20)] - E[\underline{S}(10)] \cdot E[\underline{S}(20)]$$
$$= (E[(1 + \underline{i})^2])^{10} \cdot (1 + \bar{i})^{10} - (1 + \bar{i})^{30}$$

(b) $Cov[\underline{S}(n), \underline{S}(m)]$
$$= (E[(1 + \underline{i})^2])^n \cdot (1 + \bar{i})^{m-n} - (1 + \bar{i})^{m+n}$$

5.2.20 $n = 2$: $\underset{\sim}{S}(2)$ has a 7-point distribution: $Pr[(1.08)(1.06)] = \frac{1}{9}$
        $Pr[(1.08)^2] = \frac{1}{9}$, $Pr[(1.08)(1.10)] = \frac{2}{9}$, $Pr[(1.10)^2] = \frac{1}{9}$
        $Pr[(1.10)(1.12)] = \frac{2}{9}$, $Pr[(1.12)^2] = \frac{1}{9}$, $Pr[(1.12)(1.14)] = \frac{1}{9}$
        $E[\underset{\sim}{S}(2)] = 1.210267$, $Var[\underset{\sim}{S}(2)] = .001613$
        For $n = 3$ the distribution has 16 points.

Exercises 5.3

5.3.1 $n = 20$: (a) $Var[a_{\overline{20}|}] = .1025$

5.3.3   (i) (a) $P[\underset{\sim}{Y} \le 18] .012$, $P[\underset{\sim}{Y} \le 19] = .111$, $P[\underset{\sim}{Y} \le 20.226] = .5$
        (b) $P[\underset{\sim}{Y} \le 18] .009$, $P[\underset{\sim}{Y} \le 19] = .106$, $P[\underset{\sim}{Y} \le 20.226] = .49$

5.3.5   For $n = 5$ the Chebyshev 75% interval contains 100% of the distribution.

5.3.6   Mean $= s_{\overline{10}|.12} \cdot (1.12)^{10} = 54.5037$

Exercises 5.4

5.4.4 $\sigma^2 = .0004$, $P = 0$; $\sigma^2 = 4$, $P = .48$

Exercises 6.2

6.2.1   (a) $i_{k-1,k} = \dfrac{(1 + i_{0,k})^k}{(1 + i_{0,k-1})^{k-1}} - 1$

6.2.2

k	(i)	(ii)
1	.0910	.0919
2	.0930	.0953
3	.0950	.0981
4	.0970	.1003
5	.0990	.1019
6	.1010	.1029
7	.1030	.1033
8	.1050	.1031
9	.1070	.1023
10	.1090	.1009

6.2.3   (b) (i) $i_{0,1} = .2,$ $i_{0,2} = .201,$ $i_{0,3} = .2011$
           (ii) $i_{0,1} = .2,$ $i_{0,2} = .199,$ $i_{0,3} = .1989$

Exercises 6.3

6.3.1   (a) 18.33 (b) 56.74

6.3.3 $r = .04,$ $s = .0418$

6.3.4   Let P denote the stock price on July 20
       (a) profit $= P - 111$ if $P \geq 110$ (option is exercised on July 20)
            profit $= -1$ if $P \leq 110$ (option not exercised on July 20)
       (b) 11 if $P \geq 110,$ $P - 99$ if $P \leq 110$
       (c) -6 if $P \geq 110,$ $104 - P$ if $90 \leq P \leq 110,$ 14 if $P \leq 90$
       (d) 6 if $P \geq 110,$ $P - 104$ if $90 \leq P \leq 110,$ -14 if $P \leq 90$

6.3.5   (a) $E = 45 \rightarrow P = 1.806,$ $E = 50 \rightarrow P = .00034$
          $E = 55 \rightarrow P = 0$
       (b) $E = 45 \rightarrow P = 11.798,$ $E = 50 \rightarrow P = 6.997$
          $E = 55 \rightarrow P = 2.210$

Exercises 6.5

6.5.1   (a) $i = .0593$ (b) $r = .3675$

Exercises 6.6

6.6.1   (a) 1.6332 (b) 1.6328

6.6.2 $n = 5, pmt = 79,139; n = 15, pmt = 39,442; n = 50,$
      $pmt = 30,257$ $n = 100, pmt = 30,002$
      $\Sigma t A_t v^t$: $n = 5,$ 843,038; $n = 15,$ 1,883,680; $n = 50, 3,171,124$
      $n = 100, 3,297,823$
      $\Sigma t^2 A_t v^t$: $n = 5, 5,418,640; n = 15,$ 18,312,480;
      $n = 50,$ 60,149,792; $n = 100,$ 69,036,574
      Best match occurs at $n = 15$; exact $n = 20,$ but no immunization.

6.6.6   (a) $h(.03) = 40{,}581$, $h(.08) = 2{,}170$, $h(.12) = 1{,}595$,
$h(.2) = 23{,}154$

(b) $h(.03) = -12{,}596$, $h(.08) = -690$, $h(.12) = -514$,
$h(.2) = -7{,}524$

(c) $h(.03) = -18{,}968$, $h(.08) = 994$, $h(.12) = 714$,
$h(.2) = 9{,}738$

6.6.9   (a) $A_{15} = .8053$, $A_5 = .3105$

(b) (i) $t_2 = 19.0530$, $A_{t_2} = .8432$ (ii) $A_{t_2} < 0$

(c) (i) $t_2 = 21.28$, $A_5 = .4302$ or $t_2 = 11.27$, $A_5 = .1258$

(ii) $t_2 = 31.92$, $A_5 = .5056$ (iii) no solution

(d) (i) $t_1 = 9.21$, $A_{t_2} = .2213$ (ii) no solution with $t_1 \leq 10$

(iii) no solution

(e) (i) $t_1 = 5.065$, $A_{t_1} = .3144$ (ii) no solution

(f) $t_1 = 4.74$, $t_2 = 18.30$

6.6.10 $t_0 = 16.15$, $A_{t_0} = 961{,}145$

BIBLIOGRAPHY

1. Burden, R.L. and J.D. Faires, *Numerical Analysis* (Fourth Edition). Boston: Prindle, Weber, and Schmidt, 1989.

2. Butcher, M.V. and C.J. Nesbitt, *Mathematics of Compound Interest.* Ann Arbor: Edwards Brothers, 1971.

3. Elton, E.J. and M.J. Gruber, *Modern Portfolio Theory and Investment Analysis.* New York: John Wiley and Sons, 1984.

4. Feller, W., *Introductory Probability Theory and its Applications*, Volumes I and II. New York: John Wiley and Sons, 1965.

5. Hoel, P.G., S.C. Port, and C.J. Stone, *Introduction to Probability Theory.* Boston: Houghton Mifflin, 1971.

6. Hogg, R.V. and A.T. Craig, *Introduction to Mathematical Statistics* (Fourth Edition). New York: McMillan Publishing Company, 1978.

7. Kellison, S.G., *The Theory of Interest* (Second Edition). Homewood: Richard D. Irwin, Inc., 1991.

8. McCutcheon, J.J. and W.F. Scott, *An Introduction to the Mathematics of Finance.* Oxford: Heinemann Professional Publishing, 1986.

9. Sharpe, W.F., *Investments.* Englewood Cliffs: Prentice-Hall, 1978.

10.   Venkatesh, R., Venkatesh, V., Dattatreya, R., *Interest Rate and Currency Swaps"*, Probus Publishing Company, Chicago, IL, 1995

INDEX